P9-AFB-032

GNOSIS

GNOSIS

The Nature and History of Gnosticism

KURT RUDOLPH

Translation edited by
Robert McLachlan Wilson

HARPER & ROW, PUBLISHERS

SAN FRANCISCO

Cambridge   London
Hagerstown   Mexico City
Philadelphia   São Paulo
New York   *1817*   Sydney

Translators
P. W. Coxon (pages 171–274)
K. H. Kuhn (pages 275–376)
R. McL. Wilson (translation editor; pages 1–170)

First published in the German Democratic Republic
by Koehler & Amelang, Leipzig, 1977 as
Die Gnosis: Wesen und Geschichte einer spätantiken Religion

Copyright © Koehler & Amelang, 1977

First published in the United States of America by
Harper and Row, New York, 1983.
This work is a translation from the German of the
second, revised and expanded edition (1980) of
Die Gnosis: Wesen und Geschichte einer spätantiken Religion

Copyright © T. & T. Clark Limited, Edinburgh, 1983

Published simultaneously in Canada by
Fitzhenry & Whiteside Limited, Toronto

Library of Congress Number: 81-47437
ISBN: 0-06-067017-7

ILLUSTRISSIMAE
SANCTI ANDREAE APUD SCOTOS UNIVERSITATI
OB DOCTORIS IN SANCTA THEOLOGIA DIGNITATEM AC
NOMEN SIBI OBLATUM
HUNC LIBRUM
GRATO DEVOTOQUE ANIMO
D.D.D.
KURT RUDOLFUS

CONTENTS

List of Illustrations

Illustrations in Text

the Vatican Libary. The photograph was taken after cleaning in 1975. Cf. J. Ficker, *Die altchristlichen Bildwerke im christlichen Museum des Lateran untersucht und beschrieben*, Leipzig 1890, 166–175; O. Wulff, *Die altchristliche Kunst* I, Berlin 1913, 150; M. Guarducci, La statua di "Sant' Ippolito" in Vaticano, in *Rendiconti della Pontificia Accademia Romana d'Archeologia* XLVII (1974/75), 163–190 (advocates the theory that the statue was originally not a male figure at all, but a second-century representation of Themista, a female disciple of Epicurus; the inscriptions were subsequently carved on the sides of the chair by Christians in the third century; only in the 16th century, particularly in the first description by Pirro Ligario, was it made into a statue of Hippolytus, and here the ancient coin-type of Hippocrates served as a model). The dating of the rededication of the statue through the inscriptions about 235/237, which is also the period of a persecution to which Hippolytus fell victim, goes back to information in a letter (7.1. 1977) from J. Frickel in Rome.

2 Epiphanius of Salamis, fresco from Faras, Cat. No. 57. Photo: Zbigniew Kapuścik, Warsaw. – Cf. K. Michalowski, *Faras. Die Wandbilder in den Sammlungen des Nationalmuseums zu Warschau*, Warsaw-–Dresden 1974, 257 (colour), 258 (section), 259–62 (description), 314 f. (inscriptions No. 36, 37, 38 examined by S. Jakobielski).

3–7 Ancient magic gems

3 Berlin (West), Staatliche Museen, Stiftung Preussischer Kulturbesitz, Ägyptisches Museum, inv. 9852. Green jasper with red stripes set in a ring. 0,025 : 0,0175. I owe the photograph of this hitherto unpublished gem to Dr. H. Maehler, Berlin (West).

4 Berlin (West), Staatliche Museen, Stiftung Preussischen Kulturbesitz, Ägyptisches Museum, inv. 9853. Greenish red jasper. Photo: Staatliche Museen zu Berlin (DDR). Cf. M. Pieper, Die Abraxasgemmen (in *Mitt. Dt. Inst. f. Ägypt. Altertumskunde in Kairo*, Bd. V, 1934, 119–143) 142.

5 Berlin (West), Staatliche Museen, Stiftung Preussischen Kulturbesitz, Ägyptisches Museum, inv. 9861. Greenish red jasper. Photo: Staatliche Museen zu Berlin (DDR). Cf. M. Pieper, Die Abraxasgemmen 142.

6 Berlin (West), Staatliche Museen, Stiftung Preussischen Kulturbesitz, Ägyptisches Museum, inv. 9805. Reddish brown stone. Photo: J. Leipoldt-Archiv, Universität Jena, Sektion Theologie. Cf. J. Leipoldt, Bilder zum neutestamentlichen Zeitalter (= *Umwelt des Urchristentums*, ed. J. Leipoldt and W. Grundmann, Bd. III) Berlin 1966, illustration 13.

7 Berlin (West), Staatliche Museen, Stiftung Preussischer Kulturbesitz, Ägyptisches Museum, inv. 9931. Green stone. Photo: J. Leipoldt-Archiv, Universität Jena, Sektion Theologie. Cf. J. Leipoldt, Bilder zum neutestamentlichen Zeitalter, illustration 14.

8 Alabaster bowl, in private ownership (present location unknown; it last appears in the auction catalogue of the Jacob-Hirsch-Collection from 5. Dec. 1957, Lucerne, no. 105). Height 8 cm. diam. 22 cm., depth 5.5 cm. After R. Delbrueck / W. Vollgraff, An Orphic Bowl, in *Journal of Hellenic Studies* 54 (1934) 129–139, plate III. Cf. also H. Lamer, Eine spätgriechische Schale mit orphischer Aufschrift, in *Phil. Woche* 51 (1931) 653 ff.; H. Leisegang, Das Mysterium der Schlange, in *Eranos Jahrbuch 1939*, Zürich 1940, 151–251; id. *Die Gnosis* 150 f., illustration at p. 160; P. C. Finney, Did Gnostics make Pictures? in B. Layton (ed.), *The Rediscovery of Gnosticism* I, Leiden 1980, 441.

9 Subterranean Basilica at the Porta Maggiore, Rome. Photo: Fototeca Unione, Rome. Cf. J. Carcopino *De Pythagore aux Apôtres*, Paris, 1956, 85–211.

10 View from the Djebel-el-Tarif. Photo: The Institute for Antiquity and Christianity, Claremont, Cal., December 1975.

11 North side of El-Qasr (Chenoboskion). Photo: The Institute for Antiquity and Christianity, Claremont, Cal., December 1975.

Le Coq, *Chotscho*, plate 3b (right). Photo: Volkmar Herre, Leipzig.

29, 30 Cologne Mani Codex before conservation, Institut für Altertumskunde der Universität Köln, P. Colon. inv. 4780. Photo: Institut für Altertumskunde der Universität Köln. Cf. A. Henrichs / L. Koenen, Ein griechischer Mani-Codex, 215 and plate IV.

31 Coptic Manichean manuscript (Kephalaia p. 168), Staatliche Museen zu Berlin, Papyrusabteilung, P. 15996. Photo: Staatliche Museen zu Berlin. Cf. A. Böhlig / H. J. Polotsky / C. Schmidt, *Kephalaia*, 1. Hälfte, Stuttgart 1940 (Manich. Handschriften der Staatlichen Museen Berlin Bd. 1), 168 (from chap. 69).

32 Chinese Manichean manuscript from Tun-Huang, A. Stein London Hymn-rolls 2659, lines 387–400, after E. Waldschmidt / W. Lentz, *Die Stellung Jesu im Manichäismus,* Berlin 1926 (Abh. PAW 1926, Phil.-hist. Kl. Nr. 4), plate I. Cf. op. cit. 122–124 (exposition and translation). Photo: Volkmar Herre, Leipzig.

33 Traditional Mandean sanctuary *(Mandi)* in Qal'at Salih. Photo: Kurt Rudolph (April 1969).

34 Mandean priests at the mass for the dead. Photo: Kurt Rudolph (1969).

35 Ganzibra 'Abdullah of Baghdad. Photo: Kurt Rudolph (1969).

36 Mandean baptism in the Tigris at Baghdad. Photo: Gustav Pfirrmann, Telfes (Südtirol).

37 Mandean priest in ceremonial robes. Photo: Gustav Pfirrmann, Telfes (Südtirol).

38 The holy draught of water (*mambūhā*) after baptism. Photo: Gustav Pfirrmann, Telfes (Südtirol).

39 Close of the baptismal ceremony. Photo: Gustav Pfirrmann, Telfes (Südtirol).

40, 41 Mandean magic bowl, Royal Ontario Museum, Canada, sign. 931.4.1, after W. S. McCullough, *Jewish and ·Mandaean Incarnation Bowls in the Royal Ontario Museum,* Toronto 1967, at p. 12 (Bowl C): Height 7.2 cm; diam. above 19.9 cm; diam. below 8.4 cm.

42 Mandean manuscript roll Zraztā d^eHibil Zīwā, in the possession of the author. Photo: Volkmar Herre, Leipzig. Cf. J. de Morgan, *Mission Scientifique en Perse* V/2: Textes mandaïtes, Paris 1904, 255–270. (transcription of the same text).

43 Mandean codex, Right Ginza p. 1, Bodleian Library, Oxford, Drower Collection No. 22, reproduced from a micro-film.

44–48 From the Diwan Abathur, stations on the journey of the soul, Bodleian Library, Oxford, Drower Collection No. 8, after E. S. Drower, *Diwan Abatur or Progress through the Purgatories,* Città del Vaticano 1950 (Studi e Testi 151). Another manuscript in the Vatican Library (Borgiano siriaco 175) was acquired in the 16th century by Ignatius à Jesu and published by J. Euting in 1904 after photographs taken by B. Poertner (Mandäischer Diwan, Strasbourg 1904). Both manuscripts are undated.

Abbreviations

The normal abbreviations have been used for books of the Bible.

Abh.	Abhandlung
ADAIK	Abhandlungen des Deutschen Archäologischen Instituts, Kairo (Kopt. Reihe)
AWG	Akademie der Wissenschaften zu Göttingen
BBA	Berliner Byzantinische Arbeiten
BCNH	Bibliothèque Copte de Nag Hammadi
BdKV	Bibliothek der Kirchenväter. Hrsg. von O. Bardenhewer, K. Weyman, J. Zellinger. 2. Reihe (München)
Beitr.	Beiträge
BZNW	Beihefte zur ZNW
CGL	The Coptic Gnostic Library
Corp. Herm.	Corpus Hermeticum
DAW	Deutsche Akademie der Wissenschaften; Akademie der Wissenschaften der DDR
GCS	Die griechischen christlichen Schriftsteller der ersten drei Jahrhunderte. Hrsg. von der PAW bzw. der DAW
En.	Enoch
ET	English Translation
GL	Left Ginza
GR	Right Ginza
HAW	Heidelberger Akademie der Wissenschaften
JbAC	Jahrbuch für Antike und Christentum
KlT	Kleine Texte für Vorlesungen und Übungen. Hrsg. bzw. begr. von H. Lietzmann
Mitt.	Mitteilungen
NF	Neue Folge
NHC	Nag Hammadi Codex or Codices
NHS	Nag Hammadi Studies (Leiden)
Nov Test	Novum Testamentum
NS	New Series
NTS	New Testament Studies
OLZ	Orientalistische Literaturzeitung
Pap. Ber.	Papyrus Berolinensis 8502
PAW	Preußische Akademie der Wissenschaften zu Berlin
PTS	Patristische Texte und Studien
PWRE	Pauly-Wissowa, Realencyclopädie der klassischen Altertumswissenschaften
QH	Qumran, Hymns
QS	Qumran, Manual of Discipline
RGG^2; RGG^3	Die Religion in Geschichte und Gegenwart, 2. bzw. 3. Aufl. (Tübingen)
RGGV	Religionsgeschichtliche Versuche und Vorarbeiten
SAW	Sächsische Akademie der Wissenschaften zu Leipzig
SB	Sitzungsberichte

SBL	Society of Biblical Literature
SQS	Sammlung ausgewählter kirchen- und dogmengeschichtlicher Quellenschriften. Hrsg: bzw. begr. von G. Krüger (Tübingen)
ThLZ	Theologische Literaturzeitung
ThR	Theologische Rundschau
TU	Texte und Untersuchungen zur Geschichte der altchristlichen Literatur
VigChrist.	Vigiliae Christianae
WdF	Wege der Forschung (Darmstadt)
Wiss. Beitr.	Wissenschaftliche Beiträge
WZ	Wissenschaftliche Zeitschrift
ZKG	Zeitschrift für Kirchengeschichte
ZNW	Zeitschrift für neutestamentliche Wissenschaft
ZPE	Zeitschrift für Papyrologie und Epigraphik
ZRGG	Zeitschrift für Religions- und Geistesgeschichte
ZThK	Zeitschrift für Theologie und Kirche

PREFACE TO ENGLISH EDITION

It is due to the effort and initiative of Professor R. McL. Wilson that an English translation of my book on Gnosis can be published, by the long-established Scottish firm of T. and T. Clark, so soon after the appearance of the first and second German editions. Technical terminology tends to vary from one region to another, and anyone who knows the trouble it costs to translate scientific works properly, with due regard to language, style and subject-matter, will be able to judge how much work has been involved for Professor Wilson and his collaborators, P. W. Coxon and K. H. Kuhn, in the production of this English edition. The author was regularly able to follow and control their careful and circumspect work, in particular during an unforgettable personal visit to St. Andrews. I therefore owe more than ordinary thanks to my honoured colleague R. McL. Wilson and his team – this is not the first time that they have rendered service by the translation of German works in theology and the science of religion – and especially because through them it is possible for me to express more general thanks for the stimulus which I have received from the literature in English on research into Gnosis. It is to be hoped that the worldwide range of the English language will not only be of advantage for the dissemination of the book, but will also further knowledge about Gnosis and Gnosticism in wider circles, since precisely here in my experience a mass of false and unscientific opinions and speculations is in circulation. In this regard it is certainly appropriate to reproduce in the English edition also the following passages from the Preface to the first German edition (1977), in the context of which I take the liberty of making brief and explicit reference to some older works of British and American research into Gnosis.

The growing interest, even among a wider public, in what is to be understood by "Gnosis" or "Gnosticism" is founded not only on the great discoveries of Manichean and gnostic manuscripts which have been made in this century in Turkestan (Turfan 1902–1914) and Egypt (Medinet Madi 1930 and Nag Hammadi 1945/6–1948), but also on the importance of this form of religion in late antiquity, which has been increasingly recognised in historical and critical research. A clear-cut definition of this "religion of knowledge" or of "insight", as the Greek word *gnosis* may be translated, is not easy, but should at least be briefly suggested at the very outset. We shall not go far wrong to see in it a dualistic religion, consisting of several schools and movements, which took up a definitely negative attitude towards the world and the society of the time, and proclaimed a deliverance ("redemption") of man precisely from the constraints of earthly existence through "insight" into his essential relationship, whether as "soul" or "spirit", – a relationship temporarily obscured – with a supramundane realm of freedom and of rest. Its spread through time and space, from the beginning of our era onwards, from the western part of the Near East (Syria, Palestine, Egypt, Asia Minor) to central and eastern Asia and mediaeval Europe (14th cent.) affords some indication of the role to be assigned to it, even in a modified and adapted form, in the history of religion, to say nothing of the fact that even today a remnant still exists in the Mandeans of Iraq and Iran. In other respects also manifold influences on the history of thought can be detected in European and Near Eastern traditions, be it in theology, theosophy, mysticism or philosophy.

In regard to information about Gnosis, however, the situation is none of the best, especially for the non-specialist, since for a long time there has been no major full-scale survey. We may recall the two older works of G. R. S. Mead (*Fragments of a Faith Forgotten: The Gnostics,* 1900, reprint 1960; 3 German editions 1902, 1906, 1931) and F. Legge (*Fore-runners and Rivals of Christianity from 330 B. C. to 333 A. D.*, 1915, reprint 1964). In 1932 F. C. Burkitt wrote his influential book *Church and Gnosis*. The handy monograph *Die Gnosis* by H. Leisegang, which went through four editions in German, goes back ultimately to 1924 (only a French translation has appeared: *La Gnose*. Paris 1951). In 1934, shortly before his exile from Nazi Germany, Hans Jonas published the first part of his pioneering and influential study *Gnosis und spätantiker Geist* (3rd ed. 1964). Then from his new homeland in the U.S.A. he provided for the English-speaking reader a more popular and slightly modified introduction to his position in *The Gnostic Religion* (1958, ²1963, ³1970). Basic questions of research into Gnosis, such as resulted from the influence of R. Bultmann and his school (to which Jonas also belongs), are discussed in the works of R. McL. Wilson (*The Gnostic Problem* 1958, ²1964; *Gnosis and the New Testament* 1968) and R. M. Grant (*Gnosticism and Early Christianity* 1959, [2]1966). In recent times it has been mainly collections of sources in translation, in addition to smaller summaries, which have been placed at the disposal of those interested in obtaining a comprehensive view (R. M. Grant, *Gnosticism* 1961; R. Haardt, *Die Gnosis* 1967 (unfortunately the English translation of this valuable work, *Gnosis* 1971, can be used only with caution); W. Foerster, *Die Gnosis*, 2 vols. 1969 and 1971, English translation 1972 and 1974).

My own concern with this area, extending over more than 25 years, has given me the courage to venture on a new survey which will take account of the present state of research. I have had Leisegang's valuable book in mind as a model to this extent, that it draws in the main from the sources themselves and reproduces them in detail. In contrast to him, however, I have not only chosen a completely different line of approach, which once again I owe to H. Jonas, but also have deliberately given precedence to the original works today abundantly available, above all in Coptic, and less to the heresiological reports as they are to be found in Leisegang. Further it has been my concern to offer a brief critical history of the sources as an introduction to the material, and by way of epilogue to trace to some extent the story of its later influence. More space than has hitherto been usual has been given to cultic and sociological questions. The inclusion of Manicheism and of the Mandeans (not mentioned at all by Leisegang) was undertaken quite deliberately. That my account is not complete I myself know better than anyone. An author cannot without more ado match idea with accomplishment. The editing and investigation of the new Coptic texts is still in full flow, and this imposes certain limitations and reservations. I have nowhere disavowed my own point of view with regard to basic questions or points of detail; it is founded upon a long concern with the sources and cannot always be documented in such a book as this, intended for a wider circle and setting store by overlapping connections and points of importance (occasionally the notes provide information, and more may be gathered from the bibliography). The detailed references to the sources however often offer the possibility of control. I hope that my esteemed specialist colleagues will also find profit in it.

In matters of detail the following should be noted: In the translations quoted recourse has been made throughout to the original text, which does not exclude the grateful use of existing translations (these have in each case been noted; cf. also the Translator's Note!). Round brackets () indicate insertions to facilitate comprehension, square brackets [] supplements or emendations to the original text, and angled brackets ⟨⟩ supplements from some variant form of the text. Citation of the sources follows the usual internationally known editions, about which information will be found in the Bibliography. The Nag Hammadi codices are quoted by Codex (Roman numeral), tractate (Arabic numeral), page and (when required) line (in the case of NHC II 3,4 and 5 the plate numbers of P. Labib's photographic edition of 1956 have been added in brackets). Technical terms from foreign languages are printed in italics, and for those of oriental origin (e.g. Mandean) a simplified transcription has been chosen which matches the pronunciation. The numerous cross-references are intended to facilitate looking up, and in general to promote the continuity of the presentation. The index serves the same purpose. In regard to the sources, the bibliography provides a classified survey of the translations available, with at least one edition of the text. For the remaining literature, naturally, only a selection is adduced, but it contains all that is essential. As to the chronological table, it is an attempt to fit the history of Gnosis and Manicheism into a comprehensive chronological survey, with all the inevitable gaps and uncertainties, a task which has hardly been undertaken before.

The illustrations which accompany the book are a case by themselves. Without the help of others this collection could not have been brought into being. Anyone who knows how difficult it is to gather together for this theme illustrations which are both evocative and good will be able to judge of that. Strictly speaking, we have no certain archaeological evidence for the gnostics, apart from a few inscriptions and many books or parts of books. Even the gems do not belong to that category. Attempts to claim for this purpose particular catacombs or underground chambers have so far, in my view, not entirely succeeded. The hypogeum most commonly mentioned in this context, that of the Aurelii in the Viale Manzoni in Rome, has recently been given a quite different interpretation, so that even its Christian origin has become more than questionable. In other cases of the sort I have nowhere come across anything typically gnostic. I have therefore refrained from including illustrations from this area. The picture of the subterranean basilica at the Porta Maggiore is merely an expedient, to show at *Plate 9* least conjecturally the kind of places of worship the gnostics could have used. On the other hand we have more remains of the Manicheans in Central Asia, and for that reason their monuments occupy a dominant place. From an artistic point of view they are the most precious that we possess from any gnostic religion. There is naturally an abundant supply of pictorial source-material for the Mandeans, including some in my own possession. For the rest it is mainly manuscripts that have been reproduced. This too is characteristic for Gnosis, for it is a religion of writing and of books. The Nag Hammadi discovery has impressively confirmed that once again. Professor James M. Robinson, Director of the Institute for Antiquity and Christianity at the Claremont Graduate School in California, responded generously to my request for photographs of the finds, now deposited in the Coptic Museum in Old Cairo, and of the place of discovery itself, which he and his team explored in several campaigns in 1975, 1976 and 1978. The valuable photos by Jean Doresse also come from the Claremont archives. My very special thanks are therefore due to Professor Robinson. In addition I have to thank Professor Dr. Josef Frickel of Rome for obtaining the copy for the illustration of the so-called "statue of Hippolytus" (newly cleaned and set up) and for the Semo Sancus inscription; Prof. Dr. Ludwig Koenen, formerly of Cologne and now in Ann Arbor (Michigan), for allowing the photograph of the Cologne Mani codex (in its original condition), Dr. Werner Sundermann for his help in the selection of the Manichean Turfan texts illustrated from among those in the possession of the Academy of Sciences in the German Democratic Republic; Dr. Ulrich Luft for the same assistance with the Coptic gnostic and Manichean papyri from the collection in the papyrus section of the State Museum in Berlin, and Dr. Hannelore Kischkewitz for looking after the illustrations of gems from the Egyptian Museum in Berlin. I would here express my thanks to all the museums and other institutions which have sanctioned these reproductions.

For her help in getting the book ready I am very grateful to my wife, who also took over the tedious task of preparing the index. My father-in-law, Pastor Martin Killus, and my colleague at Halle, Dr. Dr. Peter Nagel, were so kind as to take in hand a first reading of the type-script and to give their critical advice. Frau Gerda Kunzendorf worked with great devotion on the final printed version. The make-up of the book was in the experienced hands of Joachim Kölbel. Hans-Ulrich Herold drew the illustrations in the text and the maps. To them also my thanks are due.

Leipzig 1980   Kurt Rudolph

Translator's Note

Such a book as this presents certain very special problems to the translator, since a considerable part of it consists of extracts and quotations from original sources, in various ancient languages. Simply to translate the German version of these would have exposed us to the charge of producing a translation of a translation, with the attendant danger of increasing remoteness from the original. Indeed, since the Nag Hammadi texts are for the most part, if not entirely, themselves versions of Greek originals, it would have been translation of a translation of a translation! On the other hand, to have used an existing translation, quite apart from questions of copyright, would not always have yielded a satisfactory result, since such a version might have varied in some measure from that of Professor Rudolph, or proved difficult to fit into the flow of his discussion. Our solution, already applied in previous work of this kind, has been to follow the German version but at all points to have the original in view, to ensure that the translations really are English translations of the original and not just at second hand. At the present stage of research into the Nag Hammadi texts a variety of different translations is no bad thing, in order that the various possibilities for interpretation may be clearly seen. On occasion, however, and particulary in regard to the Mandean material, we have drawn upon translations made on the same principle for the English edition of Werner Foerster's two-volume anthology *Gnosis*. For permission to use these translations we are indebted to the Clarendon Press in Oxford.

We are greatly indebted to Miss Karen Fleming and Mrs. Elaine McLauchlan of St. Andrews and Mrs. Helen Marshall of Durham, who reduced our untidy and much-revised drafts to neat and legible typescript, and also to Messrs T. and T. Clark's readers, who have done so much to ensure that the book so far as possible may be free from error.

R. McL. Wilson

THE SOURCES

The Heresiological Literature
and the Older History of Research

Our knowledge and understanding of any historical phenomenon is dependent to a quite considerable extent upon the state of our sources, be they written, oral, archaeological or of some other kind. This is particularly true for the ancient religion of the so-called Gnosis or, to use the term employed by modern scholars since the 18th century, of Gnosticism. Up to quite recent times it was known almost exclusively through the work of its opponents, and the picture was therefore only a weak and distorted reflection. It was only through laborious research and some surprising new discoveries that there gradually emerged a more clearly defined picture of this religion, which was influential and significant for the history of religion in late antiquity and whose influence, through various channels, can be detected right down to modern times. One branch indeed, the Baptist sect of the Mandeans, still survives even today in Iraq.

The witness of the Church Fathers

The opponents mentioned above were in the first place Christian apologists and religious philosophers, some of them holders of episcopal office and subsequently elevated by Catholic theology to the status of "Church Fathers". They judged the deviations and opinions of their opponents from the point of view of a tradition of Christian faith and thought which was considered as firm and certain, and sought to refute them. For them it was above all a question of refuting doctrines which did not agree with the so-called apostolic tradition laid down in a lengthy process in the New Testament and in the oldest confessions of faith, since these doctrines were detrimental to the building up of a strongly organised church, relatively uniform in its leadership. For this purpose the most varied arguments and methods were employed: the demonstration of the post-Christian origin of Gnosis, the reproach of a falsification of Christian doctrine or of relapse into heathenism (in which Greek philosophy also is included), the demonstration of the lack of uniformity and the discordant nature of the opposing camp; gnostics were also accused of deceit, falsehood and magic;

finally the supernatural cause of gnostic teaching was held to be Satan himself, who in this fashion sought to corrupt the Church. The varied reports about the gnostic doctrines and schools were evaluated and interpreted accordingly, and to an increasing degree the tendency developed simply to repeat the older presentations or to copy them out. In this way much valuable source material has it is true been preserved, but by and large the work of the so-called heresiologists or "opponents of heresy" led not only to the disappearance of the gnostic communities but also to the destruction of their literary heritage. It is however the duty of the historian to understand the phenomena he is investigating in the first place on their own terms, that is on the basis of their own period; he must therefore do justice to the Church Fathers who dedicated themselves to the conflict against Gnosticism, and indeed they acted with every confidence in the justice of their cause, and were fighting for the unity of a Church threatened from different sides (including that of relations with the state); any scientific intention in the modern sense was quite alien to them. From a modern point of view the procedure of the heresiologists is indeed to be regretted, and must be assessed very critically; a contemporary view of them on the other hand leads to an understanding of their procedure, and at the same time shows how these works should be read: not as historical and critical presentations but as theological treatises. Once this is understood then the relevant works are important sources for the role of Gnosis in early Christianity; they contain also a whole range of authentic witnesses, as the historical and critical study concerned with the Church Fathers (so-called Patristics) has already established.

THE EARLY HERESIOLOGISTS AND THEIR WORKS

The oldest heresiological work of which we have any information has unfortunately not survived. It came from the pen of Justin, who died as a martyr in Rome about 165 and ranks among the most significant early Christian apologists. In his First Apology to the Roman Emperor Antoninus Pius, composed between 150 and 155, he writes at the end of chapter 26, which is concerned with the three heretics Simon, Menander and Marcion: "There is also a compilation (*Syntagma*), which we have put together against all the heresies so far; if you wish to look at it we shall set it before you". Earlier scholars made

Justin

various efforts to reconstruct this work from other contexts and quotations, but without any great success[1], and the effort has for that reason now been abandoned. It is however certain that for Justin the heretics were influenced by the demons, who even after the ascension of Christ practised their wiles among men.

One of the most comprehensive and authoritative anti-heretical documents has come down to us from the second half of the second century. Its author was the first Church Father, Ire- **Irenaeus** naeus of Lyons (Lugdunum). He originated from Asia Minor **of Lyons** and in the reign of Marcus Aurelius came to Lyons in the land of the Celts, where in 177/178 he became successor to the bishop, who had died as a martyr; it is later reported of Irenaeus too that he died in a persecution. The year of his death, like that of his birth, is unknown to us (about 130/150 to 200). His main work is the "Exposure and Refutation of the falsely so called Gnosis", consisting of five books and generally cited by the abbreviated Latin title *Adversus Haereses* ("Against Heresies"). Unfortunately this work has survived in full only in a Latin translation. The Greek original is extant only in fragments (which for the first book are almost complete). In addition there are parts in Armenian and Syriac. The work was not written all at one time but grew gradually, probably under the relatively peaceful rule of the Emperor Commodus (180–192). The occasion for it, as Irenaeus himself writes by way of introduction, was the wish of a friend to get to know the doctrines of the Valentinians. This task the author largely fulfils in the first book, in that in thirty-one chapters he deals not only with the schools of the gnostic Valentinus (especially those of Ptolemy *See below, p. 323* and Marcus) but also with other more or less gnostic sects which had in some way become known to him and all of which he traces back to Simon Magus*, a point to which we shall later re- * *cf. Acts 8* turn. This part of the book has formed since early times one of *See below, p. 294* the most important sources not only for all subsequent heresiologists, who ransacked Irenaeus for material and arguments, but also for modern scholars.

Irenaeus himself asserts that he has used written and oral utterances of the Valentinians, which has to some extent been confirmed. On closer inspection however it soon becomes evident that his knowledge was very limited and one-sided; he is best informed about the disciples of Valentinus, Ptolemy and

Marcus.[2] It was only the most recent discoveries of gnostic original sources which opened our eyes to the true extent and nature of gnostic literary work. Irenaeus' one-sided attitude towards the teachings, his attempt to classify on the basis of these and to establish a family tree of the sects and their founders, but above all his polemic and apologetic intention of exposing or "unmasking" his opponents, that is, of bringing their alleged mysteries into the open and thus proving them to be errors and lies, impose considerable limitations upon his statements. Hans von Campenhausen aptly writes "Irenaeus attempts to set out his *Refutation* as systematically and in as much detail as possible. But he himself lacks the clarity, unprejudiced objectivity and capacity for orderly presentation which were needed for the task. So the book is a typical example of an involved and tiresome attack on heretics, which through lack of intellectual superiority gropes after any argument with which the opponents can be disparaged, brought under suspicion, or caricatured. Their ridiculous pretensions, the contradictions and the absurdity of their arbitrary doctrines, the continuing dissensions between their groups and parties, and not least the unclean life and the unstable opinions of their leaders are again and again set out before us".[3] His main principle is: "not only to expose but also from every side to wound the beast"* which has penetrated into the flock of the faithful. This is done by setting over against it the "Catholic" doctrine developed by Irenaeus after older models, which is traced back to the Apostles through the succession of the bishops and which alone possesses a "sound" basis (in distinction to the "unsound" of the heretics) in the writings of the Old and New Testaments. Their reputation and testimony is greater and more reliable than that of the gnostic "fools".* He develops this Christian doctrine, which in the present context cannot be set out but which became the starting point for the subsequent orthodox theology in general, in the remaining four books of his work, which contain the real "refutation" of the heresies portrayed in the first book and stand on a higher level than this book. The gnostics have at least this merit, that they prompted our author to this influential presentation of his ideas, in the course of which, evidently without his knowing it, many of their considerations proved to be of use to him, and so have remained in the orthodox system.

The author of the next important compendium of the sects

* *Irenaeus, Adv. haer. I., 31,4*

* *op. cit. III 3,4*

and heresies which we possess, Hippolytus of Rome (died **Hippolytus** about 235), must be considered as at least an intellectual disci- **of Rome** ple of Irenaeus. He played an important part in the discussions about the discipline of Penance and the doctrine of the Trinity in the Roman Church at the beginning of the 3rd century and was even appointed as a rival bishop in the church of Rome: the schism was only brought to an end by the intervention of the emperor Maximinus Thrax (235–238), who banished both Hippolytus and his rival to Sardinia, where he evidently died. The lower part of a seated figure, found in Rome in 1551, was at that time regarded as a statue of Hippolytus, and restored accord- *Plate 1* ingly. This however has recently become very doubtful. The only thing to suggest Hippolytus is some data carved on the side walls of the chair about the year 235, on the right an Easter calendar and on the left a list of writings, which however is incomplete and also does not contain the heresiological work to which we now turn. This bears the title "Refutation of all Heresies" (Lat. *Refutatio omnium haeresium*), but from the content of the first book has also been given the title "Philosophical Teachings" (*Philosophoumena*). Under this name the book for a long time passed as a work of Origen. Down to the 19th century the remaining parts were completely lost. Only in 1842 was a manuscript discovered in a monastery on Mount Athos which contained books four to ten; here again Origen was at first suggested as their author. The second and third books have so far not been discovered. The debate about the authorship is today generally regarded as decided in favour of Hippolytus, although in recent times fresh doubts have been expressed. As the time of composition we may suggest the period after 222. In the introduction the author notes that he has already provided a short summary of the heretical opinions. This "Syntagma" is lost, but can at least in part be reconstructed. It has indeed recently been conjectured that it may perhaps be identical with the tenth book of the Refutatio, since this book is a clearly independent presentation, and not merely a digest of the preceding books (hence called Epitome).[4] The Refutatio is a kind of encyclopedia, consisting of two parts: Part 1 (books 1–4) portrays the pre-Christian ("pagan") "errors" of the Greeks, i. e. those of the philosophers, the magi, the astrologers and the mysteries; part 2 contains the Christian heresies, i. e. a description of thirty-three gnostic systems. Behind this division lies the conception maintained by Hippolytus, that the gnostics took their doctrine in the first place from the "wisdom of the heathen" and not from that of Christianity. In the interest of this view he often deals quite arbitrarily with his sources, excerpts and quotations, and in general his statements are disjointed and lacking in cohesion, and occasionally give the impression of being first drafts. At any rate his search for the origins of the heresies in Hellenism is worthy of note and anticipates some modern trends in research. Further it must be emphasised that for him the old teachings of the Greek philosophers "are more worthy of God than those of the heretics"; even their unscientific views still appeared to him probable in comparison with the "boundless folly of the heretics".[5]* The founders of the sects have taken over Greek philosophy and misused it for their own purposes. Like Irenaeus, Hippolytus is bent on bringing the heretical teachings to the light of day and exposing them as Godlessness. The sources adduced by him are in part very valuable, since we possess them only through the medium of his writings, for example the so-called "Naassene preaching" or the "Great Revelation" of Simon Magus. A critical investigation must observe here that the ascription of such gnostic documents to individual sects, whose classification is a problem in itself, is often determined by external factors and has in some measure led scholars astray. Between Hippolytus' presentation and the source adduced by him there is often a yawning contradiction, which however for the investigation of sources may provide an important tool.

Hippolytus, Refutatio

To the period between 150 and 250, evidently a high point in the debate between the Christian church and the gnostics in its midst, there belong also the antiheretical works of Tertullian, **Tertullian** Clement of Alexandria and Origen. Tertullian, the first important Latin Father (about 150 to 223/225), composed among the numerous treatises which discuss individual doctrines of the gnostics a basic dogmatic writing in which, utilising the juridical terminology familiar to him, he sought to confute the claims of the gnostic heretics. This is a "plea for the prosecution against the heretics" (*De praescriptione haereticorum*) written about 200. It is of interest not so much for knowledge of gnostic teaching but rather for the standpoint of orthodoxy, for which the standard arguments are here once and for all brought together. Tertullian lays it down that Christian doctrine rests upon Christ and his apostles alone; it is older than all the heresies and is alone determinative for the church and its interpretation of scripture. Any teaching which stands in agreement with it is to be regarded as truth; any which is not identical with it must be regarded as false. The demonstration of the older apostolic tradition is sufficient to refute any heresy as a later falsification.* Tertullian therefore does not enter into detailed argumentation or discuss the different teachings of his opponents. Their interpretation of scripture is merely individual reasoning without any value.* Like Hippolytus furthermore he sees their origin in heathen philosophy, which has been mingled with Christian ideas.* He writes: "What then has Athens to do with Jerusalem, the Academy with the Church, the heretics with the Christians? Our teaching derives from the Portico of Solomon, who himself taught that men must seek the Lord in simplicity of heart.* For my part they may, if it so pleases them, develop a Stoic, a Platonic or a dialectic Christianity. Since Jesus Christ we have no need of any further investigation, nor of any research since the Gospel has been proclaimed. If we believe then we desire nothing more beyond faith. For this is the first thing that we believe: there is nothing more which we still require to believe beyond faith itself".[6] And: "the desire for knowledge yields to faith, the search for glory yields to the salvation of the soul ... to know nothing against the rule of faith is to know all things".* This avowal of simplicity and of uncomplicated thinking had however only a limited effect. Finally Tertullian harks back to the hypothesis of the devil to explain the falsification of the apostolic teaching.* Also we find here again the argument already adduced by Irenaeus, of the lack of uniformity in doctrine and the loose manner of life of the heretics.* The sharpness and the lack of moderation in the polemic in Tertullian's writings have often been censured in the past. He does not do justice to his opponent, but is bent on making an end of him. In this process he has a keen nose for his opponent's weaknesses and knows the fundamental differences very well. Hence, as H. von Campenhausen notes, he long ago, before modern investigation gathered together the numerous groups and movements of the heresy of the period under the general designation "gnosis", had grasped their essential common elements. For him Gnosis is a "declining syncretism such as the natural spirituality of mankind loves, a spiritual and idealistic overestimate

Tertullian, De praescr. haer. 21

op. cit. 16

op. cit. 7

Wisd. 1,1

Tertullian, De praescr. haer. 14

op. cit. 40

op. cit. 41

of the self which blurs the fixed limits that separate the creature from the deity; and it is at the same time the "nihilistic" hostility against the God of reality who has created the world and has revealed himself concretely in the flesh".[7]

The discussion takes a quite different course with the two great Alexandrian theologians Clement and Origen. They have felt in themselves the stimulus of the problem, and attempt to take up in a positive way the legitimate concerns of Gnosis and to reconcile them with the basic Christian affirmations in an original fashion, which brings the two fathers themselves close **Clement** to heresy. Clement of Alexandria, about whose life we know **of Alexandria** very little indeed, not even the years of his birth and death (presumably 140/150–211/215), was one of the most educated of all the Church Fathers and can be regarded as *the* Christian gnostic. He sets out his Christian convictions in relation to the contemporary Weltanschauung and religion in three writings: the "exhortation to the Greeks", the *Paedagogus* and the "carpet bags" (*Stromata*). The latter, as the title is intended to show, is a collection of varied reflections devoted to the relation of Christian to "pagan" (Greek) wisdom. In this connection he sets over against the "heretical" or "false" gnosis the true gnosis of the Christian or perfect gnostic, who as a mature Christian in oneness with God and in ethical perfection, like the angels, represents the spiritual priesthood which Clement himself endeavours to realise along with his disciples, without breaking with the institutional church or overlooking the fundamental commandment of love to one's neighbour. "The life of the gnostic is, in my view, no other than works and words which corre-

* *Clem. Alex., Strom. VII,* spond to the tradition of the Lord".* With his conscious use of
104,2 the concept "gnosis" for the Christian knowledge of truth Clement once again attempted to overcome the breach between faith and knowledge in the Church and not to remain stuck in a mere denial of the claims of the "false" gnosis. The quotations from gnostic teachers scattered through his uncompleted Stromata, especially those from Valentinus, and the "Excerpts from (the work of the Valentinian gnostic) Theodotus" form a valuable addition to the original witnesses for this religion. To-
* *op. cit. 17, 108* wards the end of the seventh book*, with which the work breaks off, Clement gives a short summary of what he evidently wanted later to represent in detail about the gnostic movements (the Excerpta already mentioned also point to this); it is at the

same time an illustration of the principles of division which un-
derlie most heresiological presentations. "So far as the sects are
concerned, they are named after the names of their founders
like the schools of Valentinus and Marcion and Basilides, although they also boast that they present the views of Matthias.
For there was only one doctrine of all the apostles and so also
only a single tradition. Other sects are named after a place like
the Peratae, others after a people, like the sect of the Phrygi-
ans, other after their conduct like the Encratites, others after
peculiar doctrines like the Docetists and the Haematites, others after their basic ideas and what they worshipped, like the
Cainites and the so-called Ophians, others according to the
lawless practices which they venture, like the so-called Enty-
chites among the Simonians"[8].

Origen (died 253/254) also endeavoured to oppose the gnos- **Origen**
tic heresy in similar fashion. Here too, as with Clement, we can
readily identify ideas which bring him close to the Gnosis which
he opposes, such as the high estimate of knowledge over
against simple faith or the doctrine of the pre-existent soul, its
fall into matter and its return to God. Among his numerous
writings – he is the most productive of the Church Fathers – the
commentaries on biblical texts fill a large place; unfortunately
apart from a few fragments they are lost. Among those surviving are eight books of exposition of the Gospel of John, which
are important for research into Gnosis because of their discussion of the gnostic exegesis of this Gospel, a special favourite
among the Valentinians. The 48 quotations from the commentary on John by Heracleon, a distinguished disciple of Valentinus who is to be dated in the middle of the second century, are
among the most important witnesses for the gnostic interpretation of scripture. It is interesting to observe how Origen, with
the same method of interpretation as his opponent, namely that
of discovering a deeper and esoteric meaning behind the text,
endeavours to accomplish an exegesis acceptable for the
Church. By the use of this method he was able to provide a Biblical basis for his heresies which were later censured by the orthodox.

In other works too (for example in his "Contra Celsum") Origen repeatedly has occasion to speak of gnostic doctrines, but
the yield is rather less than in the case of Clement. The majority
of his works however have not survived. As he himself re-

marks, he made special efforts to obtain gnostic documents, although evidently with no great success.*

When the gnostic danger abated in the course of the 3rd and
4th centuries, and the production of gnostic literature came to
an end, the anti-heretical works also are no longer so relevant,
at least so far as concerns Gnosis in the narrower sense; however at that time began the conflict with Manicheism, to which we
shall turn later. The first Church History by Eusebius of Caesarea (died 339), which incorporates a great deal of older material, naturally also affords something for the study of Gnosis,
although not so much in the way of original quotations as in
quotations from the older heresiological literature, which to
some extent has not otherwise survived (for example the "Me-
morabilia" of Hegesippus from the second half of the second
century). Only in the fourth century are we offered once again a
comprehensive work on the history of heresy, which is to be
counted with those of Irenaeus and Hippolytus as among the
best known and most influential. Its author was Epiphanius of
Salamis (Constantia), elected in 367 as Metropolitan (arch-
bishop) of Cyprus. He was born about 315 in the neighbourhood of Eleutheropolis in Judaea and for almost thirty years
was the head of a monastery in this town, which he had founded
at the age of twenty after the pattern of Egyptian monasticism.
He died in 403 on a journey home to Salamis, where he lived.
Epiphanius was one of the most zealous defenders of orthodoxy in his time, and repeatedly played a none too honourable
role in the theological controversies of the period. It was he
who was the first to set alight the struggle against Origenism.
His part in the further course of the debate was not always very
happy, which may perhaps be excused on the ground of his
great age and a certain simple-mindedness. At any rate his
blind zeal for orthodoxy, as he himself presents it in his book
"The firmly anchored" (*Ancoratus*), can be traced everywhere
in his works. To his traditionalism there must be added his hostility to Greek science and to philosophical and theological
speculation, which brings him close to Tertullian and divides
him fundamentally from the Alexandrian theologians. His
learning (he is said among other things to have mastered not
only Greek but also Syriac, Hebrew and Coptic) was thus evidently developed in a very one-sided manner. He had no scientific method at all. This can be seen especially in his major

See below, p. 326 ff.
Eusebius
of Caesarea

Epiphanius
of Salamis

Plate 2

work, the "Medicine chest" (*Panarion*, written 374–377), which won for him the title "Patriarch of Orthodoxy". The basic idea of this book is to portray all the heretics as fierce and venomous wild beasts (especially as serpents), whose poison endangers the purity of the faith; in its defence and as an antidote for those already bitten he offers his "medicine chest". In the characterisation of the heretics he makes use, as has just been suggested, of the zoological literature of his period.[9] Linking up with Song of Solomon 6.8, he adduces in a very schematic manner eighty heresies, twenty of which are pre-Christian, and among these Greek philosophy as a whole and the Jewish sects are included. Of the sixty more or less Christian heresies he has detailed information to give about only the half. His attempt to adduce as many sects or names of sects as possible makes him act quite uncritically in his treatment of the facts, and even seduces him into invention and quite improbable reports. By this he brought the history of early Christian heresy into great confusion, and critical research has first laboriously had to separate the wheat from the chaff, a task which even today is still not complete.

Epiphanius was however an industrious collector, and in particular he ransacked the older heresiological literature (including what is now lost), above all Justin, Irenaeus and Hippolytus, who are to some extent quoted word for word. In addition he repeatedly adduces gnostic documents which in one way or another were accessible to him, and which we can only identify in part. He seeks his support however not in literary witnesses alone but also in his own personal experience. Here his experience with the sect of the Barbeliotes, who are also described simply as "gnostics", is particularly instructive.* On his visit to Egypt about 335, which brought him in particular to the Egyptian monks, he fell into the clutches of this sect and obtained knowledge of their secret doctrines and obscene rites, until he freed himself from their hands and full of indignation made a report to the Church authorities, who immediately expelled 18 members of the sect from the Church. How far these events actually took place and are not be put down to the fancy of the author may be left undecided, but the methods adopted in his heresy-hunting shed no favourable light upon him. For Epiphanius all heretics are "vain-glorious", "worthless" and "evil-minded"; their apostasy from the pure apostolic doctrine of the

* *Epiphanius, Panarion 26,17*

church condemns them to destruction. Through derivation of younger sects, or of entire movements, from older ones he sets up a family tree of heresy which has but little to do with historical reality.

Since because of its size and its prolixity the book was too inconvenient, a shorter summary was prepared soon after the author's death (*Anakephalaiosis; Recapitulatio*). This almost displaced the original and became the source for later works of the kind (e. g. by Augustine and John of Damascus).

The surviving histories of heresy from the following period afford no new material for the history of Gnosticism, although now and again we may come across some covert report which has historical value. Thus for example the prose hymns (*Mad-*

Ephraem *rashe*) of the great Syrian father Ephraem of Edessa (306–373)
of Edessa are an important source for gnostic and semi-gnostic doctrines
Theodoret in the region of Syria. Theodoret of Cyrus (about 395–466)
of Cyrus wrote a history of heresy in five books which through its arrangement, oriented to theological problems, remained influential
Augustine down to the historical writing of modern times. Augustine (354–430) wrote in addition to several anti-Manichean writings a catalogue of heresies (*De haeresibus*) which introduces 88 heresies and, as already mentioned, is heavily dependent on the Re-
John capitulatio of Pseudo-Epiphanius. John of Damascus (about
of Damascus 675–749), who ranks as the last of the Church Fathers and worked in the period of Islamic dominance, set out the history of heresies on the basis of the older patterns already mentioned. This forms the second part of his chief work, the "Source of Knowledge", and at the end (chapter 100) deals with the new sects of the "Ishmaelites, Hagarenes or Saracens", i. e. Arabic Islam. From a still later period we may mention the Scholia of the Syrian author
Theodore Theodore bar Konai deriving from 791/792, which is of great
bar Konai value for research because of its reports about the Mandeans and Manichees, but for the rest likewise only copies the Recapitulatio. This traditionalistic approach, which can be traced right down to the heresiological literature of Islam, made the catalogues of he-

1

Hippolytus of Rome (d. 235). This marble statue was found in 1551 in the crypt of Hippolytus in Rome, and the missing upper part restored. The chair and lower part of the body are ancient (2nd cent.?). The identification with the Church Father has in modern times been questioned. Probably it represents another (female?) figure. The data about Hippolytus' calendar calculations and his writings were carved upon the pedestal by his adherents (c. 235/37), but it was only in the 16th century that it was made out to be a statue of the heresiologist.

2

Epiphanius of Salamis (315–403). Fresco from the cathedral at Faras in Nubia (end of 11th cent.).
Of the Greek inscriptions on the left only the lowest is fairly legible; it relates to Manicheism,
which this contentious Father combatted among other heresies: "The devilish wickedness from the
land of the Persians thou hast exposed (?), holy Epiphanius".

3–7

Magic gems of the Abrasax or anguiped type. The figures (with cock's or ass's head and serpent feet) bear names of Hebrew or Jewish origin which are also to be found in gnostic texts as the names of gods or archons (especially the Demiurge): Jao Abrasax Sabaoth Adonaios (3), Jao (4 and 6), Abrasax (7), Sabao[th] Abrasax (5, with the boat of the Sun). Abrasax or Abraxas has the Greek letters corresponding to the number 365, and thus represents the god of the (solar) year and of eternity (*aion*), whom some gnostics (Basilides, Marcus) also took over.

8

Alabaster bowl with representation of a cultic scene (serpent worship?). 3rd/5th cent. Syria or Asia Minor. Origin disputed. A proverb on the outside points to Orphism, while the ceremony depicted (16 naked initiates worshipping a winged serpent which is surrounded by sun-rays) recalls the cult of the Ophites (see p.247).

resies not only a fixed and increasingly unrealistic constituent of apologetic and theological writing, but also a means of coming to grips with new heresies and of combatting them by referring back to the "classic" constituent of the heresy of bygone history, and to some extent by identifying them with names familiar from it.

THE OLDER SOURCES

Well into the 19th century the heresiological literature mentioned above formed our principal source for the study of the nature and the history of Gnosis and determined the course of earlier research, which was devoted in particular to the necessary source criticism. The quotations in this literature provided a range of original documents; yet in all they did not even fill fifty printed pages. This was regrettable in that it was increasingly recognised that the gnostics had produced the first Christian theological literature of all, the extent of which in the second century was evidently much greater than that in the Catholic church. This holds not only for theological works in the narrower sense, but also for poetry and the literature of simple piety, as is shown by the remains of hymns and the numerous apocryphal stories about Jesus and the apostles. Of the great gnostics of the second century, like Basilides and Valentinus, only scanty fragments are available to us, although we are to some extent informed about their extensive literary work, which included gospels, commentaries on biblical texts, letters, homilies, psalms and hymns. The same is true for their disciples.

Quotations in the heresiologists

In addition to these few authentic pieces preserved for us by the Church Fathers, some further original texts turned up in the course of time, but to begin with they did not fundamentally change the picture of Gnosis. The oldest literary work of this kind known to us is the so-called *Corpus Hermeticum*, a collection of Greek texts from the second and third centuries A. D., probably originating in Egypt, which purports to be proclamations of "Thrice great Hermes" (*Hermes Trismegistos*), behind

The Corpus Hermeticum

9
Subterranean basilica at the Porta Maggiore, Rome (1st cent. A. D.). The origin and use of this underground sanctuary are disputed. Some ascribe it to a Neopythagorean sect, others to an unknown "mystery" community. In addition to the catacombs, the gnostics could have used similar assembly halls. Epiphanius reports of the Adamites that they assembled in underground "heating vaults" (Panarion 52.2.1).

whom we may detect the Egyptian god of Wisdom, Thot. These are a typical product of the Graeco-oriental syncretism of the Roman Empire and present an occult revelation-wisdom intended to promote the effort after the vision of God, rebirth and the liberation or redemption of the soul. Here alongside mysticism, ecstasy and meditation, magic and astrology also had a part to play. Among the eighteen tractates and portions of tractates in this collection there are some which have a gnos-**The Poimandres** tic character, particularly the first, which bears the name "Poimandres" ("shepherd of men") and which for a time gave its name to the whole work. The recognition that here we have a document of non-Christian gnosis became prevalent in the 19th century, although at first only gradually, and was finally established by R. Reitzenstein. Previously the collection was regarded as exclusively a product of Neoplatonic mysticism. On the basis of a very poor manuscript tradition, it was translated into Latin for the first time in 1463 by Marsiglio Ficino, at the instance of Cosimo de Medici; printed in 1471, it exercised a great influence on Renaissance philosophy in Italy. Several editions appeared in the course of the sixteenth and seventeenth centuries, of which that of 1554 offered the Greek text for the first time. Franciscus Patricius (Patrizi) in 1591, in a book "New Philosophy" dedicated to Pope Gregory XIV, even attempted to supplant the Catholic school philosophy of Aristotle, since he saw in the teachings of Hermes something that was in conformity with Christian thought. In 1781 appeared a German translation by Dietrich Tiedemanns under the title "Hermes Trismegists Poemander oder von der göttlichen Macht und Weisheit". A serviceable and critical edition of the text was only produced after the second world war by A. D. Nock, with a French translation by A.-J. Festugière (in four volumes, 1945–1954). It also contains all the fragments which have been found elsewhere in quotations from the literature of late antiquity. Among these is a text extant only in Latin which has been **Asclepius** called "Asclepius", since it contains a revelation speech from Hermes to Asclepius. The Greek original, which is evidently to be dated to the second century, bore the title "Perfect Teaching" (*Logos Teleios*) and as we now know from Coptic discoveries was used by the gnostics.

In contrast to the Hermetic collection, which can only partially be claimed for Gnosis, four works handed down in Coptic are unmistakably products of gnostic sects. They are known to us from two manuscripts of the fourth and fifth centuries, which were acquired in the eighteenth century by two British collectors: the Codex Askewianus by the English physician Dr. Askew and the Codex Brucianus by the Scot James Bruce; the first found its way into the British Museum in London and the second to the Bodleian Library in Oxford. They were first brought to the attention of scholars by C. G. Woide in 1778. To him also is due the title "Pistis Sophia" ("Faith-Wisdom") for the document in the Codex Askewianus. A first printing of the text with a Latin translation was published in Berlin in 1851 by M. G. Schwartze. In 1895 E. Amélineau published a translation into French. The standard German translation was prepared under the auspices of the Patristic Commission of the Prussian Academy of Sciences by the Berlin church historian Carl Schmidt, who did so much for the publication of Coptic texts (1905, 3rd edition 1959); he was also responsible for the last edition of the original text (1925). The book consists of three parts and contains lengthy conversations between the risen Jesus and his male and female disciples about the fall and redemption of a heavenly being, the so-called "Pistis Sophia". A fourth part is an independent document, which likewise presents revelations of Jesus to his disciples. Both these works belong to the late phase of gnostic literary composition (third century); they are not on the highest level of inspiration, but are none the less of importance for the development of gnostic thinking and also for the text of the psalms which they incorporate.

The Pistis Sophia

To the same period we should also evidently assign the three (incomplete) texts of the Codex Brucianus, first published and translated by E. Amélineau in 1891. Shortly afterwards (1892) C. Schmidt published the edition still standard today, and a German version together with the Pistis Sophia (1905; the translation of the two manuscripts occupies 367 pages). Here we have two tractates which have passed into the literature under the name "the two Books of Jeu", since as Schmidt was the first to observe they are quoted under this title in the Pistis Sophia, with which they are also related. Their proper name however, according to the subscription contained only in the first tractate, is "Book of the great mysterious Word (*logos*)". In these the risen Jesus once again reveals to his disciples the secrets of the gnostic world beyond. By way of supplement there

The two Books of Jeu

are three fragments, of which two are prayers. The final text in the manuscript is a work handed down without title and described by Schmidt as "an unknown gnostic work". It is not a document of revelation, but an extended and fragmentary topography of the heavenly world of light and its beings, among whom Seth plays a prominent role.[9a]

Papyrus Berolinensis 8502 To these first Coptic gnostic writings, which already provided an indication of the importance of Egypt in the history of Gnosis, a further discovery was added towards the end of the 19th century. In 1896 C. Schmidt reported in the Sitzungsberichte of the Prussian Academy of Sciences on the acquisition of a Coptic papyrus volume in Cairo for the Egyptian section of the Berlin Museum, containing the three following gnostic texts: the "Gospel of Mary", of which several pages are missing, the "Apocryphon (Secret Book) of John" and the "Sophia Jesu Christi". A fourth text at the end of the Codex, "the Act of Peter", is a piece from the apocryphal Acts of Peter, which is not indeed gnostic but like other legendary literature was among the favourite reading of the gnostics.

The publication of these documents, which are of unusual importance for research into Gnosis, was dogged by singular misfortune. When the printing of the first edition, prepared by Schmidt, was almost finished it was completely destroyed by a burst water-pipe in the cellar of the printing house. War and the post-war situation prevented any new beginning, and only in 1938 did Schmidt prepare a new impression, which however was delayed through his death in the same year. Walter Till, who took over the work in 1941, completed it in 1943, but because of the war situation was unable to publish. Then after the end of the war (1946) there suddenly appeared a new discovery of Coptic gnostic books in Egypt, which also contained some texts parallel to the Berlin Codex, namely the Apocryphon of John and Sophia Jesu Christi. Till was able to take account of these to a considerable extent for the revision of his edition which had thereby become necessary, and this was finally published by the Akademie-Verlag in 1955, 59 years after the discovery, under the title *Die gnostischen Schriften des Koptischen Papyrus Berolinensis 8502*. A second edition, revised by H. M. Schenke, appeared in 1972. The significance of these documents will be discussed when we come to deal with the Nag Hammadi texts.

See below, p. 34 f.

Worthy of mention is finally a small collection of hymns in **The Odes** Syriac which are to be assigned to the area of gnostic literature **of Solomon** and are current under the name "Odes of Solomon". The Church Father Lactantius (third century) already quoted from them; through the Pistis Sophia mentioned above five complete Odes made their appearance in a Coptic version which was edited for the first time and translated into Latin by the Danish bishop F. Münter in 1812 (in the context of an invitation to a pastoral synod). In 1909 the English scholar J. Rendel Harris discovered an old Syriac manuscript which contained all but the first two of forty-two Odes; this is even today the most complete collection. These hymns are of value particularly because of their figurative language, which links them with other gnostic documents of the East; they are in addition a notable example of the close inter-relationship of Christian and Gnostic church piety. They originated probably in the second century; whether they were originally written in Greek or Aramaicis debated.

Another piece of gnostic poetry from roughly the same peri- **The Hymn** od derives from the region of Syria. This is the famous "Hymn **of the Pearl** of the Pearl", contained in the apocryphal Acts of Thomas.[*] *[*] Acts of Thomas,* The apostle Judas Thomas sings it in an Indian prison to com- *chapt. 108–113* fort his fellow prisoners. The text is extant both in Syriac and also in a Greek version. The former deserves the preference since it stands closer to the original, while the latter is a later revision. Its origin and author are both unknown. The hymn is one of the most impressive examples of gnostic poetry. It presents the fable of the sending of a prince from the East to Egypt in search of a hidden treasure, the pearl, which after a period of forgetfulness he carries off. In this way he is at the same time brought on his homeward journey, which he successfully completes. Behind the story and interwoven with it stands the gnostic myth of the liberation of the soul from darkness into the kingdom of light. The fable thus at one and the same time is a parable and has a symbolic significance.

From the other Apocryphal Acts also a whole range of gnos- **Apocryphal** tic statements can be extracted, such as the crucifixion scene in **Acts of Apostles** the Acts of John, which belongs entirely to gnostic Christology. It seems that this extensive popular literature, which is a continuation of the ancient romance literature, found a cordial welcome in the gnostic communities, since it offered ample nourishment to phantasy and delight in fable and was a means of bringing gnostic views to expression in disguised form. The heresiologists also attest the fondness of the gnostics (including the Manicheans) for this apocryphal literature.

The Mandean literature   A completely independent gnostic tradition, although one which also belongs to oriental and semitic culture, is preserved by the communities of the Mandeans already mentioned at the beginning. This is considerable in extent – corresponding roughly to that of the Old Testament. Parts of it were already brought in the 16th century to Europe through the offices of Portuguese monks; scientific concern with this literature first began in the 19th century, and in our century the fact that it belongs to a branch of oriental Gnosis has been more and more recognised. The publication of the Mandean books and documentary rolls is even today not yet complete, to say nothing of taking stock of what is actually present among the communities themselves. We shall deal with the Mandeans in a separate

See below, p. 343 ff.   chapter.

THE HISTORY OF RESEARCH[10]

The earlier phase   The situation with regard to sources which has just been discussed was decisive for earlier research into Gnosis and the resultant picture of it. After Gottfried Arnold in 1699, in his *Unparteiischen Kirchen- und Ketzerhistorie*, had passionately argued for a new view of church history which could seek the true Christianity among the outlaws and the heretics, the ground was prepared for an independent consideration of the gnostics, and in the first place in particular with the sources relating to them. The reformed theologian Isaac de Beausobre published the first modern monograph on Manicheism (1734/39), and Johann Lorenz von Mosheim undertook "several attempts" at an "independent and unprejudiced history of heresy" (1739/58), which were devoted to individual heresies – among others the Ophites. It was however the twenties of the 19th century which really formed the beginning of modern research into Gnosis, when August Neander in 1818 published a *Genetische Entwicklung der vornehmsten gnostischen Systeme* and the Frenchman J. Matter his *Histoire critique du Gnosticisme* (1828, German edition 1833). The real founder of research into gnosis was however the famous Tübingen church

historian Ferdinand Christian Baur (1792/1860), who already **Ferdinand**
in his doctoral thesis of 1827 had concerned himself with the **Christian Baur**
Christianity of the gnostics. His book *Die Christliche Gnosis*
oder die christliche Religions-Philosophie in ihrer geschichtli-
chen Entwicklung (1835), which is even today still worth reading, is a landmark in research in this field, even if his attempt to
treat the gnostics as the starting point of the Christian philosophy of religion which culminated in Hegel does not do justice to
them. Here as elsewhere Baur has not yet completely escaped
from philosophical (Hegelian) speculation.

What is specially worthy of note in these early works is the
fact that they emphasise the singular and non-Christian element in Gnosis and prefer a derivation from the "Orient", a
conception which first became fashionable again in the 20th
century. Since on the basis of the evidence available Gnosis was
regarded primarily as a philosophy, and efforts were made to
get to the bottom of its speculative system and find its origin,
the Graeco-platonic philosophy in addition provided an important background, especially in its association with Judaism, for
which in Alexandria the Jewish philosopher Philo (1st century
A.D.) is the most important witness. This view represented by
Neander, Baur and R. A. Lipsius largely determined the course
of research in the 19th century. As in research into religion in
general in this period, so in this field also a narrow delimitation
of the nature of the phenomenon along with a search for its
origin was the standard approach.

A further impulse was given to research through the work of **Adolph**
Adolph von Harnack (1851–1930), on the one hand through his **von Harnack**
contributions to the investigation of sources (his dissertation already was devoted to this theme), and on the other by the fact
that he assigned to the Gnosticism of the second century an important position in the history of Christian dogma. The latter
found its classic expression in his *Lehrbuch der Dogmenge-*
schichte, which first appeared in 1886 and set the treatment of
gnosticism under the programmatic heading: "the attempt of
the gnostics to create an apostolic doctrine of faith and a Christian theology, or: the acute secularisation of Christianity". In
this way he laid the basis for an assessment of Gnosis from the
point of view of church history, which was indeed present in
embryo in Baur, but which now first clearly emerged and became normative for almost half a century thereafter. Gnosis is

the Hellenisation of Christianity (that is what Harnack understood by "secularisation"); it was kept at a distance from the church by orthodoxy. Harnack later showed himself open to newer insights. For example he made room for the Jewish contribution to the origin of Gnosis, and indeed recognised an extra-Christian Gnosis, but he regarded this as "a Syrian vulgar-Gnosis" and assigned to it no significance for the history of Christianity. This shows that he wanted to treat Gnosis only within this church-historical framework; its history before and after was of no interest to him. This point of view has still found its representatives in more recent research (especially in the English speaking world).

Adolf Hilgenfeld   Another conception was represented by Adolf Hilgenfeld; it is summed up in his *Ketzergeschichte des Urchristentums* (1884). For him Gnosis is a non-Christian phenomenon which originated among the Samaritans, and which despite its Christianisation did not give up its own basis and was above all of influence upon Jewish Christianity. However, it lost its original universal outlook and became an esoteric "élite gnosis", and indeed a Christian heresy. One weakness which can be detected in Hilgenfeld is his unduly close adhesion to the heresiological sources.

Wilhelm Bousset   A third stage can be identified with the work *Hauptprobleme der Gnosis* (1907) by the Protestant New Testament scholar Wilhelm Bousset. He brought research into Gnosis beyond any doubt out of the narrow confines of church history into the open air of Religionsgeschichte, in that he sought to explain the origin of Gnosis from a pre-Christian mixture of Babylonian and Iranian religion, and so gave a new impulse to consideration of its early stages. His aim was pursued further by the philologist Richard Reitzenstein, who was one of the most stimulating gnostic scholars and made a great contribution to the opening up of new sources. For him too Gnosis is rooted in the Orient. Its core is an "Iranian redemption mystery" centring on the identity of God and the soul, which originated in Persia in pre-Christian times and is to be found in its purest form in Manicheism and Mandeism, but has also exercised an influence in the mystery religions of late antiquity (the idea of the universal god). By these investigations into the history of religions, the New Testament was more and more drawn into the area of research into Gnosis, particularly through works from the school

Richard Reitzenstein

of the well-known New Testament scholar Rudolph Bultmann, who made fruitful use of the concerns of the so-called "Religionsgeschichtliche Schule", to which Bousset and a number of other Protestant theologians belonged. Since then Gnosis has presented a problem for New Testament scholarship. The mutual relationships between the New Testament or primitive Christianity and early Gnosis are a hotly contested field of research.

In a book which is probably among the best known of all books on Gnosis, an attempt was made to clear up the questions of the nature and originality of Gnosis, which had been thrown up by the detailed investigations and analyses but never satisfactorily answered, and in particular the question raised by Reitzenstein of its relation to the religion of late antiquity in general. This is the work *Gnosis and spätantiker Geist* by Hans Jonas, a pupil of Bultmann and M. Heidegger, the first part of which appeared in 1934. Since Jonas was compelled by National Socialism to leave Germany, the continuation of his work had to be interrupted; it was taken up again only after the second World War (1954) with the appearance of the first half-volume of the second part, which was already complete in 1934, and even today has not yet been finished. In the interval Jonas has published also a new summary of his views in a book in English, *The Gnostic Religion* (1958). It may be said without exaggeration that Jonas introduced a new and fourth stage in modern research into Gnosis, since he sought to determine the nature of Gnosis and its statements in an analysis which was indeed based on existentialism, but in which for the first time he offered a comprehensive view of what had so far been investigated, and so provided scholarship with a means of getting a clear picture of the peculiar nature of the subject. The historical question of the origin of Gnosis is answered only in a very general way by reference to the appearance of a new "understanding of existence" in the Orient before or parallel with the rise of Christianity. But the view of the world which is provided in the numerous statements and the imagery of the gnostic systems is determined by a strict dualism which subjects everything visible or belonging to the world to criticism and rejection; the only secure foundation is a world beyond which can be described only in negative terms, and to which man belongs in a hidden part of himself, and from this alone is deliverance to be expected.

Hans Jonas

Jonas, who demonstrates this in an inspired analysis of gnostic ideas, is of the opinion that wide areas of late antiquity – "the spirit of late antiquity" – are influenced by this gnostic view of the world; he can speak of a "gnostic age". To what extent this is accurate – for example in Philo, Origen, or Plotinus – is still under discussion today. What is at any rate certain is that through Jonas Gnosis was finally liberated from its scientific "ghetto existence" and became the subject of widespread interest. This is not in any way affected by Jonas' allegiance in terms of method to Heidegger and (to some extent) Spengler, which was a sign of the times and was later modified by Jonas himself. The argument from ideological and speculative statements to man and his self-understanding which is expressed in such statements is in any case a new starting point to which Marxist research also, which however has scarcely applied itself to this area, can link on, in order to give to research into Gnosis the necessary sociological depth.

Since the work of Jonas represents the last great survey on the basis of the classical source material as we have outlined it, it forms at the same time the crown and culmination of an entire period, in particular since the beginning of the *religionsgeschichtliche* approach in Bousset and Reitzenstein. After the second World War, under the impulse of major new discoveries of material, there began a new epoch in research into Gnosis which may be regarded as a fifth stage. With this we shall be concerned in the following chapter.

The Nag Hammadi Discovery and its Significance

Qumran and Nag Hammadi The discovery of Hebrew manuscripts in 1947 on the West bank of the Dead Sea near Wadi Qumran attracted attention far beyond the circle of scholars. It belongs beyond doubt to the most important finds of this kind and for that reason was extensively described and evaluated, and not only in the specialist journals. On the other hand another discovery has aroused less of a sensation among the wider public. It was made roughly about the same time in Egypt and is of similar significance, since for the first time it brought to light an extensive quantity of original gnostic texts in the Coptic language. It is interesting to observe that these two discoveries show certain parallels. Both belong to communities which stand at the fringe and took a critical view of the official religion, the Qumran community (the Essenes) over against the Judaism of Jerusalem, the gnostics over against the orthodox church. Both collections of manuscripts were evidently concealed in times of crisis and under external pressure. In their ideology also, despite all the clear differences, there are certain points of agreement: both communities cherish a dualistic way of thinking and stand in hostility over against the world, they hope for a redemption either through an eschatological and apocalyptic victory of the "sons of light" over darkness or through the liberation of the soul, the divine spark, to the kingdom of light beyond this world. We shall see that there are also historical threads which link the two religious movements together.

In contrast to the Qumran texts, the story of the discovery of the Coptic gnostic texts is still largely veiled in obscurity, since **The story of the discovery** the place of discovery could no longer be precisely located and up to 1975 no archaeological investigation had taken place in the area. The course of the discovery and publication of this collection, as so often in the history of research into antiquity, is governed by many factors – personal, scientific and political – which could lead one to write a novel from them which would easily glide over numerous gaps and uncertainties in our information. Let us follow the course of events in broad outline; this in itself is interesting enough.[11]

On 4th October 1946 Togo Mina, then curator of the Coptic Museum in Old Cairo, purchased for 250 Egyptian pounds an incomplete and damaged Coptic papyrus codex offered to him by a Coptic teacher from the region of Nag Hammadi named Raghib Andrawus "al Quss" Abd as-Sajjid. As it later turned out, this was Codex III of the complete library. At the beginning of December in the same year, Togo Mina showed this new acquisition to two French Orientalists, Francois Daumas and Henri Corbin, who were already able to establish the gnostic character of the document on the basis of the name of one tractate, the Secret Book (Apocryphon) of John. Daumas, who first returned to Paris and there informed Antoine Guillaumont, planned an edition for the following year. In September 1947 however another Frenchman, Jean Doresse, also came to

Egypt for his studies, and was likewise informed by Togo Mina of the new discovery. Immediately on reading a few passages – among other things "Sacred Book of the Great Invisible Spirit" as well as the title "Secret Book of John" – he recognised the great importance of the codex and undertook a closer inspection. He also passed on the information to the director of the Egyptian Department of Antiquities, Etienne Drioton, and the Paris historian of religions Henri-Charles Puech. The pages of the Codex were then put under glass for security in December 1947. The public was informed for the first time by the Egyptian press on the 11/12 January 1948. The world of scholarship learned of it on the 8th of February 1948 in a report by Puech and Doresse to the Académie des Inscriptions et Belles-Lettres in Paris, and four weeks later through a report by Togo Mina in the Bulletin de l'Institut d'Egypte. With this began a new era in research into Gnosis.

The Codex Jung   In the meantime the binding and some parts of a second Codex (today listed as number I) had passed into the possession of a Belgian antiquities dealer named Albert Eid, who first, again at the end of 1947, made this available to Doresse and to Mina for examination, but then found a way to bring it out of the country, where it underwent changing fortunes. First of all it was offered to the Bollingen Foundation in New York in the winter of 1947/48 for twelve thousand dollars, then to the Bibliothèque Nationale in Paris, in both cases without success. Since in this period the owner had died, there was a danger that this valuable manuscript would disappear for years on end, or even for ever. In this situation much is due to the Dutch church historian Gilles Quispel, who had already taken over the task of mediator in the negotiations for its purchase. In order to facilitate its acquisition by the Bollingen Foundation, he had entered into alliance with the famous and influential psychologist Carl Gustav Jung, who through his agent in the negotiations, C. A. Meier, found out about the new owner and the whereabouts of the Codex. At that time (1950) it was in the safe of a bank in Brussels. In August 1951 purchase by the Bollingen Foundation was agreed. After a further checking of the authenticity of the manuscript by experts in March 1952 the purchase should have been completed, but this did not come about. At this time C. A. Meier was able to find a new Maecenas in Switzerland, George H. Page, who made the sum of thirty-five thousand

Swiss francs available for the purchase. On the 10th of May 1952 the manuscript was finally handed over in Brussels to the C. G. Jung Institute. Jung himself was to have received the valuable manuscript as a birthday gift. It was therefore given the name "Codex Jung". A report about the purchase followed, according to agreement, only on the 15th of November 1953 from H. C. Puech and G. Quispel. The first major description with a more detailed account of its contents appeared finally in 1955 in a book with the title *The Jung Codex. A Newly recovered Gnostic Papyrus*. In the same year, while he was inspecting further manuscript fragments acquired in the interval, Quispel discovered in Cairo some of the pages missing from the Codex Jung, which proved conclusively that they all belonged to the same find. By an agreement between the Coptic Museum and the owners of the Codex Jung (after Jung's death the question of ownership had become a source of dispute between his heirs and the Jung Institute), it was arranged that the Codex after publication should be returned to Cairo, in order to bring the whole discovery together there. This was for the most part done in 1975. The valuable leather binding, long regarded as lost, has in the interval become the property of the Institute for Antiquity and Christianity in Claremont (California).

In the year 1948 a further nine more or less complete papyrus books were brought to Cairo from upper Egypt by middlemen who are not identified. They were collected by a well-known antique dealer Phocion J. Tano, who was represented in the negotiations by the daughter of a noted Italian numismatist, Maria Dattari. The uncertain situation with regard to property rights in antiquities found in Egypt at that time made it necessary to handle all negotiations very delicately and avoid any sensation. Mrs. Dattari therefore first made contact with J. Doresse, who was able to make a rapid survey in October 1948 and again identified some titles ("Revelation of Adam to his Son Seth", "Gospel of Thomas", "Paraphrase of Shem" etc.) which showed these documents also to be gnostic. He informed E. Drioton and advised their purchase for the Coptic Museum in Cairo. In the spring of 1949 the volumes were handed over for inspection to Togo Mina, who asked Doresse to draw up a more detailed inventory of their contents. This inventory remained for some years the only source of information about the content of the writings and was the basis of the studies published about

The first   them by Togo Mina, Doresse and Puech. On 17th June 1949
research reports Doresse gave a report about them to the Paris Académie des
Inscriptions et Belles-Lettres of the Institut de France, and in
1950 there appeared the first comprehensive survey of the
whole discovery from the pen of H.-Ch. Puech. To protect the
valuable material from outside interference and to prevent any
loss, or perhaps their removal out of the country, Drioton decided to place it for the time being in a sealed box in his office at
the Egyptian Department of Antiquities. The Coptic Museum
was in the meantime to seek the money for the purchase from
the government. At this point political events repeatedly inter-
vened in the destiny of this discovery and delayed for years its
publication. In the first place it was indeed possible for a sum of
money to be made available – the sum of fifty thousand Egyptian pounds or fifty million (old) francs is mentioned – but the
murder of the Prime Minister, the death of Togo Mina who had
long been a sick man (1949), and finally the collapse of the mo-
narchy through the Egyptian Revolution on the 23rd July,
1952, prevented any clearing up of the situation. The famous
blind Egyptian author and scholar Taha Hussain had a short
time previously, in his capacity as Minister of Information, giv-
en permission for the manuscripts to be studied even before
their purchase. For this reason they were transferred on 9th
June, 1952 to the Coptic Museum, where the whole find has
been preserved ever since. From July 1952 to autumn 1956 the
texts remained inaccessible in the box already mentioned. The
re-organisation of the Egyptian Department of Antiquities and
of the Coptic Museum, over which Pahor Labib, an Egyptolo-
gist trained in Berlin, served as Director from 1951, led finally
to the decision that the Coptic Gnostic papyrus books should be
declared state property and the responsibility for their publication handed over to the Museum. In this way the situation with
regard to ownership was finally cleared up and the work of editing could be taken in hand.

P. Labib began in 1956 with the preparation of an inventory
and the conservation or glazing, which continued until 1961 and
in which the Egyptian Coptologist Victor Girgis and the West
German Coptologist Martin Krause had a considerable part.
The West German Archaeological Institute in Cairo made
plexiglass panels available. It emerged that the discovery consisted of thirteen volumes, of which however only eleven are

complete, while of the two others (volumes 12 and 13) only portions and fragments have survived. There is evidence to indicate that volume 12, which also has no binding, was only mutilated in modern times, that is probably after the discovery, while volume 13 was not complete even in antiquity when the library was buried. The format of the documents is on average about 35 cm by 15 cm, and only the Codex Jung is more rectangular and smaller (29 cm by 14 cm). The pages are inscribed with only a single column, and for the most part in a regular, clear and beautiful hand, which indeed in some cases may be ranked among the masterpieces of calligraphy. Of special value are the bindings of soft goatskin (which however have not been preserved complete), in a form similar to our brief-cases, which originally enclosed the papyrus leaves which had been folded and stitched together. They are so far among the oldest of their kind (4th century A.D.).

Plates 14, 16

Before we turn to the content and the lengthy story of the publication of the discovery, something must be said about its presumed origin, i.e. about the place of discovery itself. As we have seen, the documents first came by mysterious channels to Cairo, without any information being supplied about their origin. J. Doresse did not leave the matter there and on his expeditions between 1947 and 1950 to the sites of early Christian monastic settlement in Upper Egypt endeavoured to obtain information on this subject. He learned very soon, most fully in January 1950, that the manuscripts had been found in 1945 in the neighbourhood of the present small town of Nag Hammadi halfway up the Nile. Here we may introduce the impressive description given by H.-Ch. Puech in Paris in 1953:

The place of discovery

See map, p. 40

"The Djebel-el-Târif is a high cliff of chalk whose southern slope faces the bend formed by the Nile some sixty miles down stream from Luxor. With its white and bare wall it dominates a plain in which, on the left bank of the river, stands the hamlet of Nag Hammadi, while on the right are the fields of sugar-cane which surround the villages of Debba, El-Qasr and Es-Sayyad, on the very site of the ancient Shenesit-Chenoboskion where St. Pachomius founded his first monasteries in the fourth century. On the east the cliff turns abruptly to the north and looks out above the sands of the desert, always abrupt and desolate, and is pierced by numerous cavities which are as many openings of tombs. Those half-way up are Pharaonic tombs of the sixth

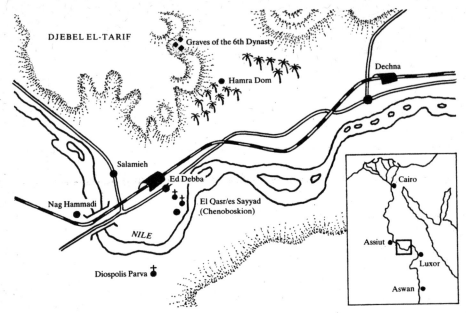

The surroundings of Nag Hammadi, with the presumed place of discovery (north-west of Hamra Dom at the foot of the Djebel-el-Tarif). The most recent investigations (1975) have yielded no evidence of graves from the Graeco-Roman period at the foot of the Djebel-el-Tarif in the neighbourhood of the finding-place. In the ancient Egyptian 6th dynasty burial ground the graves are those of officials, and not, as H. C. Puech erroneously thought (see above), of Pharaohs.

dynasty, while at the foot and up to a height of some three hundred feet are more modest tombs belonging to the Greco-Roman period. From a study made on the site by M. Jean Doresse three years ago it would seem that it was here c. 1945 that one of the most remarkable finds of our time was made.

We proceed to give in broad outlines the still very uncertain story.

The circumstances of discovery *Digging in the southern part of the cemetery, peasants from Debba and the neighbouring hamlet of Hamra-Doum chanced to light on a large jar. When they broke the vessel a number of MSS. fell out. The fellaheen attached no particular value to their discovery. Some of the pages which had come to light were torn up or burnt; the rest were sold for three Egyptian pounds and brought to Cairo where the writings were divided into three lots".* [12]

The rest of the story we know. A veil of darkness however still remained over the process of division (which is also attributed to the farmers themselves) and the intervening dealers.

Since the discovery derived from a casual grave robbery, the whole affair stood from the outset under the seal of silence, and publicity was avoided.

The circumstances of the discovery are notable enough and evidently were immediately elaborated with oriental delight in story-telling – especially where inquisitive strangers are concerned. Thus the ostensibly unsuspecting farmers are said to have used two volumes for lighting a fire. The traces of this which have been thought to be present in some texts have been explained in other ways (as due to chemical processes) and it is to be assumed that the Egyptian farmers were very well aware of the value of ancient treasures of this kind. According to another account the finder was a young man who had killed his father's murderer and had concealed himself in the deserted region of the old cemetery. One of the first who had the opportunity of seeing the find soon after the discovery is said to have been a young Coptic priest named David from the neighbourhood, who also attempted to decipher some of it. Later visits to this region by different scholars at first brought nothing fresh to light. It seemed as if the recollection of it had already faded, and most of the participants or informants were no longer alive. Only through some remarkable detective work by James M. Robinson did it become possible, in September 1975, to lift the veil of secrecy for the first time.[13] Starting from the entry in the records of the Coptic Museum regarding the purchase of Codex III from Raghib Andrawus, he made inquiries on the spot and was able not only to identify some of the intermediaries but also to find out that the real discoverer was a camel driver named Mohammed Ali es-Samman from the village of El *Plate 11* Qasr (the ancient Chenoboskion) who found the manuscripts in 1945 in a large clay jar in a cave near Hamra Dom in the neighbourhood of Nag Hammadi, while he was digging for fertiliser. Since four weeks later (January 1946) he killed his father's murderer from Hamra Dom he had never again visited this region for fear of blood vengeance. He described as the place of discovery, first of all the early Egyptian grave of Thauti, then a cave at the foot of the Djebel el-Tarif quite near the site already conjectured and photographed by Doresse in 1950. *Plate 13* Archaeological evidence however, such as fragments of the broken jar or shreds of papyrus, was not to be found in spite of intensive search. Also it was not possible to identify an ancient cemetery such as Doresse had assumed in this area. All that could be established was a few Coptic graves in the immediate vicinity of the conjectural place of discovery, so that the manu- scripts could certainly have have been buried or concealed in such a grave. The archaeological investigation of the region, which also includes a whole range of early Egyptian burial sites of the 6th dynasty (3rd century B.C.), has in the interval been undertaken by the Claremont Institute for Antiquity and Chris- tianity in three campaigns (1975, 1976, 1978), in the course of which the remains of the basilica of Pachomius at Pabau (today Faw Qibli) have in particular been investigated. This region, as already mentioned, was also the home of Christian monasti- cism.

The discovery was named after Nag Hammadi, the nearest township of any size (about 10 km distant; this is the English form of the Arabic name, which is also to be found at the rail- way station; it means "highly commendable place"); with the passing of time this name has become established. Initially it was also common for the discovery to be named after the an- cient monastic settlement of Chenoboskion, or after the two market towns El Qasr and Es-Sayyad, which today occupy its site. As we now know the village of Hamra Dom would proba- bly have had the best claim to be brought in this way to world- wide fame.

In addition to the external evidences passed on by Doresse there are also some indications in the discovery itself which at least point to the same area. These however were only disco- vered in recent times in the course of the work of preparation for publication. In one of the tractates* the temple of Diospolis is mentioned. This can mean either "little Diospolis" (Diospo- lis Parva), which lies quite close to Chenoboskion, or more probably the famous "Great Diospolis" (Diospolis Magna), the Thebes of ancient Egypt (in the neighbourhood of which the Codex Brucianus is said to have been discovered). An even stronger piece of evidence is a receipt for grain which was found in one of the bindings* and which mentions two persons, one of whom is from the district of Diospolis, the other from Dendera (between Diospolis Parva and Diospolis Magna in a bend of the Nile). Other fragments of letters and receipts, used to reinforce the bindings, give hints in regard to the probable time of manu- facture of the books: two receipts evidently bear the dates 333,

*NHC VI 6

Plate 15

*NHC VII

The date of the documents

341, 346 and 348. These data confirm the dating of the discovery already made previously, to the fourth century (about 350). The origin of the individual documents and their translation into Coptic naturally lie further back, somewhere in the second and third centuries. Since the fragments of letters in addition mention a "Father Pachom", presbyters and monks, we can infer a monastic environment. Perhaps the writings derive from the library of a monastery and were singled out and buried because of their heretical character in the course of some purging operation, or perhaps more probably they were brought to safety by interested parties and adherents. It is striking that it is just from this period that we possess the 39th Festal Letter of the pugnacious Athanasius of Alexandria, who among other things directs his attention against heretical books which falsely circulated under the names of the Apostles. This letter was translated into Coptic by the successor of Pachomius in the leadership of the monastery at Tabennisi, Theodore, and made known in 367 to the Egyptian monasteries. Even if it is not a question of an expressly anti-gnostic campaign, nevertheless hidden gnostic movements and books preserved in the desert by the hermit villages of Egypt could also have become involved in relation to the Christological conflicts of this period. For the moment we have no other information at our disposal.

As already mentioned, the content of the library was already made known between 1949 and 1950 by French scholars. As was immediately realised, it was the most comprehensive collection of gnostic writings so far, and great hopes and expectations for the future of research into Gnosis were associated with it. However the publication of the texts made very slow progress indeed, and was only brought near to completion in 1977. The inventories prepared by Doresse and Puech have in the interval been completed or corrected by more exact investigations. Great service was rendered here by the West German Coptologist Martin Krause, who from 1959 to 1961 in collaboration with the Coptic Museum in Cairo subjected the discovery to a thorough review and classification. Further improvements, especially in the fragmentary parts, resulted from the work of a research team from the Californian Institute for Antiquity and Christianity of the Claremont Graduate School under the direction of James M. Robinson. On the basis of this work the following is now established: according to the present

The writings in the Nag Hammadi discovery

state of the identification the thirteen volumes contain altogether fifty-one separate writings of varying content, with 1153 out of an original total of about 1257 pages, that is, almost ninety per cent of the library has been preserved. Of the fifty-one texts – Doresse in his time counted only forty-nine – forty-one are writings hitherto quite unknown, while the remainder are either duplicates of documents in the library itself (6) or were already known elsewhere (6 again). Ten tractates are preserved only in fragments, but the other thirty-one in good and indeed sometimes excellent condition. From these data it is clear that in the Nag Hammadi discovery we have one of the most extensive of all the finds of recent times. Even the Qumran discovery is smaller in extent and not so well preserved, although these texts are also almost five hundred years older.

Since it would exceed the limits of this book to describe the tractates in detail, we shall give here only a brief survey with a few comments.[14] In the further course of our discussion a number of them will be discussed in greater detail. These texts indeed provide the best source material which at present we possess.

Codex I ("Codex Jung")
1. A prayer of the Apostle Paul (fly-leaf, two pages).
2. An apocryphal letter of James (p. 1–16).
3. The "Gospel of Truth" (p. 16–43), a homily-like treatise which carries no title and has been named after its opening words (*Evangelium veritatis*).
4. The "Treatise (Logos) on the Resurrection" (p. 43–50), also called the "Letter to Rheginus" after the addressee mentioned in the text.
5. A "Tripartite Tractate" (p. 51–140) or "Treatise on the three natures", i.e. those of the world above, of creation and of men; it was so named because of the lack of a title.

Codex II
1. The "Secret Book (*apocryphon*) of John" (p. 1–32), which is one of the two longer versions which we now have among the three exemplars in all of this document in the library*; a fourth version is contained in the Berlin Gnostic Codex of which we have already spoken.

* cf. NHC III 1 and NHC IV 1

See above, p. 28

2. The "Gospel of Thomas" (p. 32–51), a collection of sayings of Jesus.
3. The "Gospel of Philip" (p. 51–86), a didactic or admonitory document of a "sentence" character which was evidently given only subsequently the (inappropriate) title "gospel".
4. The "Nature (*hypostasis*) of the Archons" (p. 86–97), a revelation document about the origin of the world and man, which has connections with the following tractate.
5. An anonymous document (p. 97–127), which has been given the name "On the Origin of the World".
6. The "Exegesis on the Soul" (p. 127–137), a treatise on the fall of the soul and its return to the higher world.
7. The "Book of Thomas (the athlete)" (p. 138–145), a revelation-dialogue between Jesus and Judas Thomas concerning various subjects, in particular the last things.

Codex III (the first Codex to be purchased, earlier known as number I)
1. A shorter version of the "Secret Book (*apocryphon*) of John" (p. 1–40).*   * *cf. NHC II 1*
2. The "Gospel of the Egyptians" or "Secret Book of the Great Invisible Spirit" (p. 40–69), of which there is also a parallel version in Codex IV; it deals with the destiny of the gnostics in world history.
3. A letter of "the blessed Eugnostus" (p. 70–90), which is also to be found in Codex V and has close relationships with the following "Wisdom of Jesus Christ".
4. The "Wisdom (*sophia*) of Jesus Christ" (p. 90–119), a revelation document which was already known to us from the   *See above, p. 28* Berlin papyrus.
5. The "Dialogue of the Redeemer" (p. 120–149), a revelation dialogue between Jesus and his disciples upon various themes.

Codex IV (very poorly preserved)
1. A longer version of the "Secret Book (*apocryphon*) of John" (p. 1–49).*   * *cf. NHC II 1*
2. A second version of the "Gospel of the Egyptians" (p. 50–81).*   * *cf. NHC III 2*

Codex V

1. A second but poorly preserved exemplar of the letter of the "blessed Eugnostus" (p. 1–17).* * cf. NHC III 3
2. The "Apocalypse of Paul" (p. 17–24), which tells of a rapture and heavenly journey of Paul.
3. The (first) "Revelation (Apocalypse) of James" (p. 24–44), which contains revelation dialogues between Jesus and James "the righteous".
4. The (second) "Revelation (Apocalypse) of James" (p. 44–63); it deals with the martyrdom of James, into which hymns and speeches have been introduced.
5. The "Revelation (Apocalypse) of Adam" (p. 63–85), which he hands over to Seth and which contains a kind of gnostic world history.

Codex VI

1. The "Acts of Peter and the Twelve Apostles" (p. 1–12), an apocryphal book about the Apostles without any specific gnostic content.
2. "Thunder: the perfect Mind" (p. 13–21), a revelation address by the bisexual Wisdom in "I am" style.
3. "The original (authentic) Doctrine" (p. 22–35), a homily about the destiny of the soul.
4. "The Thought (noēma) of our great Power" (p. 36–48), a gnostic Apocalypse.
5. An anonymous treatise on unrighteousness (p. 48–51), which has since been discovered to be a very poor translation of a passage from Plato's "Republic".
6. A hitherto unknown Hermetic document (p. 52–63), whose title is not extant; it is a dialogue between Father (Hermes) and son (Tat) concerning the heavenly world.
7. A prayer (p. 63–65), which belongs to the Hermetic collection and was already known to us in Greek (Papyrus Mimaut) and Latin (Asclepius ch. 41).
8. A further Hermetic text (p. 65–78), whose title has been erased; however we know this title already from the Latin version of the so-called "Asclepius", chapters 21–29. See above, p. 26

Codex VII

1. "The Paraphrase of Shem" (p. 1–49), a gnostic cosmogony

and history of salvation linking up with the primal history in the Bible.

2. "The second Logos of the Great Seth" (p. 49–70), containing information about the process of redemption through the exalted Christ, who is regarded as an incarnation of Seth, such as we know also from other Sethian writings, for example the Gospel of the Egyptians.

3. The "Revelation (apocalypse) of Peter" (p. 70–84), which presents Peter as the recipient of special revelations of Jesus before his imprisonment and (ostensible) death.

4. The "Teachings of Silvanus" (p. 84–118), a gnostic Wisdom document with a strongly world-renouncing and pessimistic basic attitude.

5. "The Three Pillars (Stelae) of Seth" (p. 118–127); they form a hymn in three parts which purports to be delivered by Dositheos.

Codex VIII (not very well preserved)

1. "Zostrianos", with the further Greek title "The Teaching of the Truth of Zostrianos, God of Truth; the Teaching of Zoroaster" (p. 1–132), a revelation document in which the teachings proclaimed are traced back to a heavenly journey by Zoroaster (understood in the ancient Graeco-Roman world as a teacher of wisdom).

2. The "Letter of Peter to Philip" (p. 132–140), introducing an apocryphal account about a conversation between the apostles and Christ and the proceedings at and after the crucifixion of Jesus.

Codex IX is extant only in fragments; after the laborious task of sorting, three treatises could be identified, the titles of which have not survived. They have been given the following names:

1. "Melchizedek" (p. 1–27), a gnostic book of revelation on the destiny of Christ and the High Priest Melchizedek.

2. "Ode about Norea" (p. 27–29)

3. "The Testimony of Truth" (p. 29–74), a polemical sermon against official (Church) Christianity and other gnostic groups.

Codex X is also in poor condition and the identification of its content so far uncertain. Possibly it contained only one document with the title:

1. "Marsanes" (p. 1–68), an apocalypse which inter alia is largely concerned with speculation on the relation of letters to parts of the soul and to angels, such as we know also from other areas of Gnosis (Marcus).

Codex XI, likewise badly preserved, evidently contains four tractates:
1. "The Interpretation of Knowledge (*gnosis*)" (p. 1–21), a didactic writing concerned with basic questions of gnostic understanding of the church (a kind of church order).
2. An anonymous document (p. 22–44), evidently of Valentinian origin, which after expositions concerning the Pleroma contains brief liturgical texts (40–44) on the anointing, baptism and the eucharist.
3. "The Alien (*allogenes*)" (p. 45–69), a revelation recorded by "Allogenes" for "my son" Messos.
4. "The High-minded (*hypsiphrone*)" (p. 69–72), likewise a (fragmentary) account of a revelation.

Codex XII contains only ten pages and fifteen fragments which allow us to infer at least two texts:
1. The "Sentences of Sextus" (p. 15–16, 27–34), a pagan collection of proverbs which had become domiciled in the Church since the second century.

* cf. NHC 13 2. Part of a version of the "Gospel of Truth".*

Codex XIII, if we are to think of it at all, is lost apart from six-
See above, p. 39 teen pages and a few fragments; they allow us to recognise two treatises:
1. "The trimorphic Protennoia" (p. 35–50), a revelation discourse in three parts by the first emanation of the primal god called Protennoia or Barbelo, concerning her three forms of manifestation as father, mother and son. A Greek addition at the end runs: "holy writing, written by the father in perfect knowledge".
2. The beginning (ten lines) of the anonymous document in
* cf. NHC II 5 Codex II* ("On the Origin of the World").

The work of After this survey the reader will ask: what texts are accessible
publication to those interested, what has so far been published and translated? This work of publication too, like the whole story of the dis-

covery, is marked by many interruptions and even today is not yet completed. Doresse and Puech, the French scholars already mentioned who first began to make a scientific assessment of the discovery, planned an edition along with Togo Mina. Then there was the Austrian Coptologist Walter Till, who in his edition of the Berlin Papyrus 8502 was already able to draw upon the parallel texts from Codex II, i. e. the "Secret Book of John" and the "Wisdom of Jesus Christ" (1955); this was really the See above, p. 28 first editorial achievement. Correctors' proofs for the French project (relating to NHC III, 1, 2 and 5) were already in circulation, but the situation already described in regard to property rights, and political events in Egypt, prevented any continuation of the plan. In 1956 an international committee of scholars which was to concern itself with the preparation for publication was indeed invited to Cairo, but the Suez crisis brought all plans to nothing and in particular made difficult any further work of collaboration with the French scholars.

In the same year Pahor Labib began with a facsimile edition, which however did not get beyond the first volume. This volume, which reproduced some pages from Codex I and also the first five tractates from Codex II, provided the basis for the first translations of these texts into various European languages. Johannes Leipoldt and Hans-Martin Schenke published their German translations of these texts in the *Theologische Literaturzeitung* in 1958/59, and made them known for the first time to the interested public.

The publication of the "Codex Jung" texts was not affected by the Cairo proceedings, although they too for financial and personal reasons were very long delayed. The first document to appear, likewise in 1956, was the Gospel of Truth, in a sumptuous edition which became the pattern for the further volumes (containing text, facsimiles, French, German and English translations). In 1963 there followed the so-called letter to Rheginus on the Resurrection, in 1968 the apocryphal Letter of James, in 1973 and 1975 the Tripartite Tractate (including the fragment of the Prayer of the Apostle Paul). The editors of the Codex Jung also published in 1959 a small bilingual edition of the Gospel of Thomas, but the complete edition has so far not yet appeared.

With the beginning of the final compilation of an inventory and the glazing of the Cairo volumes in 1959 there came also

new initiatives for publication. Pahor Labib invited a number of specialists to join in the work, and in the following years they published a number of standard editions of texts: Alexander Böhlig in 1959 and 1962 in East Germany the anonymous trea-
NHC II 5 tise from Codex II ("On the Origin of the World")* and the
NHC V 2-5 Coptic-gnostic Apocalypses from Codex V*; Walter Till in
NHC II 3 1963 in West Berlin the Gospel of Philip;*[14a] R. A. Bullard in
NHC II 4 1970 the Hypostasis of the Archons.* The latter was also published independently by Peter Nagel in 1970 in Halle (Saale). Martin Krause, who sat directly at the source and is among those best acquainted with the originals, prepared several large editions whose appearance was delayed by difficulties at the publishers: in 1962 his edition of the three versions of the Secret
NHC II 1, III 1, IV 1 Book of John came out*, in 1971 the gnostic and hermetic doc-
NHC II 6,7 uments from Codex II and Codex VI* and in 1973 four docu-
NHC VII 1-3.5 ments from Codex VII.*

In the meantime (1961) an approach had been made to UN-ESCO for assistance in the publication. A second international committee was established which was to work under the auspices of the Arabic Republic of Egypt and UNESCO. Plans were made for a facsimile edition, for which between 1962 and 1965 almost the whole library was photographed on microfilm. The colloquium on the origins of Gnosticism held in Messina in 1966 took up the initiative to press ahead with the project, which had come to a standstill. In its name the American theologian James M. Robinson took up contact with UNESCO on this question and it is due to his unwearied efforts that with the support of a new (and therefore third) international committee summoned in 1970 the "Facsimile Edition of the Nag Hammadi Codices" under the auspices of the Department of Antiquities of the Arab Republic of Egypt in association with UNESCO, estimated at ten volumes, could finally appear in Leiden. In its excellent lay-out this is a technical performance of the first rank and forms the basis for all further study of these new Coptic gnostic texts, since it reproduces the entire discovery faithfully to the original. In addition to this edition a complete translation into English under the direction of James M. Robinson has now been published, which will in time be accompanied by Coptic and English editions of separate texts with technical apparatus (The Coptic Gnostic Library). A French project has been launched by J. E. Ménard, while M. Krause is working on a

West German project.[15] In East Germany the "Berliner Arbeitskreis für koptisch-gnostische Schriften" called into being
by H. M. Schenke has since 1973 continuously published new
revisions and translations of the texts in the *Theologische Literaturzeitung*. Since 1971 there has also been a separate monograph series Nag Hammadi Studies for the publication of speci-
alised investigations and discussions of texts. We may therefore
expect that very soon the concern for the conservation and publication of the Nag Hammadi texts, which has lasted almost
thirty years, will be at an end, but the texts themselves will continue to fascinate those engaged in research into Gnosis.

The evaluation of the parts so far accessible which has already begun has shown that the significance of the Nag Hammadi Library for investigation into Gnosis is to be found in the
following points:

**The signifi-
cance of the
Nag Hammadi
Library**

1. The amount of our original sources has been unexpectedly
   enlarged and now for the first time sets research into Gnosis
   on a new basis, quite independent from the reports of the
   heresiologists. The new sources will allow us a greater control than before of the picture and the material handed down
   in the Church Fathers.
2. Since the documents derive from different "schools" and
   "movements" of Gnosis they represent such a variety of
   gnostic ways of thinking and attitudes as up to now we could
   only suspect. Alongside new insights into the development
   and the final form of Gnostic "systems" we obtain also a
   glimpse of the piety of the gnostics.
3. The discovery contains both strongly Christian and also less
   Christian and non-Christian documents; it therefore shows
   on the one hand the inter-relationship of Gnosis and Christianity, but on the other hand also their independence from
   one another. Since analyses so far undertaken on some specific Christian gnostic texts were able to show that they have
   been secondarily christianised, this provided confirmation
   for the theory of the non-Christian origin of gnosis, which
   was advocated in particular by the so called "Religionsgeschichtliche Schule" (Bousset, Reitzenstein).
4. Gnosis in its Christian form, as the library shows, understood itself as a correct interpretation of Christianity, and
   considerably advanced theological speculation, whether in
   Christological, trinitarian or cosmological respects. The op-

position of the Church Fathers becomes thereby more readily understandable than before and takes on a new depth. The development of orthodoxy was a lengthy process, which did indeed build upon certain basic statements but grew out of a very manifold variety of early Christian thought and action. This entirely valid multiplicity, to which the Christian gnostic movement also belongs, was only declared to be heretical and unorthodox in the course of the discussion, and this was a disqualification which rested purely upon theological judgements. The new texts thus have a great significance for early church history.

5. The contribution of Jewish traditions and ideas to the development of Gnosis, which had been recognised even earlier, can now be shown more clearly and more cogently.

6. Also the question of the contribution of Greek thought, particularly on its philosophical (Platonic) side, can be better and more sensibly answered with the aid of some of the new texts, and in general the contribution of contemporary philosophy emerges more strongly.

7. Finally the new sources promise to bring nearer to a solution the debated problem of the gnostic redeemer figure and its relation to the Christian. The theory of a pre-Christian or at least non-Christian redeemer conception in Gnosis proves to be correct.

8. Unfortunately even these sources do not provide sufficient material to enable us to study better than formerly the important sociological questions of the composition and structure of the gnostic communities. However even for these, as we shall show some new points of view can be obtained.

NATURE AND STRUCTURE

The main features of gnostic Ideology
and Mythology

The Church Fathers already were conscious of what was for them the frightening variety of the gnostic teachings; they compare them with the many-headed hydra of Greek legend.*[16] This picture is in fact fully and completely confirmed by the Nag Hammadi texts. At first glance the variety of the theories and speculations is confusing and discouraging. Only after long consideration do certain basic ideas emerge which again and again appear, although in varying formulation, and lead to the core of the whole. The external variety of Gnosis is naturally not accidental but evidently belongs to its very nature. As we shall see, there was no gnostic "church" or normative theology, no gnostic rule of faith nor any dogma of exclusive importance. No limits were set to free representation and theological speculation so far as they lay within the frame of the gnostic view of the world. Hence we find already in the heresiologists the most varied systems and attitudes set out under the common denominator "gnosis" and the gnostic library of Nag Hammadi offers one of the best illustrations of this situation, since here the most varied writings, with often divergent points of view, are assembled together. The gnostic communities evidently did not lay any claims to exclusiveness against one another, which probably did not exclude polemic between the teachers and founders of schools (unfortunately we know all too little of this). There was also no gnostic canon of scripture, unless it was the "holy scriptures" of other religions, like the Bible or Homer, which were employed and interpreted for the purpose of authorising the gnostics' own teachings. The fact for example that among the new Coptic gnostic texts several divergent versions of the same document can be found side by side is a clear witness for this tolerant position. The gnostics seem to have taken particular delight in bringing their teachings to expression in manifold ways, and they handled their literary production with great skill, which however for us today is sometimes difficult to understand or to appreciate. As is generally the case

The variety of gnostic systems

* Irenaeus, Adv. haer.
I 30,15;
Hippolytus,
Refutatio V, 11

we can find alongside impressive products others which are less attractive or even of little value, but everywhere one notes a masterful practice of the method of extracting as much as possible out of the thoughts and expressing it in ever new ways. In this process the interpretative method of allegory and symbolism, widely diffused in the ancient world, was freely employed. That is, a statement of the text was given a deeper meaning, or even several, in order to claim it for one's own doctrine or to display its inner richness. This method of exegesis is in Gnosis a chief means of producing one's own ideas under the cloak of the older literature – above all the sacred and canonical. What contortionist's tricks were performed in the process we shall see at various points. We may frankly speak of a "protest exegesis" in so far as it runs counter to the external text and the traditional interpretation.

The constituent elements of Gnosis   A further peculiarity of the gnostic tradition, connected with this, lies in the fact that it frequently draws its material from the most varied existing traditions, attaches itself to it, and at the same time sets it in a new frame by which this material takes on a new character and a completely new significance. Seen from the outside, the gnostic documents are often compositions and even compilations from the mythological or religious ideas of the most varied regions of religion and culture: from Greek, Jewish, Iranian, Christian (in Manicheism also Indian and from the Far East). To this extent Gnosis, as has already been repeatedly established, is a product of hellenistic syncretism, that is the mingling of Greek and Oriental traditions and ideas subsequent to the conquests of Alexander the Great. The gnostic expositions gain their thread of continuity or their consistence just through the gnostic "myth" which we shall examine more closely in what follows. The individual parts of this "myth" can be called the gnostic myths; they confront us throughout as parts of one or another gnostic sytem. Since they are built together out of older mythological material they give the impression of artificiality as compared with the old developed myths of primal times. Yet the expression "Kunstmythen" for the gnostic systems is misleading and should for preference be avoided. It is not at all a case of "artificial" and fundamentally unimportant compilations, but of illustrations of existential situations of the gnostic view of the world. Since this view of the world attaches itself in the main to the older religious imagery, almost as a parasite prospers on the soil of "host religions", it can be also described as parasitic. To this extent Gnosticism strictly speaking has no tradition of its own but only a borrowed one. Its mythology is a tradition consciously created from alien material, which it has appropriated to match its own basic conception. Considered in its own light, however, it is for Gnosticism a further confirmation of its truth, which it often traces back to a primal revelation, i. e. derives from primitive times; the knowledge of it was only temporarily extinguished or concealed.

The essential basic features of Gnosis can easily be extracted from the gnostic traditions, even if they belong to the teachings of different schools. There is first of all the idea of "gnosis" itself, a word which derives from Greek and means "knowledge" or "understanding" and in fact became a catchword of that religious movement. The New Testament already voices warnings against the teachings of the "gnosis falsely so called"*; the Church Fathers, above all Irenaeus, took up the expression as an appropriate characterisation and set over against it the "true gnosis" of the Church. The representatives of this "false gnosis" frequently called themselves "gnostics", that is "knowers, people of understanding" and there are also frequent references to "knowledge" in their writings, although in a quite special manner. They were not aiming at any ideal philosophical knowledge nor any knowledge of an intellectual or theoretical kind, but a knowledge which had at the same time a liberating and redeeming effect. The content of this knowledge or understanding is primarily religious, in so far as it circles around the background of man, the world and God, but also because it rests not upon one's own investigation but on heavenly mediation. It is a knowledge given by revelation, which has been made available only to the elect who are capable of receiving it, and therefore has an esoteric character. This knowledge freely bestowed can extend from the basic insight into the divine nature of man, his origin and his destiny, up to a complete system. All gnostic teachings are in some form a part of the redeeming knowledge which gathers together the object of knowledge (the divine nature), the means of knowledge (the redeeming gnosis) and the knower himself. The intellectual knowledge of the teaching which is offered as revealed wisdom has here a direct religious significance since it is at the same time understood

The idea of "Gnosis"

* 1 Tim. 6,20

as otherworldly and is the basis for the process of redemption. A man who possesses "gnosis" is for that reason a redeemed man: "If anyone has gnosis", it is said in the Gospel of Truth, "he is a being who comes from above ... He fulfils the will of him who has called him. He wishes to please him, he receives rest. ... He who in this manner shall have gnosis knows whence he is come and whither he goes. He knows like someone who was drunk and has become sober from his drunkenness and,

NHC I 3,22,1ff. restored again to himself, has again set his own in order".* The ignorant man in contrast is one who is a prey to forgetfulness

NHC I 3,23,35ff. and annihilation; he has no firm foundation.* In the Gospel of Philip there is the statement "He who has the knowledge (*gno-*

NHC II 3,77 (125), sis) of the truth is free. Ignorance is a slave".* But not only ig-
14f.; 84 (132), 10 norance stands in contrast to the knowledge of the gnostic, so also does faith, since it knows nothing concerning itself and remains attached to what is immediately in the foreground. It is just this opposition of "faith" and "knowledge" which was one of the central themes in the debates of the Church with the gnostic heresy. It was not only a question of the rights and the claim of faith as the only valid means of salvation, but also of the problem of the two-fold truth which became matter for discussion with the entry of the esoteric gnosis into the early Church.

Gnosis and The concept of gnosis has therefore on good grounds been
Gnosticism retained as a designation of this religious movement. Only in the eighteenth century was the form "gnosticism" created out of it – through the medium of French – and this has a disparaging ring. It has however maintained itself down to our own time and is employed in the first place for the Christian gnostic systems of the second and third centuries. Here we can probably trace the influence of Harnack. The existence of two conceptions for what is basically the same thing has frequently caused confusion in research, and in recent times has led to attempts to define the two more sharply and set them off against one anoth-

See above, p. 50 er. At the Congress on the Origins of Gnosticism in Messina in 1966 such an attempt was put forward in the form of theses for discussion by several participants.[17] According to this view we should understand by "Gnosis" a "knowledge of divine secrets which is reserved for an elite" (and thus has an esoteric character), but "Gnosticism" should be used in the above-mentioned sense for the gnostic systems of the second and third centuries.

This makes "gnosis" an uncommonly extended term, which also embraces "Gnosticism"; to this extent the latter is only a particular form of Gnosis, which is just as has already been described. This rending apart of two terms which historically and in the history of research fundamentally belong together is however not very meaningful and also has not generally prevailed. For this reason we adhere to the practice usual particularly in the German-speaking area and understand by Gnosis and Gnosticism the same thing; the first as the self-designation of a religion of redemption in late antiquity, the latter as a newer form of it. Naturally the neutral usage of "Gnosis" in the sense of philosophical knowledge or concern with theories of knowledge ("Gnoseology") remains unaffected. Gnosis in our context is in the first place a historical category, intended to comprehend a particular form of world-view in late antiquity and therefore linking up with its own self-understanding.

If we seek further for some specific elements of this Gnosis **Basic ideas of** there are a number of ideas which repeatedly occur in most of **Gnosis** the traditions and form their basic framework. It is in this sense that we understand the question of "structure" or "nature". It is a matter of the "articulation" of Gnosis.

In the Messina suggestions regarding terminology, already mentioned, the following "connected characteristics" are adduced as the central idea – the central myth – of Gnosticism: "the idea of the presence in man of a divine "spark" ..., which has proceeded from the divine world and has fallen into this world of destiny, birth and death and which must be reawakened through its own divine counterpart in order to be finally restored. This idea ... is ontologically based on the conception of a downward development of the divine whose periphery (often called *Sophia* or *Ennoia*) has fatally fallen victim to a crisis and must – even if only indirectly – produce this world, in which it then cannot be disinterested, in that it must once again recover the divine "spark" (often designated as *pneuma*, "spirit")". This description does in fact relate to an essential basic idea whose manifold variation we shall come to know more closely in the following chapters through examples from the texts.

From this quotation it is already clear that at the base of Gno- **Dualism** sis there is a dualistic view of the world which determines all its statements on a cosmological and anthropological level, and therefore this will in the first place claim our attention. This dualism is carried along or, to put it more accurately, interwoven with a monistic idea which is expressed in the already mentioned upward and downward development of the divine spark and which is the basis for the identification of man and deity (made clear in the idea of the God "Man"). Imbedded in this "dualism on a monistic background" is the doctrine of God in Gnosis, which is determined above all by the idea of the "unknown God" beyond all that is visible or sensible, and incorporates a "fullness" (*Pleroma*) of angels and other heavenly beings, be they personified ideas (abstractions) or hypostases. A **Cosmogony** prominent role is played by the creation of the world (cosmogony), which is intended to offer an explanation for the present condition of man, remote from God, and therefore occupies a considerable space in the texts. The side of this dualistic world view which is opposed to the divine pole – often described as "light" – is "darkness", which is likewise described in very varied fashion but principally in physical terms as matter and body (corpse), or psychologically as ignorance or forgetfulness. In Gnosis however the realm of this anti-divine pole is very widely extended: it reaches even into the visible heavens and includes this world and the rulers who hold it in slavery, in particular the creator of the world with his auxiliary troops, the planets and the signs of the zodiac. The whole world view of late antiquity, with its idea of the power of fate (Greek *heimarmenē*) which dominates the gods, the world and men, is here as it were bracketed together and marked with a negative sign. It becomes a prison from which there is no escape, unless the liberating act of the transcendent God and his helpers opens up a way on which man (strictly only a small part of man, namely the divine spark) can escape. Here the gnostic doctrine of redemp- **Soteriology** tion (soteriology) has its roots. This understandably claims the largest space in the systems, since it directly relates to the present situation of men. This realm of redemption is likewise depicted in manifold forms and has found different representations. Here belong not only the idea of the heavenly journey of the soul, but also the doctrine of the redeemer in Gnosis, which even today is hotly debated among scholars. This area in particular presents one of the most complicated themes of the gnostic **Eschatology** statements in the texts. Finally there is in Gnosis a "doctrine of the last things" closely connected with the cosmology and soteriology as a whole, an eschatology which consists not only in the deliverance of the heavenly soul but also has a cosmic significance.

In this outline a few main features of the gnostic ideology or mythology have been presented, which will be dealt with in greater detail in the following sections. Owing to the manifold variety already mentioned, and the abundance of the systems formed, an exhaustive presentation is not possible; we must limit ourselves to the most important features and leave many aspects out of consideration. Some things will also call for discussion in the chapter on the history of Gnosis.

As a matter of course, the structure of the gnostic communities and the cult also merit special attention, in spite of the little we know about them. Gnosis in particular gives us a typical example of the close interweaving of ideology and sociology. Strictly speaking the presentation of the historical and sociological sides of our subject ought to stand at the beginning, but within the frame of an introduction this is not practical and could be done only with numerous repetitions. In addition our primary concern is to get to know Gnosis in the ideological expressions which are characteristic for it, and this can only be done in a phenomenological survey, in which the historical, chronological and sociological problems can be for the moment set aside. We shall discuss these matters in greater detail in the chapter on the history of Gnosis, where the reader will find information about the sects mentioned in the following pages and on their background.

Cult and community

Dualism

The history of religions knows various ideas of the activity of two more or less independent deities or principles which are made responsible for the differing situations in the world. One of the best known is the Iranian Zoroastrian dualism, which sets a good and an evil god at the beginning of world history and views this history as dominated by the conflict between the two, until the good god with help of his adherents at the end of time carries off the victory. This dualism is however essentially ethically oriented, since it lays decisive importance upon religious

Iranian Zoroastrian dualism

and moral attitude and outlook, and the opposites "good" and "evil" do not coincide with those of "spiritual" and "corporeal" or "material", but also are interwoven with the latter. We shall see that this dualism had a great influence upon developing Gnosis. It is otherwise with the more strongly philosophically **The dualism of** oriented dualism of Plato, which was of great importance for **Plato** Greek thought and then for the whole of late antiquity. It knows the two levels of existence: the spiritual eternal ideas and their transitory material (spatial) counterparts, which form the cosmos; the latter do indeed signify a loss of being, but nevertheless belong to the good part of the creation (for the bad part Plato ultimately made an "evil world soul" responsible). This "ontological" or "metaphysical" dualism is likewise, as we shall show, a presupposition of the gnostic. Finally one might **Indian dualism** also refer to the Indian dualism between Being and Appearance or Becoming, which has frequently been adduced as a parallel to Gnosis but which because of its quite different orientation does not come into question (it has points in common rather with the Platonic). There is also a series of other dualisms (apart from the still more widely spread simple conceptions of duality), which are formulated in more or less radical, mixed or dialectic form and whose typology belongs to the interesting field of work of the comparative study of religion; in our context those named are sufficient.

Gnostic The gnostic dualism is distinguished from these above all in **dualism** the one essential point, that it is "anti-cosmic"; that is, its conception includes an unequivocally negative evaluation of the visible world together with its creator; it ranks as a kingdom of evil and of darkness. The identification of "evil" and "matter", which is not to be found in Iranian and Zoroastrian thought, occurs in Gnosis as a fundamental conception. In Greek thought also – apart from certain Orphic teachings, which however are of uncertain date – there is no such anticosmic development of the dualism of spirit and body. The Greek conception is unmis- **Plotinus** takably "procosmic", and no less a person than Plotinus (3rd century A.D.), the leading figure of the late or Neoplatonism, defended this position over against the gnostic depreciation of the cosmos. In his first treatise "On providence" it is said, with a clearly anti-gnostic point: "No-one therefore may find fault with our universe on the ground that it is not beautiful or not the most perfect of the beings associated with the body; nor

again quarrel with the originator of its existence, and certainly
not because it has come into existence of necessity, not on the
basis of a reflection but because the higher being brought forth
its likeness according to the law of nature".* [18] If the world also
is not perfect, since it has only a share in the highest being and is
troubled by matter, it is nevertheless as a product of the world
plan "so beautiful that there is no other that could be more
beautiful than it".* The same is true of man: he is "to this extent
a complete vessel as it is granted to him to be perfected".* A
treatise especially written "Against the Gnostics" takes issue in
particular with their view that the cosmos and its creator are
evil.[19] The descending gradation is no reason for abusing or de-
faming the lower stages of the cosmos* and stigmatising them
as "the strange earth".* The "horror story of the terrors which
according to their belief are to be played out in the heavenly
spheres" is ridiculous and erroneous, for these spheres are
"fine and beautifully prepared".* If the heavenly bodies also
originate from fire one need not fear them on that account (as
the gnostics do), for their power and influence are limited according to the law of the universe; there is no "tyranny of the
power of the stars".* At the worst they touch the "purity of the
higher world" through their magical practices (incantations).*
They find fault with providence and its lord, in that (as a consequence of their hostility to the world) they disregard all the le-
gality of this world, "the virtue whose building up goes back
over a long development from the beginning of all time, and
they make our human discipline into a mockery – in this world
there may be nothing noble to be seen – and thereby they make
discipline and righteousness of no importance".* "For of all
earthly things nothing is of value for them, but only an Other after which they will at some time strive."*

From this polemic of a Platonist the special position of the
gnostic view of the world and its consequences become very
clear. Certainly there are certain common elements between
the gnostic and Platonic views, which can now be easily pointed
out in some of the Nag Hammadi texts, be it in cosmology or in
psychology, but the dividing gulf cannot be overlooked. The
positive pole of gnostic dualism, to which Plotinus refers in the
last citation, is a higher world which, portrayed in very varied
and differing fashion, culminates in the assumption of a new
otherworldly and unknown God, who dwells beyond all visible

marginal notes:
* Plotinus, Enneads III, 2,3
* op. cit. III 2,12
* op. cit. III 2,9
* op. cit. II 9,13
* op. cit. II 9,11
* op. cit. II 9,13
* op. cit. II 9,13
* op. cit. II 9,14
* op. cit. II 9,15
* op. cit. II 9,15

The unknown God

creation and is the real lord of the universe. The world is not his work, but that of a subordinate being. But nevertheless he exercises influence in varying ways for the well-being of men, as we shall later see; it is "providence" (*pronoia*) which here comes to expression. This conception of God in Gnosis stands in contrast to all the world-gods hitherto known, who in their limitation – there is even reference to their folly – do not know the true God and therefore act as if he did not exist. The counter-god, remote from the world, who often carries the characteristic attribute of the "alien", is properly to be described only negatively or in images which are intended to express his inimitable status, free from any kind of relation to the world.

One of the most gifted of the gnostics, Basilides (second century), is said according to the account of Hippolytus to have spoken of a primal "non-existent god". The school of his later contemporary Valentinus asserted "that there is in invisible and ineffable heights a pre-existent perfect aeon (i.e. a supernatural being), whom they also call Pre-beginning, Forefather and Primal Ground (Bythos), that he is inconceivable and invisible, eternal and uncreated (or: unbegotten) and that he ex- * *Irenaeus, Adv. haer. I 1* isted in great peace and stillness in unending spaces (aeons)" * Similar ideas about the unknownness of God were already entertained by the earliest gnostics like Simon and Menander. Marcion also (first half of second century) stands in this theological tradition of Gnosis; he based his "Gospel of the alien God" (Harnack) on a sharp division of (evil) creator and (good) redeemer and he was among the most original of early Christian thinkers. Particularly impressive testimony is provided by the new Coptic texts of the most varied shades.

The Gospel of Philip develops a fundamental transmutation and revaluation of the "names", i.e. the designations, customarily given to earthly and heavenly things, on the basis of the recognition that, in face of the true world above, all earthly language is inadequate, above all when it is language established by tradition.[19a] "The names which are given to worldly (things) are the occasion of a great error; for they turn away their heart (the hearts of men) from the things which are established to those which are not established. He who hears 'God' does not perceive what is firmly established, but he has perceived what is * *NHC II 3, 53 (101), 23–29* not firmly established."* So it is also with the names "Father", "Son", "Holy Spirit", "life", "light", "resurrection" and "church", which have no meaning before eternity, the aeon.* op. cit. 53 (101), 29–54 (102), 2 The names of this world belong to error; they have been introduced by the archons (the wicked rulers of this world) to lead men astray.* * op. cit. 54 (102), 18–24

Near the beginning of the Secret Book of John there stands this statement by the exalted Christ:[20] "The [true] God, the Father of the All, the Holy [Spirit], the invisible, who is over the all, who exists in his imperishability, since he [is in] the pure light into which no eye may look. Concerning him, the Spirit, it is not fitting to think of him as a God, or that he is of a (particular) sort. For he is more excellent than the gods: he is a dominion (*archē*) over which none rules; for there is none before him, nor does he need them (the gods); he does not even need life, for he is eternal. He needs nothing, for he is not capable of being perfected, since he did not require to be perfected, but he is at all times entirely perfected. He is light. He is illimitable, since there is none before him to limit him. [He is] not subject to judgment, since there is none before him to judge him. [He is] the immeasurable, for no other who was before him has measured him. [He is] the invisible, for none has seen him. [He is] the eternal, who exists for ever. [He is] indescribable, because no-one has comprehended him in order to describe him. He is the immeasurable light, the pure, holy purity, the indescribable, perfect, imperishable. He is not perfection, nor blessedness, nor divinity, but he is something far more excellent than these. He is neither infinite nor was he ever limited, but he is something more excellent than that. He is not corporeal, he is not incorporeal. He is not great, he is not small. He is no measurable greatness, nor is he a creature: no-one can conceive him. He is nothing at all that exists, but something more excellent than that. Not as if he were excellent [in himself], but because he is his own, he has no part in an aeon (space). Time is not a property of his, for he who has part in an aeon (space), him others have formed. And time has not been assigned to him, because he has not received [anything] from any other who assigns. He also needs nothing. He who craves [only] after himself, in the perfection of light, knows the unmixed light. The immeasurable greatness, the eternal, the giver of eternity; the light, the bestower of light; the life, the giver of life; the blessed, the giver of blessedness; knowledge, the giver of knowledge; the one who is at all times good, the bestower of good, who accomplishes good; – not therefore in such a way that he has, but in such a way that he [also] gives – the compassion which shows compassion; the grace that bestows grace; the immeasurable light – what shall I say to thee concerning him, the inconceivable?"*

* Pap. Ber. 22,19–26,2

The author of the Letter of Eugnostus speaks in similar fashion about the "God of Truth", whom he proclaims as redeeming knowledge over against all other philosophical doctrines: "He who exists is indescribable, no primal power (archē) has known him, no dominion, no subordination, nor any creature since the beginning of the world, except him alone"*.[21] He is contrasted with all that has in itself transitoriness and deficiency, or is exposed to limitation or dependence. He is indeed called "Father of the All", but it is closer to the truth to say he is not "Father" but "Fore-Father". He is the beginning of all knowledge and the origin of that which is manifest.

* NHC III 3,71,13–18

The same doctrine of God is expounded at the beginning of the Valentinian fifth tractate of the Codex Jung, the so-called Tripartite Tractate, in remarkably laborious reflection. The Father already exists, "before there was anything other apart from him alone". In the image of the "root", often employed in Gnosis for the primal beginning, he is described as "root of the all", which brings forth trees, branches and fruits, by which the Pleroma is meant. "He is a single Lord and he is a God, because no-one is his God and no-one his father. He is an unbegotten one ...".* These statements are however employed only in a transferred sense (not in "legitimate fashion"). "None of the names which are understood or said or seen or conceived, none is fitting for him, even when they are very splendid, prominent, honoured. Certainly it is possible to pronounce these [names] to his glory and his honour, according to the capacity of each one among those who exalt him. He however, as he is and in what manner he finds himself, him no understanding can understand, nor can any word reproduce him, nor can any eye see him, nor any body encompass him, because of his own unapproachable greatness and his own unattainable depth and his own immeasurable height and his own inconceivable breadth".*[22]

* NHC I 5,51,24–28

* NHC I 5,54,2–23

These examples, which could be extended without difficulty – for example from the writings of the Mandeans – show that the gnostic conception of God is dictated by a contrast to all previously existing conceptions and so has a thoroughly revolutionary character. Certainly the terminology is indebted to contemporary philosophy; also it is possible to note certain agreements in the cosmology (Plotinus knew that very well), but the underlying world-denying tone cannot be mistaken. In the course of our discussion this will become still more clear. The counterpart to this highest being who can be described only in negative terms, the "unknown God", is the revelation of his secret through intermediate beings to the elect, who are thereby enabled to attain to the "knowledge" of the (hitherto) unknown one. The gnostic idea of God is therefore not only the product of a dualism hostile to the world, but it is at the same time also a consequence of the esoteric conception of knowledge: "Gnosis" mediates the secret and leads men out of their ignorance concerning the true God.

Dualism dominates the whole of gnostic cosmology, and particularly in relation to creation and its authors. The form it takes in the individual systems is however very varied, and sometimes even contradictory. This can be seen above all in the **The origin of** conception of the place of evil and of matter in the formation of **evil** the world. While in one branch of Gnosis – especially in Mandeism and in Manicheism – there are two basic principles existing from the very beginning, mythologically described as the kingdom of light and the kingdom of darkness, which are brought into contact with one another almost by accident and so set the baleful history of the world into motion, in other systems a graduated decline from the highest deity (the "unknown God") is the cause of the origin of the evil and dark powers. Hans Jonas has described the first type as the "Iranian", since it stands formally very close to the Iranian-Zoroastrian dualism. It is also best represented by the two gnostic religions already mentioned (the Hymn of the Pearl and the Odes of Solomon also belong here). That it has also influenced the remaining systems or that it was the starting point for their speculation is not affected by this. The other form Jonas called the "Syrian-Egyptian type", because of its geographical distribution. The majority of our texts, including those from Nag Hammadi, belong to this type. Their common characteristic is the idea of a downward movement, the beginning of which is variously located in the godhead itself as an internal process of self-reproduction, and which finally at the end leads to a breach in the kingdom of light, as a result of which the earthly world and the powers who hold it in subjection come into being. Evil here is not a pre-existent principle, but (according to Jonas) a "darkened level of being", a "degraded element of divinity".

The characteristic of this level, which represents the principle involved in the creation of the world, is marked as "ignorance", as particularity, as "presumption", and from this its position of opposition to God, as seen from the point of view of "knowledge", is clear. The details of this process will concern us in the following chapter. It should however be made clear that the dualism of these systems is to be seen first of all in a distinction between God and the Creator or between God and the world, not in that between God and the devil (who can also be added to the scheme). That the anti-cosmic idea lies behind this needs no further demonstration and it subsequently appears not only in the dualistic anthropology but also on the practical level in renunciation of the world. The world is the product of a divine tragedy, a disharmony in the realm of God, a baleful destiny in which man is entangled and from which he must be set free.

Matter   One idea however remains peculiar to this type, which from its basic principle of "emanation" may be called the "emanationist", namely that it reckons with a primal matter, usually described in figurative and biblical terms as chaos. There are indeed attempts to derive this too from higher powers, for example by giving an independent reality to psychological processes (passions), but they also envisage an ultimate lower antithesis to the absolute spiritual existence of the highest God. In Gnosis, as in the later Platonism, the self-alienation of the latter eventually gives rise to the realm of the transitory and the material. But this is not a natural process pre-determined by "providence" (*pronoia*), as Plotinus for example understood it, it is something effected through a crisis which has its negative consequences for the world and for man.

Anthropology   For the reasons stated, anthropology also is in Gnosis completely dominated by dualism. Here too a sharp line of distinction separates the bodily and psychic from the spiritual part of man. The latter is indeed even reduced to the "unworldly self", the original divine constituent or "spark" in man which can be activated only through "knowledge" (*gnosis*), which is the pledge of redemption. Just as the world above is characterised by a strictly unworldly aspect, and indeed one hostile to this world, so is the remnant of this divine and spiritual Beyond which remains in man. It is the same with the parallelism between the body and the world: here too the macrocosm corresponds to the microcosm and vice versa. This correspondence appears even in the terminology. It is sometimes difficult – for example in Mandean texts – to distinguish between individual and general statements about material and bodily existence: the body is described as a world (and therefore negatively) and the converse. The whole destiny of the world can be demonstrated in the figure of Adam, but so also can that of redemption. From this side also the fundamentally dualistic structure of gnostic thought can be seen.

Cosmology and Cosmogony

In regard to the external structure of the world the gnostic view is not very greatly different from that of late antiquity. Gnosis presupposes the ancient cosmic system, but interprets it in an entirely different way and introduces some new details. The earth, set according to the geocentric system at the centre of the cosmos, is surrounded by the air and the eight heavenly spheres (there are according to Ptolemy two others to provide for the precise course of the heavenly bodies, but they play no role in Gnosis). The eight spheres consist of those of the seven planets (to which the sun and the moon belong alongside Mercury, Venus, Mars, Jupiter and Saturn) and the fixed stars which close them off. Beyond them lies the realm of the "unknown God", the Pleroma (the "fullness"), with its own graduated worlds (aeons). If for late antiquity the world of the planetary spheres is the kingdom of "fate" (*heimarmenē*), which frequently controls earthly events by its influence, this is even more the case in Gnosis. For it the kingdom of the "seven" (*hebdomas*) is an inhuman and anti-divine power which, reflecting earthly circumstances, is conceived as tyranny. In mythological fashion it is inhabited by "demons", gods or spirits, who often bear the name "rulers" or "commanders" (archons); they sometimes form entire kingdoms with such an "archon" at the head. The "chief archon" and real ruler of the world is enthroned either in the seventh heaven or above it in the "eighth" (*ogdoas*), and is usual-

The view of the world

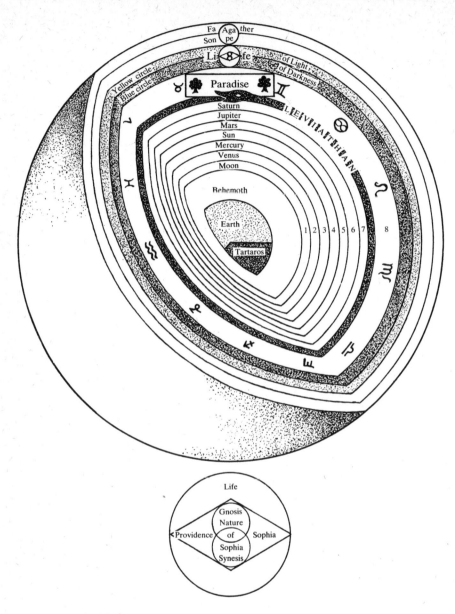

ly identical with the creator of the world (*demiurgos*). The sphere of the "eighth" is variously evaluated: either it is still a part of the powers which rule the world and then the seat of the Demiurge, occasionally also the realm of the twelve signs of the zodiac (*dodeka*), which belong to the same category as the tyrannical planets, or this sphere is an intermediate kingdom which already provides a transition to the real kingdom of light (in this capacity also it can be the dwelling place of the creator

1. The "kingdom of God" consists of pure spirit (*pneuma*) and two circles, that of the Father and that of the Son; a smaller circle represents "love" as the element which draws the Son (the Urmensch) downwards and so establishes the link with the intermediate kingdom (see below. p. 92 ff.).

2. The middle or intermediate kingdom is ruled by spirit and soul, and is marked by two colours, the yellow of the light and the blue of the darkness (evidently the limit of the visible cosmos). The small "circle of life" symbolises the realm of Sophia, from which the germ of life, i. e. the divine soul, comes to man.
In the rhomboid figure "Providence of Sophia (Wisdom)" is said to have stood, and within it in two intersecting circles "knowledge" (*gnosis*) and "insight" (*synesis*), with at the point of intersection between them "Nature of Sophia".

3. The earthly cosmos consists of body, soul and spirit. In the middle is the earth with the underworld (*tartarus*). Round it in concentric circles are: the sphere of Behemoth (named after the primeval monster of extra-biblical Jewish tradition, cf. Gen. 1.1; 4 Esdras 6.49; Baruch 29.4) or the atmosphere; then the spheres of the seven planets and the circle of the serpent biting its own tail (Leviathan), the lord of the world who gives expression to the malevolent character of the cosmos; beyond these is the circle of the fixed stars, in which are the signs of the zodiac and in which paradise is located. The latter is marked as a rectangle in which stand the tree of life and that of the knowledge of good and evil (see below, p. 98 ff.); the "flaming, turning sword" (cf. Gen. 3.24) separates paradise from the sphere of the fixed stars and perhaps also (following a passage in Philo) symbolises the turning of these spheres.

of the world; some systems see in the "eighth" already the beginning of "freedom" from the lower spheres). We possess a description of a diagram of this universe, the so-called "diagram of the Ophians (Ophites)" which both Celsus, the opponent of Christianity, and also his critic the Church Father Origen have handed down to us; the two use it for different ends in their debate.

Unfortunately the diagram is difficult to interpret, and also not completely reproduced. There have been several attempts to reconstruct it, among them that by H. Leisegang,[23] which we reproduce with a short explanation. From it can be clearly seen the tripartite division of the cosmos which was standard for most gnostic sects, into the kingdom of light or of God, the intermediate kingdom, and the earthly world with the spheres of the stars and the planets which enclose it, shut off from the kingdom above by the serpent Leviathan.

The whole world system, the cosmos, is thus for the gnostic a **Criticism of the** system of constraint, which he therefore can describe as "dark- **cosmos** ness", "death", "deception", "wickedness". "The cosmos is the fullness of evil."* Its origin goes back to lower powers, hostile *Corp. Herm. VI 4* to God, who above all press hard upon man, who finds himself in this "dwelling place" without at first having ways and means of escaping from it. Only with the aid of his insight into the situation, imparted to him in various ways but above all in regard to the origin of the world system (cosmogony) and the part of the supreme kingdom of God therein, has he any chance of overcoming the opposition and of escape. The heart of the matter is that man is subordinated to the earthly sphere and hence to its powers only in part, namely in his physical existence; in another part, admittedly only a small one, he belongs to the supramundane spiritual realm. This part of man, often described as the "true" or "inner man", "spirit" (*pneuma*), "soul" or "reason" (*nous*) is, over against the body which encloses him, in the same situation as the whole man over against the cosmos. Here we find the roots of the comparison, often used in Gnosis, of

See above, p. 67 microcosm and macrocosm which we have already mentioned.

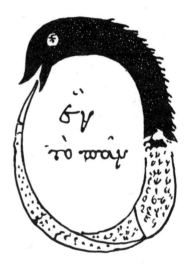

The universe as a serpent in an alchemical manuscript of the 14th century, with the Greek inscription "One is the all" (*hen to pan*). The dark upper part of the serpent biting its own tail represents the earth, the light lower part the starry heaven. The whole is an ancient symbol for the cycle of eternal becoming, which Gnosis also used to characterise the cosmos. For a similar drawing, see below, p. 223.

Cosmogonies and anthropogonies   The problem of how man with his superior element could "decline" into the body and the world is answered by the gnostic cosmogonies and anthropogonies. They are therefore broadly depicted and just because of their illuminating character form a centre of all gnostic systems. In these is crystallised an essential part of the gnostic myth, the knowledge of which at the same time possesses a redeeming function. It imparts the "insight" (this word is the best equivalent for the concept "gnosis") into the background of the cosmic event and is therefore repeatedly described as a "revelation", which the "redeemer" or heavenly "emissary" presents in one form or another. Over against this stands the "ignorance" (*agnoia*) or "lack of knowledge" (*agnosia*) of the non-gnostics, who have not yet been "awakened" to the truth. It is a trait typical for Gnosis that it also traces back the origin of the world to an act of ignorance, which entered in already at the very beginning and the removal of which through knowledge is the aim of the gnostic doctrine of redemption. If in the following account we divide these processes up into individual sections, this is done only for practical reasons. Fundamentally the gnostic myth is a unity of cosmogony, anthropogony and soteriology, which is indeed variously presented and often only hinted at, but forms in itself a closely interlocked system for appropriation by the gnostic, who is thereby assured of his deliverance from the world. It gives the redeeming answer to the questions which stir mankind, as they are preserved for us in a gnostic extract in Clement of Alexandria: "Who were we? What have we become? Where were we? Whither have we been cast? Whither do we hasten? From what have we been set free?"* The texts are in one way or another related to this, even if not all parts of the myth find expression. They can only be correctly appreciated when this background is taken into account (even if it is a case only of a collection of sayings or of hymns). Gnostic texts therefore, more than other ancient writings, are also to be read between the lines.

* *Clem. Alex., Ex Theodoto 78,2*

Gnostic cosmogonies

The gnostic doctrines of the origin of the world, because of their central importance, are very richly developed, so that it is not easy to organise them systematically. Frequently they are presented in some way as free interpretations or transcriptions (paraphrases) of the biblical creation story, with at the same time the use of cosmogonies from other spheres of influence. Essentially it is always a question of the downward development from the highest being, already mentioned, which leads by ways usually described in very complicated fashion on the one hand to the creation of the world, but at the same time on the other hand to the embodiment of a divine and spiritual particle (which really makes possible the very creation itself, but is also a pledge of the later redemption). If we fix attention upon the bearer of the "devolution", the primary principle of the fall into the lower regions, we can (so far as there is detailed reflection on this point) find either a male or a female being represented. The former predominates in the so called "Iranian" systems, classically represented in Manicheism, where the

See below, p. 336 "Urmensch" meets the attack of darkness at the behest of the king of light and introduces the cosmological development. The female figure is dominant in almost all the so-called "Syrian-Egyptian" or "emanationist" doctrines, although even here there are some exceptions, as is shown above all by the first tractate in the Hermetic collection (Poimandres) and the so-called "Naassene Preaching"[24].

The origin of the world according to the Anonymous Treatise in NHC II

We shall now illustrate what has been said by a few examples. The "anonymous treatise" ("On the Origin of the World")[25] begins with a polemic against traditional cosmogonies: "Since all, the gods of the cosmos and men, say that there is nothing before chaos, I will demonstrate that they are all in error, since they do not know [the constitution] of chaos and its root ... It (chaos) is something from a shadow; it was called "darkness". But the shadow derives from a work which was there from the beginning. It is therefore evident that it was already there when chaos had not yet come into being; but this followed the first work ...".* The sequel then goes on to deal with this origin of chaos: "But when the nature (*physis*) of the immortals had been completed out of the boundless one, there flowed a likeness out of Pistis (i.e. Faith), which was called Sophia (Wisdom). It willed and became a work which is like the light which first existed. And immediately its will became manifest: a heavenly image of inconceivable greatness which is now between the immortals and those who came into being after them according to the fashion of the things above: it is a curtain which separates men and the heavenly things. But the region (*aeon*) of truth has no shadow in its inward part, for the immeasurable light fills it entirely. But its outward part is shadow and therefore it was called "darkness". A power (*dynamis*) appeared over the darkness. The powers which came into being thereafter however called the shadow "the boundless chaos". From it sprouted the race of the Gods ..., so that a race of dung appeared after the first work. The abyss (thus) originated from the Pistis, of which we have spoken".*

* NHC II 5,97 (145), 24–98 (146), 11

* NHC II 5, 98 (146), 11–99 (147), 2

In this way, for our author, the proof is provided that Pistis (Sophia) through her work, a curtain, was the originator of chaos, which again is only the shadow of the curtain. The development takes place outside the "nature of the immortals", that is, the beings of light, in the "aeon of truth", but was set in motion by the self-willed act of one of the beings of light. In a parallel text, the Hypostasis of the Archons, the description is shorter but the tendency is even more strongly emphasised: "Sophia (Wisdom) which is called "Pistis" wished to create a work alone without her consort. And her work became an image of heaven, (so that) a curtain exists between the heavenly and the lower regions (aeons). And a shadow came into being beneath the curtain, and that shadow became matter".*

NHC II 4,94 (142), 5–13

This origin of matter is thus described in the text first quoted: "Thereupon the shadow took note that there was something stronger than itself. It became envious and immediately it gave birth to envy, after it had become pregnant from itself. From that day on the beginning (archē) of envy made its appearance in all the regions (aeons) and their worlds. But that envy was found to be an abortion, in which there was no [divine] spirit. It originated like the shadow in a great watery substance. Then the hatred (= envy) which originated from the shadow was cast into a part of chaos ... As with a woman who gives birth to a child all her superfluous matter falls away, so the matter (hylē) which originated from the shadow was cast into a part of chaos, and it came forth from chaos no [more] ..."*

NHC II 5,99 (147), 2–22

Matter accordingly originated from a negative psychic action on the part of the "shadow"; thereby it is discounted from the beginning. Behind this there evidently lies the idea attested in Philo of Alexandria (1st century A.D.) of the "shadow of God", which functions as a tool at the creation. In Gnosis however this idea is quite clearly employed in a derogatory sense. Close upon the origin of matter there follows that of the world creator (Demiurge), who here as in many other gnostic documents bears the name Jaldabaoth.* The word is of Semitic (Aramaic) origin and probably means "begetter of Sabaoth (= Abaoth)" i. e. "the (heavenly) powers";[26] evidently an esoteric description of the God of the Jews who corresponding to the biblical tradition occupies in the gnostic systems the role of the creator. Celsus, already mentioned, reports that the gnostics – he considers them Christians – called the God of the Jews the "accursed God", since he created the visible world and withheld knowledge from men.*

NHC II 5,100 (148), 14

Origen, C. Celsum VI 28

"When this had happened, then Pistis came and showed herself to the matter (hylē) of chaos which had been cast out like an abortion, for there was no spirit (pneuma) in it. In consequence this whole is a boundless darkness and a bottomless water. But

when Pistis had seen what had happened through her error she
was disturbed. The disturbance caused a "work of terror" to
make its appearance, which however fled into chaos. But she
turned herself to it in order [to breathe] into its face in the abyss
which is [beneath all] the heavens. When [Pis]tis Sophia now
wished that that which was without spirit (*pneuma*) should assume form (*typos*) and rule over matter (*hyle*) and all its powers, then there appeared out of the water first a "ruler" (archon), which was in the form of a lion [and] bi-sexual and possessed a great power in himself, but did not know whence he
had originated. But when Pistis Sophia saw how he moved in
the depth of the water, she said to him: "Young man, pass over
to this place", for which the interpretation is "Jaldabaoth" ...
The ruler Jaldabaoth now did not know the power of Pistis, nor
had he seen her face, but only her likeness which spoke with
him in the water, and after that voice he called himself "Jaldabaoth". But the perfect call him "Ariel", since he had the form
of a lion. After he had come into being and had the power over
matter (*hyle*), Pistis Sophia withdrew up to her light".*

* NHC II 5,99 (147),
23–100 (148), 29

Now begins the creative activity of the Demiurge, which because of its breadth of detail we can reproduce only in extracts:
"When the ruler (archon) saw his greatness, and saw only himself and no other apart from water and darkness, then he
thought that he alone existed. His th[ought] was completed
through the word. It became manifest in a spirit (*pneuma*)
which moved to and fro upon the water.* But when that spirit
appeared, the ruler separated the watery substance to one part
and the dry was separated to another part, and out of matter
(*hyle*) he created for himself a dwelling place; he called it
"heaven". And out of matter the ruler created a footstool and
called it "earth".* Thereafter there follows through his word
the creation of his six bi-sexual sons, who accordingly bear male
and female names (including Jao, Sabaoth, Adonaios, Eloaios,
Oraios, Sophia which are of Semitic or Jewish origin and are also known from parallel texts). Each of these "archons" receives
his own "heaven" as a dwelling place, with thrones, glories,
temples, chariots, "spiritual maidens", "hosts of divine powers", angels and archangels, "innumerable myriads". These are
the heavenly realms or spheres of the rulers of this world, of
which we have spoken. There is also a report of a first "disturbance" of these worlds through the "troubler", which is

* cf. Gen. 1,2

* NHC II 5,100 (148),
29–103 (151), 2

brought to an end by the intervention of Pistis; her breath banishes him to Tartarus. Evidently we have here a development of the Greek mythology of the war with the Titans. Then comes an important episode which recurs in all similar texts: the presumption (*hybris*) of the Demiurge:

"When thus the heavens and their powers had been established together with all their organisation, then the First-begetter (*archigenetor*) exalted himself and received praise from the entire host of the angels; and all the gods and their angels blessed and praised him. But he rejoiced in his heart and boasted continually, saying to them: "I have need of no-one". He said [further]: "I am God and there is no other apart from me".* But when he said this he sinned against all the immortals, who took note of it and preserved him. When now Pistis saw the godlessness of the great ruler (archon) she became enraged. Invisibly she said to him: "You are mistaken, Samael!" – i. e. "the blind god". – "An immortal man of light is before you who will make himself known in your images. He will trample you down as clay is trodden, and you will descend with those who are yours to your mother, the abyss. For at the end of your works the whole deficiency will be dissolved, which has come forth from truth into appearance. It will pass away and become like that which never existed". When Pistis had said this she showed in the water the image of her greatness. And then she withdrew back to her light".*

* cf. Is. 45,21; 46,9

* NHC II 5, 103 (151), 3–32

In this incident we already have an intimation of the beginning of a change in circumstances which leads through the revelation of the "man of light" to the anthropogony, with which we will be concerned in the next chapter. Our text picks up the thread again after a long insertion which deals with the repentance and enthronement of Sabaoth, *[26a] and portrays the confusion of the demiurge at the existence of a being before and above him. "He was ashamed of his error". But his folly prompts him to the demand: "If there is anyone before me, let him reveal himself, that we may see his light". Immediately there comes a "light from the ogdoad above, which passed through all the heavens of the earth". When he perceives the beauty of the light, he is again ashamed. In the light there now appears a human figure, which admittedly is visible only to Jaldabaoth, but which with its glory sets all the heavenly powers in confusion. A fresh insertion tells of the unfulfilled relationship

* NHC II 5,107 (155), 17–108 (156), 14

between the "Pronoia" (providence) of the Demiurge and the figure of light, who is called "Light-Adam"; out of this originates Eros (Love). Eros however is the cause of the creation of

• NHC II 5,108 (156), 14–28

paradise, plants and animals.* The "Light-Adam" remains two days on earth and then returns into the Kingdom of Light. "Immediately the darkness became entirely without [reason] (*nous*)". His complete return is however not possible because of his contact with the lower world. He can no longer reach the ogdoad, but must create for himself a world (aeon) of his own in "the endless region between the ogdoad and the chaos beneath", which is however more excellent than the lower

• NHC II 5,111 (159), 29–112 (160), 25

worlds.* By this is evidently meant the realm of the fixed stars. The sequel is then formed by the creation of man.

See below, p. 94

These texts give a good insight into the method of gnostic speculation, which with the aid of traditional material brings to expression a new kind of conception of the origin of the world. The world of the creator is subordinated to a world which lies before it in space and time, and at the same time is thereby devaluated; its origin is to be explained from a disharmony which somehow enters in at the margin of the upper world. A female

"Wisdom"
(Sophia)

being is responsible for this, who bears the name "Wisdom" (Sophia) and "Faith" (Pistis) – the first evidently with an eye on the figure of "Wisdom" known from the Jewish wisdom litera-

• Wisd. 9; Prov. 8,22–31

ture, who functions as the assistant of God in creation*, but also in disappointment at the folly of mankind flees from the world into heaven, as it is related in the Ethiopic Book of

• Enoch 28

Enoch.* Since for the gnostics "faith" plays only a provisional role over against "knowledge", it can be employed as a description of the divided and not completely integrated being, which has "ignorance" and therefore the creation for its sequel. The Valentinian school developed the fall, the repentance and the redemption of Sophia in their system into a grandiose doctrine which is regarded also as the pattern for the redemption of man. In the lengthy expositions of the Coptic Pistis Sophia we have a final product of this type of speculation. The beginning

See below, p. 294 f.

we possess in the myth, brought into assocation with Simon Magus, of the fall of a female being, who bears various names.

**The cosmogony
of the Secret
Book of John**

This conception has taken a form evidently classical for many schools in the wellknown Apocryphon of John, to which we now turn.[27]

After the description, reproduced above, of the Father of All

surrounded by light the proceedings in the Pleroma are related
thus: "He knew his own image when he saw it in the pure water *See above, p. 63f.*
of light which surrounded him. And his thought (*ennoia*) accomplished a work, it revealed itself. It stood before him out of
the glory of the light: this is the power which is before the all,
which revealed itself, the perfect providence (*pronoia*) of the
all, the light, the likeness of the light, the image of the invisible.
She is the perfect power Barbēlo, the perfect aeon of glory ...
She is the first thought (*ennoia*), his (the Father's) image. She
became a first "man", which is the virgin spirit (*pneuma*) ...
And Barbēlo asked of him to give her a first knowledge; he
granted it. When he granted it, the first knowledge was manifested. She took her stand with thought (*ennoia*) – that is providence (*pronoia*) – praising the Invisible and the perfect power
Barbēlo, because they had come into being through them"*. In * *Pap. Ber. 27,1–36,15*
the same fashion (prayer, assent, manifestation) other aeons
also come into being: "incorruptibility", "eternal life" (the formation of a second Ennoia has evidently dropped out of our
text); altogether they form a bisexual "pentad of the aeons of
the father" or a "decad". Then a further action begins: Barbēlo
after "steadfast looking" at the Father brings forth a "blessed
spark of light", which is described as "only-begotten (*monogenēs*)", "divine self-begotten (*autogenēs*)", "first-born son of
the all" and is identified with the heavenly Christ (interpreted
as "kindly" = *chrēstos*).* * *op. cit. 30,15ff.*

The sequence of the aeons is continued by him with the aid of
the invisible spirit;* mind (*nous*), will and the word (*logos*) * *op. cit. 31,1ff.*
come into being. The God of Truth then sets him over the all
and causes four great lights to proceed from him and incorruptibility. These are on the one hand designated as "grace", "insight", "perception" and "prudence", but on the other hand
bear (Semitic) angel names (Harmozēl, Oroiaēl, Daveithe,
Eleleth) and each consists of three aeons, making a total of
twelve aeons.* These aeons belong to the self-begotten son * *op. cit. 33,7–34,7*
(Christ). There is here no arrangement in pairs such as Irenaeus
for example reports; however it is presupposed in what follows,
so that we must reckon with the possibility of a later alteration
of the context. The continuation reports first of the begetting of
the heavenly Adam, who appears as "perfect true man" and at
the command of God, the spirit and the son originated from
First Knowledge and Understanding (*nous*).* Christ sets him, * *op. cit. 34,19–36,15*

his son Seth and his descendants ("the souls of the holy ones" = the gnostics) over the four lights already mentioned. With this the narrative about the pleroma is complete and now begins the description of the behaviour of Sophia, i. e. the critical event which suddenly alters the whole of the development hitherto.

"Our sister Sophia, who is an Aeon, thought a thought of herself. And through the thought of the spirit (*pneuma*) and the first knowledge she wanted to reveal the likeness (of her thought) out of herself, although the spirit had not consented or granted [it], nor again had her partner consented, the male virgin spirit. So she did not find one in harmony (*symphonos*) with her, when she was about to concede it without the consent of the spirit and the knowledge of her own partner, when she became strong (pregnant) in consequence of the passion that was in her. Her thought could not remain inactive, and [so] her work came forth: imperfect, hateful in appearance, since she had made it without her consort (*syzygos*). And it was not like the appearance of the mother, since it was of another form. But she looked upon it in her consideration that it was of the stamp of a different appearance, since it had the external (appearance) of a serpent and a lion; its [eyes] shone with fire. She cast it away from herself, out of those places, that none of the immortals might see it, since she had borne it in ignorance. She bound with it a cloud of light, set a throne in the midst of the cloud, that none might see it except the holy spirit – whom they call "life" (*zoē*), the mother of all – and gave him the name "Jaldabaoth". This is the first archon. He drew much power from the mother, removed himself from her, and turned himself away from the place in which he had been born. He took possession of another place. He made for himself an aeon flaming with shining fire, in which he now dwells". *

* op. cit. 36,16–39,4

The Demiurge thus involuntarily brought into being now begins to create his own world: "He united himself with the unreason (*aponoia*) which is with him. He brought into being the powers which are under him, the twelve angels, each one of them for his [own] aeon according to the pattern of the incorruptible aeons. And he created for each one of them seven angels and for the angels three powers, so that all who are under him produce three hundred and sixty angelic beings . . . When the powers made their appearance out of the first begetter (*archigenetor*), the first archon of darkness, out of the ignorance of him who begot them, their names were these: the first is Jaōth, the second is Hermas ... the third is Galila, the fourth is Jōbēl, the fifth is Adōnaios, the sixth is Sabaoth, the seventh is Kainan and Kaē who is called Cain – that is the sun – the eight is Abiressine, the ninth is Jōbēl(!), the tenth is Harmupiaēl, the eleventh is Adōnin, the twelfth is Belias". *

* *op. cit. 39,4–44,18*

Further names for these derive "from the passion and from wrath", but they also bear names which correspond to their "true nature", i. e. as signs of the zodiac, which they are. Jaldabaoth, who now also bears the name "Saklas", i. e. "fool", then appoints seven kings over the seven heavens and five over the "chaos of the underworld". The first, the planets, bear "names of glory" and have the appearance of animals: 1. Jaōth, the lion-faced, 2. Elōaios, the ass-faced, 3. Astaphaios, the hyena-faced, 4. Jaō, the serpent-faced with seven heads, 5. Adōnaios, the dragon-faced, 6. Adōni, the ape-faced, 7. Sabbataios, with the face of flaming fire. "These are they who control the world". The names, which – as far as Astaphaios – are older and later names for the God of the Jews, show like the description of their outward appearance what a deep contempt is now displayed towards the biblical God of creation and his government of the world. They are found also in other systems, for example in that of the so called Ophites.* "But Jaldabaoth, Saklas, the many-formed, so that he can show himself with any face, gave to them (the planets) of the fire which belongs to him; but he did not give them of the pure light of the power which he had drawn from the mother. For this reason he ruled over them, because of the glory which was in him from the power [of the light] from the mother. For this reason he had himself called "God", in that he resisted the nature (*hypostasis*) from which he had come into being. And he bound seven powers with the principalities".* These subordinate powers bear the following names: "Providence" (*pronoia*), "Divinity", "Lordship", "Fire", "Kingdom", "Insight" (*synesis*), "Wisdom" (*sophia*). Later they give the man created by them his psychic powers. After the work is complete the Demiurge exalts himself with the familiar arrogance: "He saw the creation that was beneath him and the multitude of angels under him and said to them "I am a jealous God, apart from me there is none".* Thereby he indicated to the angels under him that there is another God; for if there was no other, of whom should he be jealous?"*

* *Origen, C. Celsum VI 31 f.*

* *Pap. Ber. 42,10–43,7*

See below, p. 96f.

* *cf. Exod. 20,5; Is. 45,5; 46,9*

* *Pap. Ber. 44,9–18*

* op. cit. 44,19–47,16

The narrative now turns again to Sophia and portrays her repentance, suffering and restoration into the Pleroma.* She begins to be agitated when she recognises her deficiency and the loss of her perfection. (The movement "to and fro in the darkness of ignorance", occasioned by the repentance, is explained by a bold interpretation of Genesis 1.2. in the Greek translation). Her son the Demiurge is so taken up with himself and his work that he is aware only of his mother and not of the "multitude" of the Pleroma superior to her. "But when the mother recognised that the abortion of darkness was not perfect, because her consort (*syzygos*) had not concurred with her, she repented and wept bitterly. He (the spirit) heard the prayer of her repentance and the brethren prayed for her. The holy invisible spirit assented ... he poured out upon her a spirit (*pneuma*) from the perfection. Her consort came down to her in order to put right her deficiency ... And she was not brought back to her own aeon, but because of the very great ignorance which had become manifest in her she is in the nonad (i. e. between the Pleroma and the realm of the Demiurge) until she puts right her deficiency. A voice came to her: "Man exists and the son of Man". By this the highest God and the Only-begotten are meant. The sequel contains the anthropogony.

See below, p. 94 ff.

Behind this system lies a similar structure to that of the anonymous document On the Origin of the World.* The church fathers already called the representatives of this movement "Barbelognostics" or "Barbeliotes" after the first emanation of the Father of all, who bears the name Barbēlo (difficult to explain but certainly an artificial Semitic or Aramic word). It is one of the largest groups in Gnosis, but not however uniform, as the new Coptic texts make clear. Barbēlo represents the female aspect of the Father and is a kind of gnostic mother goddess. Probably she was from the beginning one person with Sophia, as the new document The Three Pillars of Seth expresses it.* She has at the same time also however bisexual features; she is "the first male virgin aeon".* For the gnostics bisexuality is an expression of perfection; it is only the earthly creation which leads to a separation of the original divine unity, which holds for the whole Pleroma. The uncontrolled "passion" of Sophia is also a violation of this unity; it has accordingly fateful consequences for her and for the cosmos. In the statements of the Valentinian Theodotus, as Clement has transcribed them, we

* NHC II 5

Barbēlo and Sophia

* NHC VII 5,123,16f.

* NHC VII 5,121,20f.

are told that the creator is a product of the "passions of desire".* This twofold position of Sophia has led in Valentinianism to the conception of a higher ("incorruptible") and a lower
fallen Sophia, of whom the latter is also called "little Sophia" or
"Sophia of death".* Her dual role becomes visible also in the
creation of man in so far as she has a part in it through the implanting of the divine spark (usually of the female sex). The
destiny of this spark in the world of the body is like that of Sophia after her fall, for which reason a number of witnesses draw
the two together into one figure and illustrate by it the unity of
opposites or the transitoriness of earthly ("unenlightened")
judgment. Such an example is afforded by the Nag Hammadi
document Thunder: the perfect Mind.* Here in the form of a
revelation address there is reference to the two sides of a female
figure who has been sent by the power, that she may be sought
and found. Behind her is evidently concealed Sophia, but also
the soul, both in their two manners of existence: as perfect, divine and redeeming power, and as fallen phenomenon exposed
to deficiency: [28]

*Clem. Alex.,
Ex Theodoto 33,3–4*

NHC II 3, 60 (108), 12–15

„Thunder: the perfect Mind"

NHC VI 2

"I am the honoured / and the despised.
I am the prostitute / and the respectable woman.
I am the wife / and the virgin.
I am the mother / and the daughter.
I am the members of my mother.*
. . .

NHC VI 2,13,16–22

I am the silence / which is unattainable,
the insight (*epinoia*), / which much (in the world) recalls.
I am the voice / whose sound is manifold,
and the logos / which has many images.*
. . .

NHC VI 2,14,9–13

I am knowledge / and ignorance.
I am shame / and boldness.
I am shameless / and I am ashamed.
I am strength / and I am fear.*
. . .

NHC VI 2,14,26–31

I am she who is in all terrors / and [I am] boldness in trem-
bling.

I am she who is weak / and I am safe in a place of pleasure.
I am unreasoning / and I am wise.*

* NHC VI 2,15,25–30

. . .

Yea, I am the wisdom (*Sophia*) of the Greeks / and the knowledge (*gnosis*) of the barbarians.
I am the Law of the Greeks / and of the barbarians.
I am she who has many images in Egypt / and who has no image among the barbarians.
I am she who was everywhere hated / and she who was everywhere beloved.
I am she who is called "life" / and [yet] you have called [me] "death".
I am she who is called "law" / and [yet] you have called [me] "lawlessness".
I am she whom you have sought / and I am she whom you have grasped.
I am she whom you have scattered / and [yet] you have gathered me together.
I am she before whom you have been ashamed / and [yet] you were shameless before me.*

* NHC VI 2,16,3–22

. . .

I am the mind of those [who understand] / and the rest of him [who sleeps].
I am the knowledge to which enquiring after me leads / and the finding for those who seek after me, and the command for those who entreat me.*

* NHC VI 2,18,9–13

. . .

I am the union / and the dissolution.
I am the remaining / and I am the releasing.
I am what is beneath, / and to me will they come up.
I am judgement and forgiveness.
I am sinless and [yet] the root of sin comes from me.
I am the desire in the vision / and [yet] the mastery of the heart dwells in me".*

* NHC VI 2,19,10–20

Thus "wisdom" is for the gnostic a many-sided phenomenon which unites in itself many aspects of his view of the world, both negative and positive. Perhaps we may deduce from this why

Sophia plays such a large part in many gnostic systems and documents. She belongs to the oldest and most important elements
of the structure of Gnosis.

The gnostic idea of the origin of the world appears in a con-
cise form, stripped of its mythological colouring, in the (Valentinian) Gospel of Philip: "The world came into being through a
transgression. For he who created it wanted to create it imperishable and immortal. He failed and did not attain to his hope. For
the incorruption of the world did not exist and the incorruption
of him who made the world did not exist".* The Gospel of
Truth has worked over this whole process in meditative fashion
by interpreting the origin of the world as the consequence of
psychological processes of a universal or cosmological significance, the reversal of which constitutes Gnosis: "The all was
within the inconceivable, incomprehensible, who is exalted
above any thought, while the ignorance about the Father produced anguish and terror. And the anguish thickened like a
mist, so that none could see. Therefore error (*planē*) gained
strength. She set to work upon her "matter" (*hylē*) in vain, for
she did not know the truth. She began on a creature (*plasma*) to
establish with vigour the substitute for the truth in beauty. But
this was not a humiliation for him, the inconceivable, incomprehensible, for the anguish, the forgetfulness and the creature
of deceit were nothing, whereas the abiding truth is unchangeable and unperturbed and has no need of adornment. Therefore
despise error! Thus it is with her: she has no root, she came into
being in a mist (= ignorance) with regard to the Father. Since
she [now] is, she prepares works, forgetfulness and fears, in
order that with these she may beguile those who belong to the
Midst (i. e. evidently the beings of the intermediate kingdom)
and take them captive (in matter) . . . The forgetfulness did not
come into being with the Father although it came into being because of him. What comes into being within him is knowledge
(*gnosis*), which was made manifest that the forgetfulness might
be dissolved and the Father be known. Since the forgetfulness
came into being because the Father was not known, then from
the moment when the Father is known the forgetfulness will no
longer exist".*

The origin of
the world
according to
the Gospel of
Philip and the
Gospel of
Truth

* NHC II 3, 75 (123), 2–9

* NHC I 3,17,6–18,11

Presumably the "passions" mentioned are only circumlocutions for things which are otherwise abundantly described in
mythological terms, for example "error" as an image for the

Demiurge, "ignorance", "anguish" and "terror" as references to the behaviour of Sophia. In the sequel there is repeatedly reference to "deficiency", which attaches to the all because it is in ignorance of the true Father.* Its perfection lies therefore in a return, i. e. in the knowledge of the Father and the annihilation of the error.* To this end the Father sends his son (Christ) that he may show the (fallen) aeons the way to their origin and to rest. This is tantamount to the dissolution of the cosmos. "In that he (Christ) filled (i. e. removed) the deficiency, he destroyed the form (= outer appearance); its (the deficiency's) form, in which he (Christ) served, is the cosmos. For the place where there is envy and strife is deficiency. But the place where there is unity is perfect. Since the deficiency came into being because they did not know the Father, then when they know the Father the deficiency will no longer exist. Just as any man's ignorance immediately disappears when he attains to knowledge, as darkness disappears when the light appears, so the deficiency disappears in the perfection".* From the parallel formulations it is very clear that "forgetfulness" and "deficiency" mean the same thing, which characterises earthly and worldly existence and which can only be overcome through knowledge. The text also shows how closely the cosmology or cosmogony is tied up with redemption; the two processes for the gnostic are not to be separated.

The three-principle systems In the previous section we have dealt in detail with a "female" type of speculation to which the thought of emanation from a primal origin belongs. Other systems, which we can only briefly touch upon, reckon with three primal principles or, as the gnostics are fond of saying, "roots", which condition the forming of the world. The majority of these are reported to us by Hippolytus, but not always completely. In some these "roots" have themselves proceeded from an earlier origin or "seed". The existence of chaos is always presupposed, and this represents darkness or matter, frequently designated as a separate fourth power. "He who says that the universe proceeds from one (principle) is mistaken; he who says from three, speaks the truth and gives the right explanation of the all." So runs a fundamental statement of the Naassenes according to Hippolytus.* This movement, which received its name because of the prominence given to the serpent (Hebrew *nahash*, Grecised into *naas*) speaks of the "pre-existent", "self-originate"

Margin notes:
* NHC I 3,18,35–19,17
* NHC I 3,21,8–22,33
* NHC I 3,24,20–25,3
* Hippolytus, Refutatio V 8,1

and "chaos", to which is added also the Demiurge Esaldaios as a "fourth power". The latter created the cosmos, the "nothing", without the help and knowledge of the first three, but thereby – which is only presupposed – shut up the vital middle principle, the world soul or (inner) "man" (*anthropos*), in chaos. The destiny of this part is the subject of a lengthy document, the so-called Naassene Homily, on which we shall touch in the next chapter.

The Sethians (named after Seth the son of Adam) also have a doctrine of three principles: "light", "spirit" and "darkness" (so Hippolytus). This agrees with the Paraphrase of Shem: "there was light and darkness, and spirit (*pneuma*) was between them".* The operation of these three "roots" is described by means of a lengthy and distorted interpretation of Genesis 1: chaos (darkness) below, the spirit above it and at the top the light. "The light was thought, filled with hearing and word (*logos*). They were united in a single form. And the darkness was wind in waters; it possessed reason (*nous*), clothed with a restless fire. And the spirit between them was a mild, humble light".* While the light in which the "greatness" dwells knows about the baseness and the confusion of darkness, the latter does not know itself and its position. Through a movement by it the spirit is alarmed and lifts itself up to its place, from which it sees both the darkness below and also the light above it. The latter reveals itself to him in the form of a being which is described as the image and "son of the undefiled limitless light" and is identical with the revealer of the entire doctrine, Derdekeas. It is his task to carry up to the higher light the light shut up in darkness ("nature" and chaos) in the form of "understanding" (*nous*), in order that the separation now introduced may become perfect. This is only partially brought about, since nature (*physis*) strives against it and retains a part of the light. The cosmogony follows in the course of the (not always very lucid) effort towards the liberation of the light, in the interplay of the different powers (among others there is reference to the "womb" and the hymen). The struggle continues in the history of the world, which is orientated to certain specific biblical events but with an evaluation which is entirely contrary to the Bible, and will come to an end only in the "time of consummation": nature perishes, and her "thoughts" separate from her to enter into the light.

* *NHC VII 1,1,26f.*

* *NHC VII 1,1,32–2,5*

From this brief survey it is clear that these systems have no "Sophia myth", but either simply presuppose, or even postulate, the cosmogonic fall from the present state of the world or understand it as merely the act of a supramundane and generally masculine being. A further characteristic is a certain circular movement which is bound up with it: what is above descends below, in order finally to return to its old position (this time however once and for all, in contrast for example to the Indian systems). This idea is indeed part of Gnosis as a whole – it is the monistic basic structure in its dualistic view of the world – but it has a particularly prominent presentation in the three-principle systems. As an illustration, reference is made to the ocean, which flows "downwards" and "upwards": the first signifies the origin of men, the second that of "gods", i.e. the divine element in man finds its way back to its origin (so in the Naassene homily). With other groups (the so-called Peratae) the image is that of the serpent moving this way and that, which symbolises the turning of the middle principle from above downwards and the reverse. The first principle remains always unaffected; it is the static pole of what has come to pass, the goal of becoming. The disturbing factor in the "circle" is the power of darkness and of evil, which is a basic presupposition in all systems. Hence the negative judgement of the world is brought more or less to expression. Its creator and ruler is described as a "murderer from the beginning"*, since his work brings corruption and death (so the Peratae in Hippolytus)*. The stars are "the gods of corruption" who enslave mankind and expose them to the unavoidable becoming and passing away.* (This statement is linked up with an interpretation of Old Testament stories.)

cf. John 8,44

Hippolytus, Refutatio V 17,7

op. cit. 16,6ff.

The cosmogony of Poimandres

Finally we may glance at the cosmogony contained in the Poimandres, which despite its purely hellenistic-gnostic colouring also draws upon the Jewish creation story. The author is granted the following vision*[29]: alongside the primal "serene and friendly light" there appears "gradually and downward tending a fearful and terrifying darkness, wound in a coil, so that I compared it to a snake. Then the darkness changed itself into a kind of moist nature (*physis*), unspeakably confused, giving off smoke as from a fire, and uttering an inexpressibly doleful sound ... but from the light (...) there came a holy word (*logos*) upon the nature and unmixed fire shot up from the moist nature to the height. For it was light, quick and vigorous all at

Corp. Herm. I 4–11

once, and the air, being light, followed the spirit as it ascended
from earth and water up to the fire, so that it seemed to me to be
hanging from it. But earth and water remained mixed together
by themselves, so that the earth was not to be seen for water.
But they (the elements) were stirred through the spiritual word
(*logos*) which moved upon them,* so that it became audi- * *cf. Gen. 1,2*
ble(?)".

The interpretation of this vision by Poimandres is as follows:
the light is "understanding" (*nous*) or the "Father God" (= Poimandres), the logos of light which originated from him is the
"son of God", who at the same time is what the visionary "sees
and hears"; these two – Nous and Logos – belong together:
"their union is life". The question as to the origin of the elements is answered thus: "From the will (*boulē*) of God, which
received the word (*logos*) and saw the beautiful (invisible) cosmos and copied it; it formed itself into a cosmos through its own
elements and through the souls generated by it". Then it is said
"the god Nous, being bisexual life and light, brought forth
through another word a demiurge understanding (*nous*), which
as god of the fire and the spirit created seven administrators,
who encompass the invisible world in circles and whose administration is called "destiny" (*heimarmenē*). Then the divine
word (*logos*) sprang at once out of the downward-tending elements into the pure creation of nature and united with the creator understanding (*nous*), for it was like him. And the irrational
downward tending elements of nature were left to themselves,
so that they were mere matter (*hylē*)".

With this the process of separation is for the moment at an
end and the Demiurge can now with the logos set the spheres in
motion. This circling motion brings out of the lower elements
corresponding irrational beasts, and living beings come into existence in the air, in the water and on the earth.* As a final act * *cf. Gen. 1,24*
there follows the creation of man, first of all that of the divine *See below, p. 107ff.*
image. Only as a result of this act and its further consequences
does the gnostic character of the document become evident,
since otherwise it breathes the atmosphere of late Greek philosophy (visible in the positive cosmology) and can be assessed as
a product from the beginnings of Gnosis.

Anthropology and Anthropogony

The dualistic view of the world just described also determines the gnostic view of man and indeed finds in it its central means of expression. Man is for Gnosis, as for all religions, at the centre of history; in him the opposing powers who dominate the cosmos can be exhibited in a special degree. The verdict with

Devaluation of material existence

regard to the earthly and visible world includes on the anthropological level a negative judgment upon the whole of bodily and psychic existence. This earthly material existence, like the world itself, is a product of the Demiurge and correspondingly is a sphere hostile to God, dominated by evil powers which are evident and active in the passions and desires. The psychic part of man is therefore represented as a product of evil powers (above all the planets) and through this man is not only the object but also the subject of the activity of such powers. The "demonistic conception of the world" thus corresponds to the "demonistic conception of the soul" (H. Jonas). Valentinus writes in one of his letters that the human heart is the abode of evil spirits who prevent its becoming pure, and instead treat it disgracefully through "unseemly desires"; it is comparable to

Clem. Alex., Strom. II 114,3–5

an inn, which is full of filth and dissolute men.*

This view of the relation of man to the world and his imprisonment therein is however only one side. The other side is that which corresponds on the macrocosmic level to the kingdom of

The unworldly "I"

the "unknown God": it is the deep and hidden relation to this higher world. Gnosis described this transcendent level in many images and expressions since, like the highest being, it has no connection with this world and in practice can only be described in negative terms. In the Greek and Coptic texts the dominant concept is "spirit" (*pneuma*), in the relevant Hermetica "understanding" (*nous*), and in the oriental or Semitic "soul". A designation to which we shall have to give closer attention is "inner man". Probably the most appropriate is the expression "spark" (Greek *spinthēr*), which occurs here and there. "Seed of light" is also found for it. In order to make use of a uniform expression scholars have become accustomed to speak of the "self" or "I", and here the reproduction of a Manichean, Iranian term has played a part. The "incomparable self" in man

I

Manichean book illustration (miniature) from Turkestan (Chotsko, Turfan oasis). Above: "elect" (*electi*) reading and teaching; below: the faithful ("hearers" or "catechumens") listening.

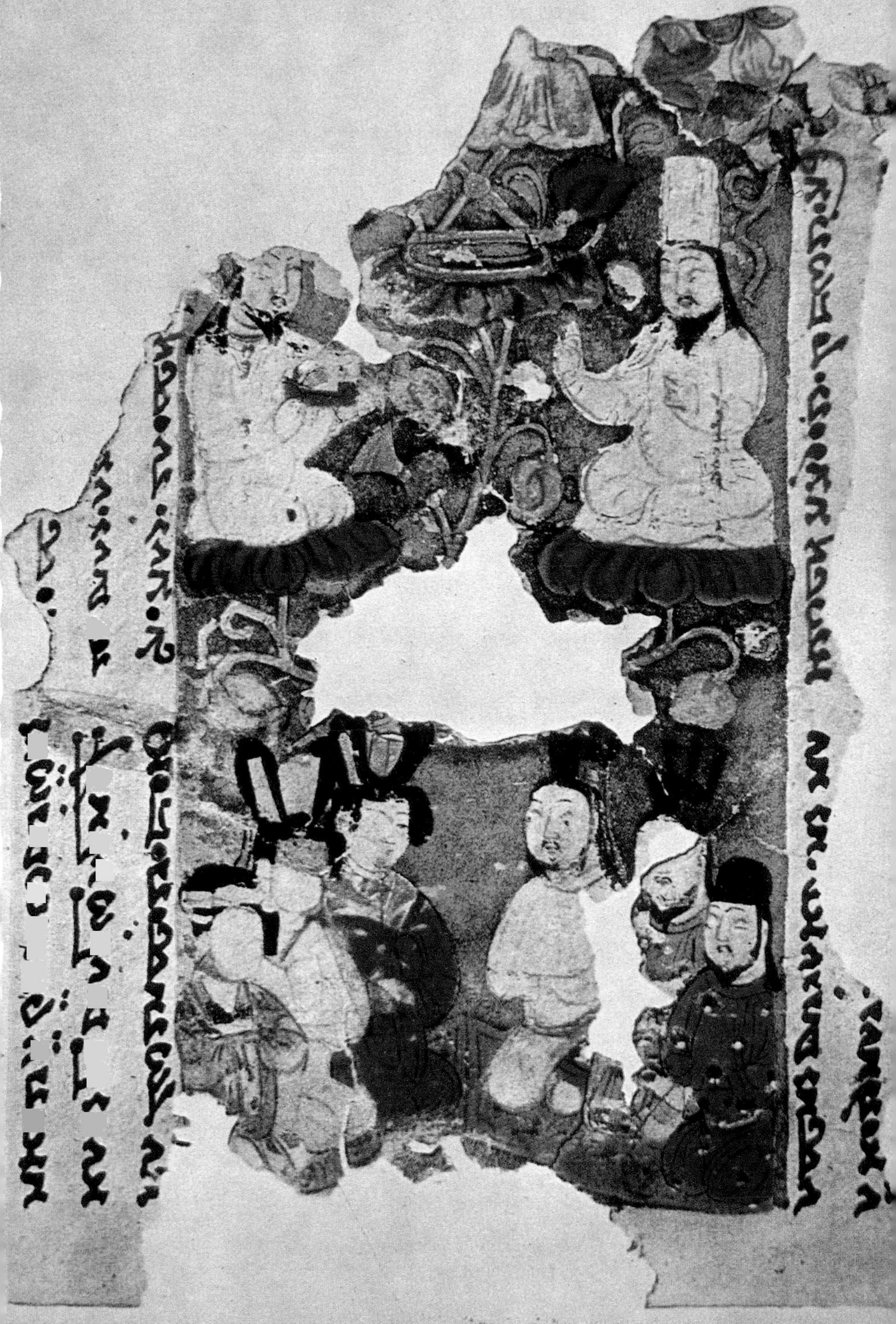

forms the third anthropological element for Gnosis, alongside body and soul. Gnostic anthropology is therefore basically tripartite, although in distinction to similar contemporary conceptions a clear line is drawn between the material and psychic and the spiritual part. The terminology used, especially for the transcendent core of man, is externally indebted to the philosophical tradition, but in its deeper understanding is at variance with it, as is shown above all by the ambivalent use of "soul" (*psychē*) and "spirit" (*pneuma*). When in oriental texts, especially the Mandean, the term "soul" is used, the expression for "spirit" stands on the lower level and corresponds to the "soul" (*psychē*) in the hellenistic sources. Thus here too we have a trichotomy and the internal agreement in the position of the "self" is preserved.

It is this "self" with which the anthropogony and the later soteriology are particularly concerned. The man to whom the knowledge of an otherworldly core of his being has been granted asks about the origin of this core, and the anthropogony gives the answer. One must also bear in mind that only through this divine basis in man is Gnosis possible at all, i. e. the knowledge is on the one side a function of the unworldly "I", but on the other side it is directed to this in order to discover it and to experience it as a guarantee of release from the cosmos. The whole gnostic doctrine of redemption centres upon the restoration to its origin of this divine spark of light, which through fatal events has "fallen" into the world, a restoration mythologically represented as an "ascent of the soul". This eschatological act, which takes place after death, is the real means of the liberation of the "self", since at this point the concealing wrapper of the bodily and psychic existence falls away and the potential freedom of the authentic "I" is realised. It is clear from this that gnostic anthropology is basically on two levels, related to cosmic and to acosmic existence, but that through the tendency to extend the realm of the cosmic as wide as possible and to draw into it the psychic existence of man as well, it is led to introduce the acosmic "I" as a third principle. Here too very clear expression is given to the dualistic basis of Gnosis.

The gnostic anthropology is reflected in the division of men into two or three classes: the "spiritual" (pneumatic), the psychic, and the "fleshly" (sarkic, from Greek *sarx* "flesh, body") or "earthly" (choic, from Greek *choikos* "earthly"), also called

Spirit, soul, body and their representatives

"hylic" (Greek *hylē*, "matter"). "There are three men and their races to the end of the world: the spiritual (pneumatic), the psychic and the earthly (choic)", it is said in the anonymous treatise,* which accordingly also distinguishes three Adam figures: the first or pneumatic, the second or psychic and the third or earthly.* All three have indeed originated in succession, but they are united in the one first man; they form the three constituents of every man. The one which in each case predominates determines the type of man to which one belongs. Strictly only the pneumatic and hylic stand in opposition, since the psychic belong to the latter and are reckoned among the "ignorant". Only the pneumatics are gnostics and capable of redemption. This intermediate position of the "psychic" can also be explained from a historical situation: in Christian Gnosis these were held to include the mass of ordinary Christians, who stood between the heathen and the gnostics and were the target for missionary effort. This does not signify any weakening of the dualistic principle, but its consistent application in a changed situation; the esoteric gnostic understanding of salvation is preserved even with regard to the ordinary Christians.[30]

* NHC II 5, 122 (170), 6–9

* NHC II 5, 117 (165), 28–35

The God "Man"

The central position occupied by man in gnostic theology led to a particularly important complex of ideas, customarily described as the "doctrine of the God 'Man'". It is also known under the name of "Urmensch myth" or (from the Greek word for "man") "Anthropos myth". The basic idea lies in the close relation or kinship of nature between the highest God and the inner core of man. This relationship, evidently with an eye on the biblical statements*, is understood as a relationship of copy to original, i.e. the (earthly) man is a copy of the divine pattern, which likewise often bears the name "man". One text refers to him as "the Father of truth, the Man of the greatness".* The often very complicated doctrine can be reduced to two basic types:[31] in one the highest being himself is the first or primal man (*anthropos*), who through his appearance to the creator powers gives them a pattern or model for the creation of the earthly (and therefore second) man, in the other the highest God produces first of all a heavenly man of like nature (frequently called "son of man"), who is then the direct prototype of the earthly (and therefore third) man. In the second version there is often also the idea that the (second) heavenly primal man allows himself to be seduced into taking up residence in

* cf. Gen. 1,26

* NHC VII 2,53,3–5

the earthly (bodily) man; he is then regarded as an "inner man" and at the same time represents the divine substance in man already mentioned (the "pneuma"). The rich language of gnostic imagery does not always clearly distinguish which man is in view; the divine attributes can be applied both to the heavenly and also to the earthly man who is by nature united with him – generally illustrated by Adam. The idea of the fall of a heavenly being and his dispersal in the earthly world is one of the basic conceptions of Gnosis and received its most sublime and clearest formulation in Manicheism.

See below, p. 335 ff.

Behind this idea of the divine "Man", who dwells both above and in the world, there is an entirely new conception of anthropology. This becomes clear above all in the higher estimate of man in comparison with the Demiurge: it is not only that the (first) man, i.e. the unknown God, exists before him – the earthly man also, who is his product, is superior to him by reason of his supramundane divine relationship and substance. H. Jonas aptly says "this exaltation of "man" into a supramundane God who – if not the first – is at any rate earlier and more exalted than the Demiurge, is one of the most important aspects of gnostic mythology in the general history of religions. It unites speculations so widely separated as those of the Poimandres and Mani; it indicates a new metaphysical status of man in the order of existence, and it is instruction on this theme which assigns the creator and ruler of nature to his proper place".[32] Behind this is expressed the whole revolutionary spirit of Gnosis in its rejection of the traditional values and ideas of faith, which we shall encounter also in other contexts.

The god-like place of man on the basis of his natural origin is very clearly formulated in some passages: "God created men, and men created God. So is it also in the world, since men created gods and worship them as their creations. It would be fitting that the gods should worship men".* The earliest known gnostics, like Simon Magus, Menander and Epiphanes, put this into practice and – at least according to the Church Fathers – allowed themselves to be worshipped as gods. The Greek conception of the sea as the place of origin of gods and men* is interpreted in the Naassene homily in the sense that the flow from the heavenly to the earthly ocean signifies the coming into being of men, while the route in the opposite direction is that of gods,* that is, man takes the place appropriate to his nature, for

* *NHC II 3,71 (119), 35–72 (120),4*

* *Homer, Iliad 14,201*

* *Hippolytus, Refutatio V 7,36*

* Ps. 82,6 which the psalm verse "you are gods, all sons of the most high"* is immediately pressed into service. "The beginning of perfection is the knowledge of man, but the knowledge of God is com-

* Hippolytus,
Refutatio V 6,6; 8,38 plete perfection".* The true knowledge of God begins with knowledge of man as a being related to God. The "tree of knowledge" in paradise according to various gnostic texts imparts to Adam his appropriate god-like status over against the lower creator god, who pronounced his prohibition of the enjoyment of this tree only out of envy. In the same way the serpent of paradise functions in some systems at the behest of the highest God for the instruction of the first man in paradise, and thus has a positive task. Some sources speak of the terror of the lower powers when they recognise the true character of the man created by them. Thus for them the creation of man has a boomerang effect: "the first begetter (*archigenetor*) of ignorance ... created a man after my (the primal Father's) image, but without knowing that that would become for him a destroying judgment, nor recognising the power which is in him (the

* NHC XIII 1,40,23–29 man)".*

The creation   With this we have already touched on the theme of the an-
and awakening thropogony proper, to which we have still to add something be-
of Adam   fore we discuss the texts themselves. It is presented predomi-
nantly by use of the Old Testament narrative of Adam and Eve, although generally in a very strange fashion, such as is typical of the gnostic interpretation of biblical statements. Here not only the canonical texts have their part, but also post-biblical Jewish ideas, and above all the myth of the quickening of Adam's body (Golem) by the spirit of God. It provided a good model for the gnostic theologians, in clothing some of their ideas about the origins of man and his dual nature in a literary garb. From this arose a "basic type of gnostic Urmensch-Adam speculation",[33] which recurs in many branches of the movement down to the Mandeans and Manichees. Naturally it stands in close connection with the "Anthropos myth". Both are indeed indebted to

* Gen. 1 the same biblical tradition* or relate to it. The most important features of this Adam story are the following: the body of Adam is moulded by the creator and his angels (archons, planets) from the elements (linking up with the plural used in

* Gen. 1,26 the Bible*); since however he has no real life in him, he is equipped by the highest being in a secret or mediated fashion with the divine spirit, i.e. the pneuma substance, which exalts

him above the creator God and bestows upon him the capacity for redemption. Redemption consists in the awakening of Adam to the knowledge of his true origin and of the worthlessness of the Demiurge.

This occurrence is usually connected with the biblical paradise story, the statements of which however are transformed into their opposites, since they are expressed on the level of the creator who considers Adam as his creature and does not know of his higher destiny. On the basis of this myth, worked out in various ways in the several documents, the destiny of man in his two-fold nature is programmatically presented. Adam or the first earthly man is for Gnosis the prototype of men in general; his destiny anticipates that of the mankind which is to follow. For this reason all these narratives have not only an illustrative but above all an existential significance. They are expressions of knowledge about the whence and the whither of mankind.

Let us now illustrate what has been said once more by a few extracts from the original sources, which for this part of gnostic theology are available in considerable quantity. We recall that in the "anonymous document", towards the end of the cosmogonic part, there is a report of the appearance of the "Adam of light". This already leads into the anthropogony proper, since these two sections of this "primal history" belong closely together and are only artifically separated by us. The dark powers under the leadership of the "first begetter" (Demiurge) begin the creation of man first of all as a counterblast to the inroads of the world of light: "Before the Adam of light had returned from the chaos the powers observed him and mocked at the first begetter (*archigenetor*), because he had lied when he said: "I am God. There is none before me". When they came to him they said: "Is perhaps this the God who has destroyed our work?" He answered and said: "Yes! If you wish that he should not be able (completely) to destroy our work, come, let us form a man out of the earth after the image of our body and after the likeness of this one (i. e. the Adam of light), that he may serve us, in order that this one when he sees his likeness may love it. He will no longer destroy our work, but we shall make those who shall be brought forth out of the light our servants during the whole period of this age". * The powers of light however use this plan for their own purposes, for they act after wise providence and create a spiritual man, "the instructor": "All this happened

The primal history according to the Anonymous Treatise in NHC II

See above, p. 75 ff.

* *NHC II 5,112 (160), 25–113 (161),5*

according to the providence (*pronoia*) of "faith" (*pistis*), in order that the man (of light) might appear before his likeness and condemn them (the powers) through their own creature (*plasma*)[a]; and their creature became a hedge of light. When then the powers took knowledge that they should form man, "wisdom life" (*sophia zoë*) forestalled them ... and she laughed at their resolve: "Blind they are in ignorance, they have formed him (the man) against themselves and know not what they will do". For this reason she anticipated them and first formed her man that he might instruct their (the powers') creature. Just as it (the creature) will despise them, so will it also be delivered from them".* The origin of the "instructor" comes about in a complicated manner: A "drop of light" flows from Sophia upon the water and there becomes a womb, called "Eve of life" or "instructress of life", from which then a "bisexual man" is born, whom the Greeks called Hermaphrodites, but the dark powers "the beast", which is the later serpent of paradise who instructs Adam.*

* NHC II 5,113 (161), 5–114 (162), 24

* NHC II 5,113 (161), 21 –114 (162), 2

The creation of the earthly Adam begins after some interruptions of the original connection: the Archigenetor issues a decree with regard to the man to be formed, and each of the powers "cast his seed upon the midst of the navel of the earth. From that day on the seven commanders (archons) formed the man, his body being indeed like their body, but his appearance like the man (of light) who had shown himself to them. His creature came into being according to the individual parts of each (of the archons). But their chief formed the brain and the marrow. Then he made his appearance like (the one) before him, (and) became a psychic man*, and he was called "Adam", that is the father, after the name of him who was before him. So when they had completed Adam, he (the chief archon) placed in him a vessel because he was shaped like the abortions, since there was no spirit (*pneuma*) in him. Therefore when the chief archon thought of the word of "faith" (*pistis*) he was afraid lest perhaps the true man might come into his creature and become master of it. Therefore he left his creature forty days without soul (*psychē*) and withdrew himself and let it be. But in these forty days "wisdom life" (*sophia zoë*) sent her breath into Adam, in whom there was still no soul. He began to move upon the earth,

* cf. Gen. 2,7

---

[a] "Creature" throughout this context renders the Greek loan-word *plasma*, i. e. the body *moulded* by the archons (Tr.).

but could not stand up. When the seven "commanders" (archons) came and saw him they were greatly disturbed; they came to him, seized him and said to the breath that was in him: "Who are you? And whence have you come to these places?" He answered (and) said: "I have come through the power of the man (of light) for the destruction of your work" ... When they had heard this they praised him, since he had given to them rest from the fear and the anxiety in which they were (since he was indeed imprisoned in Adam) ... But when they saw that Adam could not stand up they rejoiced, took him away, set him in paradise and returned back to their heavens."* *NHC II 5,114 (162), 24–115 (163), 30

The next act introduces the awakening of Adam, which takes its course in two stages: first comes the awakening through the heavenly Eve*, whose origin from Sophia has already been re- *NHC II 5,115 (163), 30–116 (164), 33 lated and whose name is etymologically interpreted as "instruc- *NHC II 5,113 (161), 32–34 tress of life"*. In another version she is called "the spiritual woman"*. Behind this evidently stands the idea that as "moth- *NHC II 4,89 (137), 11f. er of life" she is also the mother of Adam and hence of mankind. As it is said in other passages in our text*, she is virgin, *NHC II 5,116 (164), 4–15 wife and mother in one person and thus represents the female aspect of the kingdom of light, which is already visible in Sophia (as a form of whom she ultimately appears). The attempt of the powers to restrict the process of the first awakening through a binding of Eve to Adam fails*. Only the likeness of the spiritual *NHC II 5,116 (164), 2–33 Eve, i.e. the earthly Eve, remains with Adam; she herself transforms herself into the "tree of knowledge" of paradise. Her defilement by the archons* affects only the earthly likeness *NHC II 5,116 (164), 34–117 (165), 28 (in the Hypostasis of the Archons it is only her "shadow"*), *NHC II 4,89 (137), 25f. which thus becomes mother of the sons of Adam, who therefore likewise have a dual nature*. According to this Adam him- *NHC II 5,117 (165), 15–24 self begets no children (it is different in the version of the Hypostasis of the Archons*). The second act of the illumination of *NHC II 4,91 (139), 11f. Adam* follows in the garden of paradise with the aid of the ser- *NHC II 5,118 (166), 7–121 (169), 13 pent, who as an incarnation of the bisexual "instructor" (who is a product of the spiritual Eve) plays a thoroughly positive role; See above, p. 95f. the famous "apple tree" which becomes a snare for Eve is for the gnostics a symbol of the good supreme God (in our text an incarnation of the spiritual Eve). In the Hypostasis of the Archons the "spiritual woman" is active also in the form of the ser- pent.* The paradise story ends with the cursing and expulsion *NHC II 4,89 (137), 31–90 (138), 12 of the first human couple,* to which however that of their origi- *NHC II 5,120 (168), 3–12

* NHC II 5,121 (169),
27–35
nators themselves is added.* With this the story of the primeval
age reaches a dramatic end (the final eschatological perspective
of our document will concern us later).

"Thereafter . . . "wisdom life" (*sophia zoē*) sent her daughter
who is called "Eve" as an instructor to awaken Adam in whom
there was [still] no soul, that his descendants might become ves-
sels of the light. [When] Eve saw her likeness lying there she
had compassion on him and said: "Adam! Live! Lift yourself
up from the earth!" Immediately her word became a work.
When Adam had risen up he immediately opened his eyes.
When he saw her he said: "You shall be called the mother of the
* cf. Gen. 3,20 living, because you have given me life".* Thereupon the powers came to know that their creature lived and had raised himself up. They fell into great confusion [and] sent seven archangels to see what had happened. They came to Adam, [and]
when they saw Eve speaking with him they said to one another:
"What is this light? She too is like that form which showed itself
to us in the light. Come now, let us take hold of her and cast our
seed into her, that when she is defiled she may not be able to ascend to her light but those born from her will be subject to us.
Let us not say to Adam that he is not one of us, but let us bring
upon him a sleep of forgetfulness and say to him in his sleep that
* cf. Gen. 2,21 she (Eve) originated from his rib,* that the woman may be subject [to him] and he be lord over her". Then Eve laughed at
their purpose, since she was powerful. She blinded their eyes,
left her likeness secretly with Adam, went [herself] into the tree
of knowledge (*gnosis*) [and] remained there. But they (the
powers) followed her and she showed to them that she had entered into the tree, had become a tree. When they fell into great
terror the blind fled. Thereafter [when] they awoke out of their
sleep of forgetfulness (strictly: from their blindness) they came
to [Adam and] when they saw the form of this (Eve) with him
they were disturbed, because they thought that this was the true
Eve, and they waxed bold, went to her, seized her, cast their
seed upon her and practised roguery with her . . . but they
erred, since they did not know that they had defiled their own
(the powers') body. It is the likeness which the powers and their
angels have defiled in every manner. She became pregnant first
with Abel from the first archon, and from the seven powers and
their angels with the remaining sons whom she bore. But all this
happened according to the providence of the first begetter (*ar-*

chigenetor), that the first mother might bring into existence in herself every seed which is mixed and was to be fitted into the destiny (*heimarmenē*) of the world with its phenomena (the signs of the zodiac) and into (earthly) "righteousness". But a plan came into being because of (the earthly) Eve, that the creatures of the powers might become a hedge of the light; then it (the light) will judge them (the powers) through their creatures ... When the "commanders" (archons) saw that he (Adam) and she who was with him wandered about in ignorance like cattle, they were very glad. When they recognised that the immortal "man" would not neglect them (Adam and Eve) but that they would also fear her who had become a tree, they fell into confusion; they said: "Is this perhaps the true "man" who blinded us and has instructed us about the defiled one, in that she is like him, that they may overcome us?" Thereupon they took counsel, seven in number, went in fear to Adam and Eve [and] said to him (!): "All the trees which are in paradise are created for you, to eat their fruit. But the tree of knowledge (*gnosis*), beware that you do not eat of it. If you should eat [of it] you will die".* After they had put into them a great fear they returned to their powers. Then came he who is wiser than all of them, who is called "the beast" (i.e. the serpent), and when he saw the form of their mother Eve he said to her "What did God say to you: Eat not of the tree of knowledge (*gnosis*)?". She said: He said not only "Do not eat of it", but "Do not touch it, that you may not die". He said to them: "Be not afraid! You shall [not die] the death. For [he knows] that if you eat of it your understanding (*nous*) will become sober and you will be like gods, since you know the difference which exists between evil and good men. He said this to you because he is envious, that you should not eat of it". But Eve trusted in the words of the instructor. She looked at the tree; she saw that it was beautiful and tall; she became enamoured of it; she took of its fruit, ate and gave also to her husband, (who) also ate. Then their understanding (*nous*) was opened: for when they had eaten the light of knowledge (*gnosis*) illuminated them. When they had put on shame, they recognised that they were denuded of knowledge (*gnosis*). When they had become sober they saw that they were naked; they loved one another. When they saw that their fashioners were in the form of animals, they felt revulsion for them and became very understanding. When then

cf. Gen. 2,16f.

See above, p. 96f.

the commanders (archons) recognised that they had transgressed their commandment they came with earthquake and great terror into paradise to Adam and Eve, in order to see the outcome of the help. Then Adam and Eve were greatly troubled; they hid themselves among the trees which are in paradise. Then the commanders (archons) did not know where they were. They said: "Adam, where are you?" He said: "I am here. Out of fear of you I hid myself, because I was ashamed". But they said to him in ignorance: "Who has spoken to you [concerning] the shame which you have put on, if you have not [eaten] of this tree?" He said: "The woman whom thou (!) didst give me, she gave to me [and] I ate". But then [they said]: "What have you done?" She (Eve) answered [and] said: "The instructor enticed me (and) I ate". Thereupon the archons went to the instructor. Their eyes had been blinded by him (and) they were not able to do anything to him; they (only) cursed him because they were without power. Then they went to the woman and cursed her and her children. After the woman they cursed Adam (also), and because of him the earth and the fruits. And they cursed all the things which they had formed; there is no kind of blessing with them. They could not bring forth anything good because of evil. From that day the powers perceived that there really was a stronger over against them . . . They brought great envy into the world just because of the immortal "man". And when the archons saw their Adam, that he had attained to another knowledge (*gnosis*), they wished to tempt him . . .

(This happens through the naming of the animals, which Adam accomplishes to the dismay of the powers; they conclude from it): "See, Adam has become like one of us, so that he knows the distinction of light and darkness. Lest he now be led astray as at the "tree of knowledge" and also go to the "tree of life" and eat of it, become immortal and become lord and despise us and make little of us and all our glory – then will he judge us and the cosmos – come, let us cast him out from the paradise down upon the earth from which he was brought forth, that from now on he may not know anything better than us". And they cast Adam and his wife out of the paradise. And what they had done was not sufficient for them, but they were (again) afraid, went to the "tree of life", surrounded it with great terror, fiery creatures which are called Cherubim, and set a fiery sword in their midst, which turns with fearful terror at all times, that none of the earthly ones might ever attain to that place ... Then when "wisdom life" (*sophia zoē*) saw that the archons of darkness had cursed her (Wisdom's) likenesses she was enraged. And after she had come down with all her powers from the first heaven (counting from above), she drove the archons out of their heavens and cast them down into the sinful cosmos, that they might there become like the wicked [demons] on the earth".*

* NHC II 5,115 (163), 30–121 (169), 35

In this situation the powers do not remain inactive; they lead the world still further into error and contribute to its enslavement: "They created for themselves angels, that is many demons, that they might serve (them). But these taught men many errors: magic, witchcraft (*pharmakeia*), idolatry, the shedding of blood, altars, temples, offerings and drink offerings for all the demons of the earth. They had as their collaborator "fate" (*heimarmenē*), who came into being by agreement through the gods of unrighteousness and "righteousness". And when the cosmos was thus brought into confusion it entered into error: for just as at all times all men on the earth served the demons, from the foundation to the consummation ..., so the cosmos came into confusion in ignorance and forgetting. They all went astray until the coming of the true "man".* This catalogue of disaster for the world and men, which as we shall see is only the outward side of a secret *Heilsgeschichte*, does not derive from any lack of purpose, but corresponds to the providence of the highest God, as our document expressly affirms. "By reason of matter (*hylē*) the archons have become masters over the cosmos, when it had already become full (of things and men), i. e. they held it in ignorance. What is the reason for this? It is this: Because the immortal Father knows that a deficiency arose out of the truth in the aeons and their cosmos, therefore when he wished to deprive the archons of corruption of their power through their creatures, he sent your images (those of the gnostics addressed) into the cosmos of corruption, i. e. the innocent spirits, the little blessed ones; they are not strange to knowledge (*gnosis*)".*

* NHC II 5,123 (171), 7–24

* NHC II 5,124 (172), 1–12

With this, like almost every gnostic treatise, this account also passes on to an assurance of salvation and introduces the doctrine of salvation (soteriology) and the conceptions of the end (eschatology). The anthropogony is fundamentally only a means, despite the muddled situation of the present, of helping the will of the world of light to make its breakthrough. Hence the gnostic sees in Adam his own destiny (fall, knowledge, redemption) anticipated.

We can trace this also on the basis of the Secret Book of John, which we left above after the restoration of the fallen Sophia. In this document too there is reference to the coming into being of three men: the psychic, the pneumatic and the earthly. Their binding together is once again portrayed in a very detailed but considered fashion. First of all we have the "psychic Adam", whom the demiurge Jaldabaoth with his "seven emissaries" (Genesis 1.26 is drawn upon here also) creates after the image, reflected in the water of chaos, of the "holy perfect Father, the first man in the form of a man".* Thus the device of imitation is again made to serve the powers of darkness, but of necessity it must be imperfect and finally needs the help of the powers of light, who thereby are able to ensure the fulfilment of the secret purpose of the plan of salvation. Our text is a particularly impressive example of the opposition of the two basic powers, since every move of the one side is matched by a countermove on the other, until in the course of the development a certain pendulum effect is established. Corresponding to the ancient idea of the part played by the planets in the formation of the psychic body of man, the seven powers contribute from their own elements the following "souls" for Adam:* the "bone-soul", the "sinew-soul", the "flesh-soul", the "marrow-soul", the "blood-soul", the "skin-soul", and the "hair-soul". These "souls of the body" correspond, as is frequently the case in gnostic thought, to macrocosmic powers (providence, divinity, lordship, fire, kingdom, insight, wisdom). Behind this evidently lies the idea of the psychic capacities of man, belonging to the earthly intellectual (immaterial) sphere, in contrast to the supramundane intellectual element which is a gracious gift from the world above. In spite of the skill devoted to the formation of this psychic body it remains immobile and it is not possible to make him stand upright.* This gives "Wisdom" (*sophia*) opportunity to intervene in order to win back the power which through her error she had lost to her son the Demiurge. She prays "the Father of the all" for help; he has recourse to deception (this is evidently quite permissible in dealing with the evil powers): "By a holy decree he sent the "self-originate" (*auto-*

Margin notes:

See above, p. 80

The primal history according to the Apocryphon of John

* Pap. Ber. 48,4–51, 5

* op. cit. 49,9–50, 11

* op. cit. 50,11–18

genēs)[34] and the four lights in the form of the angels of the first archon. They gave him advice, that they might bring out from him the power of the mother. They said to him: "Breathe into his face (something) of the spirit (*pneuma*) which is in you, and the thing will raise itself up". And (so) he breathed into him of his spirit – it is the power from the mother – into the body, and it moved at once ..."* In this way the pneumatic seed finds its way into the psychic Adam, and is thus no longer subject exclusively to the control of the powers of darkness. To achieve this end a stratagem was therefore necessary, an idea widespread in almost all gnostic systems (including that of Mani).

Our text now goes on to a counter-move on the part of the lower powers, in that the psychic Adam is imprisoned in the earthly body: when they observed that Adam was superior to them in wisdom and understanding, and also free from "wickedness", "they took him and brought him down to the regions beneath all matter (*hylē*)".* The response to this by the kingdom of light is: "But the holy Father is a merciful benefactor; he took pity on the power [of the mother] ...; he sent out the good spirit (*pneuma*) and his great mercy as a helper for the first who had come down, who was called "Adam", (namely) the "insight" (*epinoia*) of light, who was called by him (Adam) "life" (*zoē*, i.e. Eve). But it is she who works at the whole creation, labouring at it, setting it in her own perfect temple and enlightening it concerning the origin of its deficiency, and showing it its way upward. And the insight (*epinoia*) of light was hidden in him (Adam), that the archons might not know [her] but our sister, "Wisdom" (*sophia*), who [is like] us, might put right her deficiency through the insight (*epinoia*) of light. And the man shone because of the shadow of the light which is in him. And his thought was exalted above those who had created him. And they (the archons) nodded (in agreement): they saw that the man had exalted himself above them".* In reaction to this they set about the making of a further creature out of the four material elements (earth, water, fire and wind), i.e. out of matter (*hylē*), darkness, desire and the "antagonist spirit" (*antikeimenon pneuma*). "This is the fetter, this the tomb of the creature of the body, which was put upon man as a fetter of matter (*hylē*). This is the first who came down, and his first disruption. But the power of thought (*ennoia;* in a variant: insight, *epinoia*) of the first light is in him; it awakens his thought".*

* op. cit. 51,8–52, 1

* op. cit. 52,1–17

* op. cit. 52,17–54, 8

* op. cit. 55,9–18

Thereupon the chief archon transfers Adam to paradise, which however offers only a deceptive "bliss". For the archons' fruit "is poison against which there is no remedy, and their promise is death for him. But their tree was appointed as "a tree

op. cit. 56,3–11 of life""*. About this alleged tree of life there is however the following comment: "Its root is bitter, its branches are shadows of death, its leaves hatred and deception, its sap (or: oil) is a balm of wickedness, and its fruit the desire of death; its seed drinks of those who taste it, the underworld is their dwelling

op. cit. 56,17–57,7 place".* The "life" which it is to impart is a "counterfeit" or "false spirit" which will turn Adam away from the light, "that

op. cit. 56,14–17 he may not know his perfection".* Over against this the "tree of the knowledge of good and evil" is the insight (*epinoia*) of light, "because of which they gave command not to eat (of it), that is, not to listen to it, since the command is directed against him (Adam), that he may not look upwards to his perfection and

op. cit. 57,8–19 recognise his deprivation of perfection".* In our document however the serpent is left with its biblical evaluation, in that it remains linked with the false "tree of life" and teaches Adam "the procreation of the passion of the defilement and corruption", which is useful only to the archons (we have here therefore an indication of aversion to procreation).

op. cit. 58,16–59,1 The creator now causes Adam to fall asleep,* an image frequently used in Gnosis for the paralysing of man's capacity for knowledge, to which is opposed the awakening through the call of the revealer or through knowledge. By covering his (Adam's) mind with a veil and weighing him down with a stupor, he attempts to gain possession of the unattainable "insight of light", and indeed by the creation of a corresponding female

op. cit. 59,6–19 being, the earthly Eve, from the rib of Adam.* "Immediately he became sober from the intoxication of darkness. She, the "insight of light", took away the veil which was upon his mind. At once when he knew his substance (in the woman who was of like nature to him; a variant has: his fellow-being which was like him), he said: "This is now bone of my bone and flesh of my

op. cit. 59,20–60,7; flesh""* Only now follows the imparting of knowledge to them
cf. Gen. 2,23, through the "tree of knowledge": "Through the authority of
also 2,24 the height and the revelation the "insight" (*epinoia*) taught him knowledge; through the tree in the form of an eagle she instructed him to eat of knowledge (of the tree?) that he might remember his perfection; for the fault of the two was ignor-

ance".* The answer of the Demiurge to this turning away of his *Pap. Ber. 60,16–61,7*
creatures from him is their cursing and expulsion from paradise
into "darkness".* *op. cit. 61,7–62,2*

A further act of vengeance on his part is the violation of the
"maiden who stood beside Adam": * he begets from her two fig- *op. cit. 62,3–12*
ures who bear the two names of God which appear in the Old
Testament, Jahweh and Elohim, and are designated as "Jave,
with the face of a bear, and Eloim, with the face of a cat".
"Eloim is the righteous, Jave is the unrighteous".* The first *op. cit. 62,13 f.*
rules over fire and wind, the latter over water and earth. "These
are they who among the races of all mankind down to the present day are called Cain and Abel." Together they rule over the
primal elements (*archai*) and thus over the "tomb", i.e. over
the body and matter. In this account we have a particularly instructive example of the gnostic "interpretation" of biblical tradition. The "desire of procreation" is implanted in Adam by the
Demiurge (who is thus represented by the serpent!) and
through it he begets his first son Seth, who according to the
view of a widespread gnostic movement was the ancestor of the
"incorruptible race", the redeemed mankind, and therefore of
the gnostics themselves, for which reason they received from
the heresiologists the name "Sethians" (a large part of our new
documents belongs to this movement). With this the gnostic
world history really begins. It consists of the conflict between
the spiritual powers of light and the earthly powers of darkness,
usually illustrated by using the primeval history in the Bible. In
our document Wisdom (*sophia*) first sends her spirit (*pneuma*)
down upon Eve (the name does not occur, but she is the "being" who is like Adam) that she may have descendants corresponding to the spirit, who strive after knowledge and perfection; in the further course of the history also it is the spirit who
awakens men out of the "wickedness of the grave", the earthly
world, and prepares their perfection in the world of light, i.e. it
has an eschatological function. The darkness naturally does not
remain inactive: with the aid of an opposing spirit, the "counterfeit spirit" as it is called, it seeks to lead mankind away from
the true path. Actually this begins already with the desire for
procreation, and works out in "all wickedness and temptations to evil" to which susceptible souls are exposed. If they are
governed by the counterfeit spirit, they must undergo punishment and purification; if the power and spirit of life has entered

See further below, p. 183ff.

into them, they belong to the redeemed race of mankind.

A particularly far-reaching means adopted by the darkness to achieve its ends is the setting up of the well-known sidereal power of fate or Heimarmenē. According to our text it is a creation of the Demiurge in opposition to the successful work among men of the spirit, or of the Epinoia of light which is identical with it.* In order to gain possession of their "power of thought", the chief archon forms a resolve with his powers: "They caused Heimarmenē to come into being, and with a measure, times and seasons they bound the gods of heaven, the angels, demons and men, that they might all be in its (Heimarmenē's) fetter and it be lord over them all: a plan wicked and perverse". Since this device also does not entirely succeed, the chief archon attempts to achieve his purpose by destroying the presumptuous men through the Flood, but through the deliverance of Noah this likewise fails.

* Pap. Ber. 71,5–72,12

See below, p. 134f.

The witness of the Church Fathers

The original sources thus far adduced at length, it may be noted, in part confirm what the Church Fathers also report concerning the gnostic doctrines of the origin of the world and of man, even if the full riches and the deeper content of this literature have only now become known to us. Evidently the basic ideas of the anthropology portrayed belong to the oldest conceptions of the gnostics. Irenaeus ascribes them to early representatives like Saturninus (or Saturnilus) and Menander.* Of the latter Tertullian* reports that he taught: "This (our) worthless and wretched body, which they are not ashamed 'to describe as the evil, was nevertheless a creation of the angels." The doctrine is not strange either to the so-called Naassene Homily, although without the full apparatus of the supramundane proceedings and the "female element". Here, as also in some other systems, the light in the form of the heavenly "man" (*anthropos*) falls directly into the earthly body of Adam. The process is thus accomplished in a very simple and lucid conception, although it is accompanied by a complicated foray through the myths of various peoples which are employed, with the aid of the familiar bold interpretation, for the purpose of finding everywhere the gnostic doctrine of the "inner man" or imprisoned soul. The first man, to whom the several peoples give different names (the Chaldeans "Adam") was born from the earth; "but he lay there without breath, without motion, without stirring, like a statue, an image of that "man" above

* Irenaeus, Adv. haer. I 24,1

* Tertullian, De carne 5

praised in song, Adamas (i. e. "the man of steel"), who originated from many powers ... Now in order that the great Man
from on high might be completely held fast ... the soul (*psychē*)
also was given to him (the image), that enslaved through the
soul the creation of the most beautiful, perfect and great Man
might suffer and be punished."* "From the blessed being on
high, Man or Primal Man or Adamas, the Logos (the rational
"word" as a circumlocution for the seed of light) fell down into
the "moulded figure of clay" to serve the artificer of this creation, Esaldaios the fiery god, the fourth in number (of the primal principles)".* In another passage there is reference to Adamas as the "inner man"* who according to an interpretation of
some biblical passages was laid down "at the foundations of
Zion". These are now further interpreted, drawing on a passage in Homer*, as the "hedge of the teeth", "that is, the wall
and rampart in which is the inner man, fallen down there from
the primal man Adamas, cut out on high without hands to cut
and brought down into the creature of forgetfulness, the earthly, the potsherd."*

* *Hippolytus, Refutatio V 7,6f.*

* *op. cit. V 7,30*

* *2 Cor. 4,16*

* *Homer, Iliad 4,350*

* *Hippolytus, Refutatio V 7,35f. See above, p. 86f.*

A similar idea evidently lies behind the Poimandres, to which
we shall return once again. After the completion of the creation
of the world a second drama begins, once again moving from
above downward, and relating to the birth of the "man":

The anthropogony of the Poimandres

"The Father of all, the "understanding" (*nous*), who is life and
light, brought forth a man (*anthropos*) who was like him. He
loved him as his own child, for he was very beautiful, since he
had his father's image. Actually, even God loved his own form.
He handed over to him all his creatures.* And when he (the
man) observed the creation of the Demiurge in the fire (so
probably instead of "Father"), he wished himself also to create,
and it was granted him by the Father. When he came into the
demiurgic sphere, he who was to have all the authority, he observed the creations of his brother (i. e. the seven planets); but
they fell in love with him, and each gave him something of his
own order. And when he had learned their essence and partak-
en of their nature, he wished to break through the periphery of
the circles and contemplate the power of him who is appointed
over the fire (i. e. the Demiurge). And he who had full authority over the world of mortals and of the irrational beasts stooped
down through the harmony (of the spheres), breaking through
the vault, and showed to the lower nature (*physis*) the beautiful

* *cf. Gen. 1,26-28*

form of God. Seeing him in his immeasurable beauty, having in himself all the power (energy) of the (seven) administrators and the form of God, she smiled at him in love, since she saw the image of the most beautiful form of the Man in the water and his shadow on the earth. But he, seeing this form that was like him in the water, loved it and wished to dwell (in it). At the same time as the will came action, and he inhabited the irrational form. But nature receiving her lover enfolded him completely and they were united, for they were in love."*

Corp. Herm. I 12–15

The dual nature of man is the result of this union, as the text very impressively formulates it in the immediate sequel: "And because of this man, in contrast to all living creatures on earth, is twofold: mortal through the body, but immortal because of the essential Man (*anthropos*). For although he is immortal and has power over all things, he experiences the mortal lot, being subject to fate (*heimarmenē*). Although he is above the harmony, he has become a slave within the harmony. Bisexual from a bisexual father, unsleeping from one who needs no sleep, he is mastered [by love and sleep].

The origin of mankind results from this mixed nature, first seven bisexual men corresponding to the "nature of the harmony of the seven (planets)", which the Anthropos carried in himself. The separation of the sexes comes at the end of the period of creation, according to the will (*boulē*) of God, and then begins the multiplication of living things (here the Old Testament is quoted.*). "He who has understanding (*nous*), let him recognise himself as immortal, and love (*eros*) as the cause of death ..."*This moral drawn from what is set out is constantly repeated, and underlines the existential reference of the whole revelation of the events of primal history. "He who knows himself has attained to the overflowing good; but he who loves the body which originated from the error of love (*eros*) remains in the darkness, wandering about, sensibly suffering what belongs to death".* Thus the destiny of the Urmensch is the guarantee of the redemption of the gnostic, in that he comprehends his essential membership in him, and thereby in God who is indeed light, spirit, life, soul.

Gen. 1, 12.28

Corp. Herm. I 18

op. cit. I 19

How this Hermetic Gnosis, here appearing in hellenistic dress, was understood even later is shown by a fourth-century alchemist named Zosimus (from Panopolis in Egypt), who stands in this tradition. In the extant 24th book ("Omega") of

Zosimus

his "Chemeutika" he presents the following teaching: The first man, also called "inner Adam", "pneumatic man" or "light" (Adam of Light), is persuaded by the archons in paradise to put on, and so quicken to life, the "external (bodily) Adam" created by them, which consists of "the power of fate (*heimarmenē*)" and the four elements. The use of gnostic ideas, and especially those which centre upon the god "Man", has found an echo right down to modern times in alchemy, of which Zosimus is our first identifiable representative.

The entrance into the body, or the darkness, of the "seed of light", the "inner man", or whatever may be the title of the supramundane element, marks the beginning of its suffering, as the Poimandres expressly says. The goal of liberation can be attained only gradually with the aid of divine messengers and redeemers, and lies either in death (of the body) or at the end of the world itself. In the interval the destiny of the "soul" is accomplished, if we may for once use this idea for the divine spark already mentioned. The world is its "prison" , the "house", the "dark place" – all expressions used alternatively and in rich variety by the gnostic texts to describe the situation. The portrayal of this condition of the soul occupies considerable space, since it gives expression to the state of past and present as they appear in the gnostic view of the world. The idea of the "migration of the soul" is also not alien to Gnosis: the "decanting" of the soul from one body into another, especially when it is a question of the punishment of sinful and unawakened souls. That in Gnosis the relation between the destiny of the individual soul and that of mankind as a whole is not always logically defined is something which it shares with all religions. The "soul" of the individual is part of the "universal soul", which is caught up precisely in the image of the "inner" or "spiritual man" and forms the secret backbone of mankind, without which there would be no redemption. In the Mandean hymns of the dead the macrocosmic and microcosmic levels are closely interwoven. The body of Adam is the body of the world, and the soul of Adam is the totality of the souls.

The earthly destiny of the soul

See below, p. 111 ff.

The discovery at Nag Hammadi has bequeathed to us a series of texts which present the theme of the destiny of the soul in an impressive manner. Among these is in particular the "Exegesis on the Soul", from which we would cite a few passages.[35] Drawing on passages from the Bible and Homer, this document por-

The Exegesis on the Soul (NHC II 6)

trays the fall of the originally bisexual soul from its "father's house" into the earthly world, where it loses its virginity and has to endure a mean and wretched existence. After its repentance its lot is altered through the compassion of the Father, in that he sends to her as her bridegroom her "consort", the "firstborn", once lost, with whom she is united in the bridal chamber after purification (baptism) and so attains her rebirth, a process which is interpreted as "resurrection", ascension to heaven, and deliverance from imprisonment. It remains uncertain to what school this document belongs; scholars have thought both of the Valentinian and the Simonian. In its oldest form it evidently belongs to a relatively early stage of gnostic literary work, which had still scarcely come into contact with Christian ideas. A striking feature is its erotic and sexual tenor, which however is often to be found in gnostic texts in the description of life in this world.

"The wise who were before us gave to the soul (*psychē*) a female name. Since she is truly, even in her nature, a woman, she has also a womb. So long as she is alone with the Father she is a virgin, and a bisexual being in her appearance. But when she fell into the body and came into this life, then she fell into the hands of many robbers. And the insolent tossed her to one another and [defiled] her. Some used her [violently], others persuaded her by a deceitful gift. In brief, they dishonoured her. [So] she lost her virginity and played the harlot with her body and gave herself to everyone ... at the end of all this they abandon her and go. But she becomes a poor deserted widow who has no help. She also gains no hearing in her suffering, for she received nothing from them except the defilements which they gave her when they consorted with her ... But when the Father who is above in heaven observes her searching and looks down upon her [and] sees how she sighs because of her passions and defilements, and how she repents of the harlotry which she has committed, and how she begins to call upon his name that he may help her ... and says: "Deliver me, my father. Behold I will give account to you [as to why] I have forsaken my house and have fled from my maiden chamber; once again I turn to you" – when he sees her in this condition, then will he resolve to make her worthy of his compassion ..."*

* NHC II 6,127,19–129,4

This forgetting of her origin on the part of the soul, which is described as "drunkenness", "sleep" or even, as in our example, as sexual aberration, is a standing part of the repertoire of this type of text, which describes the suffering of the soul. It is the dark and evil powers who wish to hold the soul fast in their realm and therefore infatuate it, lull it to sleep, make it drunk. Only the act of knowledge and the help of the redeemer can deliver her from it; this is the great theme of gnostic soteriology, which will occupy us in the next section.

To conclude this chapter we may add a few examples from the Mandean literature, which contains especially poetic descriptions on the theme of the soul, frequently illustrated from the Urmensch Adam as the prototype of human destiny.[36] The evil powers, i. e. the wicked spirit (*rūhā*) and the planets, forge plans and say:

From the Mandean texts

"We shall capture Adam and seize him
and detain him with us in the world.
. . .

We shall take a snare
and shall practise embracing in the world
. . .

We shall install him in our assembly,
we shall seize and lay hold of his heart.
We shall capture him with horns and flutes
(so that) he cannot escape from us".*

Right Ginza III

This purpose is prevented by the beings of light, in that they create for Adam a "companion" and impart to him the secrets of the world. Above all in the hymns from the ritual of the dead such descriptions are constantly to be met with:

"A mana (spiritual being = soul) am I of the great Life.
Who brought me out of the House of Life?
From the House of Life who brought me,
Who sent me into the Tibil (the earthly world) and made me
live (there)?
Who made me live in the Tibil,
and who made me stay in the house of my enemies?
Who made me stay in the house of my enemies,
so that my treasurers (in the sense of guardians) knew nothing of me?

My treasurers knew nothing of me,

* Left Ginza II 18 so that I had to stay in the house of my enemies".*

The "treasure of life", as the soul is also described, has been brought into the world by "simple" beings of light:

"They put it in filth
and clothe it in the colours of the flesh.
They put it in filth
* Right Ginza III and clothe it with a perishable garment"*

In another passage the soul is reluctant to enter into the body (of Adam), "it weeps, laments and sheds tears"; only the persuasive arts of its brothers, the beings of light, move it to do so:

"O soul, arise, go forth,
enter the body and be chained in the palace.
The rebellious lion will be chained by you,
the rebellious unruly lion.
The dragon will be chained by you,
the evil one will be slain where it is.
By you the King of Darkness will be bound,
* Left Ginza III 1 against whose might no one can prevail".*

As weapons it receives the Mandean wisdom (Nasirutha) and "the true words" from the world of light:

"I proceeded and entered the body
and let myself be fettered in the palace.
From the day on which I entered the body,
I was his bride in the ages (or: generations).
His bride was I in the ages,
* Left Ginza III 9 and the evil ones from the depths were angry with me".*

For the soul the body is "a rapacious sea which robs and devours sheep. It is a dragon, a wicked one who has seven heads", i.e. corresponds to the planets. Here the interweaving of microcosm and macrocosm mentioned above is clearly to be seen. In the same way it can be said in a lament by Adam:

"Alas, alas, that my brothers beguiled me, removed me from their midst, and brought, cast and hurled me into a stinking body, to the destructive lions, the rebellious, unruly lions. They led me and hurled me to the dragon, who surrounds the whole world. They brought, cast and hurled me amongst the evil planets, who daily provoke uproar (?). Daily they forge weapons against me. They built idol shrines from clay, false images, and day after day slaughter (or curse) before them and (play) on drums and flutes, to entice me into apostasy in their midst. In the strength of the Great Life I sat down and walked among them, but I was no companion of theirs and took no part in them". *

* Left Ginza I 2

The Doctrine of Redemption and the Redeemer

Gnosis is a religion of redemption. The cosmogonical and anthropogonical teachings so far set out may already convey some impression of it. The word "gnosis" itself, as we have seen, has a predominantly soteriological value and in itself already clearly expresses the understanding of redemption. It is the act of self-recognition which introduces the "deliverance" from the situation encountered and guarantees man salvation. For this reason the famous Delphic slogan "know thyself" is popular also in Gnosis and was employed in numerous ways, especially in the Hermetic gnostic texts. Just as the Platonic school already interpreted this proverb in the sense of knowledge of the divine soul in man, so here it was understood to mean a knowledge of the divine spirit (*nous*) which forms the true nature of man, thus his divine nature. "God the Father, from whom "man" (*anthropos*) came, is light and life. If you therefore learn that he consists of life and light and that you derive from him, you will again attain to life", says Poimandres.* In the Book of Thomas (the Contender) Christ says at the very beginning to his "twin brother" Judas Thomas: "Examine yourself and know who you are and how you were and or how you shall be ... You have already come to knowledge, and you will be called "the one who knows himself", for he who has not known himself has known nothing. But he who has known himself has already come to knowledge concerning the depth of the All." *[37]

Ignorance or darkness, which comes to the same thing, pre-

The role of self-knowledge

See above, p. 108

See pages 108 ff., 186 ff.

* Cor. Herm. I 21

* NHC II 7,138,8–18

The conflict of knowledge and ignorance

vents man from coming to knowledge of himself, as the seventh Hermetic tractate forcefully portrays it: "But first you must tear up the garment you are wearing, the fabric of ignorance, the base of evil, the bond of corruption, the dark wall, the living death, the perceptible corpse, the grave you carry around with you, the robber within you, who hates through what he loves and envies through what he hates. Such is the enemy whom you have put on [as] a robe, who drags you by the throat downwards towards himself, so that you may not look up and see the beauty of the truth and the good that lies therein, and hate his own wickedness and perceive his plot which he has laid against you, he who makes insensitive the organs of sense which are such [but are not held to be such], blocking them with much matter and filling them with filthy desire, so that you neither hear what you ought to hear nor see what you ought to see."* The Gospel of Philip compares the removal of this "wicked ignorance" by knowledge with the laying open of the entrails, which leads to death, or the uncovering of the roots which leads to the withering of the tree: "For so long as the root of wickedness is hidden it is strong, but when it is recognised it is dissolved, but when it becomes visible it perishes ... But Jesus plucked out the root of the whole place (i.e. the world); but others only partially. As for us: let each one of us dig down after the root of evil which is in him [and] pluck [it] out of his heart to the root. But it will be plucked out if we recognise it. But if we do not recognise it, it strikes root in us and brings forth its fruit in our hearts ..."* Gnosis thus has a directly exposing and soteriological function; it *is* redemption.

* Corp. Herm. VII 2.3

* NHC II 3,83 (131),1–11

The conflict between knowledge and ignorance is a universal one, deliberately appointed by the Father to make the victory of "gnosis" manifest. So the Original Teaching sees it: "Now he, the Father, since he wished to reveal his riches and his glory, set this great conflict (*agon*) in the world because he wished that the contenders should become manifest [and] all those contending should through an elevated and unattainable knowledge leave behind them what has come into being and despise it, that they should press on to that which exists (the true Being). And those who strive with us as adversaries warring against us, we are to counter their ignorance through our knowledge, since we already know about the unattainable from whom we have come forth. We possess nothing in this world (the cosmos), that the power of this world which has come into being may not hold us back in the heavenly worlds (cosmos) in which universal death resides . . ."* The latter is an allusion to the dangers of the "journey of the soul" through the supramundane spheres, to which we shall return.

NHC VI 3,26,8–32

See below, p. 173 ff.

The process, introduced by "gnosis", of bringing back the particles of light from darkness into the realm of light can naturally only be realised at death, when "spirit" or "soul" (as descriptions of the divine particle of light) are separated from the body. Then begins the real liberation to which the gnostic aspires. "But when all the chosen ones lay aside the animal existence (i. e. the body) then will the light withdraw to its true being", it is said in the Book of Thomas the Contender*. That this final act has danger in it, since indeed the powers of this world seek to prevent this liberation, is a matter which will concern us later. The "ascent of the soul" here referred to is an inseparable constituent of the gnostic hope of redemption; it is regarded as its eschatological component, which makes real what the gnostic has already attained through knowledge. The present and the future aspects of salvation are therefore often very closely linked in the gnostic texts. The gnostic is already redeemed, although the completion of the redemption is still outstanding. The laying aside of ignorance guarantees his freedom. In the sequel to the passage quoted from the Gospel of Philip it is said: "Truth is like ignorance: when it is hidden it rests in itself. But when it is revealed and recognised it is praised, inasmuch as it is stronger than ignorance and error. It gives freedom* . . . Ignorance is a slave. Knowledge is freedom. When we recognise the truth we shall find the fruits of the truth in us. If we unite with it, it will bring our fulfilment".* Hippolytus hands down the following eschatological hope from the so-called Peratae, who are known only from his work: "If any of those who are here is able to comprehend that he is a character of the Father (another expression for "image") brought down from above and put into a body here, then just like a lamb in the womb which became white through the rod, entirely like the Father in heaven, so will such a one ascend to that place. But he who does not receive this teaching nor recognise the necessity of becoming (i. e. the earthly world) is like an abortion born by night and will (also) perish by night".*

The recovery of the particles of light

NHC II 7,139,28–30

See below, p. 172 ff.

cf. John 8,32

NHC II 3,84 (132),2–13

Hippolytus, Refutatio V 17,6

It is a logical consequence of the status of "knowledge" thus

Knowledge as the way to redemption

presented that the act of cognition for the individual is regarded as a reversal of the misconduct, the error or the deficiency, which once stood at the beginning of the cosmic process. The individual act of cognition thus has a universal significance, a conception best expressed by the Valentinians and also by Manicheism. Of the former Irenaeus already relates that "the perfect redemption is the simple knowledge of the ineffable greatness (of the Father)", and thus needs no other mediation (such as a cultic). "For since through "ignorance" "deficiency" and "passion" came into being, so through "knowledge" the whole situation deriving from "ignorance" is resolved. Hence "knowledge" is the redemption of the "inner man". It (the redemption) is not corporeal, for the body is perishable, nor psychic, for the soul (*psychē*) also derives from the "deficiency" and is only like a residence of the spirit (*pneuma*); the redemption must therefore be spiritual (pneumatic). For through knowledge the inner spiritual "man" (*anthropos*) is redeemed. Thus the knowledge of the All is sufficient for them, and this is the true redemption".* This corresponds with what is said in the Gospel of Truth: "Since the deficiency originated because they (the powers) did not know the Father, then when they know the Father the deficiency from this time on will no longer exist. Just as a man's ignorance is dissolved of itself when he comes to know, as darkness dissolves when the light appears, so also the deficiency dissolves in the perfection. From this time on the (external) "form" is no longer visible, but it will be dissolved in the union with the oneness ... at the time in which unity will perfect the "spaces" (i. e. the aeons). From the unity each one will (again) receive himself. Through knowledge he will unify himself out of diversity into unity, devouring the matter in himself like a fire, darkness through light, death through life".* Here the universal, macrocosmic starting-point of the statement has returned once more to an individual, microcosmic context. The two are united by the same eschatological direction towards the realisation of the redemption grasped "in knowledge", which consists in the removal of deficiency as the cause of the world and a return to the divine unity. The gnostic redemption is a deliverance from the world and the body, not as in Christianity from sin and guilt, mainly in so far as the earthly and corporeal world as such represents the sin into which the divine soul had innocently fallen; through its involvement with

* *Irenaeus, Adv. haer. I 21,4*

* *NHC I 3,24,28–25,19*

the cosmic powers, however, it has become guilty, and it can be freed from this guilt only through insight and at the same time repentance. The ethical problems connected with this will concern us later.

The Church Fathers already drew from the testimonies the conclusion that the gnostics are strictly "redeemed by nature", since they belong in substance with the world of light, i. e. they carry the guarantee of redemption within themselves. Research into Gnosis has long maintained this interpretation. Only through the new texts have certain doubts been voiced against it.[38] For from these texts it is clear that the "pneuma-nature" of the gnostic can on the one hand be understood also as the grace of God, while on the other hand salvation is not automatically assured, but must be accompanied by a corresponding way of life which matches the acquired condition of one "redeemed". Behind the descriptions "spirit", "soul" or "body", which sound mythological and substantial, there often lie concealed only definitions of nature which are oriented either to the story of Adam or to the anthropology, and are intended to characterise man in his position between light and darkness, salvation and damnation. Gnosis is not a "theology of salvation by nature", as the heresiologists caricature it; it is rather thoroughly conscious of the provisional situation of the redeemed up to the realisation of redemption after death. Otherwise the extant literature which relates to existential and ethical behaviour is inexplicable. Naturally the fact remains that the pneumatic element cannot perish and its entry into the Pleroma is preordained, but the why and the how are not independent of the right conduct of its bearer. The pneumatic seed needs a certain education (or "training", as it is sometimes called), beginning with its awakening through coming to consciousness, up to the purification from psychic or bodily defilement (in ascetic movements). The gnostic also must prove himself in the conflict with the passions of his bodily and psychic nature and the deceptive arts (the "snares" and "traps") of the archons. The anonymous treatise says "For each one will reveal his nature (*physis*) through his practice (*praxis*) and his knowledge (*gnosis*)".* In contrast to the slavery in which the unredeemed (i. e. the "fleshly") find themselves, and to those who are brought to salvation by "constraint, force and threat" (evidently the merely "psychic"), "he who is entirely from the superior origin of the

The nature of redemption

* *NHC II 5,127 (175),16f.*

Fatherhood (i. e. the pneumatic) requires no protection, since he himself preserves that which is with him (= what is his own), without any word or constraint, (and) since he unites himself (entirely) with his will which belongs alone to the insight (*ennoia*) of the Fatherhood, that it (the Fatherhood) may (again) become perfect ..." – so the Second Logos of the great Seth.*

• NHC VII 2,61,24–36

The gnostic thus acts in conformity with his nature and destiny; he is enabled to do so by the freedom from the constraint and tyranny of the cosmos which he has recovered. There is for him no redemption given by nature which he has not achieved for himself. At the end of the Poimandres the visionary cries out to the Father of all "Let me never fall away from the knowledge (*gnosis*) which accords with our being, grant it and give me power. With this grace I will enlighten those who are in ignorance, my brothers, thy sons. Therefore I believe and testify: I go to life and to light. Blessed art thou, Father, thy man (*anthropos*) wishes with thee to partake in the work of sanctification, as thou hast granted him all authority".*

* Corp. Herm. I 32

Self-redemption and redemption by another   In the discussion of the way of salvation thus portrayed, the question soon arises as to whether man is actually in a position to find this way of himself through mere self-knowledge. Here we touch upon the vexed question of the gnostic doctrine of the redeemer, which we must consider in greater detail.

Both in the older and in more recent research it has frequently been disputed that Gnosis had any idea of its own of the redeemer. As an argument on the one hand there is reference to the fundamental act of "self-knowledge", on the other the thesis that the redeemer was first introduced into Gnosis through Christianity: Gnosis would then be basically a religion of self-redemption, not of redemption by another. Now the concept **The figure of the redeemer** "redeemer" is actually somewhat vague, since one may understand by it either very much or very little. For Christianity the redeemer Christ is an indispensable presupposition of the hope of redemption, since faith relates to the saving act which he accomplished at God's behest, which is identical with his person. In the area of Christian Gnosis the idea is certainly to be found, but it is only one form and not the normative one. Preponderant in Gnosis are quite other conceptions, which are clearly distinct from the Christian and therefore cannot derive from Christianity. Whether or not one should subsume these likewise under the word "redeemer" remains merely a question of definition. The ancient idea of the "redeemer" corresponds more to the concept of "liberator" or "deliverer", and this actually fits the gnostic "redeemer"-figures also. They are those who for the first time show to men in general the way to liberation from the cosmos. One may call them just as well revealers or emissaries or messengers, who at the command of the supreme God impart the saving message of the redeeming knowledge. Since however this is beyond doubt an act of redemption, they can also with justice be described as "redeemers" (some of them indeed are active as "helpers" in the accomplishment of the ascent of the soul). In a Mandean hymn from the collection of the daily prayers it is said about the work of the emissary of light:

> "You came from the house of life,
> you came: what did you bring us?
> I brought you, that you shall not die,
> that your souls shall not be restrained (in the ascent).
> I brought you life for the day of death
> And joy for the day of gloom.
> I brought you repose,
> in which the disquiet of nations is not to be found." *

* Mandean Liturgies 196 f.

The gnostic concept of the redeemer is not simply dependent on Christianity, but also forms a fundamental element in the structure of the gnostic view of the world. Man can only become aware of his calamitous situation because it has been made known to him by means of revelation. The gnostic view of the world simply demands a revelation which comes from outside the cosmos and displays the possibility of deliverance; for of himself man cannot escape from his prison in which according to this religion he is shut up. He is not only imprisoned but is "asleep" or "drunken". Only a "call" from outside can "awaken" him or make him "sober", i. e. drive out his ignorance. This call is in Gnosis the simplest representation of the redeemer, its minimal form so to speak. It can be expanded into a complete system which as a document of revelation takes over the role of imparting gnosis. In many cases a gnostic doctrine is only the unfolding of the original awakening call to the sleeping soul, a process which we find exemplified on the basis of the Adam story. It is a question of the awakening of the "seed of light" in the

The "call"

thought of men, and this can come about in various forms and is repeated again and again wherever the call to conversion or repentance is heard: "Still are you asleep and dreaming. Wake up, turn about, taste and eat the true food! Impart the word (*logos*) and the water of life! Cease from the evil desires and wishes and the (things) which are unlike (you) ..." * In the letter to the Ephesians a gnostic call has survived in Christian form: "Awake, thou that sleepest, and rise up from the dead, and Christ shall shine upon you". * The Gospel of Truth deals with the significance of the call in connection with the bestowal of names; it understands this as a kind of call: "Therefore he who has knowledge is one who comes from above. When he is called he hears, answers and turns to him who calls him, ascends to him and knows how he is called. Since he has knowledge, he fulfils the will of him who called him ... He who thus shall attain knowledge knows whence he is come and whither he goes. He knows like one who was drunk and has departed from his drunkenness; he brought his own (again) into order after he had returned to himself". * In the apocryphal Acts of John there is this statement by the redeemer to his disciples: "You could by no means understand what you suffer if I had not been sent to you as a word (*logos*) from the Father". *

    It is only through the call that the gnostic also, by reacting to it, becomes a herald of gnostic wisdom, and thus a bearer of the call who continues the work of liberation, as it is clearly expressed in the tractate Poimandres. After receiving instruction from Poimandres, who in this text plays the role of the redeemer and is identical with the "understanding" (*nous*) which bestows knowledge, the recipient goes on "to proclaim to men the beauty of piety and knowledge (*gnosis*): "You people, earthborn men, who have given yourselves up to drunkenness and sleep and to ignorance of God, sober up, stop being drunk, bewitched by unreasoning sleep". * How in this tractate the role of the redeeming "understanding" as the presupposition of knowledge is retained becomes clear from the following remarkable passage, which answers the question whether all men do not have this "understanding" (*nous*) which is necessary for the knowledge of one's self: "Cease such talk! I, the understanding (*nous*), am near the pious, good, pure, pitiful, reverent ones and my presence becomes aid, and at once they perceive the all, they propitiate the Father by love and give thanks,

* NHC VI 4,39,33–40,7

* Eph. 5,14

* NHC I 3,22,2–19

* Acts of John 96

* Corp. Herm. I 27

praising him and singing hymns directed towards him as it is fitting".* In another treatise in the Hermetic collection there is an   *op. cit. I 22
evangelistic address corresponding to an extended call, which
urges men to seek a "guide" who will lead to the gates of knowledge, "where the bright light is, uncontaminated with darkness, where not one is drunk but all are sober, because they
look with their heart at him who wishes to be seen".* We shall   *Corp. Herm. VII 2
see later that in other texts the "word" or "logos" has a redeeming function which is equivalent to that of "understanding" in
the Hermetica.

The gnostic doctrine of the redeemer has many ramifications   **Unity and diversity in the redeemer doctrine**
and cannot be compressed without more ado into a uniform
picture. From the point of view of function it is indeed very uniform, starting with the awakening call and going on to the proclamation ("revelation") of the doctrines and secret traditions,
but the various schools and writings have different views about
the figures and the form of the redeemer or emissary of light.
Here the superimposing of different traditions plays a large
part, especially in the texts which have been subsequently
"christianised", i. e. those in which Christ has only secondarily
been given a place. A whole series of the new Coptic texts belong here. However, attempts were already made earlier to reduce the gnostic doctrine of the redeemer to a uniform conception, a "redeemer myth". For this R. Reitzenstein introduced
the concept "redeemed redeemer".[39] By this he understood the   **The "redeemed redeemer"**
idea, which occurs above all in Manicheism, that a heavenly being (the son of God or of "Man") falls into darkness and is there
held captive, and can return again only after leaving behind
some part of his being; this part forms the soul of light scattered
in the world of the body (through the creation of the world and
man), and for its redemption the part which returned to the
beyond descends once again as a redeemer in order to redeem
("to gather together") the rest of his nature and so restore his
original totality. As an image for this process the "gathering of
the body" or of the "members" through the "head" (= the redeemer) is used. In the precise form given this myth, as already
said, can be seen only in Manichean texts and Reitzenstein
merely read it into many gnostic traditions. However the basic
idea is not alien to Gnosis, on the contrary Manicheism only
drew a consequence from its soteriology, and a whole range of
statements only become comprehensible when we start from

this, that the idea of a redeemer who sets free the "souls", as particles of light identical with his nature, by means of the knowledge of this identity and thereby suffers the same fate as these souls or particles of light, actually does play a part. "But Jesus too was in need of redemption, that he might not be held back by the "insight" (*ennoia*) of deficiency in which he had been placed, brought thereto by "wisdom" (*sophia*), as Theodotus says" (thus the Valentinian excerpts in Clement of Alexandria).* A confirmation may be found in a passage of almost the same tenor in the Tripartite Tractate: "He too (Christ), the son, who was appointed as a place of redemption for the all, was himself in need of redemption, in that he had become man ..."* In the same way it is briefly stated in the Gospel of Philip: "Again he (Jesus) was redeemed, again he redeemed".* The apocryphal and strongly gnostic Acts of John expresses the same idea in a hymn which Christ sings: "I will be saved and I will save. Amen. I will be redeemed and I will redeem. Amen."* In the Odes of Solomon there is an echo of this: "(Be) beloved in the beloved (i. e. Christ) and such as are preserved in him who lives (Christ), and redeemed in him who is redeemed".* After his own deliverance Christ delivered his own from the prison (the world): "They received my blessing and became alive, and they gathered themselves around me and were redeemed; for they have become my members and I their head".* The whole of the so- called "Hymn of the Pearl" and a series of Mandean texts cannot be understood without the idea that the redeemer (*salvator*) and the one to be redeemed (*salvandus*) belong closely together and are sometimes difficult to keep apart, since the point of view may swiftly change, from "saviour" to "saved" (*salvatus*) or "to be saved" (*salvandus*) and vice versa. Behind this stands the conception, fundamental to gnostic soteriology, that both partners, Salvator and Salvandus, are of one nature, i. e. form parts of the world of light. In

Marginal notes:
* Clem. Alex., Ex Theodoto 22,7
* NHC I 5,124,32–125,2
* NHC II 3,71 (119),2f.
* Acts of John 95,1
* Od. Sol. 8,22
* op. cit. 17,14f.

10

View from the Djebel-el-Tarif into the Nile valley at El-Qasr and Es-Sayyad (Chenoboskion). The presumed place of discovery of the Nag Hammadi Codices lies below the cliff edge visible in the foreground.

11

North side of El-Qasr (Chenoboskion) with a view towards the Djebel-el-Tarif and the monastery church of Apa Palamon (left) and the new church of Abu Sayfayn (St Mercurius) (right). On the right in the foreground the finder of the manuscripts, Mohammed Ali es Samman, at that time (1945) 25 years old.

12
Massif of Djebel-el-Tarif, at the foot of which the
Coptic manuscripts were found, from the
north-west.

13
The place of discovery below the Djebel-el-Tarif.
According to his own account the finder discovered
the jar with the codices under the right side of the
broken boulder at the foot of the second cliff in the
background, where the shadow can be seen.

14
The Nag Hammadi Codices, from a
photo taken by Jean Doresse in Cairo
in 1949. Left: pages from Codices I and
XII. Middle (from above): Codices II,
VII, VIII, III, XI (lying in front). Right
(from above): Codices V, IX, VI, IV, X;
in front, pages from Codex XIII.

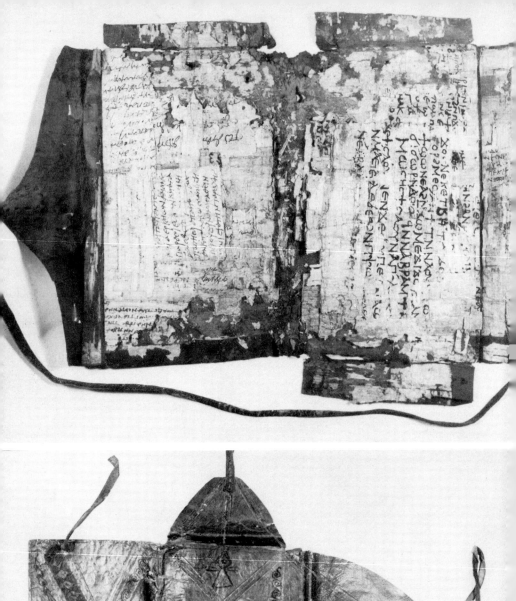

15

Inside of the open cover of Codex VII. The papyrus fragments used for backing contain the remains of receipts, accounts and letters, with important information about the date and place of manufacture of the manuscripts (see p.42).

(see p.42)

16

Outside of the leather cover of Codex II. This is artistically the most valuable cover in the collection, its decoration consisting of incised lines and ornament tinted with ink (rhombs, snails, heartshaped leaves, ankh signs).

17

The open Codex IV, showing pages 49, 37, 41. The Secret Book of John.

ⲙⲡⲓϩⲱⲃ̣ . . . . ⲛ̣

ⲛⲥⲉϯ . ⲟⲩⲧⲉⲉⲧⲥⲛ̄ⲛ̣

ⲣ̣ . . . . ⲁⲩ . . ⲁⲩⲏⲣⲉⲙⲡⲛⲟⲩ

ⲧⲉ . . ⲉϥϣⲟⲟⲡ̣ⲙⲉⲛⲛ̄ⲛⲟⳓⲡ̄ⲛⲟ̄ⳓ

. . . . . . ⲟⲓⲡⲏ̄ⲥⲧ̄ⲡⲁⲧⲡⲉⲧⲥ̄ⲏⲛⲉⲧ

ⲉⲥⲩ̣ⲛⲉⲧ̄ⲡ̄ⲛⲟⳓ̄ⲁ̄ⲗ̄ⲗⲁⲟⲩⲉⲉⲧⲣⲉ

ⲩ̣ⲟⲙⲉϥϣⲱⲡⲉⲉⲙⲁ̄ⲗ̄ⲗⲉϥϣⲛⲉ

ⲓ̄ⲛⲥⲟⲩⲟⲑⲉⲟⲩⲛⲧⲉϥⳓⲁ̄ⲍ̄ⲛ̄ⲛⲉ

ⲉ̄ⲅⲉⲛ̄ⲩ̄ϯ̄ⲉⲛ̄ⲛⲉⲧ̄ϭ̄ⲣ̄ⲱⲥ · ⲛ̄ⲧⲟⲕ

. ⲟⲩⲟⲕⲉⲕϣⲁⲧⲟ̄ⲃ̄ⲙ̄ⲡ̄ⲛ̄ⲟⲩⲧⲉ

ⲛⲁ̄ϯ̄ⲛⲉⲕⲉⲛ̄ⲥ̄ⲙ̄ⲡⲉⲕⲥⲏ̄ⲧ̄ⲡⲧ̄

ⲣ̄ϥⲉⲕ̄ϣⲁⲛ̄ϯ̄ⲙ̄ⲡⲉⲕⲟ · ⲉⲓⲕⲛ̄

ⲛⲉⲧⲥⲕⲁⲉⲓⲧ̄ · ⲡⲧ̄ⲙⲉⲛⲟⲩⲕⲟⲩ

ⲡⲉⲧⲉⲡ̄ⲡⲣⲟⲑⲩⲙⲓⲁⲁⲉⲟⲩⲛⲟⳓ

ⲧⲉϣⲱⲧⲏⲡ̄ⲛⲟⲩⲧⲉ · ⲡⲧ̄ⲉⲧⲙⲉ

ⲉⲩⲍⲉⲙⲛ̄ⲁⲁⲩⲱϣⲟⲟⲡ̄ⲓ̄ⲛ̄ⲁⳓⲣ̄ⲛ̄

ⲡⲛⲟⲩⲧⲉ · ⲡⲉⲉⲓϭⲁⳓⲣⲉⲛⲉⲧⲛⲟⲩ

ⲧⲉ · ⲡⲉⲧⲧⲟⲛ̄ⲛⲛ̄ⲡⲉⲥⲏⲧⲉ

ⲡⲛⲟⲩⲧⲉⲕⲁⲧⲁⲧⲉϥϭⲟⲙ · ⲡⲉⲓ

ⲉⲉⲧⲣ̄ⲧⲓⲙⲁ̄ · ⲙ̄ⲡ̄ⲛⲟⲩⲧⲉⲁⲗ̄ⲗⲱ

ⲛⲟⲩⲧⲉⲙⲉⲛⲅ̄ⲭ̄ⲣⲭⲣⲓⲁⲉⲛⲛⲛⲁ

ⲉϣⲣⲙⲉ̣ⲇⲉⲉϫ̄ⲛ̄ⲛⲉⲧϯⲛ̄ⲛⲉⲧ

ⲣ̣ⲟ̣ⲱϣ̣ⲙ̄ⲡⲓⲥⲧⲟⲥⲙⲉⲩϫⲉⲥⲁ̄

ϣⲁϫ̣ⲉ̣ . ⲉⲩϯⲏⲉⲇⲉⲛⲁ̣ⲩⲱ

. . ⲛⲉ̣ϥ . ⲟⲥⲙ̄ⲙⲁⲉⲓϫⲓ̄ⲥ̄ⲃ̄ⲱ

ⲉⲓ̈ⲡⲉⲡⲉⲣⲅ̣ⲁ̣ⲧ̣ⲏⲥ̄ⲛ̄ⲧⲁⲗⲏⲑ̣ⲓ̄

18
Codex XII p. 33. The Sentences of Sextus.

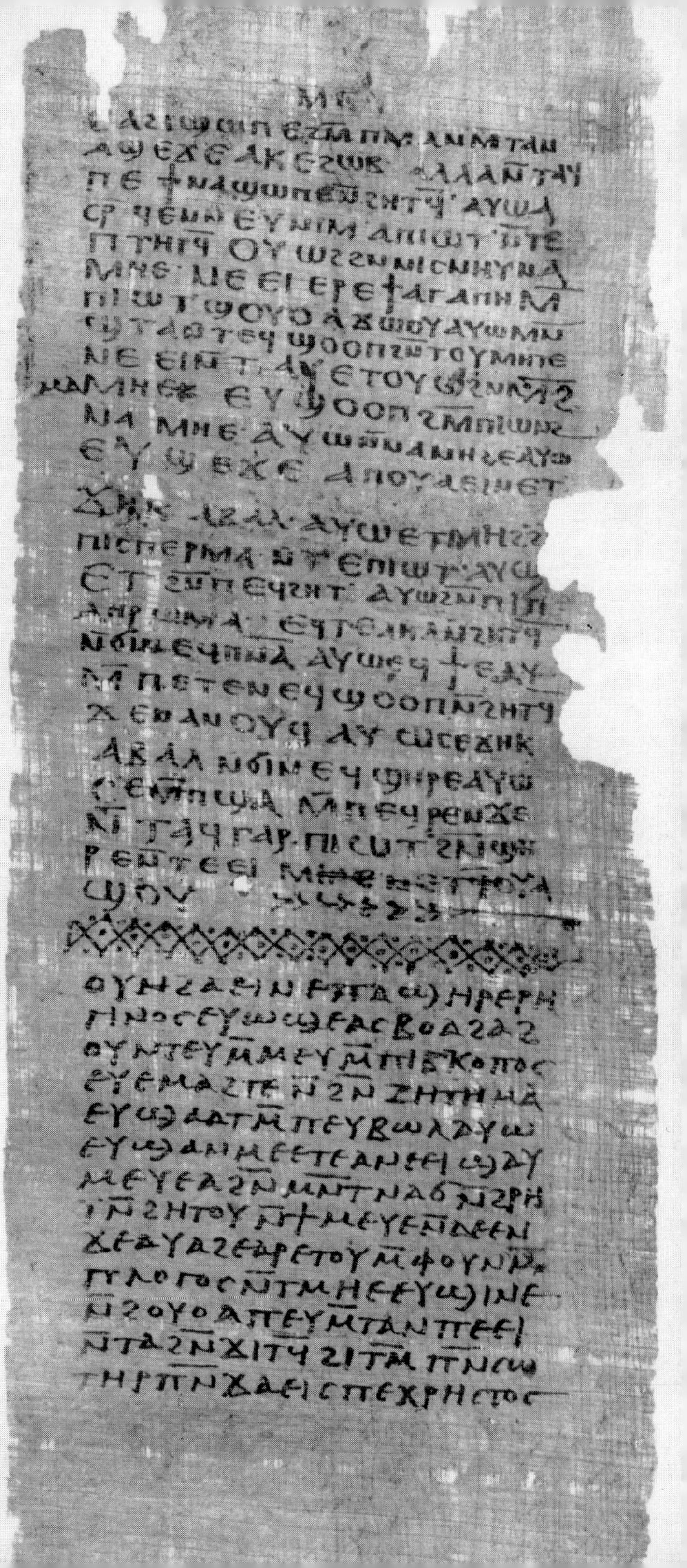

19
Codex I p. 43. End of the Gospel of Truth and beginning of the treatise On the Resurrection. It can be clearly seen here that two scribes with different handwriting worked on this manuscript.

20
The Coptic gnostic Papyrus Berolinensis 8502, p. 77. End of the Apocryphon of John and beginning of the Sophia Jesu Christi.

the process of redemption they represent two poles which must indeed be kept apart, but through their consubstantiality they have from the beginning removed or "unyoked" the distinction between the two which otherwise is usual in the history of religion. Hence the Christ who appears as a Seth Redivivus in the Second Logos of the Great Seth can say: "When I had come to my own and united myself with them and me, there was no need for many words, for our insight (*ennoia*) was with their insight (*ennoia*), for which reason they understood all that I said".* * *NHC VII 2,59,9–15*

The idea of the "redeemed redeemer" is therefore indeed a logical and characteristic formulation of the gnostic redeemer conception, which unites redeemer and redeemed very closely together, but it is only one variation of this. There is no uniform gnostic "redeemer myth", such as theologians in particular **Further ideas** have imagined. The Nag Hammadi texts have shown us what **of redemption** breadth of variation we must assume in the redeemer conceptions of Gnosis. They have also finally taught us that we must depart from the theory of a Christian origin of gnostic soteriology (which is admittedly very difficult for some scholars, especially theologians). If we consider the figures under which we meet with the gnostic redeemer in the texts, we find both persons and also concepts, both in the first instance drawn from the biblical tradition. Among the first are the (heavenly) Adam (a name often identified with the Greek word "adamas", i. e. the "man of steel"), the (heavenly) Eve, the sons of Adam Abel (Mandean Hibil), Seth (Mandean Sitil) and Enosh (Anosh), the high priest Melchizedek*, the angel Baruch, the "great an- * *NHC IX 1* gel Elelēth", and some anonymous biblical figures like the three men who came to visit Abraham*, who according to the * *Gen. 18,1 ff.* Apocalypse of Adam appeared to Adam.* * *NHC V 5*

Among the abstract entities which have a soteriological function there are in the first place wisdom (*sophia*), then the spirit (of truth or life or holiness), the understanding (*nous*), the insight (*epinoia*) or power of thought (*ennoia*), both as expressions of the illuminating knowledge; further the word (*logos*), the illuminator or light-bearer (*phōstēr*), the angel of gnosis and others. The Paraphrase of Shem* traces the content of its * *NHC VII 1* revelation back to a heavenly being named Derdekeas, probably (from Aramaic) "child, boy". Among the Mandeans the re- *See above, p. 85* deeming knowledge has become an independent person called "knowledge of life" (*manda dehaijī*). In the Hermetic texts the "thrice great Hermes" or "shepherd of men" (*Poimandres*) is the redeemer or revealer. Christian Gnosis naturally sets Christ in this position, which could not be done without some tension with ecclesiastical Christology and the gnostic systems themselves. Other historical figures of this kind who play a redeeming role in Gnosis are Simon Magus and Zoroaster (Zostrianos). The gnostic religious founder Mani accepted a great number of Old Testament personalities into the chain of the revealers or "apostles of light", but also Zoroaster, Buddha and Jesus. What is offered by Gnosis in this area is therefore very rich, and it shows that it quite shamelessly exploited the most varied traditions and ideas for its own purposes. Purely mythical beings stand along-side more or less historical figures. It is to be assumed that the former belong to the oldest constituent and that a "historicising" of the redeemer figure set in only later, particularly in connection with the introduction of the figure of Christ into Gnosis.

This view also imposes itself when we consider the temporal appearance of the redeemer or revealer in the framework of gnostic world history. Two points or periods of the time can be adduced for this, which are usually closely coupled together: first the appearance in the primeval times at the beginning of history, and secondly a continuous revelation in history. The

The primal revelation

first, which may be called "primal revelation", is familiar to us already from the portrayal of the events relating to the origin of Adam. As we have seen on the basis of the extracts, it is played out in very varied fashion and the Old Testament narratives are exploited for it: the serpent, the "tree of knowledge", the "spiritual Eve". How complicated the presentation of this process

See above, p. 103 ff.

can be is shown very impressively by the Secret Book of John. The "insight (*epinoia*) of light" comes down in order to en-

* *Pap. Ber. 53,15*
** *op. cit. 59,20f.*

lighten Adam* and drive away his "drunkenness";** in this

* *op. cit. 53,6*
** *op. cit. 53f.*

work of assistance* she is active both in Adam or in man** and also, after his incorporation and transference into paradise, in

* *op. cit. 57,8ff.; 60f.*

the "tree of knowledge";* finally she is active to help also in the

* *op. cit. 72f.*

deliverance of Noah.* As her name already shows, she is the personified spiritual "insight" or gnosis, which in various ways frees man's "power of thought" and delivers him from the ar-

* *NHC II 5*

chons. In the anonymous treatise* it is the heavenly (spiritual) Eve who functions at the behest of Sophia, her mother, as the instructor and awakener of Adam, but also in the form of the serpent continues or repeats the process of redemption in paradise. The same conception appears also in the Hypostasis of the Archons.* Behind the dual role played here by the female redemptive power there stands evidently the connection of the "inner" self-knowledge with the "external" imparting of knowledge by the "call", which is apposite for Gnosis as a whole. Among the Mandeans and Manichees also the primal revelation is the decisive act of redemption; it is normative for the time which follows, and offers to the gnostic the guarantee of his own redemption, for in its events he sees himself involved in respect of his own destiny.

See above, p. 96ff.
* *NHC II 4,89 (137), 31–90 (138), 19*

The continuing revelation

This first redeeming revelation however requires repetition, since only in this way can the seed of light, imprisoned by the aggressive powers of darkness, be helped to its final deliverance. For this reason the gnostic systems have given expression in various forms to the idea of a continuing activity of revelation, variously linked up with a simple periodisation or speculation about the ages of the world. Here it may be a question of ideas which were developed in association with the biblical *Heilsgeschichte* (in the main of the pre-Mosaic period), or of the presence, in some way not precisely defined, of beings of light who assist the gnostic in some form, especially in the ascent of the soul (as for example among the Mandeans). The first conception is widely diffused, but again it can be represented in various ways. Either it is always the same redeemer figure (e.g. Baruch, Seth, the Phōstēr, Nous, Logos or others), or there is a series of changing figures (e.g. the sons of Adam among the Mandeans) who from time to time descend from above to illuminate the ages. It is however also possible that the coming of the redeeming power took place once and for all in the primal era, and that it remains thereafter in the world as a helper, like the "insight" (*epinoia*) of light" or the "spirit of truth" (in the Hypostasis of the Archons*).

See above, p. 103f.
* *NHC II 4*

The whole world of ideas in this central area of gnostic theology is often difficult to penetrate, to say nothing of systematising it. In some of the new Coptic texts there is reference to a three-fold "coming" of the redeemer, by whom either Seth himself or one of his intermediate angels is understood; in this capacity they bear the title of "illuminators" or "bearers of light" (*phōstēres*). What is meant by the three-fold appearance can only be recognised with difficulty, since there is no uniform interpretation to be found. Presumably it was originally a matter of the redeeming activity of Seth, who is also described as "the great saviour" (*Sotēr*), in the three ages or "aeons" after Adam on behalf of his race, the Sethian gnostics. Here the Flood and the burning of Sodom and later, after the Christianisation of the sect, the condemnation of Jesus by the rulers of the world marked the special stages. Similar ideas are found in the old Mandean sources where the heavenly sons of Adam, Abel, Seth and Enosh, are responsible for individual ages and have to hold their ground victoriously on behalf of their "race" in the face of specific catastrophes (sword, fire, water). In several texts the world of light makes use of various figures in order to help the "perfect race" of the gnostics: by "guardians" or "watchers", by prophets or angels. There is thus a confusing variety of redeeming powers which the gnostic summons to his assistance in order to escape from the destiny of the wicked world.

We shall once again illustrate what has been said by means of a few chosen passages from the sources. As already mentioned, **The Flood** the biblical story of the Flood attracts considerable attention, in **among the** that it is evaluated as an example of the deliverance of an up-**Gnostics** right gnostic from the attempts of the evil rulers of the world to destroy him. Here there are various references to a female being named Norea, who ranks as the wife either of Seth or of Noah. She is a recipient of revelation and there was accordingly a series of documents current under her name, of which a frag-*NHC IX 2* ment has turned up in Nag Hammadi*. In the Hypostasis of the Archons, already often adduced, the following version is presented, which has been put together secondarily out of two tra-*NHC II 4,92 (140),* ditions*:[40]
3–97 (145), 21

First of all the archons bring the flood upon mankind. Noah is warned by the "ruler (*archon*) of the powers" (i. e. Sabaoth, the penitent son of the Demiurge, transferred into the seventh *NHC II 4,95 (143), 13–25* heaven)* and accordingly builds the ark. Then comes Norea, a *NHC II 4,91 (139),* daughter of Adam and Eve, "helper for all the races of man",*
33–92 (140), 3 and demands admission into the ark, which she is refused, whereupon she burns up the ark with her breath and Noah is compelled to build it all over again. Now the archons come to *NHC II 4,89 (137), 18–31* seduce Norea, as they had done with her mother.* In her dis-*See above, p. 98 ff.* tress she turns to the power of God:

"She cried out with a loud voice [and said to] the holy one,

the God of the All: "Help me against the archons of unrighteousness and deliver me out of their hands!". At once the angel
came down from heaven and said to her: "Why are you crying
up to God? Why do you importune the holy spirit?" Norea
said: "Who are you?" − the archons of unrighteousness had departed from her − He said: I am Elelēth (i. e. "goddess"), the
wisdom, the great angel, who stands before the holy spirit. I
have been sent to speak with you and to rescue you out of the
hands of these lawless ones. And I shall teach you about your
root (origin)"."

   The text now* begins a narrative in the first person in which
Norea herself portrays the supernatural appearance of the angel ("his form was like pure gold and his garment like snow"),
and then passes on to a fresh introduction of Elelēth and three
revelation speeches which answer Norea's questions about the
origin and nature of the evil powers (archons), her own origin,
and the coming of the "true man" (evidently Seth-Christ) at the
end of time. The cosmogonic information we know from the
parallel version in the anonymous treatise*. It is as we have earlier explained an essential constituent of the message of redemption, and answers the questions of the gnostic in search of
knowledge. Norea's question as to whether she also belongs to
matter (hylē) is answered as follows: "You with your children
belong to the Father who is from the beginning. Their souls
came from above, out of the incorruptible light. Therefore the
powers will not be able to approach them, because of the spirit
of truth which dwells in them. But all who have known this way
are immortal in the midst of mortal men".*

   A kind of gnostic world history, which is at the same time a
Heilsgeschichte, is contained in the Revelation of Adam to his
son Seth.[41] This document works together very skilfully several
traditions and is certainly a witness of early Gnosis, since it still
stands very near to the Jewish apocalyptic literature and has no
Christian tenor. Our concern here is the basic idea of the cyclic
revelation, which is maintained throughout. The binding together of different levels by literary frame-stories is quite typical for a gnostic revelation document, since in this way it can
demonstrate its soteriological character. First of all Adam in
the seven hundredth year (!) imparts to his son Seth what he experienced before and after his fall*, and then what he has
learned about the destiny of Seth's descendants, i. e. the men of

Margin notes:

* NHC II 4,93 (141), 14

* NHC II 5
  See above, p. 72 ff.

* NHC II 4,96 (144), 19–27

**World history
according to
the Apocalypse
of Adam**

* NHC V 5,64,5–67,14

NHC V 5,67,14–85,18 gnosis, by a communication from the three supernatural men.* In the first part it is reported that Adam and Eve were originally "eternal angels", who stood above the creator God. Adam received from Eve the knowledge of the eternal God, just as we know it from other documents which portray the "spiritual Eve" as an imparter of revelation. The paradisal condition and the "eternal knowledge of the God of truth" were lost through the wrathful activity of the Demiurge and they became "two aeons", i.e. they fell into the power of the "ruler (*archon*) of the aeons and powers (of this world)" and had to serve him; as "men" they were instructed only about "dead things". The "first knowledge which breathed in us" went on the other hand into the "great race" of Seth. To free Adam and Eve from their slavery and spiritual darkness the three men now appear and say: "Adam, stand up from the sleep of death and hear about the aeon and the seed of that man (Seth) to whom life has attained, who has come forth from you and your consort Eve". The Demiurge however prevents this deliverance by once again spreading darkness over them and implanting in Adam a desire for Eve: "Then the keenness of our eternal knowledge left us, and weakness followed us". Since Adam feels his end draw near, he wishes now to hand on to Seth the revelation imparted to him (which he thus can still remember very well!).

First of all the deliverance of the men of gnosis during the *NHC V 5,67,22–73,24* Flood is reported.* While Noah is saved with his family by the creator god, thus as in the Old Testament with the aid of the ark, it is "great angels" of the world of light who preserve the men of gnosis (the Sethians) from the Flood and bring them to a secure place, "where the spirit of life is". By their preservation Noah and his descendants are obliged to serve the Demiurge. When however those men of gnosis unite themselves to them, the Demiurge angrily calls Noah to account, but he naturally denies that they derive from him. The "God of Truth" then brings his representatives once again into safety in a "holy dwelling place", where they are to live for six hundred years without sin and only in the knowledge of God. During this period the earth is divided between the sons of Noah, Ham, Shem and Japhet, and called upon to obey the creator god. But 400,000 descendants of Ham and Japhet associate themselves with "those men who originated from the great eternal knowledge; for the shadow of their power will preserve those who take up their dwelling with them from all evil works and all filthy passions. Then will the seed of Ham and Japhet form twelve kingdoms . . ." A second attempt by the Demiurge Saklas, i.e. "fool", to put a stop to this development by a fresh catastrophe, this time with the aid of fire, brimstone and asphalt (evidently an echo of the biblical story of Sodom and Gomorrah*) is unsuccessful. The "great men" are delivered by the   * *Gen. 19,1–29* clouds of light Abrasax, Sablō and Gamaliēl, who come down to them and transport them "above the angels and the authorities of the powers" into an "incorruptible aeon". "The men will be like those (holy) angels, for they are not alien to them but work upon the incorruptible seed". A further, third redemption is then added:* it is the coming of the "illuminator (*phōs-*   * *NHC V 5,76,9–77,27* *tēr*) of knowledge". He delivers from death those of the seed of Noah, Ham and Japhet who "think of the knowledge of the eternal God in their hearts". At the same time he confuses the creator god through his signs and wonders, and the creator's attempts to destroy him are unsuccessful because they affect only his "flesh" and he sees in him only a phantom.

Now begins a kind of excursus, which deals with thirteen kingdoms and a "kingless race", each of whom has a different statement to make about the origin of the "illuminator".* This   * *NHC V 5,77,27–83,4* passage is one of the most remarkable and not easy to interpret. Evidently, at least in the present context, Seth the redeemer is meant by the "illuminator", and his appearance is expressed by the use of various mythological traditions from contemporary ideas of the saviour or redeemer (especially the Iranian). The only correct view however is that of the kingless race, by whom are meant the gnostics (here the Sethians; we know this self-designation from other texts also). It runs: "God has chosen him (the illuminator) from all aeons. He caused him to come into being through a knowledge (*gnosis*) of the undefiled (God) of truth. It said: "[The great] illuminator proceeded from a strange ether, [from a] great aeon. [He caused the race] of those men whom he had chosen to shine so that they might illumine the whole aeon"".* In contrast to this we may give the   * *NHC V 5,82,19–83,4* statement by the second kingdom, which seems to derive from an old fairytale motif: "He originated from a great prophet. And a bird came, took the child which had been born, [and] carried him [off] to a high mountain; and he was nurtured by the bird of heaven. An angel appeared there [and] said to him:

"Stand up! God has honoured you". He received honour and
NHC V 5,78,6–17 power, and so he came upon the water",* i.e. appeared in this
world (perhaps with some kind of allusion to baptism). The
fifth kingdom says of him: "He arose out of a drop from heaven
which was cast into the sea. The abyss received him, gave birth
to him, [and] raised him up to heaven. He received honour and
NHC V 5,79,19–27 power, and so he [came] upon [the water]".* The description
by the tenth kingdom is more drastic: "His god loved a cloud of
desire; he begat him (through Onanism) in his hand and cast of
the drop upon the clouds beside him and he was born. He received honour and power in that place, and so he came upon
NHC V 5,81,14–23 the water".* The idea of the twelfth kingdom is quite simple:
"He originated from two illuminators (*phōstēres*), was nurtured, received glory and power, and so he came upon the wa-
NHC V 5,82,4–10 ter".* The thought which lies concealed behind these fourteen
statements about the gnostic redeemer is naturally that of the
continuing revelation, for the kingdoms are evidently to be
considered also as a horizontal succession which culminates in
the last place in which the "illuminator", who under various
forms is still always the same, makes his appearance. Thereafter the last time already begins, opening with the repentance of
the peoples at their lack of understanding towards the men of
gnosis and a condemnation of the angels responsible for it. Only those can attain to deliverance who have taken to heart the
"words of the God of the aeons" and who "know the eternal
God in a wisdom of knowledge (*gnosis*) and a doctrine of angels
NHC V 5,85,1–18 in eternity".* So ends "the secret knowledge of Adam which he
imparted to Seth". The "eternal knowledge (*gnosis*)" is imparted to the gnostics, as it is said in an addition at the end, through
the "logos-born and incorruptible illuminators, who proceeded
from the holy seed (the men of Seth)".

The redeemer   The manner in which the redeemer Seth cares for his race up-
Seth in the   on earth, to protect it, is narrated by the Gospel of the Egyp-
Gospel of the tians[42], deriving from the same gnostic school: "Then the great
Egyptians   Seth saw the activity of the devil (*diabolos*), his manifoldness
and his plans, which were to come upon his incorruptible unwavering race, the persecutions through his (the devil's) powers and angels and their misguidance (*planē*); (he saw) how
they waxed bold against themselves ... and he requested
watchers for his seed. Then there came from the aeons four
hundred ethereal angels and with them the great ether Osiēl

and the great Selmechēl, to watch over the great incorruptible race, his fruit, and [thus over] the great men of the great Seth, from this point and moment of truth and righteousness to the consummation of the aeon and its rulers (archons), whom the great judges have [already] condemned to death".* The same text also presents the remarkable view that one of the sacred dwelling places of the men of Seth was Sodom and Gomorrah, i. e. the cities condemned by the biblical tradition have for the gnostics a positive ring, because they belong to the *Heilsgeschichte*. Irenaeus mentions that one gnostic movement considered itself as kinsmen of Cain, Esau and the Sodomites.* We shall meet with such transmutations of Jewish history in various forms; it is a result of the rejection of the biblical creator as a lower and hostile being. "Then came the great Seth and brought his seed, and it was sown in the ages (aeons) which have come to be [in the transitory world], whose number is the measure of Sodom. Some say that Sodom is the pasture [for the seed] of the great Seth, which is Gomorrah. Others on the other hand [say] that the great Seth took his planting from Gomorrah and planted it in the second place, to which he gave the name Sodom".*

* NHC III 2,61,16–62,24

* Irenaeus, Adv. haer. I 31,1

* NHC III 2,60,9–18

The appendix in the longer version of the Secret Book of John[43] speaks of a threefold descent of the redeemer figure, here designated by "providence" (*pronoia*) and according to the final redaction of the document identified with Christ.* The passage shows at the same time the manner in which Gnosis conceived of this descent: as a journey into darkness, chaos, the underworld, by which this world is described. In the process the redeemer remains at first unrecognised by the powers. This "magic hood" motif is one of the typical marks of the gnostic redeemer myths and we shall often meet with it. The disturbance which the coming of the redeemer sets into motion lays hold of the entire cosmos, for it is the intrusion of another world into the area encompassed by Fate. In other texts this is portrayed as a breach through the "walls" and "bars" which surround the world. A battle with the rulers of darkness can also form part of this (as for example in the Mandean literature), and the conquest and imprisonment of these powers expresses the confidence of the gnostic community in the victory of the light. At the beginning of our text the close connection of redeemer and redeemed (the "seed") is maintained: the entrance of the seed

The redeemer in the Apocryphon of John

* NHC II 1,30,11–31,27

of light into this world is at the same time the first descent of the redeeming power. At the end the description accordingly passes into the timeless awakening call to men in need of redemption, and to their deliverance:

"But I am the perfect providence (*pronoia*) of the all. I transformed myself into my seed (i. e. descendants), for I was first there, walking upon all ways. For I am the riches of the light. I am the recollection of the (heavenly) fullness (*pleroma*), but I went into the great darkness and endured until I came into the midst of the prison. And the foundations of chaos shook and I hid myself before them (the powers) because of their wickedness, and they knew me not. Again I turned myself for a second time [into the darkness] and went and came forth from those who belong to the light, I who am the recollection of the providence (*pronoia*). I went into the midst of the darkness and the inner part of the underworld, following out my saving plan. And the foundations of chaos shook, that they might fall upon those who are in chaos and destroy them. And I hastened up again to my root of light, that they might not be destroyed before the time. Further I went for the third time, I who am the light which is in the light, [and] the recollection of the providence (*pronoia*), to enter into the midst of the darkness and the inner part of the underworld. I filled my countenance with the light of the perfection of their (the powers') age (aeon) and went into the midst of their prison, that is the prison of the body, and said: "He who hears, let him rise up from the deep sleep!". Then he wept (the man to be redeemed) and shed great tears. He wiped them away and said: "Who is it who calls my name, and whence has this hope come to me while I am in the fetters of the prison?" And I said: "I am the providence (*pronoia*) of the pure light, I am the thought of the virgin spirit who raises you up to the exalted place. Stand up and remember that you are the one who has heard (this) and follow your root – which is I, the merciful – and secure yourself against the angels of poverty and the demons of chaos and all who attach to you, and be watchful against the deep sleep and against involvement in the inner part of the underworld". And I set him upright and sealed him in water of light with five seals, that death henceforth might no more have any power over him".

Another presentation of the soteriology related to this passage, as with the Sethian movement in general, is offered by the as yet little known Nag Hammadi document the Trimorphic **The doctrine of** Protennoia, which evidently derives from a codex already lost **the redeemer** in antiquity (usually described as Codex XIII).[44] In three sec- **in the** tions, frequently in hymnic form, – the "doctrine of the Epi- **Trimorphic** phany" – the cosmological and soteriological role of the person- **Protennoia** ified "first thought" of the primal Father is developed in the *See above, p. 48* form of a trinitarian doctrine. "The call (of redemption) rings out in three dwelling places"* in a threefold revelation in the * *NHC XIII 1,37,21–23* form of father, mother (or wife) and son. While the mother rep- resents the "first thought"herself and among other names is al- so called Barbēlo,* the son is the "word" (*logos*); he has origi- * *NHC XIII 1,38,9* nated out of her "call" and continues her work as a final revela- tion (the last editor of the document links him with the figure of Christ). Behind the Protennoia there also stand features of a universal deity, such as the gnostics frequently employ for their dialectic thinking; we recall the figure of Wisdom. A detailed *See above, p. 71ff.* reproduction of this very remarkable text, which however is often damaged and therefore not always easy to understand, cannot be given here, but some passages give excellent testimo- nies for our theme, especially for the fundamental idea of the "call". First of all the first descent, the "primal revelation" of Protennoia as a father figure:

"I [came down into the] midst of the underworld. I shone out [over the] darkness. I am he who caused the [water] (of knowl- edge?) to pour forth. I am he who is hidden in the [shining] wa- ters. I am he who has come forth to the all. . . I am he who is full of the call. Through me does knowledge (*gnosis*) come forth, I who am in the inexpressible and unknowable (aeons). I am per- ception and knowledge, I who cause a call to go forth by means of a thought. I am the actual call which causes a call to resound in each one, and thus they recognise [me] through it (know- ledge), since a seed (of light) is in [them]. I am the thought of the Father, [and] through me [the c]all first came forth,that is the knowledge of the unending – I who am the thought of the all and who am united with the unknowable and inconceivable thought. It is I who appeared in all who have known me, for it is I who am united with each one through the hidden thought and through an exalted call".* After the creation of the world and * *NHC XIII 1,36,4–26* men through the "great demon", who as in similar texts is a pro- duct of "wisdom" or the "insight (*epinoia*) of light",* there fol- * *NHC XIII 1,* lows a further descent of the "power of thought" in order to *39,30f.; 40,15f.*

help the imprisoned particles of light and to ensure their deliverance:

"But now I came down and reached the chaos, and I was [with] my own who are in that place ... (context in part destroyed) ... I will impart to you (addressed to the community) an inexpressible and indescribable secret: out of my "providence" (*pronoia*) I have loosed all your bonds for you, and I have smashed the chains of the demons of the underworld which fettered my members, in order to move themselves (?); and the high walls of darkness have I destroyed; and the strong gates of the merciless have I shattered; and their bars I have dashed in pieces; and (even so I compelled) the evil working power (energy) and him who smites you and him who hinders you, and the tyrant and the adversary, and him who is king (of darkness) and the authentic enemy. All this I have caused my own to know, who are the sons of the light, so that they may dissolve all these (powers) and be freed from all these bonds and enter into the place in which they were at first. I am the first who came down because of my part, which is the spirit (*pneuma*) which is in the soul (*psychē*) ... I spoke with the archons and powers in their speech, for I descended (through them); but my secrets I said (only) to my own, (for it is) a hidden secret. And they released themselves from the bonds and from the eternal lack of capacity for knowledge (or: from the eternal sleep). And I brought forth fruit in them, which is the recollection of the unchangeable aeon and (of) my home and (that) of [their] father ..."*

* NHC XIII 1, 40,29–41,32

In the second "teaching" the Protennoia appears in "the form of a woman" in order to speak about the "end of the age" (aeon). At the beginning she again introduces herself: "I am the call which was revealed through my thought. For I am the consort, I am called the "thought of the invisible" (and) I am called the "unchangeable voice". I am called "the consort". I am a single one who am undefiled. I am the mother of the call which I speak in varied fashion, I who fulfil (or: complete) the all, who possess knowledge in myself, the knowledge of the eternities. I am the speech which is in every creature, and I am recognised from out of the all. I am the one who causes the sound of the call to sound in the ears of those who have known me, that is the sons of light".* It is part of the gnostic world of ideas that the call of the being of light is alien and incompre-

* NHC XIII 1, 42,4–16

hensible to the lower powers, and they therefore cannot attain
to true knowledge (in the present case in regard to their immi-
nent destruction). "For that call which we have heard is strange
to us and we do not understand it, nor do we know whence it
comes. It came (and) brought fear into our midst, and weakness into the members of our limbs".*   * NHC XIII 1,44,6–10

In the third section finally the son speaks in the form of the
word (*logos*); it is the third form of manifestation of the Protennoia. This part has been described as "a substantial parallel to
the prologue of the Fourth Gospel";[45]
"I am [the wor]d (*logos*), which dwells [in the] inexpressible
[light] . . .* I alone am the inexpressible, undefiled, immeasura-   * NHC XIII 1,46,5f.
ble, inconceivable word (*logos*).

It is a hidden light which bears living fruit (and) causes living
water to spring forth out of the invisible, undefiled, and immeasurable source. That is, (I am) the unrepeatable call of the
glory of the mother, the glory of the creation of God, a male virgin from a hidden understanding (*nous*). That is, (I am) the inimitable silence hidden from the all; an immeasurable light; the
source of the all; the root of the whole aeon; the foundation
which bears every movement of the aeons (and) belongs to the
mighty glory; the foundation of every basis; the breath (of life)
of the powers; the eye of the three dwelling places (places of
manifestation); as a call originated from a thought and (as) a
word (*logos*) through a voice which was sent out to enlighten
those who dwell in the darkness* . . . And I showed myself (to   * NHC XIII 1,46,14–33
the archons) in the likeness of their (external) image, and I
wore the clothing of them all. [And] I hid myself in them, and
they did not know him who bestowed power upon me. For I exist in all authorities and powers and in the angels and in every
movement which exists in the whole of matter (*hylē*). And I hid
myself in them until I revealed myself to my brothers. And
none of them knew me, al[though] I am he who is active in
them, but [they thou]ght that the all had been created [by
them], because they are ignorant [and] do not know [their] root,
the place from which they have grown. [I] am the light which il-
lumines the all. I am the light which delights in my brothers. For
I came into the world (*kosmos*) [of mortals] because of the spirit (*pneuma*) which is left [in it] . . . which had come forth from
the [harmless] wisdom (*sophia*) . . ."* The working of the word   * NHC XIII 1,47,15–34
of redemption takes place in secret and is adapted to the situa-

tion in the cosmos: "[For when I] was in that place I clothed myself in the [manner of a] son of the first begetter (*archigenetor*) and was like him to the end of his judgment, that is (the end) of the ignorance of chaos. And I showed myself among the angels in their form, and among the powers as if I was one of them, but among the sons of men as if I were a son of man. Although I am the father of each one of them, I hid myself in them all until I showed myself [only] in my members. And I instructed them about the ineffable ordinances and about the brothers. But they are inexpressible to every power and every dominant (archontic) might, except only the sons of the light ..."* By these "ordinances" are meant the (cultic) mysteries of the community (the "five seals") which thus are likewise traced back to an institution by the revealer.

* NHC XIII 1,49,11–26

The redemptive function of the Logos   The manner in which the redeeming function of the Logos is seen to operate without assuming any personal figure is shown by the Hermetic texts already mentioned (where however the "understanding" has the same function), but also very impressively by the Nag Hammadi document The Original Teaching[46]: "Our soul is truly sick, for it dwells in a house of poverty (i. e. the body), [and] matter wounded its eyes, wishing to make it (the soul) blind. Because of this it hastens after the word (*logos*) and lays it upon its eyes like a medicament, swallowing them and casting [the blindness] from itself ... (context destroyed) ... and that one if he finds himself in ignorance is then entirely dark and a hylic. So it is with the soul, if it at all times [receives] a word (*logos*), to lay it like a medicament upon its eyes that it may see (again), and its light hide the enemies who strive with it, and it may blind them with the light, imprison them at its coming, bring them down into sleeplessness, and become confident in its power and its sceptre. While its enemies look upon it in shame, it hastens upwards into its treasure-house, in which its understanding (*nous*, as a heavenly counterpart) dwells, and into its secure storehouse".* To this is added a parable which compares the life of the gnostics, or their souls, with fish which are hunted by a fisherman (who is expressly described as an "adversary") with nets and hooks.*

* NHC VI 3,27,25–28,26

* NHC VI 3,29,3–25

Revelation in the Book Baruch   Finally one other example may be given of the idea of a continuing revelation, this time drawn from the report of a Church Father. Hippolytus in his Refutation of all Heresies adduces among others a gnostic Justin, who composed a book with the title "Baruch".* From this work, which he considers the most * Hippolytus, Refutatio V 24 abominable of all the books which he has read, he quotes a long passage, interspersed with his own paraphrases, which is one of the most original and probably also the oldest testimonies of Gnosis.* Although it is not possible to go more deeply into the * op. cit. V 26–27 problems of this "Baruch-gnosis", we should like to look for a moment at the doctrine of revelation. The underlying system is still strongly indebted to its Jewish basis, and finds confirmation for its views in the Old Testament. Of the three primal powers the prescient "Good" as the highest deity, the male, limited and creator principle Elohim (i.e. the Old Testament God) and the female power named Edem (i.e. "earth"), the latter two gave birth to twelve paternal and twelve maternal angels who are the counterparts of each other and thus represent the good and the evil side of the cosmos. In particular the third angel on each side plays a special role. On the father's side he is called Baruch (Hebrew "blessed"), on the side of Edem on the other hand Naas (Hebrew *nachas* "serpent"). The two also represent the two trees of paradise: the first the tree of life, the second the baleful tree of the knowledge of good and evil. In this system the biblical view of the serpent is thus preserved. Man is created by the angels in collaboration, and for this purpose the upper parts of Edem, which are in human form, are used, while her serpentine lower body serves for the creation of the beasts. As a symbol of their unity and love Elohim sets in the first human couple the spirit (*pneuma*) and Edem the soul (*psyche*). After the creation Elohim ascends with his angels to heaven and there discovers the good God "at the upper limit of heaven". He remains with him and wishes to serve only the Good, but before that to destroy his world again, "for my spirit was fettered to men, and I wish to take it again to myself". The Good however rejects this; the world is to remain for Edem as her possession. In revenge for the disappearance of her partner Edem now sets her angels against the spirit of man, in that she causes them to instigate discord or "division", and as beings of the zodiac to encircle the world. Naas in particular, the third angel, receives "great power to torment the spirit of Elohim which is in man with all punishments". "When the father Elohim saw all this he sent Baruch, the third of his angels, to help the spirit which is in all men". He warns the man, who is still in paradise (Hebrew *eden* "garden", with an echo of *"Edem"*), against the serpent (*naas*) who is in the tree of knowledge and represents lawlessness. The serpent however succeeds in deceiving Adam and Eve, which leads to the origin of adultery and paederasty. "From then on evil and good held sway over men, springing from one primal cause, that of the father. For when the father (Elohim) ascended to the Good he showed the way to those who wished (likewise) to ascend; but in that he abandoned Edem, he created the cause of evil for the spirit of the father which is in men". This makes necessary a continuing activity of redemption on the part of Baruch, which here corresponds in a positive way to the biblical *Heilsgeschichte* (in contrast to other systems) but is destroyed by the machinations of the serpent: "Baruch was now sent to Moses, and through him he spoke to the children of Israel that they should turn to the Good. But the third [angel of Edem, Naas (the serpent)], through the soul which since Edem dwells in Moses as also in all men, darkened the commandments of Baruch and brought it about that they should listen to his own (i. e. the law of Moses is not from the highest God!). For this reason the soul is set against the spirit and the spirit against the soul . . . both dwell in all men, in man and woman. Once again Baruch was then sent to the prophets, that through them the spirit that dwells in man might hear and flee from Edem and the wicked creature (the creation) just as the father Elohim once fled. But in the same way and with the same intent Naas brought about the fall of the prophets through the soul . . . They were all brought down and did not listen to the words of Baruch which Elohim had commanded. Finally Elohim chose Heracles as a prophet among the uncircumcised (i. e. the heathen) and sent him, that he might prevail against the twelve angels of Edem and free the father from the twelve evil angels of the creation: these are the twelve labours of Heracles which Heracles accomplished in order . . . When he thought that he had already conquered (the twelve angels), Omphale, who is Babel or Aphrodite, fastened upon him, seduced him and deprived him of his power, (i. e.) the commands of Baruch which Elohim had commanded, and she clothed him with her own garment, i. e. the power of Edem, the lower power, and so the prophecy of Heracles and his work remained incomplete. Finally Baruch was sent again by Elohim "in the days of Herod" * and came to Nazareth, and found Jesus the son of Joseph and Mary keeping sheep, a twelve year old

* *cf. Luke 1,5*

boy, and proclaimed to him from the beginning everything that had happened, from Edem and Elohim, and what was to happen thereafter, and said: "All the prophets before thee were led astray. Strive now, Jesus son of man, not to let yourself be seduced, but proclaim to men this doctrine (*logos*) and announce to them the things concerning the Father and concerning the Good, and ascend to the Good and sit down there together with Elohim, the father of us all". And Jesus obeyed the angel and said: "Lord, I will do everything", and he preached. Naas now wished to seduce him also but was not able, for he remained faithful to Baruch. Then Naas became enraged because he could not seduce him, and caused him to be crucified. But he left the body of Edem (the earthly physical body) on the wood (of the cross) and ascended up to the Good. But to Edem he said: "Woman, thou hast thy son",* i. e. the "psychic and earthly man". But he himself gave up the spirit into the hand of the father* and went up to the Good".   * *cf. John 19,26*

* *cf. Luke 23,46*

We can see how in this text the figure of Christ has been organically built into the gnostic redeemer's continuing activity of revelation. Before we look more closely at the gnostic conception of Christ, we should note a further extract from one of the **The** new Coptic texts, which abandons the Jewish *Heilsgeschichte* to **devaluation** ridicule in the face of gnostic possession of the truth, and thus **of the Jewish** represents a certain counterpart to the Book of Baruch just ***Heilsgeschichte*** quoted (although in this too there is a clear criticism of the Old Testament figures, in that they are all unable to resist the temptations of the earthly and psychic powers). In the Second Logos of the great Seth it is stated in the framework of the revelation of Seth-Christ*:[47] "For Adam was a matter of ridicule, who was   * *NHC VII 2,62,27–65,2* created by the seventh (the Demiurge) according to the character of a human form, as if he had become powerful over me and my brothers; (but) over against him we are without wickedness (and) have not sinned (as he).

Matter of ridicule were Abraham, Isaac and Jacob, in that the "fathers" gave to them names according to (their) character through the seventh, as if he had become powerful over me and my brothers ... (again as above).

Matter of ridicule was David, in that his son was called "Son of man", which was occasioned by the seventh, as if he had become powerful over me and those like me ... (as above).

Matter of ridicule was Solomon, in that he thought he was an "anointed one" (*Christus*) and became proud through the seventh, as if he had become powerful over me and my brothers ... (as above).

Matter of ridicule were the twelve prophets, in that they appeared as imitators of the true prophets (and) arose according to (their) character through the seventh, as if ... (as above).

Matter of ridicule was Moses, an (alleged) "faithful servant", who was called "friend (of God)", (since) because of him impious testimony was laid down, who never knew me, neither he nor those who were before him. From Adam to Moses and John the Baptist none of them has known me, not even my brothers. For what they possessed was (only) a doctrine of angels, to observe (the regulations about) foods, and a bitter slavery. Never have they known any truth, nor will they recognise any such, for a great deception lies upon their soul so that they never have the power to obtain an understanding (*nous*) of freedom to recognise him. But because of my father I am he whom the world has not known and therefore he (the Demiurge) exalted himself above me and my brothers ... (as above).

Matter of ridicule was this ruler (*archon*), because he said: "I am God and there is none who is greater than I. I alone am the father, the Lord ..."*, as if he had become powerful over me and my brothers ... (as above). Since we became masters over his teaching, so he is in a vain glory and does not agree with our (true) father. And so we make ourselves masters of his doctrine by means of our friendship, since he is proud in idle boasting and does not agree with our father. For he was a matter of ridicule with (self) judgment and false prophecy".

To this is added the awakening call to those who are still "blind", i. e. the ignorant. The redeeming knowledge which the redeemer imparts is an esoteric possession for the elect, and cannot be known by the evil powers of the world, since it belongs to another and "alien" world.

cf. Is. 45,5; 44,6f.; cf. also Exod. 20,5

The figure of Christ in Gnosis

It has already been said that the gnostic doctrine of the redeemer evidently arose independently of Christianity, but at the same time the figure of Christ is present in many systems or documents. Various investigations on the basis of the new texts have shown with a fair degree of certainty that in several cases Christ has only secondarily been built into the context (for example in the Secret Book of John,* the Wisdom of Jesus Christ etc.*). This is achieved for one thing by presenting the docu-

NHC II 1

NHC III 4, Pap. Ber.

ment as a revelation of the exalted Christ to his disciples, using a dialogue pattern according to which the disciples, generally ignorant, are instructed by their Lord through their questions about the secrets of gnostic doctrine, or again by the identification of the figure of Christ with one of the more prominent beings of light, in the first place with the "son" of the primal Father, who is at the same time the first revealer or redeemer, i. e. Christ became an important member of the gnostic Pleroma and of the soteriology. This process naturally had several consequences, in the first place for the gnostic doctrine itself and then for the conception of Christ, i. e. for Christology, and finally for the official Christian theology, whether in a positive or negative respect. As we have established, the gnostic soteriology consists essentially of two parts, the primal revelation and the continuing revelation. Both were transferred to Christ, as we have already seen from some witnesses. The New Testament also offers examples which belong to the earliest testimonies for this remarkable two-sided process, on the one hand the Christianising of gnostic ideas and on the other the gnosticising of Christian conceptions. For the doctrine of the primal revelation we may recall the beginning of the Gospel of John*, where the Logos shows a gnostic background, and probably also derives from a gnostic hymn.[48] The Hymn of Christ in Philippians* also belongs to this category.[49] At the same time the idea of the continuing redemptive activity is necessarily bound up with this, in that the revelation of Christ is either presented as the keystone of all redeeming activity or is transposed from primal times into the "midst of the time". It is under this head that we should deal for example with the doctrine of the "spirit of truth" or "comforter" (paraclete) in the same Gospel of John, or the hymns in Colossians*; in Hebrews also features of the advancing revelation may be found in association with the people of God in search of "the rest", such as is the case in gnostic texts referring to the "true" or "perfect" race. We shall not however concern ourselves with these New Testament problems, but with some characteristic features of the gnostic Christology, in the process adhering especially once more to the new original texts.

The introduction of the Christian redeemer figure into gnostic soteriology led in the first place to three characteristic phenomena which we would describe as 1. "historicising" of the

See above, p. 132 ff.

* *cf. esp. John 1,1–5. 9–12*

* *Phil. 2,6–8*

* *Col. 1,15–20; 2,13–15*

gnostic redeemer, 2. as a "splitting" of the Christ figure and 3. as "Docetism" or a conception of a merely phantom body.

The historicising of the gnostic redeemer figure

As can be seen from the testimonies already adduced, the gnostic conception of the redeemer in both its basic types has expressly mythological features. Its representatives are either anonymous spiritual potencies or legendary Old Testament figures. Any association with historical persons occurs only seldom, and if it does so only in a very vague way, as for example in the Nag Hammadi document Zostrianos,* where the ancient Iranian prophet is portrayed, in accordance with the ideas of late antiquity, as the proclaimer of secret doctrines. His wisdom he obtains in the course of a heavenly journey which he experiences in the desert, when in despair at his unproductive search at the feet of his gods for the truth about the world he is near to death. An angel of knowledge (*gnosis*) leads him into the world beyond, where various beings of light reveal to him the mysteries of gnostic or Sethian doctrine, which he is to proclaim to men. The text then draws to an end with a speech of repentance and conversion. In a similar fashion the Samaritan sect-founder Dositheos appears as a revealer in the Three Steles of Seth*, in which connection it should be noticed that according to some heresiological reports he also played the godfather in the formation of gnostic schools. The historical linking of the gnostic message of redemption is still more clear in the two leaders Simon Magus and Menander (first century A.D.), at least according to the reports of the Church Fathers. According to these they claimed divinity for themselves and appeared as redeemers, in the process understanding themselves as the antipodes of the Christian redeemer. Behind this lies evidently a gnostic protest conception, evoked by the historical conditioning of Christian soteriology. We can demonstrate this process very clearly in the Mandean tradition where, as distinct from the older mythological conceptions of the redeemer, one of the Mandean redeemers, who elsewhere plays a role in primeval times (the reference is to Abel, Mandean Hibil, or Enosh or Anosh) takes on "historical" features as the opponent of Jesus Christ in Jerusalem.

* NHC VIII 1

* NHC VII 5

See below, p. 296

See further below, pp. 294, 298

Gnosis however not only developed such historicising protest ideas against Christianity, but also itself incorporated the figure of Christ and so adopted a new element into its soteriology, which entailed in some measure its new formation. The gnostic *Heilsgeschichte* thereby received a new caesura, and Christ became, entirely in a Christian spirit, its fulfilment. In Christian Gnosis, as this area is usually called to distinguish it from the pre-Christian and post-Christian gnostic streams, Christ has become the central redeemer figure, which is to be distinguished from the official church one only through its special significance (sometimes however only with difficulty). This process, which in its details is still not clearly comprehensible and to which we shall return again in the context of the historical presentation, has however still another side: if one may on the one hand speak of a kind of "historicising" of the gnostic idea of the redeemer through the acceptance of Jesus Christ, on the other side, i. e. from the point of view of Christianity, we must speak of a "mythologising" of the figure of Christ which is almost unsurpassed in its extent. It was this side of the development above all which prevented Gnosis from obtaining permanent right of domicile in Christian thought, even if there were again and again – even today – movements in that direction. Through his insertion into the fundamentally mythological apparatus of the gnostic doctrine of the world and of salvation, Christ was made into a strictly mythological being, which as we have indicated above has already left its deposit in the New Testament. In order to bring the two aspects – the historical and the mythological – under a common denominator, the gnostic theologians brought about a division of the Christian redeemer into two completely separate beings, namely the earthly and transitory Jesus of Nazareth and the heavenly and eternal Christ, and thereby created one of the most remarkable pieces of gnostic teaching. In this way it was possible to appoint the Christian redeemer for several tasks in the gnostic systems.

First of all Jesus is the revealer and proclaimer of gnostic wisdom, usually in the form of secret traditions which he imparts to his elect, often through the mediation of privileged disciples like Peter, James, John or Thomas, or in response to their questions. The favourite period for such revelations is the forty days between the resurrection and the (final) ascension, but other events from the life of Jesus are also used, such as the transfiguration scene.* Several documents finally, for example the Secret Book of John, affirm that the heavenly Christ appeared to one of the disciples in a vision and imparted to him the content of the document in question.* No limits are set to the fantasy of

See below, p. 299 ff.

The mythologising of the figure of Christ

The earthly Jesus as Revealer

* Mark 9; Matth. 17; Luke 9

* NHC II 1; Pap. Ber.

* NHC II 2

this "apocryphal", i. e. "hidden" literature; it serves to sanction the gnostic doctrine as "true" Christianity over against the claims of the Catholic Church. The Gospel of Thomas* presents the ancient material of the sayings and parables of Jesus in a gnostic interpretation and adds new material of the same sort. The superscription gives succinct expression to both claim and promise: "These are the secret words which the living Jesus spoke and Didymus (twin) Judas Thomas wrote them down and said: "He who shall find the interpretation of these words shall not taste of death"." The gnostic men of letters were frequently leaders in the production of such "gospels"; only a fragment of this material has come down to us. Of the school of Basilides it is said: "The Gospel (good news) is according to them the knowledge (*gnosis*) of the supramundane things ...,

* Hippolytus,
Refutatio VII 27,7

which the great (world-) ruler (archon) did not understand".*

**The Christ of
the Naassene
Psalm**

The redeemer function of Christ is correspondingly conceived entirely in a gnostic spirit; he ranks as an incarnation of the "call" and as the liberator of the soul. In a psalm of the so-called Naassenes ("serpent people") preserved by Hippolytus (unfortunately not without flaws) this task is very impressively described:[50]

"The law that engendered the all was the first[-born] Nous;
  the second after the first-born was the outpoured chaos;
  thirdly the soul (*psyche*) received an active (?) law;
  therefore girt about with the form of a hind (or: a mean form)
  it toils laboriously in the power of death (?):
  Now possessed of sovereignty it sees the light,
  now cast into misery it mourns,
  now it is mourned and rejoices,
  now it is judged and dies,
  now it has no further escape (?):
  wandering the wretched one falls into a labyrinth of evils.
  But Jesus said: "Look, Father,
  upon this being pursued by evils, which on the earth
  wanders about, far from thy breath.
  It seeks to escape from the bitter chaos
  and knows not how it shall win through.
  For its sake send me, Father!
  Possessing the seals I will descend,
  all the aeons will I pass through,

all secrets will I reveal,
the forms of the gods will I disclose
and the hidden things of the holy way,
which I have called "knowledge" (*gnosis*), I will impart"".*

* *Hippolytus,
Refutatio V, 10,2*

The Wisdom of Jesus Christ contained in the Berlin papyrus **The**
8502[51] portrays the soteriological task of the redeemer (*sotēr*) **Christology**
Jesus Christ as follows in an address to his disciples at the end: **of the Sophia**
"I am come from the first, who was sent that I might reveal to **Jesu Christi**
you what was from the beginning, because of the pride of the
first begetter (*archigenetor*) and his angels, since they say of
themselves that they are gods. But I am come to lead them
(mankind) out of their blindness, that I may show to all the
(true) God who is over the all. Do you now trample upon their
(the powers') graves. Tread down their (alleged) "providence"
(*pronoia*), smash their yoke and raise up what is mine! For I
have given to you the power over all things as children of the
light, that you may trample upon their power with your feet".*   * *Pap. Ber. 125,10–126,16*

The Gospel of Philip gives expression to the activity of Christ **Christ in the**
in similar fashion, but with a stronger Christian emphasis and **Gospel of**
using the imagery of the redeeming of a pledge, by which is to **Philip**
be understood the soul which fell in primal times:
"Christ came that he might ransom some, deliver others, and
redeem others. Those who were strangers he ransomed, he
made them his own and separated his own whom he had laid
down as pledges (= souls) according to his will. It was not only
when he appeared that he laid down the soul as he wished, but
since the world (cosmos) exists he laid down the soul (as a
pledge). When the time came near at which he wanted (it), then
he came for the first time to take it back (again), since that
which had been left behind as a pledge had fallen among the
robbers and had been carried off as a captive. But he delivered
it and redeemed both the good in the world and the evil".*   * *NHC II 3,52 (100),
35–53 (101), 14*

The descriptions of the redeemer's acts correspond on the
one hand completely to gnostic ideas, but on the other side also
show how profoundly Christian ideas have been linked up with
them. As already mentioned, the separation of the earthly-Je- **Christian**
sus and the heavenly Christ gave gnostic Christology an expe- **and gnostic**
dient for doing justice both to the genuinely gnostic and also to **soteriolgy**
Christian soteriology. We have already seen from the example *See above, p. 146f.*
of the book Baruch of the gnostic Justin how Jesus acts at the

behest of the angel Baruch and remains faithful to him. In the Sethian texts it is the heavenly Seth who appears in Jesus, as in the Gospel of the Egyptians where "the great incorruptible

* NHC III 2,51,20f.
Seth, the son of the incorruptible man Adamas"* is on the one
* NHC III 2,54,20
side evidently identified with the "great Christ"* but on the other side "has put on Jesus the living ... and (so) nailed the powers of the thirteen aeons (of the Demiurge) to (the
* NHC III 2,64,1–4
cross)".* In the same way it is said of Seth-Christ at the end of the Trimorphic Protennoia: "I myself have put on Jesus. I brought him from the wood (of the cross) which is cursed and
* NHC XIII 1,50,9–12
placed him in the dwelling places of his father".* While Jesus as the temporary earthly manifestation of Christ takes over the above-mentioned task as revealer of gnostic teaching, Christ is a higher being of light who from the very beginning dwells in the pleroma with the Father and is usually described as his "image", as the "self-originate", "son", "first born" (or identified
See above, p. 77
with these). In this capacity he plays a role in the world of light which does indeed in some texts clearly conflict with that of other and older beings of light, but has become characteristic for a whole series of schools in Christian Gnosis. Thus in the Christian redaction of the Secret Book of John there is already
See above, p. 80
the statement that the restoration of the fallen Sophia is effected by Christ, her "consort" (*syzygos*). This position of Christ is also clear from the Wisdom of Jesus Christ, where he forms the male part of the first-born of the "first man" (= God the Father) and his consort the "great Sophia", while the female is the (little) Sophia. This redemptive role of Christ in relation to Sophia was strongly developed, particularly in the Valentinian school, and made a prototype and symbol of the soteriological work of Christ in general. Here one may speak of a regular transfer of the central Christian saving events from earth into the world beyond: they are events within the pleroma and thus prototypes of those which subsequently take place in the historical earthly realm in relation to Jesus of Nazareth. "Redemption", "crucifixion" and "resurrection" are for Gnosis largely understood as symbolic incidents of cosmic significance and accordingly were subjected to entirely new interpretations which often become visible only on a closer inspection. This was one of the facts which demonstrated the danger of the gnostic teachings for an orthodox Christian understanding. Irenaeus remarks about the Valentinians: "Certainly they confess with

their tongues the one Jesus Christ, but in their minds (*sententia*) they divide him"* (in three parts, as he correctly states). *Irenaeus Adv. haer. III 16,1*

According to the teaching of Valentinus, as it is preserved in the many branches of his school, **Christ together** with the Holy Spirit forms a separate pair of aeons **which** originated together with the remaining 30 bisexual **pairs of aeons** for the stabilising of the peace of the pleroma. This was made necessary as a result of the disturbance which had entered in through the fall of the "higher Sophia", the last offspring in the kingdom of light. Driven by her passionate search for the supreme Father, which her partner could not prevent, she became ensnared and would almost have perished if she had not been restrained by the "limit" (*horos*) between the higher and the lower worlds and at the same time purified (from her desire). This "limit" also bears the designations "cross", "redeemer", "absolver", "limit-setter" and "bringer back after conflict", and thus has a soteriological significance. "The cross is a sign of the limit (*horos*) in the pleroma. For it separates the unfaithful from the faithful even as that separates the world from the pleroma".* Further there is a report of the bringing forth of a "second Christ" as the common act of the pleroma: "This was the most perfect beauty and star of the pleroma, the perfect fruit, Jesus, who is also called Saviour (*sotēr*), Christ, word (*logos*) after the name of the Father, and the all because he derived from all (the aeons)".* He is the one who will appear in Jesus of Nazareth. But it is not only within the pleroma that a saving activity of Christ is assumed; there is also one outside, and once again in connection with the (lower) Sophia or, as she is called from the corresponding Semitic word, Achamoth. The passion (*pathos*) and reflection (*enthymesis*) of Sophia are separated off in the incident in the pleroma and "of necessity cast (strictly skimmed off) into the places of shadow and of emptiness". Thus this shapeless and formless "premature birth" of Sophia finds itself ⏌ide of the light. "Then the (higher) Christ took pity on it, extended himself through the cross (*horos*) and formed it by his power into a figure, but only according to nature, not according to knowledge (*gnosis*). Thereafter he returned above, withdrawing his power (from it), and abandoned it that it might perceive the passion attaching to it because of its separation from the pleroma, and feel yearning for what was of a different kind, for indeed it possessed a certain savour of immortality which Christ

The heavenly Christ in Valentinus

Clem. Alex., Ex Theodoto 42,1

Irenaeus, Adv. haer. I 2,6

* Irenaeus, Adv. haer. I 4,1 and the Holy Spirit had left to it".* It becomes conscious of its situation and seeks to turn about, but is unable to do so because of the limit (*horos*), which cannot allow any passion to pass into the pleroma, and therefore falls into manifold passions, sorrow, fear, distress, but all in ignorance. From these results the psychic and bodily creation, with which we are not here further concerned. Finally Achamoth appeals to Christ to help her. "He had ascended up into the pleroma and naturally had no desire to descend [again] a second time, but he sent the "comforter" (paraclete), i. e. the saviour (*sotēr*), to whom the Father had handed over all power and set everything under his author-* cf. Col. 1,16 ity . . . "* He comes to her with his angels, and through him she is this time moulded "according to knowledge" also and freed from her passions (these are banished into the world of the body and here form two kinds of earthly passions). "But Achamoth, freed from the passions, enjoyed with delight the vision of the lights (= angels) who had come with him (the Sotēr), had intercourse with them, and became pregnant with fruit after * Irenaeus, Adv. haer. I 4,5 their likeness . . ."*

This supernatural redeeming activity of the heavenly Christ for the benefit of Sophia, who ranks as "mother" of the seed of light and so of the gnostics, was given extended treatment particularly in the Coptic Pistis Sophia, where considerable space is devoted to the lament and to the journeys of Sophia, through * Pistis Sophia, chs. 30–58 psalms which have been inserted.* Here too she is delivered by Jesus, who first of all through a power of light causes her to be transposed from chaos into a higher place, and finally himself comes down to lead her back to her old place, the thirteenth aeon. In gratitude she offers up a series of hymns to the "first * op. cit., chs. 58–62 mystery",* and these as the account proceeds are interpreted by the disciples of Jesus, with specific reference to the fate of * op. cit., chs. 63–82 Sophia.*

The figure of   It was certainly Mani who drew the most consistent conclu-
Christ in   sions from the gnostic Christology, and with the systematic
Manicheism   power that was all his own developed a three-fold form of the
Christian redeemer: the "Jesus of Glory" as a continuation of the heavenly Christ of Gnosis is responsible for the whole event of redemption; the earthly Jesus, in whom as in all the prophets the "reason (*nous*) of light" which emanates from the Jesus of glory is deposited, is a precursor of Mani as a revealer or "apostle of light"; the soul of light imprisoned and suffering in the

world corresponds to the "suffering Jesus", who is thus understood in a purely cosmic and symbolic fashion (this third figure of Jesus may also be a secondary conception of North African Manicheism, which however has its starting points in Mani himself and takes account of the basic understanding of suffering in Gnosis).

The so-called Docetism has been named above as a third **Docetism** peculiarity of the gnostic Christology. The name was already current among the Church Fathers and is derived from the Greek word for "appearance" (*dokēsis*), "to appear" or "have the appearance of" (*dokeo*). What is meant is the idea widespread among the Christian gnostics that Christ appeared only "in semblance" (*dokēsei*) as a man or in the flesh, and correspondingly neither suffered nor was really crucified. This conception is for Gnosis a necessary inference from its anti-cosmic dualism, according to which a clear devaluation attaches to what is earthly and bodily, and it therefore cannot enter into any serious mingling with what is spiritual and other-worldly. Indeed it is the whole aim of gnostic effort to reverse the temporary binding together of body and spirit or "seed of light", which has resulted from a guilt-laden destiny. The redeemer who introduces this act through his revelation cannot indeed avoid showing himself "in the flesh" in order to adapt himself to earthly conditions, but this happens for him, as the authoritative representative of the "unworldly" higher world, only for a time and in terms of external appearance (which however is plain and comprehensible only to those of insight). For this reason Gnosis has to attain to a new interpretation of the Christian theology of suffering and the Cross. This however came out in very different ways and may extend from a radically docetic to an almost completely undocetic conception. Here a large part is played by the "magic hood" motif which we have already men- *See above, p. 139* tioned, in that the redeemer on his descent through the spheres (aeons) of the archons must ensure for himself unimpeded passage. By adapting himself to the respective spheres and through a change in his outward appearance he outwits the demiurgic powers and then after completing his task of redemption is able on his return to overcome them openly and triumphantly. Thus the docetic conception at the same time also serves to put the creator to shame, since he attempts by the crucifixion of Christ to destroy the redeemer. The change in his outward appearance is expressly assessed as a means of adapting the redeemer to the conceptual horizon of his environment: "He (Jesus) did not show himself as he [really] was, but he showed himself as people were able to see him. He showed himself to all [creatures]: To the great he showed himself as great, to the small he showed himself as small. [To the] angels [he showed himself] as an angel, and to men as a man. Hence his word (*logos*) concealed itself from all. Some indeed saw him, but thought that they were seeing themselves. But when he showed himself to his disciples on the mount (of Olives)* he was not small, he had become great. But he made the disciples great that they might be able to see how great he is".* This capacity for transformation on the part of the gnostic Christ is repeatedly found in the texts, for example in the form that he can reveal himself both as a child and as an old man, i. e. he possesses the power of timelessness or eternity.

° *cf. Matth. 17,1 ff.*

* *NHC II 3,57 (105), 29–58 (106), 10*

Early Christian Christology in relation to the gnostic   It has been repeatedly a disadvantage in assessment of the gnostic idea of the "semblance body" that it has been treated far too much in the light of later ecclesiastical Christology, and through this the opposition of the gnostic and Christian conceptions has occupied the foreground. A historical treatment however leds to a different picture. Adolf von Harnack in his History of Dogma repeatedly pointed out that the Christian communities down into the second century frequently took no offence whatever at gnostic Docetism, since they themselves advocated in their Christology a "naive Docetism".[52] It was only in the debate with Gnosticism that this was gradually eliminated and replaced by a complicated doctrine of the two natures. When in primitive and early Christianity there is any more detailed reflection about the relationship of God and man in Christ, this takes place for the most part in two ways.[53] Either Jesus is a man chosen by God who was equipped with the Spirit of God and at the end of his career was adopted by God to the place of Son and correspondingly set at the right hand of God (the so-called "Adoptionist" Christology) or, in Harnack's words, "Jesus ranks as a heavenly spiritual being (or the highest heavenly being after God, the "second God", who however is one with God), who, older than the world, took on flesh and after the completion of his work on earth has returned again to heaven" (pneumatic or better hypostatic Christology). The second type, the so-called "spirit or pneuma Christology", is fundamentally an idea close to the docetic understanding since generally there is no more detailed reflection concerning the bodily and human side. In other words, docetism is only a variation of the "pneuma Christology". For both Christ is a heavenly divine being (whether as spirit or as an angel) temporarily clothed with flesh, i. e. appearing in human form. Harnack rightly called this form a "mythological transformation".[54]

It is therefore not surprising if there is between gnostic and Christian Christology no such deep gulf as has been repeatedly asserted – especially in more recent theological research. Paul already reckons only with the "risen", i. e. the heavenly pre-existent Christ who has returned to God; the earthly Jesus has for him no longer any significance.* The Johannine view of * 2. Cor. 5,16 Christ stands still closer to the gnostic: it is not his earthly appearance which is decisive but his heavenly and otherwordly origin which only faith can perceive. That he has come "in the flesh" * means only this, that he has entered into the earthly and * John 1,14 human sphere, just as Gnosis also assumes with regard to the redeemer. But the "fleshly Christ" is not the true one, it is the non-fleshly, the Christ of glory, the Logos.* This dualism of the * John 1,1ff. two forms of appearance, that of men of the world (illustrated by the attitude of the Jews) and that of the believer, corresponds entirely to gnostic views. One may not indeed describe this Christology, which is fully built into the Johannine dualism of light and darkness, as an outright docetic one, but through the distance from the world which is here brought to expression it stands very close to it; in no case is it, as is usually asserted, "antidocetic". The Gospel of John shows very clearly how fluid are the limits between primitive Christian and gnostic conceptions at this point; it is, as has recently been shown once again, "the first system known to us in detail of a Gnosis which adapts Christian tradition to itself".[55] Its revealer as the believer sees him "is without restriction to be called a gnostic revealer. John describes this revealer Jesus exclusively in relation to the poles of a gnostic dualism: in statements of his relationship to the Father and to the world".[56] We cannot follow this development further here, but the great Alexandrian theologian Clement still cherished docetic conceptions, which at his time were by no means reckoned to be expressly heretical.

This picture is entirely confirmed by a series of Nag Hammadi documents. The Gospel of Truth offers a view of Christ related

The Christology in the Gospel of Truth

to the "spirit Christology" and to the Gospel of John.[57] We cannot unambiguously read from it either Docetism or anti-Docetism. The document evidently operates with a transformed "flesh-conception" intended to give expression to the special nature of Christ which is visible only to the initiate, a "spiritualised flesh" so to speak. The decisive passage unfortunately cannot be translated for certain, but is to be reproduced somewhat as follows: "[The people] of matter (*hylē*) were alien (to him, i.e. Jesus), they did not see his form and did not recognise him, for he came down (out of the Pleroma) in (or by means of) a fleshly form, nothing hindering his course, since incorruptibility is incapable of comprehension (or: because it – the flesh – is incorruptibility and incomprehensibility)".* The same text however also includes an expressly positive evaluation of the suffering and death of Jesus on the Cross, which omits scarcely anything of a Christian spirit; in general this gospel has an expressly Christocentric content: "None of those who believed in the redemption could become manifest before that book (of life) had appeared. Therefore the merciful and faithful Jesus was patient, enduring suffering, until he took that book, since he knew that his death is life for many. As with a testament which is still unpublished the possession of the deceased master is hidden, so the all remained hidden because the Father of the all was (still) invisible ... Therefore Jesus revealed himself. He clothed himself with that book (or according to an emendation: he opened that book). He was nailed to a tree. He nailed the decree of the Father to the Cross. Oh what a great and glorious teaching! He humbled himself even to death although eternal life clothed him. After he had laid aside these perishable rags (i.e. the body), he clothed himself with incorruptibility which no one can take from him".*

* NHC I 3,31,1–6

* NHC I 3,20,6–34

The Christ of the Letter to Rheginus

Concern for a balanced relationship of the two natures in Christ appears also in the Treatise on the Resurrection (Epistle to Rheginus), where the argument again makes use of a special kind of "flesh" which also remains the property of the spirit which returns into the Pleroma ("the risen") in that it is transformed. The resurrection of Jesus is for the author a decisive event which conquers death, i.e. the "law of nature".* "The Son of God, Rheginus, was (at the same time) Son of Man. He compassed them (the natures) both, since he possessed manhood and Godhead (in himself), that on the one hand by the

* NHC I 4,44,20

fact that he was Son of God he might conquer death, but on the other hand through the Son of Man the restoration (*apokatastasis*) to the Pleroma might be brought about, since he was at first from above, a "seed of truth", even before the (world) system had come into being . . ." * The manhood which Christ bears, as * *NHC I 4,44,22–36* is clear from the remainder of the context, is however a special one transformed through the divine nature; only so can it bring eternal life (the "resurrection"). Another Coptic document (the Thought of our great Power) states only briefly that the ruler of the lower world sought in vain to hold Christ fast, since he was not in a position to discover "the (special) nature of his flesh". *   * *NHC VI 4,41,30–42,4*

If we compare with these statements those made concerning **Christ in the** the same problem by the apocryphal Letter of the Apostles **Epistula** (*Epistula Apostolorum*), usually described as anti-gnostic, it **Apostolorum** can be seen how open all the fronts were on this question, and that a separation into "orthodoxy" and "heresy" is inappropriate for the first two centuries. In the Ethiopic version of this document it is said, as a statement of Christ to his disciples:[58] "While I was coming from the Father of all, passing over the heavens, during which I put on the wisdom of the Father and and in his power clothed myself with his power, I was in the heavens. And passing by the angels and archangels, in their form and like one of them, I passed over to the classes, lordships and princes, possessing in myself the measure of the wisdom of the Father who sent me . . ." * "Therefore have I fulfilled *Epistula Apostolorum 13* all compassion: without being begotten I am born of man (or: begotten), and without having flesh I have put on flesh and grown up, that I might (belong to) you who are begotten in flesh and that you in the rebirth might obtain the resurrection in your flesh, a garment that will not pass away . . ." * This is also * *op. cit. 21* the view of the Letter to Rheginus.

That there were in the gnostic schools also varying conceptions of the nature of Christ can not only be discovered from our sources themselves, but is expressly attested in a fragmen- **The Document** tary document from the Nag Hammadi library which has been **Melchizedek** called Melchizedek.[59] "[People] will appear in his (Jesus') name and say [about him]: "He is unborn", although he is yet born; "he does [not] eat", although he is does indeed eat; "[he] does not drink", although he does drink; "he is uncircumcised" although he is circumcised; "he is unfleshly", although he is come in the flesh; "he did not subject himself to suffering", although he did submit to suffering; "he is not risen from the dead", although he is risen fro[m the] dead".* Here therefore in a gnostic document a standpoint corresponding to that of the Church is adopted in opposition to an extreme Docetism, which seems clearly to coincide with what we have learned from the Gospel of Truth and the letter to Rheginus.

* NHC IX 1,5,1–11

The suffering of Christ among the gnostics   There were thus gnostic movements which ascribed a saving value to the Passion of Christ (including his death on the Cross), and did not deny it or take it in merely symbolic fashion. To what extent this goes back to accommodation to the broad but still not uniform Christian community is difficult to determine. We must start from the fact that the gnostics also entertained very varied opinions on a question which in Christianity at large was still new and in debate. At any rate their share in the development of Christology was considerable, both in a negative and delimiting and also in a positive and progressive sense. Harnack therefore was not entirely incorrect when he once wrote: "It is not Docetism (in the strict sense) which is the characteristic of gnostic Christology, but the two-nature doctrine, i. e. the distinction between Jesus and Christ, or the doctrine that the redeemer as redeemer did not become man".[60] That means, he was in the first place a heavenly being, such as was appropriate to gnostic soteriology from the outset, and such a being naturally was immortal. To this extent Docetism is naturally the appropriate expression of the gnostic hope of redemption. The Teachings of Silvanus excellently express this basic conviction in one passage: "Thus Christ also, even when he is in deficiency, is yet without deficiency. And even if he was begotten he is yet unbegotten. Thus Christ, even when he is comprehended, is in his nature incomprehensible."* With this paradox Christian Gnosis had to rest content.

* NHC VII 4, 101,33–102,4

Gnostic witnesses for docetism   Against this background the well-known Docetic expressions of gnostic literature can now also be understood. In the main they see Jesus as merely the temporary habitation of Christ or the saviour, who descended upon Jesus (in the form of the dove) at his baptism and then separated from him again before the crucifixion. A birth of Christ is accordingly quite out of

Manichean book illustration (miniature) from Turkestan (Chotsko, Turfan oasis): Electi writing.

the question. This according to the tradition of Irenaeus was already the position of the first Docetic, Cerinthus from Asia Minor (first half of second century): "Jesus was not born of the virgin, but rather he was the son of Joseph and Mary, just like all other men, but more powerful in righteousness, intelligence and wisdom. After the baptism Christ descended upon him from the authority which is above all in the form of a dove and thereafter proclaimed the unknown Father and accomplished wonders. But at the end Christ again departed from Jesus and (only) Jesus suffered, (i. e. was crucified) and rose again (from the dead); Christ however remained impassible, since he was a spiritual being".* In similar fashion another contemporary, Basilides, taught that the light of the gospel (i. e. Christ) "descended upon Jesus the son of Mary and he was illumined and kindled by the light which shone upon him".* Thereafter everything took place as it stands written in the Gospels. "But this came about that Jesus might become the firstfruit of the division of kinds of the things which had been mixed".* It was only his bodily part which suffered, and this fell back again into "formlessness"; what rose again was the "psychic part" originating from the hebdomad, the sphere of the planets, which returned to its origin; whatever else belonged to the higher spheres was carried back by Jesus to its own place, above all the seed of light (here described as "a third sonship") was purified through him and restored to the Pleroma. Jesus is thus the one who brings everything to its place, "his suffering came about for no other purpose than to separate what had been mingled".* The report of Irenaeus* does not fit very well into this picture as Hippolytus presents it, since according to that Basilides taught that it was not Christ who suffered but Simon of Cyrene.* "The latter was crucified out of ignorance and error after he had been transformed by him (Christ) so that he was thought to be Jesus. But Jesus himself took the form of Simon and stood by laughing at them. For since he was an incorporeal power and the understanding (*nous*) of the unbegotten Father he could transform himself as he wished, and so he ascended to him who had sent him, mocking at them (the Jews or the archons), since he could not be held fast and was invisible to them all. Therefore those who know this are freed from the demiurgic powers. And one ought (therefore) not to confess the crucified, but the one who came in human form and who was thought (*putatus*) to have

Cerinthus

* *Irenaeus, Adv. haer. I 26,1*

Basilides

Hippolytus, Refutatio VII 26,8

* *op. cit. VII 27,8*

* *op. cit. VII 27,8–12*

* *Irenaeus, Adv. haer. I 24,3–7*

* *cf. Mark. 15,21; Matth. 27,32; Luke 23,26*

been crucified, who was called Jesus and was sent by the Father to destroy the works of the creator through this dispensation. Thus when anyone, he says, confesses the crucified, he is still a slave and under the power of those who created bodies. But he who denies (him), he is freed from them and knows the dispensation of the unbegotten Father".* We shall later come to know similar reports about the events of the crucifixion.

Irenaeus, Adv. haer. I 24,4

The Valentinian Christology

The Christology of the Valentinians is more complicated, since precisely in this area they were at variance among themselves. In general they reckon with three Christ figures, the spiritual, the psychic and the bodily, each of whom has his separate significance and function.* According to Irenaeus Valentinians (of the Italian school) put forward the following conception: "Some say that he (the creator) brought forth Christ, his own son, but only as psychic, and spoke about him through the prophets. This however was the one who passed through Mary just as water flows through a pipe, and upon him the saviour (*sotēr*) formed from the Pleroma of all (the aeons) descended at the baptism (of Jesus) in the form of a dove; in him also was the spiritual seed of Achamoth. Our Lord therefore, as they say, was compounded of these four parts and thus preserved the pattern (*typos*) of the original primary tetrad (*tetraktys*): from the spiritual, what came from Achamoth; from the psychic, what came from the creator; from the dispensation (*oikonomia*), what was created with inexpressible skill, and from the redeemer (*sotēr*) the element which came upon him (Jesus) as a dove. And this one (*sotēr*) remained impassible – for he could not suffer since he was inconceivable and invisible. For this reason, when he (Jesus) was brought before Pilate, the spirit of Christ which had been put into him was taken away from him. But also the seed deriving from the mother (Sophia), so they say, did not suffer, for it too was incapable of suffering, being spiritual (pneumatic), and invisible to the creator. Thus according to them (only) the psychic Christ suffered and the one mysteriously prepared from the saving dispensation (*oikonomia*), that the mother (Sophia) through him might display the image of that higher Christ who extended himself out over the cross (*stauros*) and formed Achamoth (the lower Sophia) according to her nature".* Another large section of the Valentinians, the oriental, taught on the other hand "that the body of the saviour (*sotēr*) was spiritual. For holy spirit, i. e. Sophia,

Hippolytus, Refutatio VI 36,4

See above, p. 155f.

See above, p. 155

Irenaeus, Adv. haer. I 7,2

came upon Mary and the power of the Most High, the creative art, that that which was given by the spirit to Mary might be formed".* According to this the earthly Jesus evidently appeared as some kind of spirit or phantom.

Hippolytus, Refutatio VI 35,7

Related to the Valentinian view is that of the so-called Docetae, of whom Hippolytus and Clement of Alexandria report. Only the first however gives any detailed account* and asserts that they gave themselves this name. According to Clement** a certain Julius Cassianus (second half of second century), who was counted a disciple of Valentinus, was their founder. For them the heavenly Christ, who possessed the fullness of the aeons, only came down upon earth by stripping himself of all glory, and making himself quite small, like "a lightning flash in a minute body". "That he might also put on the outer darkness – what is meant is the flesh – an angel accompanied him from above and announced to Mary, as it is written.* Her offspring was born as it is written. When it was born he (Christ) coming from above took it and accomplished everything as it is written in the gospels: he washed (baptised) himself in the Jordan, he washed himself and received in the water the image (*typos*) and the seal of the body born from the virgin, that when the ruler (*archon*) should condemn his own creature to death, to the Cross, that soul which had been brought up in the body might strip off the body and nail it to the wood of the Cross, and through it triumph over the powers and dominions* and (yet) not be found naked, but instead of that flesh put on the body which had been formed in the water when he was baptised ... He put on from the thirty aeons of the Pleroma thirty images. Therefore that eternal one was thirty years on earth, each aeon evidently being the image for a year".*

The docetists

Hippolytus, Refutatio VIII 8,2–10,11

** *Clem. Alex., Strom. III 91,1; 102,3*

* *cf. Luke 1,26ff.*

* *cf. Col. 2,14f.*

* *Hippolytus, Refutatio VIII 10,5–8*

These passages from the Church Fathers are in many respects confirmed by the new Coptic texts, although not in the details of the various schools. We should like to adduce some very remarkable passages from among them, in order to round off the picture of Docetic Christology from this side also.

The first **Apocalypse** of James has the following word of consolation come through the exalted Christ at his reappearance to James, who is grieved over the suffering of the Lord: "James, be not concerned for my sake nor for this people (the Jews). I am the one who was in me. Never have I experienced any kind of suffering, nor was I (ever) tormented, and this people no-

Docetism in the Nag Hammadi texts

where **did any evil**. This (suffering) was however reserved for a
form (*typos*; **what is meant is the** body) of the archons, and it

NHC V 3,31,15–26   was good that it was destroyed by them". * The Second Logos of
the great Seth expresses itself in the same way with regard to
this problem, emphasising the false view of the powers of the
world and of darkness; according to this text, as with Basilides,
Simon of Cyrene was a substitute for the suffering of Christ:[61]
"But I was in the jaws of lions ... I was not delivered up to them
as they thought. I did not suffer at all. They sought to punish
me, and I died, (but) not in reality but (only) in appearance,
that I might not be put to shame through them ... I suffered no
insult and was not afraid of that which was to befall me at their
hand ... But I suffered (only) according to their view and conception, that no word need further be wasted concerning them.
For my death, of which they think that it is accomplished, consists (only) in their error and their blindness, when they nailed
their man to their death. Their insight (*ennoia*) did not see me,
for they were deaf and blind. Since however they do this, they
judge themselves. I was indeed seen by them and tortured by
them (but) another – their father – was the one who drank the
gall and the vinegar. It was not I whom they smote with the
reed. It was another who bore the cross upon his shoulders,
namely Simon. It was another upon whose head they set the
crown of thorns. But I rejoiced in the height over all the (vain)
riches of the archons and the seed of their error (and) their idle

NHC VII 2,55,9–56,19   boasting. And I laughed at their ignorance ..." * Somewhat later this theme is taken up once again, evidently from another
tradition, but at the same time something more is said about the
understanding of the passion; it is the coming in flesh as such:
"O you who do not see, do not see your blindness, that he
whom they did not recognise has never been recognised nor understood. They did not receive a reliable hearing (from him),
therefore they eagerly practised a judgement of error and lifted
up their soiled, murdering hands against him, as if they were
beating the air ... I am an anointed one (*Christus*), the Son of
man, who derives from you. I am (at the same time) in you, in
that I was despised for your sakes that you too might forget that

NHC VII 2,65,2–23   which is changeable". *

In the still little known Letter of Peter to Philip the fate of Jesus is portrayed in very biblical fashion, but immediately understood in a docetic, i. e. "impassible", sense and only the suffer-

ing of the disciples is emphasised. Peter says to the disciples: "Our illuminator (*phōstēr*) Jesus [came] down and was crucified. And he wo[re a] crown of thorns and put on a purple robe and was [hanged] on a tree (= crucified) and laid in [a] grave and he rose again from the dead. My brothers, Jesus is an alien to this suffering; but we are those who have suffered because of the transgressions of the mother (that is, Sophia)"* * *NHC VIII 2,139,15–24*

Judas Iscariot

Another strongly apocalyptic text, the Thought of our great Power, refers to Judas Iscariot, the betrayer of Jesus, which is seldom the case elsewhere in Gnosis. He is portrayed as possessed by the archons, who wanted thereby to get Christ in their grasp, but naturally expose themselves in that because of the "nature of his flesh" they could not grasp him. Judas himself is banished to the underworld and handed over to the judges there. It is remarkable how in this text the work of Christ is described as the turn of the aeons which already introduces the final period. "His word (*logos*) dissolved the law of the aeon. He came from the word (*logos*), the power of life, and it was stronger than the command of the archons, and they were not able to do anything against their work to become master of it".* * *NHC VI 4,42,5–11*

Christ as an onlooker at the crucifixion of Jesus

As we have seen, the docetic conception made it possible to have Christ represented at the crucifixion through a substitute, be it the earthly and bodily Jesus or another man. A particularly delicate touch in these descriptions is the parodoxical situation in which Christ looks on at his own (apparent) crucifixion and is amused at it. The best-known account of this kind so far is in the gnostic Acts of John.[62] Here the Lord, already risen from the body, gives to the disciple John who has fled to the Mount of Olives a vision and interpretation of the "cross of light", while below them the actual crucifixion is in process: "John, for the men below I am crucified in Jerusalem and pierced with lances and with reeds and given to drink of vinegar and gall . . ."* This cross of wood is not the true "cross of light", * *Acts of John chs. 97–104* which has a cosmic and symbolic function and power (which is like that of the Valentinian *horos*). "Also I am not the one on the cross, I whom now you do not see but whose voice you only hear. I was taken to be what I am not, I who am not what I was for many others. Rather what they will say of me is mean and not worthy of me . . . The multitude about the cross that is ⟨not⟩ of one form is the lower nature . . ." "I have thus suffered nothing of that which they will say about me; but also that suf-

* op. cit. chs. 94–96

See below, p. 251
fering which I showed to you and the others in my dance*, I will
have it called a mystery ... You hear that I have suffered – and
yet I have not suffered –, that I have not suffered – and yet I
have suffered –, that I was pierced – and yet I have not been
struck –, that blood flowed from me – and yet it did not flow –,
in brief that I have not had what those men say of me ...".
There follows a symbolic interpretation of the death on the
Cross; then the passage closes with the injunction: "First, then,
you must know the Logos (i.e. the heavenly Christ), then you
will know the Lord, and thirdly the man and what he suf-
* op. cit. ch. 101
fered."*

A similar situation, although without these interpretations,
is described by the Revelation of Peter.[63] Here the saviour (sotēr) reveals to Peter, who sees everything before him as in a vision, his own fate upon the Cross: "'What do I see, O Lord, is it
you yourself whom they grasp and [yet] you hold me [by the
hand]? Or who is he who on the wood (the cross) is glad and
laughs, and [who is] the other whom they strike on feet and
hands?' The redeemer (sotēr) said to me: 'He whom you see on
the wood (cross) glad and laughing, this is the living Jesus. But
he in whose hands and feet they drive nails is his fleshly [like-
ness], it is the substitute (or: the ransom), whom (or: which)
they put to shame, the one who originated after his likeness.
But look on him and me [for comparison]!' But when I had
looked (sufficiently) I said: 'Lord, no-one sees thee, let us flee
from this place!' And he said to me: 'I have told you that they
are blind. Let them alone! And see how they do not understand
what they say: for they have put to shame the son of their (so-
called) glory in the place of my servant'. But I saw one who
drew near to us, and he was like him and the one who laughed
on the cross; (his appearance) however was painted (or: wov-
en) in holy spirit, and he is the saviour. There was however a
great ineffable light which surrounded them, and the host of in-
* NHC VII 3,81,3–82,14
describable and invisible angels, who sang praises to them ..."*
In an appended interpretation of the vision by the saviour it is
stated that "he who was nailed up is the first birth, the house of
the demons and the clay vessel (?) in whom they dwell, [the
man] of Elohim (the God of creation and the law) and of the
* NHC VII 3,82,17–83,15
cross which is under the law".* The other however who stood
by is the "living saviour" who must again be set free and who
rejoices at the lack of understanding, the disunity and the blind-

ness of his adversaries. "Accordingly (only) that which is capable of suffering (the body) will [suffer], in that the body is the substitute (or: the ransom). He however who was set free is my bodiless body; for I am (only) perceptible spirit which is full of radiant light, he whom thou hast seen as he came to me ..."

In Christian Gnosis also Cross and Resurrection belong **Crucifixion and** closely together, but in such a way that the latter already takes **resurrection** place before or at the same time as the crucifixion; it is the liberation of the spirit and the destruction of the flesh in one. For this reason the gnostic can say in an inverted sense that Jesus came "to crucify the world".* "Blessed is he who has crucified ° *NHC II 3,63 (III),24* the world, and not allowed the world to crucify him" is the proclamation of the "living Jesus" to his disciples in the First Book of Jeu, and this crucifixion consists in the hearing and carrying out of what he has to impart to them as secret knowledge.

The ascent of the soul and the end of the world

The redemption guaranteed by means of "knowledge", in the **The release of** sense of an escape from the entanglements of earthly existence, **soul** is first realized by the gnostic at the time of his death, for at this moment he encounters the everlasting, rewakening fact of release from the fetters of the body, and is able to set out on the way to his true home. This process, familiar also in other religions, is called the "ascent of the soul" or the "heavenly journey of the soul". For Gnosis death is thus very definitely an act of liberation. The Mandeans used an expression of their own: "the day of escape" (or: "release"), and placed their main soteriological emphasis in the sphere which was entered after death. With this object in mind Gnosis is primarily concerned with a man's personal destiny; expressed somewhat differently: the eschatology of the individual, i.e. the doctrine of the fate of individuals after death, is of primary importance. In no way does this exclude a "universal eschatology" which understands the end of the world in a collective sense, as is sometimes supposed. On the contrary, Gnosis is interested not only in the final end of mankind but also in that of the cosmos, for both are

ordered in accordance with its cosmology. The coming into being of the world, which is regarded as calamitous, has its goal in
an end which restores the beginning.

Eschatology of Our first concern however is with the "eschatology of indi-
individuals viduals". The path of the soul to the kingdom of light or to
"rest", as this objective is often described, is the same as that
which the soul traversed at the beginning. Taking up the words
Heraclitus, Frag. B 90 of the ancient Greek philosopher Heraclitus* it is recorded in
one section of the Three Stelae of Seth: "The way of ascent is
NHC VII 5,127,20f. (like) the way of descent"*, which refers here to the elevation
to the pleroma achieved by prayer. The redeemer must also tra-
verse this path, and so both are frequently likened to each other: the redeemer prepares or shows the soul the way; he has, as
the Mandeans say, "established the path". However, gnostic
theology here faces an initial problem of conflicting interests.
Only rarely is the ascent of the soul accomplished automatically, but requires help and support. The reason for this lies in the
existence of the powers which rule the world, the Archons, who
try to impede the soul's return in order to prevent the perfecting of the world of light and thus protract the world process.

Dangers on the The description of the menace to be encountered on the jour-
journey of the ney is a central theme in numerous gnostic traditions, as is also
soul that of the overcoming of these obstacles. At this point magic
and cult intrude for a number of gnostic schools, media which
really run counter to gnostic self-understanding, but which do
show that such practices also have their own decisive importance in Gnosis. One must not rely only on the saving nature of
"knowledge" and the "natural" redemption process, but on
See below, p. 244 palpable elements, like protective and distinguishing signs and
symbols ("seals"), magical sayings and death ceremonies.

Magic and the The classical opponent of Christianity Celsus (2 cent.) had
ascent of the these practices in mind when he derided the Christian gnostics
soul (Ophites): "If you are seeking a guide for this way (to God),
then you must avoid the conjurers and sorcerers and the exor-
cists." He regrets that they are persecuted and crucified
(referring to the anti-Christian pogrom of 178–180), "because
of ... the demonic words addressed to the lion, the animal with
double forms (amphibian), and the one shaped like an ass, and
the other illustrious doorkeepers, whose names you hapless
Origen, C. Celsum VII 40 folk have wretchedly learnt by heart".* Origen annotates these
remarks, correctly tracing them back to gnostic Ophite models,

and reproduces more detailed associations, namely the ascent of the soul through the demonic planetary spheres.* The ascending soul, after it has crossed the "barrier of evil", i. e. the firmament, by traversing the "eternally chained gates of the Archons" has to acquire the favour of each of the guardians of the planetary stations by prayers of entreaty. The address to Astaphaeus (= Venus) is an example: "Astaphaeus, lord of the third gate, overseer of the primeval source of water, look upon one initiate who has been purified by the spirit of a virgin (Sophia), let me pass, thou who dost behold the world's essence. May grace be with me, father, let it be with me!" This is a picture of the underworld as the ancient Egyptians depicted it in their description of the journey of the dead, which has been transferred by Gnosis to the supernatural intermediate world. The departed soul, as Celsus likewise reported, was surrounded by seven angelic archons, but it is also surrounded by "angels of light" who are willing to help it.*

* op. cit. VI 30 f.
Diagram, p. 68
* Origen, C. Celsum VI 27

These events are extensively treated in the two books of Jeu, which belong to a late stage of Gnosis. In them the "marks" (characters) and "seals" of the upper "treasures", i. e. the stations of the pleroma, are described in detail and represented pictorially as well those of the lower aeons which the soul has to traverse hurriedly. Jesus supplies his disciples with precise instructions for this, e. g. for the first aeon the following: "When you come forth from the body and reach the first aeon and the archons of that aeon appear before you, seal yourselves with this seal: This is its name: *Zōzezē*, say it but once, seize this number: 1119, with your two hands. When you seal yourself with this seal and have pronounced its name just once, then vindicate yourself with this recitation (apology): 'fall back *protethpersomphon chūs* (a secret name), you archons of the first aeon, because I challenge *ēaza zēōzaz zōzeōz*'. Now when the archons of the first aeon hear those names they will be terrified and draw back and flee in the direction of the west on the left and you will be able to ascend."* This is repeated in similar fashion, only with different "seals" and oath formulae, as far as the eleventh aeon. The twelfth aeon sets up the pleroma of the "invisible" and "unbegotten" gods to whom seal, number and name must also be declared, until finally after the 14th aeon the holiest of all begins, which must be entered only with the "mystery of the forgiveness of sins".

See above, p. 27 f.
Diagram, p. 174
* 2nd Book of Jeu. ch. 52

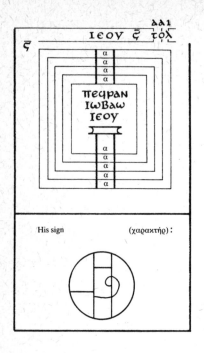

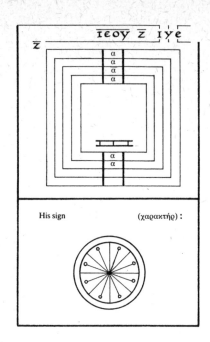

"Signs" (characters) and "seals" of the aeons according to the two Coptic books of Jeu.

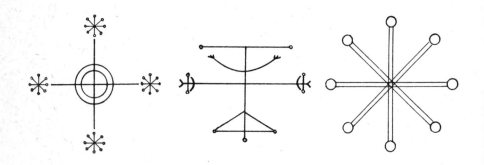

* Irenaeus,
Adv. haer. I 21,5
See below, p. 244 f.

Irenaeus also discussed the motif of the ascent of souls using secret agencies and describes an actual ceremony for the dead which was organized for this purpose.* Secret sayings were imparted to the dead man which he had to recite against the "powers" in order to ascend on high. One of the many new discoveries which the Nag Hammadi texts have given us, the first "Apocalypse of James", contains a passage which has close connections with that referred to in Irenaeus, albeit in another context, namely a conversation between the risen Jesus and James

the Just. Jesus imparts to his disciple the following secret revelation about the way[64]: "[Beh]old I shall reveal to you your re-
demp[tion]. When [you] are seized and you undergo these
(death) pangs, a multitude (of Archons) will turn against you,
that they may seize you. And in particular three of them will
seize you, (namely) those who sit there as (supernatural) toll
collectors, not only demanding toll, but also taking away souls
by force. When you come into their power, one of them who is
their keeper (overseer) will say to you: 'Who are you, or where
are you from?' You are (then) to say to him: 'I am a son and I
am from the Father!' He will say to you: 'What sort of son are
you and to what Father do you belong?' You are to say to him:
'I am from the Father who [was] pre-existent, and [I am] a son
through him who was pre-existent'. [He will say] to you: '[Why]
were you [sent out?]' You are to [say to him: 'I came] from the
one [who was pre-existent,] that I might behold [all that are
ours and that are alien!' He will say to you: 'what are] these
alien things?' You are to say to him: 'They are not entirely alien
but they are from [Acha]moth, i.e. the female; and she produced these when she brought this race down (in substance)
from the pre-existent one. So then they are not alien, but they
are ours. They are indeed ours because she who is mistress of
them (i.e. Achamoth or Sophia) is from the pre-existent one.
At the same time they are alien because the pre-existent one
did not combine with her, when she later produced them.'
When he also says to you: 'Where will you go?' you are to say to
him: 'To the place whence I came, there shall I return'. And if
you respond in this manner, you will escape their attacks. But
when you encounter [these] three detainers [who] take away
souls by fo[rce] in that place ... you are [to say to them: 'I am] a
vess[el] more [worthy] than [the female who produced y]ou ...
You for your [part] will not be sober. But I shall call on the imperishable knowledge (*gnosis*), which is Sophia who is in the
Father, (and) who is the mother of Achamoth ...' Then they
will fall into disorder (and) will raise a clamour against their
root and the race of their mother. [But] you will go up to [what
is] yours ..."*

* NHC V 3,32,29–35,25

The ascent of souls in Mandean literature

Mandaean literature provides the largest and most impressive witness for our topic. Whole books or tractates describe
the journey of the soul through the super-terrestrial "watch-
houses" or "infernal regions". In one particular Diwan, the

"Diwan (of) Abathur", there is a pictorial representation. Af-
Plates 42–48 ter death the soul must embark on a long (42 days) journey es-
corted by the prayers and rites of the community on earth. This
See below, p. 362 ascent (*masiqta*), as the event itself together with the vital rite
which goes with it is called, a sort of mass for the dead, leads
through the celestial "watch-stations" of the planets and creatures of the zodiac which allow only pure and sinless souls to
pass, while the others are held and punished and have to suffer
"purgatory" (*purgatorium*). Finally the soul has to face the ordeal of the scales on which the required measure of weight, the
piety of the soul, determines entry into the kingdom of light. In
addition to piety and good works, means which guarantee a
passage through are the signs, "names" and baptisms" of cultic
practice. In one of the texts in question from the Book of the
Songs of the Dead or of the Soul, Adam is given certain direc-
tions by the messenger who intends to fetch him from his life on
earth but at first encounters resistance[65]: "The way which we
must take is long and has no end. Parasangs are not measured
on it, and it is not marked by milestones. Torturers are left behind on it, watch-house keepers and toll-keepers sit on it. The
weapons (or: chains) are forged and held in readiness, the irons
are polished and set at hand; the cauldrons, which guard the
souls of the wicked, simmer. On the road is an ocean which has
no passage. Each one is brought to it and conveyed across by his
own donations and almsgiving. His works precede him as his
messenger. The way which we must take is crammed with this-
tles and thorns. Seven walls encircle it (and) mountains, in
which there is no gap. The scales are set up there and from
1,000 (souls) they choose one soul that is good and enlightened
* Left Ginza I 2 ..."*

In poetic form this journey is described in a number of ways
in the "Songs of Ascent" of the same book[66], which at the same
time constitutes a remarkable testimonial to gnostic piety:

I fly and proceed thither,
Until I reach the watch-house of the sun,
I cry:
'Who will guide me past the watch-house of the sun?'
'Your reward, your works, your alms, and your goodness
will guide you past the watch-house of the sun.'
How greatly I rejoice,

how greatly my heart rejoices.
How much I look forward
to the day when my struggle is over,
to the day when my struggle is over
and my course is set towards the Place of Life.
I hasten and proceed thither,
until I reach the watch-house of the moon,
(... continues as above)
... until I reach the watch-house of fire,
... until I reach the watch-house of the Seven,
... until I reach the watch-house of Rūhā (the evil spirit)
... until I reach the water-brooks.

When I arrived at the water-brooks,
a discharge of radiance met me.
It took me by the palm of my right hand
and brought me over the streams.
Radiance was brought and I was clothed in it,
light was brought and I was wrapped in it.

The Life supported the Life
the Life found Its Own
Its Own did the Life find,
and my soul found that for which it yearned."*

* Left Ginza III 12

Thus the return home of the soul is a restoration to the World of Light, from which it once – according to Mandean beliefs – fell through no fault of its own. Hence the frequent mention of the "first dwelling-place" or the "first earth" to which the soul longs to return. There it becomes once more a being of light (*uthra*) or a "luminary" and praises the Life, as the highest being of the Mandeans is called. The support which the departing soul enjoys from its "planter" or "helper" plays an important role; he encourages the soul's ascent and helps it through all dangers because it is his "counterpart". "You are my counterpart, I shall cause you to ascend and keep you safe in my garment", speaks the helper to the "mana", a specific Mandean designation for the particle of light in man which amounts almost to "spirit", "divine being". The redemption event in these texts lies completely in the sphere of the ascent and is connected with the return home of the soul. The theme of the call and the awakening of the sleeping soul, as we have come to recognize it, figures

The "helper"

frequently as an image for the activity of the guides of souls,
who at the same time fulfil the role of angels of death.

> "He (the messenger) stood there in radiance
> and appeared to the mana, the son of the Mighty (Life).
> He cried and made his voice heard,
> and set his heart up on its support:
> 'Shine forth and illuminate, mana!
> I have come to you and will not leave you.
> When you are called,
> (Then) rise to the Place of Light.
> (The Life; or: one) planted me,
> and sent me to you.
> Arise, depart, mana,
> from the trunk, into which you were cast,
> the trunk, in which you grew up,
> and which has no hands or feet.
> Ascend, rise up to your former home,
> to your fine abode with the uthras.
> Live among the uthras, your brothers,
> sit there as you were taught to do.
> Seek the house of your Father
> and curse the world of falsehood where you lived.
> May your radiance protect you,
> may you be raised in your hidden light.
> May your radiance go before you,
> And your light be established (or: set up) behind you.
> May your throne be set up, just as it used to be,
> and the seven (planets) be without favour.'"*

Left Ginza II 1

In another such **hymn Mana** who often, as here, alternates with
Adam, is invoked:

> "'Rise, **mana**, leave this world!
> The perversity which pained you, will their own lords
> receive.
> The sleep from which you woke,
> will return and overwhelm them.
> Rise, clothe yourself with great radiance
> and wrap yourself in beloved (or costly) light.
> Put on the girdle of open eyes,
> which is all eye.'

The mana rose up from them,
and the planets gave themselves over to lamentation."*   * Left Ginza II 8

A common conception in Mandean literature is that of the re-   **The seven**
lease of the soul from the charge of the evil forces, i. e. the "Sev-   **planets and**
en" (planets), by an act of force on the part of the "helper" or   **their penal**
messenger of light. Not only does the idea of the wall of the fir-   **stations**
mament, which has to be breached, play a role here, but also
that of the super-terrestrial penal stations, on which the sinful
are detained; they can be redeemed only by a feat of the world
of light (assisted in no small measure by the prayers and ceremonies of the earthly community!):

"My measure is full, and I depart,
and the Seven confronted me on the way.
They closed the gates before me,
that they might detain me on the way.
The wicked speak about me:
'We shall cut him off (from the light) and keep him with us.'
But I raised my eyes on high,
I looked out and beheld the House of Life.
The Life answered me from the fruits,
the Radiance answered me from afar.
The Great Life was pleased
and sent the son of Life to me.
He sent the man to me,
who made me hear his voice.
He opened the doors for me and came,
he split the firmament and revealed himself.
He opened the doors and came,
He opened the gates before me and drove the Seven from my
path.
He clothed me with radiance
and wrapped me with light.
He gave a wreath of radiance to me
and my form shone forth more than all the worlds."*   * Left Ginza III 56

According to another version the seven demons surround the
body and try to detain the believer (who stands here for the
soul) in the "house of the toll keeper", in the assumption that
no one could provide help for him. "Immediately there was a

tremor in this world." A being of light (*uthra*) was commissioned to bring assistance.

> He smashed their watch-houses
> and made a breach in their fortress.
> He made a breach in their fortress
> and the Seven fled from his path.
> He brought radiance and clothed me in it,
> and brought me forth in glory from the world.
> The Seven with their demons and phantoms,
> sit in lamentation.
> They all sit in lamentation
> for the man who has escaped from the earth,
> for the man who has escaped from the earth,
> and made a breach in their fortress.
> He made a breach in their fortress
> and was brought (or: they brought him) forth with glory
> from the world.
> When the Seven saw this,
> They saw themselves as powerless, they turned back and set forth
> again on their way.
> The chosen ones and the uthras ascended with their praise
> and viewed the Place of Light."*

* Left Ginza III 15

The punishment of the wicked The Mandean evidence makes it clear that the supramundane purgatories or "hells" are a means to punish sinful souls, as in general they are for all unbelievers and non-Mandeans. In this way the problem is solved as to what happens to those who have not attained to "knowledge" or have offended against it. Purification has to be undergone as a means of punishment by the forces of darkness. The final fate of these "souls" will then eventually be decided at the end of the world. Certainly the possibility of a "second death", i.e. a final annihilation and confinement in darkness is understood throughout. What is more, souls can be lost forever in as much as they are unable to free themselves from the clothes and activities which bespeak the contamination of earthly wickedness. In this way the pleroma sustains injury in relation to its primordial origin. Other strands of Gnosis also take account of this view. In the Gospel of Truth it is put thus: "For he who is ignorant until the end is a

creature of oblivion, and he will be scattered along with it".*   * *NHC I 3,21,34–37*
We cite only a few examples from the rich hymnic tradition of
the Mandeans:[67] The highest messenger of light, the "Knowledge of Life" addresses the soul:

> "O soul! When I cried to you, you gave me no answer,
>   now, when you cry, who shall give you an answer?
> Because you loved gold and silver,
>   you will be locked up in the innermost Sheol.
> Because you loved dreams and phantoms,
>   you will sink into the cauldron, as it seethes.
> On the other hand if your debts are settled
>   and all your sins are removed,
> you will rise on the ascent (*masiqta*),
>   by which the perfect ascend.
> If your sins are not removed
>   and your debts are not settled,
> you, soul, will die a second death,
>   and your eyes will not see the light."*

      * *Left Ginza III 57*

But then, if the soul pays attention to what the messenger imparts to him by following the virtuous path of the Mandeans, it
is guided by him over the "Great Sea", is brought to the "watch-
house", to the "flames of fire, whose smoke ascends and
reaches to the firmament", and to the "deeply dug pits"; the
"high mountain" is made passable for it and a breach is made in
the "iron wall" which surrounds the world – the whole description serving to illustrate the dangerous journey which only the
chosen ones complete successfully.

    Another image for one of the punishment stations is the
"great Reed-(*sūf-*) Sea" which has its origin in the biblical
Reed-Sea legend* and is interpreted in popular Mandean verse   *Exod. 14*
as the "Ocean of the End (*sūf*)."

> "The wicked fall through their (own) will
>   into the great Ocean of Sūf.
> They will be housed in the darkness,
>   and the mountain of darkness will receive them,
> until the day, the day of judgement,
>   until the hour, the hour of salvation."*

      * *Right Ginza II 3*

The redeemer appears in the supramundane "prisons" to save individual souls:

"I passed the gate of those who were fettered,
and my radiance filled their prison.
My radiance filled their prison,
and they were made fragrant by my smell.
By my smell they were made fragrant,
and Hell was illumined by my radiance.
The (imprisoned) souls perceived it,
they weep, lament, and shed (tears).
I cry out to the prison warder:
'Open the gate for the souls.'
He replies:
'How many shall I set free of the thousands,
how many shall I let go of the tens of thousands?'
He opened the gate for me
and put a sign on the passport.
He opened the gate for me
and gave them (the freed souls) the recompense for their
chains."*

* *Left Ginza III 24*

The messenger is also concerned about the punishment:

"I conversed and spoke
to the warder of all the prisoners:
'Torment the wicked for their deeds
and watch over their souls,
until the Great (Life) sits in judgement,
(until) the wicked come and are questioned.'"*

* *Left Ginza III 23*

The upramundane purgatories

* *Left Ginza I 4*

A more detailed portrayal of particular watch-houses serving as punishment stations and of their inmates is provided by some prose texts in the Left Ginza.* In the first watch-house encountered by the ascending soul "instruments of torture, torment, and affliction are deposited" and "sinful souls are judged with unjust judgement". "[Sorcerers and] witches are tormented by a fiery whip, and are dispatched like vermin into the mouths of the ovens. As it stood there this soul trembled and shook, and its whole form trembled in its raiment, and it cried to the great and sublime Life and said: 'Where is the Life, whom I have loved? Where is Kušta, (truth) who dwelt in my heart? Where are the alms which I carry in my pocket?' And one says (or: they [the watchers] say) to it: 'O Soul! You are ascending to the Place of Light, wherefore do you cry to the great and sublime Life? Give your name and your sign which you received from the waves of water, from the treasures (or: thoughts) of radiance, from the great and high crater, from the great Jordan of healing powers and from the great springs of light.' When this soul stands in its place it opens (its mouth), cries out, and presents itself, giving its name, its sign, its blessing, and its baptism and everything that this soul has received from the waves of water ... (see above) ... and from the great and sublime Life. And the accursed fell on their faces and spoke to it: 'Go forth, soul, hasten and proceed thither, flee, ascend, conduct your lawsuit, and be victorious (in it), speak and gain a favourable hearing, remember us before the great and sublime Life!'" The beings of light escorting the soul instruct it about this first watch-house and who is "bound fast" in it (*inter alia* priests, sacrificers, givers of oracles, "Pharisees", adulterers). The soul has to wander through seven such stations and thereby experience all the horrors of these places and view those who have to suffer in them (among whom number Christians, ascetics or monks, venal potentates and judges, apostate Mandeans). Finally, once it has passed the "scales" which balance works and reward against one another, joining the spirit (the lesser part) if the balance proves satisfactory, the soul reaches the World of Light, of which once more it becomes part.

Other texts also take the problem of the deliverance and non-deliverance or the damnation of soul into consideration. In the Apocryphon of John the same kind of questions are put to Christ the Revealer and are answered by him in a number of ways.* Apart from the immediate ascent of the soul we have to reckon with a process of purification (perhaps by the migration of the soul) and with a final damnation of fallen souls at the last judgement. Here also allowance is made for a loss of "elements of light". The reason for this lies in the activity of an "antagonist spirit" which as the product of the dark forces seduces souls and leads them astray from the true path prescribed by the "Spirit of Life". It is a form of the Satan, the great "adversary" of biblical mythology, which confronts us here. For Gnosis too, the question of steadfastness is decisive, not merely the "knowledge" of the true nature of man.

Deliverance and damnation

* *Pap. Ber. 64–70*

See above, p. 105 f.

See below, p. 260 f.

First the promise of salvation extends to those "on whom the spirit of life comes down and who have united with the power (of light)" (i. e. the chosen!); "they will become worthy to go up to those great lights ..."* It is expressly stated that those who possess this "spirit of life ... will in any case live and come out of wickedness". "The power (i. e. the soul) comes into every (!) man, for without it they could not stand. But after it has been born then the 'spirit of life' is brought to it. Now if this strong divine spirit (*pneuma*) has come to life, it strengthens the power (of light) – which is the soul – and it does not go astray to evil. But with those into whom the 'counterfeit spirit' enters, it (the soul) is seduced by it and goes astray."* The soul strengthened by the spirit goes to the place allotted to it; "it escapes from the works of wickedness and through the imperishable oversight it is delivered and brought up to the repose of the aeons".* But over those who do not possess knowledge "a counterfeit spirit gained the mastery as they stumbled. And in this way it weighs down their soul and draws it to the works of wickedness, and thus brings it to oblivion (of Gnosis). After it has unclothed itself (of the body), it (the counterfeit spirit) hands it over to the powers which came into being under the archon (demiurge). Again they are flung into chains and led around (i. e. implanted in a body), until they are delivered from the oblivion and receive knowledge (and) so become perfect and saved."* Thus there are no further travels for the soul.* On the other hand the souls of apostate gnostics are kept for the last judgement: "They will go to the place to which the angels of poverty will withdraw, to whom no repentance has been accorded. They will be kept until the day on which they are punished. Everyone who has spoken against the Holy Spirit will be tormented in eternal punishment."*

Hell   In this way Gnosis also admitted the conception of hell as it was disseminated in hellenistic and Christian popular beliefs. The new Book of Thomas which contains various eschatological elements attests the development. In a "woe" oracle Christ describes the lot of the unbeliever:[68] "He will be handed over to the ruler (archon) above, who rules over all the powers ... and he will seize that man and cast him down from heaven into the abyss and he will be confined in a cramped dark place. He will not be able to turn or move because of the great depth of Tartaros and the griev[ous suf]fering of the underworld, which is se-

Side notes:

* *Pap. Ber. 65,3ff.*

* *op. cit. 67,1–18*

* *op. cit. 68,4–13*

* *op. cit. 68,17–69,13*
* *op. cit. 70,7f.*

* *op. cit. 70,12–71,2*

cured … [your stupid]ity will not be forgiven […], they will persecute you and [will] hand you over to [the an]gel, the lord of Tartaros […] pursuing them with whips of fire which fling sparks into the face of him who is pursued. If he flees to the west, he finds the fire. If he turns to the south, he finds it again there. If he turns to the north, the seething threat of fire meets him. But he cannot find the way to the east, to flee there and save himself. For he did not find it on the day when he was in the body, that he might find it on the day of judgement."* But the promise to those who remain steadfast (pneumatics) is: "When you come forth from the labours and sufferings of the body you will obtain rest through the Good and reign with the king, and you will be one with him and he one with you from now to [all] eternity."*

NHC II 7,142,27–143,7

NHC II 7,145,12–16

Late Simonian ideas

Another description which deals with the question of the redemption of the soul – whether this be as a whole or only in part, – is supplied by the late Simonian school in a document of theirs entitled the "Great Proclamation" (sections of which are preserved in Hippolytus*). According to this the "infinite power" (= what is divine) is present in man "potentially but not actually", and needs to be "fully formed" and grown in order to lead to salvation; in the hereafter it will once more be "in substance, in power, in greatness and in effective action" one and the same with the "ingenerate, unalterable, infinite power".* It will become "an infinite and unalterable Aeon which no longer enters into becoming."* On the other hand if it remains only as a potentiality "and be not fully formed (or remains a likeness), then he disappears and is lost, like the power of doing grammar or geometry in the human soul. For if this power acquires the proper skill (technique), it illuminates what comes to pass. But if it fails to acquire it, lack of skill and obscurity result, and just as if it never existed, it perishes with the man at his death."* Redemption will thus belong only to those who have actualised their divine tendency through knowledge, the others go the way of destruction, the end destined for matter (*hylē*).

Hippolytus, Refutatio VI 9–18

See below, p. 295f.

Hippolytus, Refutatio VI 12,2–4

op. cit. VI 14,6

op. cit. VI 12,4

The same conclusion was reached by those gnostics who took for granted the notion that "two kinds of men were formed by the angels, the one wicked, and the other good" as Irenaeus* reported of the early gnostic school of Saturninus (or Satornilos). The Redeemer came only to "discomfort" evil men together with the demons who supported them, and to lead good

Irenaeus, Adv. haer. I 24,2

men to salvation. This two-fold predestination is thus an early development in Gnosis and is connected closely with an esoteric interpretation of salvation.

The gnostic tendencies which take account of three classes of men (or, considered microcosmically, with three constituent elements in man) – the pneumatics, psychics and hylics, – go in **Valentinian** a completely different direction. Thus the Valentinians* as**conceptions** sume that the "earthly man" (choics, hylics) or "the earthly" *Irenaeus.* will perish with all that is material, the "psychic man" or "psy*Adv. haer. I 6,1; 7,1,5* chic" first enters the realm of the demiurge (the Hebdomad) but then if he (or it) chooses what is "better, he (or it) will find repose in the place of the Middle (i. e. the Ogdoad)", if he throws in his (or its) lot with the wicked, he (or it) will share the fate of the "earthly ones"; the "pneumatic man" or "the pneumatic" on the other hand, "which Achamoth sowed in righteous souls up till now will be 'fully formed' and brought up here (upon earth)" in order that after the laying aside of the body at death he may rise up together with the "psychic beings" to the "place of the Middle" (the residence of his mother, Acha*See below, p. 196* moth), from where at the end of the world, leaving behind the psychic, he is then finally drawn into the "bridal chamber" of the Pleroma. This conception starts out from the gnostic "natural order" of the cosmos and results in the restoration of its constituent elements to their place of origin; in the end the prospect of complete salvation or destruction is held out. And so a journey incumbent on the soul finds a place in Valentinianism.

The ascent of   The ascent of the soul as we understand it at present can also **the soul** result in a more sublimated form, one which is related to that of **according to** the late Hellenistic milieu which likewise held strongly to the **Poimandres** belief. The main concern in this area has to do with the gradual laying aside of the material – psychic coating which envelops the divine element and its restitution to the cosmic spheres to which it corresponds. Actually it is the birth process in reverse: everything that was by chance contributed by the planetary spheres to the creation of the human body will be surrendered back to them, until the spiritual or divine element returns to God pure and undefiled. The well-known book of Poimandres which belongs to the Hermetic writings and to which we have *See above,* referred repeatedly presupposes this idea. The "shepherd of *pages 86 ff., 107 ff.* men" gives the following information on the question of the "ascent": "First, at the dissolution of the material body you surrender the body to change, and the (outer) form you have disappears, and you surrender (your) character (*ethos*) to the daemon as no longer effectual. The sensory organs of the body return to their origins (sources), they become separate parts and (with the formation of a new body) are compounded again for effectiveness. Passion and desire go into the irrational nature. And so he then goes upwards through the harmony (of the spheres): To the first zone he gives the capacity to grow or to diminish, to the second (zone) his evil machinations, an (henceforth) ineffectual cunning, to the third (zone) the deceit of (henceforth) ineffectual lust, to the fourth (zone) ineffectual greedy love of power, to the fifth (zone) unholy boldness and rash audacity, to the sixth (zone) ineffectual evil strivings after riches, and to the seventh (zone) the lurking lie. And then stripped of all the activities of the harmony (of the spheres), he reaches the nature of the Ogdoad (*ogdoas*) (now) with his own power, and with those who are there he praises the Father. Those who are present rejoice together that this one has come and becoming like those with him he hears also the sweet sounds of certain powers lingering over the nature of the Ogdoad and praising God. Then in order they go up to the Father, change themselves into powers, and having become powers they (themselves) come to be in God."* On the other hand for the "foolish, bad, corrupt, jealous, covetous, murderous and impious" the text holds the prospect of an avenging demon who torments them with fire both here and in the future life.**

* *Corp. Herm. I 24–26*

** *Corp. Herm. I 23; s. also NHC II 7,142 f.*

See above, p. 184 f.

The return of the body

The laying aside of the body is for Gnosis not only tantamount to a release of the "soul" but is equally a judgement against the forces which created the body. It is a victory for the world of light and heralds the final destruction of darkness. Descriptions of this process are often very vivid, particularly in the Mandean literature, although corresponding sections are not lacking among the new Coptic writings. The Authoritative Teaching provides the following impressive description:[69] The soul "surrendered the body to those who had given it to her. They were ashamed while those who deal in bodies sat weeping because they were not able to do any business with that body, nor did they find any (other) merchandise for it. They exerted themselves to the utmost until they had shaped the body of this soul, wishing to throw down the invisible soul. They were therefore ashamed of their (own) work. They suffered the loss of the one for whom they had worked so hard. They did not realize that she (the soul) had an invisible spiritual (pneumatic) body. They thought (rather): 'We are her shepherd who feeds her!' But they did not realize that she knows another way, which is hidden from them, which her true shepherd taught her in knowledge."*

* NCH VI 3,32,16–33,3

The purification of the soul   The austere notion of purity which Gnosis associates with its kingdom of light or "pleroma" makes it essential that the element of light which comes forth from the earthly darkness is thoroughly purged of all dross associated with this life before it can make an entry. Above all washings or "baptisms" as they are depicted in various writings, serve this purpose. For the baptismal sect of the Mandeans this is of course a foregone conclusion:

"He (Adam) rose up and ascended to the House of Life:
They (the beings of light) washed him in the (heavenly)
Jordan and protected him.
They washed him and protected him in the Jordan;
They placed their right hand on him.
They baptized him with their baptism
and strengthened him with their pure words."*

* Left Ginza II 21

Similarly in the tractate The Trimorphic Protennoia where the "enthronement" of the soul is depicted after its ceremonial ascent:[70] "When you enter this (light) you will receive radiance from those who impart radiance, and those who enthrone will enthrone you. You will receive garments from those who give garments and the baptizers will baptize you and you will be full of radiance. This is the (light) in which you once were when you were enlightened."* The same proceedings are found once more at the close of the tractate.* The spirit here obtains "garments of light" in place of his earthly garment, he is baptized "in the spring of the water of Life", receives a "throne of glory" and the "glory of the fatherhood". Another tractate from the gnostic Coptic library, Zostrianos*, depicts a heavenly journey of Zoroaster through the ether, the seven spheres of the archons, the "place of repentance" (Sophia, corresponding to the Ogdoad) and finally the levels of the aeons of light. But he can enter these only when he has subjected himself to various baptisms which not only make him equal to the various be-

* NHC XIII 1,45,13–20
* NHC XIII 1,48,13–35

* NHC VIII 1

ings of light but admit him into the heavenly mysteries. The baptisms are thus in the nature of an initiation (where progress from one stage to the next is also an advance in spiritual insight).

The eschatological "benefits" mentioned in these utterances are somewhat similar in the gnostic texts. It is primarily a matter of the integration into true being of a constituent element that has been temporarily lost, most frequently employing terminology dealing with light. Other metaphors are often the obtaining of "rest", i. e. the victory over the "unrest" and "strife" of the world, the "bridal chamber" and sacred marriage, interpreted spiritually, between the soul and the redeemer, also understood as the uniting of separate elements or the reclamation of androgynous unity. At the end of the Authoritative Teaching it is said that the "rational soul" who attained to "knowledge about God" labouring with inquiry and enduring distress in the body, "found her rising: she came to rest in the one who is rest; she reclined in the bridal chamber; she ate of the meal for which she had hungered; she partook of the immortal food. She found what she had looked for. She received rest from her labours, while the light that shines over her does not sink ..."* "In return for all the shame and contempt that she received in this world (*kosmos*) she receives ten thousand times the grace and glory."*

The heavenly benefits

* *NHC VI 3,34,32–35,18*

* *NHC VI 3,32,12–15*

It remains to discuss a particularly characteristic concept of Gnosis within the framework of personal eschatology, namely that of "resurrection". As is well known, belief in the "resurrection of the dead" is an unqualified universal eschatological hope, first of Iranian then of Jewish – Christian tradition. But the gnostics very early reshaped it into a personal eschatology, probably in contact with older, perhaps Jewish models, which possessed a spiritualized interpretation of this concept and its association with the redemption of individuals after death. Another point of contact might have been the resurrection of Jesus within the framework of the events of Easter and the Ascension. And reference may be made to the mysterious interpretation of the event of baptism as "death" and "resurrection"* which is also found in Gnosis. At all events Paul already is evidently being confronted* with the gnostic exegesis of the hope of the resurrection and so especially are his disciples, as the Second Epistle to Timothy* proves. Thus there were Chris-

The gnostic belief in resurrection

* *cf. Rom. 6,3f.*

* *cf. I Cor. 15,12*

* *2 Tim. 2,18*

tians who maintained "that the resurrection is past already". This is an obvious allusion to the gnostic understanding of the doctrine of resurrection which interpreted the "release of the soul" through knowledge as an act of "resurrection from the dead" (= those without knowledge). Such an understanding is a necessary deduction from the view of the physical body nurtured by Gnosis; the view advanced by Paul holds for it too: "Flesh and blood cannot inherit the kingdom of God".* For the gnostic any resurrection of the dead was excluded from the outset; the flesh or the substance (*hylē*) is destined to perish. "There is no resurrection of the flesh, but only of the soul", say the so-called Archontics, a late gnostic group in Palestine.* And this "resurrection" of the soul is understood by Gnosis in a two-fold manner: for one thing as a "resuscitation" of the spark of light from "forgetfulness" and "ignorance" (both of which are understood as a figure of death) through the call of the redeemer and through self-knowledge, and secondly as an "ascent" of the spark of light to the pleroma. (Add to this that the Greek word for "resurrection" also means "rising, awakening, re-awakening" as well as "raising, setting up"). Both aspects often merge with one another because the liberating "knowledge" can already signify an anticipation of the end and its realization is already achieved in time.

The Exegesis concerning the Soul expresses this very clearly: The "re-birth" of the soul, represented as the outcome of an association between soul and spirit (= Redeemer), is presupposed but so also is the realization of its redemption: The soul "received the divine nature from the Father for her rejuvenation, so that she might be restored to the place where originally she had been: This is the 'resurrection' from the dead; this is the ransom from captivity; this is the rising up to heaven; this is the way of ascent to the Father."* The Naassenes in a sermon attributed to them* hold a similar view when they designate the unawakened "spiritual man" a corpse "since he is buried in the body as if in a tomb and a sepulchre", and they utilize the following exegesis: "This is what the words 'You are whited sepulchres filled with dead men's bones'* mean, because the living man is not in you; and again it is said: 'The dead shall leap up from the grave'*, that is, from their earthly bodies, being regenerated as 'spiritual men' (pneumatics), not carnal (sarcics). This is the 'resurrection' which comes to pass through the gate

* 1 Cor. 15,50

* Epiphanius, Panarion 40,2,5

* NHC II 6,134,9–15

* Hippolytus, Refutatio V 8,22–24

* Matth. 23,27

* John 5,28f.

of heaven, and those who do not enter by it remain dead." At
the end it is said that by this "resurrection" the gnostic becomes
"God".   *See above, p. 93 f.*

It is on the basis of this "spiritual" understanding of the resurrection that the at first sight paradoxical statements of the Gospel of Philip are to be understood: "Those who say: 'The Lord
(Christ) died first and (then) rose' are wrong. For he rose first
and (then) died. If anyone does not first obtain the resurrec-
tion, he will not die."* And again: "Those who say: 'First one   * *NHC II 3,56 (104),15–19*
will die and (then) rise' are wrong. If men do not first expe-
rience the resurrection while they are alive, they will not re-
ceive anything when they die."* Above all the soul must be   ° *NHC II 3,73 (121),1–4*
awakened from the sleep of death before it can finally be re-
leased after death. In other passages of the "Gospel" resurrection is likened to baptism which effects the "release" into the
bridal chamber.* One can be (in Valentinian fashion) either in   * *NHC II 3,67 (115),*
this world (i. e. remain in ignorance) or in the resurrection (i. e.   *14–18; 69 (117), 24–28*
experience release) or in the "places that are in the middle"
(the intermediate realm of the psychics).* "As long as we are in   * *NHC II 3,66 (114), 7–25*
this world (*kosmos*), it is fitting for us that we acquire the resurrection for ourselves, that when we strip off the flesh we may be
found in (the place of) rest (and) not walk in the middle (the intermediate realm) . . ." Because the latter, it is said, is death.

We have among the Nag Hammadi writings a special Trea-   **The Treatise**
tise (*logos*) on the Resurrection which purports to be a letter   **on the**
from an anonymous author to Rheginus. It contains clear evi-   **Resurrection**
dence of the attempts on the part of the gnostic understanding
of resurrection to grapple with that of the belief of the Christian
community; and also the problems which Gnosis encountered
in dealing with the question – at the outset it is expressly stated
that the question of resurrection occasioned the treatise.[71] The
author starts by noting that "the redeemer (*sotēr*) swallowed up
death . . . for he laid aside the world (*kosmos*) that perishes and
transformed himself into an incorruptible aeon and rose up,
when he had swallowed up the visible by the invisible, and
(thus) he gave us the way of our immortality."* The belief and   * *NHC I 4,45,14–23*
assurance of one's own release and "resurrection" is based on
this: "But if we are manifest in this world (*kosmos*) as people
who bear him (the redeemer) (in themselves), we are his beams
and we are held by him until our (bodily) setting, which is our
death in this life. We are (then) drawn into heaven by him as the

beams by the sun, not being restrained by any thing: this is "spiritual (pneumatic) resurrection" which swallows up the psychic as well as the fleshly (sarcic)."

The author accordingly distinguishes three kinds of 'resurrection' of which the 'spiritual' is the crucial one. It is the one which is peculiar to the "pneumatic" as the actual blessing of salvation and is granted on the basis of his knowledge and predestination: "The thought of those who are saved shall not perish: the mind (*nous*) of those who have known him (the redeemer) shall not perish. Therefore we are (indeed) chosen for salvation and redemption: we were ordained from the beginning not to fall into the folly of those who are without knowledge

* NHC I 4,46,21–29

..."* This is the unequivocal gnostic assurance of redemption which is founded on the fixed "system of the Pleroma" from which only a "small part detached itself and became the

* NHC I 4,46,35–38
* NHC I 4,47,2f.

world",* and finally came back. There ought to be no doubt concerning the resurrection.* For "it is the revelation of those who have (now already) risen ... It is not an illusion (phantasy) but truth! But rather it is fitting to say that the world (*kosmos*)

* NHC I 4,48,4–16

is more an illusion than the resurrection ..."* It "is the truth that is established and the revelation of that which (really) is

* NHC I 4,48,33–35

..."* So the letter-writer challenges his addressee: "Come away from the divisions (in this world) and the fetters and already you have the resurrection";* in this sense he should look

* NHC I 4,49,15f.
* NHC I 4,49,22f.,25f.

upon himself as already risen.*

The author is indeed confronted by the problem of the physical – psychic resurrection and this entices him into a somewhat involved argumentation which really must have run contrary to the gnostic spirit, although it was not entirely unfamiliar; ostensibly it was an accommodation to official Christianity and proved readily instructive for the flexibility of gnostic thought. First: in our text the resurrection is understood on two levels only: one takes place on earth and the other after death, and there is none at the end of the world (instead there is mention

* NHC I 4,44,30–33
See below, p. 194 ff.

only of "the restoration to the Pleroma"*). The resurrection after death which signifies the ascent of the released spirit necessitates the existence of a special bearer, a "body of resurrection" or a kind of "spiritual flesh". The author clearly has this in mind when he writes to his partner: "For if you were (once still) not in the flesh, but (first) received flesh when you came into the world, why should you not (also) receive flesh when you ascend into the aeon? That which (like the aeon) is more excellent than the flesh is for it the cause of life. That which comes into being for your sake (like the body of flesh) is it not yours? Is that which is yours not (of necessity) bound up with you? But while you are in this place (the world) what are you lacking? ... The outer covering (or: afterbirth) of the body is old age, and you are corruption. Absence is therefore for you a gain, for you will not surrender that which is excellent when you depart. That which is bad (the body) is (indeed) diminishing, but it owes thanks (for it). Nothing (earthly) redeems us from this place (the world), but (only) the All which we are (ourselves) – we are already saved, we have received complete salvation."* But to * *NHC I 4,47,4–29* those who have misgivings, who want to know whether "he who is saved, when he quits his body, will be saved at once"* it is re- * *NHC I 4,47,30–36* marked: "Do not let anyone doubt concerning this. In the old fetters (? of the body) the visible members which are dead shall not be saved; but (only) the living mem[bers] which are in them shall arise:"* The outer frame shall certainly disappear at * *NHC I 4,47,36–48,3* death, but the inner spiritual form is preserved when it is re-   *For sequel,* leased from the body, thereby ensuring the continuity and iden-   *see above, p. 192* tity of the redeemed even beyond death. It is in this light that the concept cited above of the "spiritual resurrection swallowing up" the psychic and the fleshly, as well as the redeemer "swallowing up" the visible by the invisible, must be understood. As is attested elsewhere the resurrection has to do with "the transformation of things and a transition into newness." "For incorruption de[scends] upon corruption and the light flows down upon the darkness, swallowing it up, and the Pleroma fills the lack. These are the tokens and images of the resurrection."* * *NHC I 4,48,35–49,7*

This conception of a transformed "spiritual" body is found **The "spiritual"** again in other writings and indicates that Gnosis (above all **resurrection** Christian Gnosis) even in this question was unable to adhere **body** completely to the principle of the abhorrent nature of the body, but produced some contradictory statements. From the Authoritative Teaching we already know the idea that the soul   *See above, p. 187f.* "possesses an invisible spiritual body" which the Archons were unable to perceive.* The Gospel of Philip even speaks of a * *NHC VI 3,32,32* "true flesh" which Christ wore of which ours is only a likeness.* * *NHC II 3,68 (116), 31–37* In a longer exposition of the same treatise it is maintained in opposition to those who fear "lest they rise naked (and) therefore desire to rise in the flesh": "They do not know that those who wear the flesh are naked (and) those who [prepare] themselves to strip are not naked."* In the exposition of a passage in I Corinthians** the flesh which shall not be able to inherit the kingdom of God is equated with what is earthly and human, while that which shall inherit the kingdom is equated with the (sacramental) flesh of Jesus.* The view that the flesh shall not rise is censured. But then what will rise? "You say: 'It is the spirit in the flesh and also this light in the flesh.' (But) this too is a 'word' (*logos*) that is in the flesh, for whatever you will say (on this) you say nothing apart from the flesh. It is (therefore) needful to rise in this flesh as everything is (layed out?) in it." The passage is not easy to understand, but indicates that here too a "spiritual resurrection body" is presupposed which, after discarding the earthly body, "clothes" the ascending spirit in a new way. According to the testimony of the Church Fathers the Valentinian school, from which the Gospel of Philip and the Letter to Rheginos originated, gave a good deal of consideration to the problem of the resurrection and also spoke of a "spiritual body (or flesh)". Epiphanius notes briefly in this connection: "They deny the resurrection of the dead, saying something mysterious and ridiculous, that it is not this body which rises, but another one rises from it, which they call 'spiritual' (pneumatic)"*. Finally it may be mentioned that the Mandeans endeavoured by means of one of their ceremonies for the dead to furnish the soul with a new body, with which it could enter the realm of light.

Universal eschatology   The eschatological ideas of Gnosis are not limited to the "ascent of the soul" and the concomitant problems, but as we have already indicated also include the end of the cosmos. In gnostic studies this is not always appreciated sufficiently. It seems that it was the Nag Hammadi texts which first opened our eyes to this perspective of the gnostic view of history. This interpretation of history is a linear one, as in the Bible, i.e. as far as the cosmos is concerned it operates with an unequivocal beginning and end to a time span dominated by an unrepeatable process leading irresistibly towards a goal. This process is controlled, if one can say so, by the successive restoration of estranged particles of light to the Pleroma, which thereby "makes good" its "deficiency". To this extent world history is *Heilsgeschichte* which is finally accomplished when all the particles of light (at

Margin notes:
* NHC II 3,56 (104), 26–57 (105), 19
* 1 Cor. 15,50

* cf. John 6,53

* Epiphanius, Panarion 31,7,6.7,10

least all those which are able to participate in the liberation) have returned and the condition which prevailed at the beginning – the separation of light and darkness, "divine" and "nondivine", "spirit and body", good and bad, and "above" and "below" – has been re-established. It is a matter of a "process of separation" with its own inner dynamic which eventually comes to a standstill when the alienation of the "spirit" is annulled. Consequently H. Jonas was perfectly justified in his precise formulation: "Gnostic myth is eschatological not only in its content but also in its formal structure."[72] This fundamental tendency of Gnosis towards the *Endzeit* thus includes the fate of the individual soul and that of the totality of "souls" yet to be saved, and this can only be brought about in a final act which affects the cosmos as a whole. Added to this, the idea of purification, either in the form of the souls' journey or of some other punishment of impure souls, also necessitates such a conclusion.

As far as we can tell from the source material at present available Gnosis nowhere envisaged a repetition of the world-cycle – such as for example in Greek or Indian teaching on the succession of world epochs. A cyclic conception of the world process is foreign to it. Of course there are phenomena within the concept of history considered on the macrocosmic level which have a certain cyclic character, as for example in the systems involving three principles or the acceptance of several world ages with a catastrophic outcome for mankind (e. g. the flood). And furthermore, on an individual level, there is the doctrine of the transmigration of souls as a process of purification. But these events constitute no exception to the rule of the gnostic view of time in which the course of history was determined by a linear theory. The circumscribed character of time that is inexorably orientated towards an end remains intact. The termination (or oblivion) which the cosmos meets at the end of time is irreversible and does not allows for a fresh start in the cosmic process: This would indeed signify a renewed alienation of the light.

The most important phases in the eschatological drama are first the deliverance of the remaining purified or "perfected" particles of light, and then the punishment of the powers or their partial rehabilitation (which varies in the different schools of Gnosis); and finally the "confinement" or destruction of

Cyclic and linear concepts of world history

See above, p. 84 f.

See above, p. 134 ff.

nature, which in several gnostic systems is brought about by a universal conflagration and is already introduced by the apocalyptic events at the beginning of the *Endzeit*. In the following selection of descriptions these characteristics confront us in more or less pronounced form. That here contemporary ideas from Jewish-Christian, hellenistic and Iranian traditions are discovered in Gnosis indicates that on this point too it is a child of its time.

The end of the world according to the Valentinians

In Valentinian Gnosis – according to Irenaeus – the end of the world takes place "when all that is 'spiritual' (pneumatic) is shaped and perfected through knowledge (*gnosis*). 'All that is spiritual' are the 'spiritual men' (pneumatics) who possess the perfect knowledge of God and are initiated into the mysteries of Achamoth – they claim that they themselves are these persons."* When the education process of the "spiritual" is completed on earth and in the intermediate realm ("place of the Middle") then the "spirits" are detached from their "souls" and enter the Pleroma together with their mother, Achamoth, as "pure spirits" and "will be bestowed as brides on the angels around the Saviour". The Demiurge along with the souls of the righteous passes into the place of the Middle where they find repose "for nothing psychic enters the Pleroma". "When this has taken place then the fire that is hidden in the world will blaze forth and burn: when it has consumed all matter it will be consumed with it and pass into nonexistence."* The so-called Tripartite Tractate* has by and large confirmed these statements.

* *Irenaeus, Adv.haer. I 6,1*

* *op. cit. I 7,1*
* *NHC I 5, esp. 126–240*

The Apocatastasis

For the assembly of the particles of light at the *Endzeit* and the dissolution of the world the gnostics variously utilized the concept of the "bringing back (of all things)" or *Apocatastasis* (properly "restoration"), which originated in the hellenistic (primarily Stoic) and Jewish-Christian teaching about the *Endzeit* and which had an explicitly cosmological character. In Gnosis it is related purely to the spiritual world: to the "restoration of the Pleroma".* The gnostic Heracleon** interprets John 4.36 with this in mind in his commentary on John's Gospel and so too does Marcus the Magician, likewise a descendant of the Valentinian school, use it.* A related concept is that of the

* *NHC I 4,44,30–33; NHC I 5,123,21f.*

** *Heracleon Fragment 34*

* *Irenaeus, Adv.haer. I 14,1*

Manichean book illustration (miniature) from Turkestan (Chotsko, Turfan oasis). Recitation with musical accompaniment.

"collection of members (= souls)" without which the Pleroma   *See also above,*
or its representative, the Redeemer, is not fully redeemed.*   *p. 121f.*
The Ophites believed, according to Irenaeus, that the "con-   • *Acts of John 100*
summation" shall come "when the whole trace of the spirit of
light is gathered together and taken up into the aeon of imperishability."* For the "Pistis Sophia" the "consummation of the   • *Irenaeus,*
Aeon" or "dissolution of the All" is identical with the "collec-   *Adv. haer. I 30, 14*
tive ascent of the number of perfected souls of the inheritance
of light."* The formulation repeatedly used by the Mandeans   • *Pistis Sophia,*
for this proceeding is a striking one: *ch. 86, 126, 31–34*

"On the day when the light rises up
   the darkness will return to its place."

Extensive universal portrayals of the *Endzeit* are seldom en-   **Apocalyptic**
countered in the gnostic texts (apart from the Manichean); at   **conceptions**
present some of the Nag Hammadi writings provide the most
detailed descriptions. We do however find eschatological descriptions or motifs in other connections than that dealing with
the end of the world; one example is that of the "ascent of the
soul" which is certainly an eschatological event, another is the
appearance (epiphany) of the Redeemer, although here it is a
question of final world catastrophe. Speaking in graphic terms,
the vertical penetration by the world of light, in the form of its
messenger, into the horizontal level of the cosmic course of history for the benefit of the particles of light anticipates the *Endzeit* and proclaims that the process is irrevocable. The Mandean
texts are particularly helpful here as the following example tak-
en from one of the daily prayers shows. It describes the power
of the saving call:[73]

"At my voice the earth trembled,
   at my radiance the heavens tottered.
   The seas completely dry up,
   and streams fall into the wastes.
   The fortresses (evil powers or potentates) are destroyed,
   and the strong men (or potentates) of the earth (Tibil) are
      tormented.

   The mountains, however high,
   will crumble like bridges.

As for the wicked who revolt against me,
there is a man who will torment them.
Not by my strength,

* *Mandean Liturgies 205 f.*   but by the strength of the Mighty Life."*

Similarly the "time of the consummation" was not only announced to the archons by the "call" of the "Trimorphic First
Thought (*protennoia*)" in the tractate of that name, but it was
already initiated: the travails of the *Endzeit* in wholly apocalyptic fashion have already come into operation:[74] "When [the
gre]at powers realized that the time of consummation had appeared – just as the pangs of a woman giving birth make themselves (suddenly) felt, so also the destruction approached – all
the elements began to tremble, and the foundations of the underworld and the ceilings of chaos shook. A great fire burst
forth from their midst and the rocks and the plain were shaken
like a reed shaken by the wind. And the lots of fateful power
(*heimarmenē*) and those who apportion the (heavenly) dwell-
ings were profoundly disturbed over a mighty thunder. And the
thrones of the powers were shaken and overthrown; and their

* *NHC XIII 1,43,4–17*   king was afraid ..."* The custodians of the Heimarmenē and
the powers are perplexed over these events which are occa-
sioned "by the call of a sublime voice", and they ask the Demiurge (*archigenetor*) but he is unable to give them any information. Thereupon they resolve, lamenting and sorrowing, first to
continue the circuit of the fate-determining spheres until they
meet their end in the "bosom of the underworld". "For already
the slackening of our fetters has arrived and our time has been
fulfilled, and the weeping over our destruction has come near

* *op. cit. 44,14–18*   ..."*

Another Nag Hammadi text, the Concept (*noēma*) of our
Great Power, contains a not entirely lucid and evidently fragmentary view of history which takes account of a sequence of
ages (aeons) which are eventually terminated by a catastrophic
judgement: the "fleshly aeon" by the Flood, the "psychic
aeon" by a universal conflagration in which only the souls of the
gnostics are saved (the "spiritual aeon" which ought now to
begin is not dealt with in the treatise).[75] Here too the signs of
the *Endzeit*, crammed with contemporary historical allusions
(*inter alia* the so-called Jewish War, 66–73 A.D.) and other
apocalyptic themes (Antichrist, apostasy etc.), begin before

the time and reach their climax in the end of the world. This again begins with natural catastrophes (the drying up of heaven and earth, the exhausting of springs and rivers, the laying bare of the abyss, transformations in the realm of stars). Then follows the salvation of pure souls by the redeemer (Christ) before the universal conflagration begins, "to destroy everything". The impure souls are punished until they are purified and their "imprisonment" at an end. "When the fire has consumed them all and finds nothing else to burn then it will die out by its own hand ... Then the firmaments [will plunge down] into the depth (or underworld). Then [the] sons of matter will perish and will henceforth cease to exist. Then will the souls be manifest who are pure through the light of the Power, who is exalted above all powers ... And they will be in the aeon of beauty [i. e.] the aeon of the bridal chamber adorned with 'wisdom' (*sophia*), having praised him who is in the unique incomprehensible unity and having (also) seen him because of his love which is in them. And they became reflections in his light (and) all began to shine. They found rest in his rest."* The exact opposite is the fate of the souls who remain impure: They will be punished in the place of purification and can only gaze at the "holy ones"; from the fire (?) and the "[prod]igious pit" they plead for mercy, but all in vain, because they are corrupted by their adherence to the "creations of the archons". *NHC VI 4,45,29–47,26*

A very complete picture of the *Endzeit* which includes some of its most significant features is found at the end of the anonymous treatise which we mentioned in the section on anthropogony. The "perfect ones" or gnostics make their appearance at the judgement of the "gods of chaos and their powers" while the latter are unmasked as sham rulers; thus they have already forfeited their power and lost their dominion.* The consequences at the end are inexorable: "Before the en[d of the ae]on the whole place will be shaken by [a mig]hty thunde[r]. Then the archons will lament cry[ing out on account of] th[eir] death, the angels will mourn for their men, the demons will weep for their times, their men will lament and cry out on account of their death. Then the aeon will begin to stagger, its kings will be drunk from the flaming sword and they will make war against one another, so that the earth will be drunk from the blood which is shed, and the seas will be agitated by that war. Then the sun will be darkened, the moon will lose its light and the

See above, p. 92

NHC II 5,125 (173), 7–32

stars of heaven will abandon their course. And a mighty thunder will come forth from a great power above the heavens of all the powers of chaos, where the firmament of the woman is situated. When she has created the first work she will lay aside the wise fire of insight and put on senseless wrath. Then she will pursue the gods of chaos whom she created together with the Archigenetor and cast them into the abyss: they will be blotted out by their (own) injustice. They will become like the volcanoes and will devour one another until they are destroyed by their Archigenetor. When he has destroyed them he will turn against himself and destroy himself until he is destroyed. And their heavens will dash against one another and their powers will burn and their aeons will be devastated. And his hea[ven] will cave in and be shattered. His worl[d], h[owever], will fall down to the earth [but the earth will not] be able to bear them (all); (thus) they will r[ush dow]n to the abyss a[n]d the [abys]s will be destroyed. The light will [be separated from the dark]-ness and it will wipe it out and it will be as though it had not come into being. And the work which the darkness followed will be broken up and the deficiency will be rooted out (and hurled) down into the darkness. And the light will return up to its root. And the glory of the unbegotten will make an appearance, and will fill all the aeons, when the prophetic utterance and the report concerning those who are kings have been ratified and have been fulfilled by those who are called perfect. But those who were not perfected in the unbegotten Father will receive their glories in their aeons and in the immortal kingdoms, but they will never enter into the kingless realm. Because it is necessary that everyone goes to the place from whence he came. Because each one by his deed and his knowledge will disclose his nature."*[76]

° *NHC II 5,125 (173), 32–127 (175), 17*

The destruction of darkness   The end of the cosmos does not simply signal the separation of two basically opposing principles but results in the destruction of one of them. The primeval state is thereby restored, for inasmuch as the tractate cited describes chaos as a "work" which had its origin in the "shadow" of the curtain between the inside and outside of the realm of light it was something which was created and could also be destroyed. That this does not resolve all the problems is quite understandable, because the gnostic reflections on primeval origins are shot through with doubts about the concept of "nothingness": one is always left with "something", whether it be "chaos" or "the root" (= principle). The main tendency in gnostic eschatological thought is directed towards the view that the process of world evolution is finished once and for all. It also involves the complete elimination of the presuppositions which led to the origin of the unhappy cosmos. The impression is given that the situation at the end of time is not merely a bare restoration of the primeval condition but that it surpasses it by the constantly repeated affirmation of the "destruction", "dissolution" and "tearing-out" of the "root of darkness".

The utterances of the Paraphrase of Shem are quite clear in this respect since they hold out the prospect of a radical "destruction of Nature (*physis*)":[77]

"And in the last day the forms of nature (*physis*) and the winds and all their demons will be eliminated. They will become a dark lump, just as they were in the beginning. And the sweet waters which were oppressed by the demons will be dried up ... The other works of nature will no (more) make an appearance; they will mix with the infinite waters of darkness and all their forms will cease to exist in the middle region (between light and chaos)."* The concept of the "lump", which nature becomes, was known hitherto only from the Manichaeans, where the residue of the material world (stripped of the particles of light) together with the demons and the souls damned eternally, vanishes into a "lump" (Gk. *bolos*, Lat. *globus*) or "pit" which is then sealed up, to be rendered for ever harmless. Our text certainly follows the same idea. In it "nature", destined for destruction, is devoid of all spiritual elements: "When the consummation comes and nature is destroyed then their minds will be separated from the darkness. Nature has oppressed them for a short period. And they (the minds = particles of light) will be in the ineffable light of the unbegotten spirit where they will not possess a form (any more)."*

The deliverance of the very last particles of light present in the world is represented frequently by an act of "cauterizing" and demonstrates the positive aspect of the universal conflagration. This idea which is primarily an Iranian one originates in the old legal concept of the ordeal which is found already in the inventory of final events in Zarathustra (men must cross a molten stream of metal which served as a means of purification). The Manicheans counted on a burning of this sort lasting

NHC VII 1,45,14–31

See below, p. 339

NHC VII 1,48,19–28

The purification of the particles of light

almost 1500 years which would not only consume the material world but would liberate the divine elements which were yet to be saved; whatever part of God himself "cannot be purifed will be chained by an eternal penal chain when the end of the world comes."* The Pistis Sophia assigns the function of dissolving the "Mixture" to Jesus; he will give the order "that they bring all tyrant gods who have not given up what is purified of their light, and will give commandment to the wise fire, over which the perfect pass, to eat into those tyrants until they give up the last purification of their light."*

Augustine, Epistulae 236,2

Pistis Sophia, ch. 45; 48,33–49,4

In contrast to other sources a complete "restoration" appears to be envisaged here. The Mandeans who take account of a "second death" of sinful souls sentenced at the last judgement have in mind at the same time a restitution of the fallen Demiurge (Ptahil) and other beings of light (among others the one who weighs souls in the scales); they are judged but are then taken out of this world by "radiant Hibil (Abel)" and baptized in the Jordan to gain entry into the World of Light:*[78]

The restitution of the Demiurge

Right Ginza XV 3

> "When the world passes away
> and the firmament of the angels is rolled up,
> when the ⟨firmament⟩ of the angels is rolled up,
> and sun and moon are no more,
> when the sun and moon are no more
> and [radiance and] brightness are taken from them,
> when radiance and brightness are taken from them,
> and guardians are given charge of them and the stars shine
>   no more,
> when these works are destroyed,
> then Ptahil's garment will be ready for him.
> A garment will be ready for Ptahil,
> and he will be baptized here in the Jordan."*

Left Ginza II 4

Community, cult and social practice (Ethics)

Gnosis is not simply a body of teaching but may also be understood as designating a special community of people with certain behaviour patterns. This aspect is more or less familiar to the heresiologists through the number of "sects" whose names they determined in accordance with characteristic features, or after founding members etc. (cf. the citation from Clement of Alexandria), or which even go back to the self-designations of the sects themselves (which, in some cases, is not always demonstrable). "All these", writes Hippolytus, "prefer to be called 'the knowing (ones)' (gnostics) for they alone have stumbled onto the wondrous 'knowledge' (*gnosis*) of the perfect and good."* This pronouncement which is certainly to the point was naturally taken by the Church Fathers to highlight the absurd. Epiphanius more than anyone took pleasure in exaggerating the number and lack of unity of the gnostic groups and in inventing additional names. Thus be says in one passage of his "Medicine-chest" that the leaders "of Gnosis falsely so-called have begun their evil growth upon the world, namely the so-called gnostics and Phibionites and the followers of Epiphanes, and the Stratiotici and Levitici and Borborians and the rest. For each of these (leaders) has contrived his own sect to suit his own passions and has devised thousands (!) of ways of evil."* He also maintains that the same sects bear different names, like the "Borborians", whom others call "Coddians", or the people who are called Stratioci and Phibionites in Egypt while others call them "Zacchaeans" or "Babelites". Little confidence can be vouchsafed to such statements of the Church Fathers; it is important to look to the gnostic texts themselves. Thanks to the Nag Hammadi material this is now a more fruitful exercise than was possible earlier.

Strikingly, one scarcely ever comes across the designations used by the Church Fathers. In one of the new texts* a (very damaged) catalogue of heresies is preserved which, from the standpoint of a Christian-gnostic "orthodoxy", criticizes the teachings of Valentinus and his disciples who are also called "Valentinians", Basilides and his "pupils" and the "Simonians".[79] It is indeed a strongly polemical tractate. On the other hand, most of the Coptic gnostic sources have quite different names for their communities which are not attached to historical founders of schools but are acquired from the theological contents of their teachings and lend expression to their self-understanding. Such expressions are well-known self-designations, like "chosen", "children (or sons) of the Light", (who stand over against the "children of darkness" of this world),

The gnostics in the heresiologists

See above, p. 17

* *Hippolytus, Refutatio V 23,3*

See above, p. 18ff.

* *Epiphanius, Panarion 25,2,1*

Evidence from the gnostic texts

* *NHC IX 3*

"spiritual ones" or "those who possess the spirit" (pneumatics), "watchful", "perfect", "truthful", "holy", "alien" and "free" (with regard to this world). In addition there are circumlocutions which enhance the character of the "constant generation" (or "seed" of the world of light) which has existed since time began. For the gnostics conceived themselves as a kind of "primordial generation" who, since the origin of the earthly material world, represented the élite of mankind. Correspondingly they see in Adam and Eve their first representatives, and in particular Seth the son of Adam was deeply revered as their ancestor by a large group who called themselves after him the "children" or "generation" of Seth, a name which corresponds to that of the "Sethians" of the Church Fathers and which is the only one of this kind that can be attested in the sources up to the present moment. Similarly there are also references to the See above, p.139 "generation of Shem" or the "good seed" of the Sodomites. With this background tradition and "other-worldly" parentage the gnostics saw themselves as "children of the unbegotten father", as "children of God" (the "unknown God" is the one referred to) or "the ones belonging to him", as the "generation of perfect eternal men of light", "having their origin in an unchanging aeon"; they are the "unwavering", the "true", the "cultivated, perfect, homogeneous generation" (thus the tradition passed on by the so-called Peratae). This concept of community finds expression in the salutations exchanged between "brother" and "sister", expressions used also in allusions to the redeemer or messengers of light and indeed associated with the idea of a great family which shares the same origin (the "har- See below, p.266f. mony of souls" is understood quite literally). A title repeatedly used, the "generation which knows no tyranny" or the "kingless generation", exhibits a special kind of social awareness and * NHC II 5,124 (172), 21–125 (173), 14 functions as the highest rank in gnostic society*. In this way the gnostics believed themselves to be the only ones who belonged to the highest God, and not dependent on any earthly or supramundane power.

The Christian gnostics   The Christian gnostics considered themselves to be Christians and not "pagans" and by using the appellation severely vexed their ecclesiastical rivals (the Valentinians, for example, were the "disciples of Christ", a term seldom used in their time). The shrewd opponent of Christianity, Celsus (2. Cent.) made no distinction between the two. It is no wonder therefore that the concept of the "church" (*ekklesia*) was adopted by **The idea of the** Gnosis and was made use of in their self-understanding: the **church** "church" is the society of the "elect", the pneumatics, the seed of light. The "blessed ones", i. e. the messengers of light, "appeared distinctively, and each one of them proclaimed from their earth (of light) their knowledge (*gnosis*) of the 'church' which appeared in the moulded bodies of corruption. It was found to have every seed (of light) because of the seed of the powers which was mixed [with it] ..."* The concept of the * *NHC II 5,124 (172),* church played a significant role in the Valentinian school in par- *25–32* ticular. An actual pair of aeons bearing the names of "Man" (*anthropos*) and "Church" (*ekklesia*) were produced from the union of "Word" (*logos*) and "Life" (*zoë*). This aeon is the "church above", the pre-existent image of the earthly community and identical with the seed of light.* Thus the "Church" is li- * *Irenaeus,* mited to the "spirits" which existed already with the primeval *Adv. haer. I 1,1.5,6* Father before the creation and are reborn in the pneumatics. For the Valentinians the "spirit", i. e. the immortal seed of light, is by this token "poured out upon all in the Church (below); therefore the signs of the spirit – healings and prophesyings – are accomplished through the Church."* The Tripartite * *Clem. Alex.,* Tractate describes the pre-existence of the Church in the fol- *Ex Theodoto 24,1* lowing way:[80] "Not only does the son exist from the beginning but the Church also exists from the beginning. Now whoever thinks when he ascertains that the son is an only son he contradicts the word – because of the mystery (*mysterion*) of the matter it is not so ... (as the Father notwithstanding his son is a unity and remains so for himself alone, so too the son in regard to the Church and the Church in regard to the "many men" which exist in it) ... it (the Church) exists before the aeons and is properly called 'the aeons of the aeons'; such is the nature (*physis*) of the imperishable holy spirits (*pneuma*), upon which the son rests since his essence is like that of the Father who rests upon the son ... The Church exists in (or through) the laws and the virtues in which the Father and son exist ..."* * *NHC I 5,57,34–59,5*

Unfortunately very little is known about the form and com- **The** position of the "earthly" society. The heresiologists expatiate **composition** garrulously on the teachings but their statements on the inner **of the** life of the gnostic communities are woefully inadequate. Cer- **community** tainly that life, for different reasons, was largely inaccessible because the gnostics practised a more or less rigid code of secrecy (the so-called arcane discipline). Moreover the original sources, including the Nag Hammadi texts, have revealed nothing dramatically new on this aspect, apart from insights into the piety and cultic practice of the gnostic communities and what they thought of themselves. Consequently we can only surmise about the social structure and composition of the common rule. A "sociology of Gnosis" is therefore at the moment still only in its infancy. We can only look into a few characteristic features here.

The social context In the preface to his work Adversus Haereses Irenaeus speaks of the "inexperienced ones" (*inexpertiores*) who fell victim to the "pretexts" of the gnostic missionaries. According to this it was only the "uneducated" or "semi-educated", as the word may also be understood, who made up the majority of the gnostic communities, a picture which is not entirely accurate but which at any rate points in the right direction, namely that there was a polarization in the structure of the community: in contrast to the really "knowledgeable ones" and the leaders is a relatively uneducated and uninitiated community. Expressed in gnostic terminology one can also speak of "pneumatics" or "perfect ones" and of "psychics". This double structure appears very clearly in Manicheism where the "chosen ones" are

See below, p. 340 f. strictly distinguished from the "hearers" or "catechumens". The esoteric tendency in the gnostic concept of redemption is also worked out inside the chosen community. The Book of Thomas makes a distinction, apart from "blind men" in general,

* *NHC II 7,138,35*
** *NHC II 7,139,11*
* *NHC II, 7,139,12;*
140,10 f.
** *NHC II 7,139,28* al, between two groups which evidently form one community: the "beginners"* or "small ones"** and the "perfect ones"* or "chosen ones"**. This corresponds to the threefold division of

See above, p. 91 f. mankind used elsewhere. When Tertullian mockingly observes with regard to the heretics "the catechumens are 'perfect' (*per-*

* *Tertullian, Praescr., ch. 41* *fecti*) before they have received full instruction"* this represents the viewpoint of the fossilized hierarchical mother church rather than that of the gnostic conception of the community which was differently constituted. Allowance was made for example, for participation by "laity" and "women" (Tertullian waxes wroth about this too), on the basis of their "gifts of grace" (charismas) and both were permitted to take leading positions. In 1881 G. Koffmane had attempted to correct the older viewpoint,[81] that "the gnostics were proud spiritual aristocrats and like philosophers they would have been interested only in

sharing their lofty wisdom with a few experts; as with the Pythagoreans such schools would also have admitted religious practices and rites. The opponents of heresy teach us something different; they report that not only men with spiritual capital but
also those of sufficiently low standing may be 'led astray'". He
then draws his conclusion: "One can do justice to Gnosis only if
one understands it primarily as a religious community".

The social class to which the individual member belonged is
open to conjecture. The "elite", particularly the founders of
the sects and authors of texts, certainly belonged to a level familiar with hellenistic and Jewish culture. To use modern
terms, to all appearances they were rootless intellectuals with
no political influence, who had a more or less philosophical
and,- above all, mythological culture, which won adherents
from the plebeian classes. We have yet to see that they probably adopted as a starting point the position of the Jewish wisdom teachers, who formed a kind of "scribal" or "lay-intellec-
tualism" (M. Weber). Tertullian spitefully observes of the he-   *See below, p. 292f.*
retics that "they hold intercourse with magicians, charlatans,
astrologers and philosophers and the reason is that they are
men who devote themselves to curious questions (*curiosita-
ti*)."* Such a portrayal certainly belongs to the fixed inventory   *Tertullian, Praescr., ch. 43*
of the heresiologists and one can find similar expressions in al-
most all the well-known opponents of heresy, but it is not whol-
ly without foundation. Already one of the first founders of a   *See above, p. 9f.*
gnostic school was given the epithet "magician" (Simon Ma-
gus), and one of the disciples of Valentinus, Marcus, evidently   *See below, p. 294f.*
gave greater scope to magical practice and numerical specula-
tion than was usual in Gnosis. The gnostics are not an unusual
phenomenon in this respect but are firmly rooted in the contemporary scene in which the practice of sorcery, astrology and
numerical speculation – in addition to philosophical eclecticism
– was not a rarity even in the highest circles. Repeatedly in the
Nag Hammadi texts one finds passages which belong to these
categories. In addition to this the magical literature of late antiquity affords a rich supplement of related material, be it in the
existence of demons and nomenclature held in common or in
similar mythological traditions (e. g. the "release of Adam from
the coercion of fate [*anankē*]"). Irenaeus affirms that in the
Simonian school not only the "mystery priests" but also each
member "performed sorceries (magic)". "They practise exor-

cisms·and incantations, love potions and erotic magic; familiar spirits and dream-inducers, and whatever other occult things exist, are zealously cultivated among them."*

* Irenaeus,
Adv. haer. I 23,4

Founders of the sects   On the other hand the great personalities like Valentinus, Basilides or even Mani proffer another picture. They represent the elite in Gnosis, were known by the Church Fathers and waged grievous battle with them. Tertullian who in general is hostile to much reflection and meditation notes with disapproval, as we saw above, the traffic with philosophers and those who pander to (intellectual) "curiosity" (*curiositas*), a testimony to the standing of the great gnostics in the world in which they lived. Gnostic teachers in Alexandria, the stronghold of Greek culture, like Basilides and Valentinus represent a high level of erudition (the same goes for their close disciples); they are without doubt the peers of Origen and Clement who operated in the same place and in many respects they surpass their petty orthodox opponents like Irenaeus and Hippolytus. Deserving mention in this connection is the remaining gnostic literature which unfortunately is largely anonymous but does maintain a relatively high standard to judge by comparisons with contemporary pagan and Christian (i. e. orthodox church) literature. The same goes for the activity in translation which played a leading role in Gnosis and encouraged its proliferation. It involved translation from Aramaic and Syriac into Greek, from Greek or from Syriac directly into Coptic. This evidently required whole schools of translators such as we must presuppose for Coptic material in Upper Egypt (around Asyut). The Upper Egyptian dialect into which these gnostic and Manichean texts were transmitted was at the same time elevated to the level of a literary language and sociologically may even be regarded as the "heretical dialect" of Coptic. The effectiveness of Manichean literary activity is even more evident, with translations into Iranian, Chinese and Turkish. The Mandeans likewise had their own special language and script, peculiar to this gnostic community.

The social origin of the communities   These facts prevent us from seeing in the gnostic communities merely insignificant conventicles of people "semi-educated" and "led astray", as church tradition would have us believe, although in actual fact the seriousness of the polemic against them gives the lie to this assessment. Unfortunately we do not have a clear picture of the social structure of the communities.

In general they are not very different from the other Christian communities and in many respects they are very close to them indeed. Thus recruits were obtained from every level of society: some of the leading thinkers probably from the higher circles, but the majority of adherents from the middle and lower classes (particularly skilled artisans and merchants). Actually the only person of whose profession we have some knowledge is Marcion (first half of the 2nd C.), the radical disciple of Paul who stands very close to Gnosis and who like his father is said to have been a "shipowner". The "Syrian philosopher" Bardaisan (Bardesanes, 154–222) who likewise had gnostic sympathies was a teacher and lived at the court of an eastern petty prince. Finally Mani the great gnostic, according to tradition, was even related to the Arsacid royal family; he also resided for a time at court and later in that of the Sassanians. We have no information about the other founders of sects. Of the Valentinian sect leader Marcus it is said that he was "devoted" to women, "especially those of high rank, clothed in purple and wealthy", not only to win them but also to lead them into prophesying. In another instance Eusebius* discourses on an erstwhile Valentinian called Ambrose who was sufficiently well-to-do to defray the expenses of his teacher Origen by obtaining the services of amanuenses and copyists – affording a valuable clue to the financing of gnostic literary publications. To the best of my knowledge membership of slaves is not attested, although it is quite probable that it did take place as in the case of the mother church. Certain social features attested by some writers, the "rich" and the "poor", "free men" and "slaves", "rulers" and "people", taken as distinctions which pertain to the corruptible earth, allow us to suppose that groups of the exploited and suppressed classes are here speaking for themselves.

Eusebius, HE VI 23,1f.

See further below, p. 264 f.

The position of women

The percentage of women was evidently very high and reveals that Gnosis held out prospects otherwise barred to them, especially in the official church. They frequently occupied leading positions either as teachers, prophetesses, missionaries or played a leading role in cultic ceremonies (baptism, eucharist) and magical practices (exorcisms). One example is that of Marcellina who circa 150 propagated the doctrines of the gnostic Carpocrates in Rome.* The important disciple of Valentinus, Ptolemaeus, wrote a detailed letter, still extant, to an educated lady whom he calls "sister Flora" on questions dealing with the

* *Irenaeus, Adv. haer. I 26,6*

See below, p. 259

Tomb inscription of Flavia Sophe. Rome, 3rd cent.

See illustration

interpretation of the Mosaic law. Also preserved is the tomb inscription of a gnostic woman called Flavia Sophē:

> "You, who did yearn for the paternal light,
> Sister, spouse, my Sophē,
> Anointed in the baths of Christ with everlasting, holy oil,
> Hasten to gaze at the divine features of the aeons,
> The great Angel of the great council (i. e. the Redeemer),
> The true Son;
> You entered the bridal chamber and deathless ascended
> To the bosom of the Father."[82]

In the apocryphal Acts of the Apostles which emanate mostly from gnostic circles women frequently play a large role. Presumably the prominent position of Sophia and other female beings in the gnostic systems is also connected with this. Consequently sex is not the determining factor although, as we shall See below, p. 270 ff. see, ideologically women are not granted equal rights. The heresiologists naturally took offence at the special status of women in the gnostic communities and either subjected them For examples see below, p. 249 ff., 256 ff., 270 ff. to ridicule or made them the object of smutty remarks. Relations with women were usually treated under the subject of "temptation" (also in the sexual sense) and their participation in the ceremonies represented accordingly.

Likewise we have only a sketchy knowledge of the organization of the gnostic communities. Naturally it does not have any centralized administration, and to that extent there is no gnostic "church". At the centre stands the community of individual aims or "schools". At its head stand first the founders, to some of whom charismatic or prophetic qualities were ascribed and who were regarded as the counterparts of the "divine men" (*theios anēr*) of antiquity. Lucian (120–180 A.D.) evidently describes such a sect leader with mocking disdain in his burlesque "The Death of Peregrine".* This figure who was happy to call himself Proteus "became closely acquainted with the peculiar wisdom of the Christians when he saw a good deal of their priests and scribes in Palestine. And, incredible as it may sound, within a short while he convinced them of his superiority; he was prophet, elder (*thiasiarch*), ruler of the synagogue and everything in one person. He expounded their books, commented on them, and wrote books himself; in short they took him for a divine being (literally: God), made him their law-giver and declared him their leader (*prostatēs*)." A similar picture emerges from the reports about Marcus (mentioned above), community leader, prophet and magician or priest all in one person. His disciples also, in thoroughly gnostic fashion, claimed perfection and the highest knowledge, far beyond that of the Church's apostles. "They claim that they have more knowledge than all others, and that they alone have attained the greatness of the knowledge of the ineffable power."* When the founder or leader died leadership evidently passed to disciples, a process which often led to divisions in the originally unified community, as we can see very clearly in the school of Valentinus which split into several branches (two in particular). To judge by the number of the communities or schools which are reflected in the sundry items of literature, this must frequently have been the case. A certain independence of thought in confronting the many open problems of gnostic teaching may have played a significant part. This would also include the lack of a rigid discipline and standardized instruction (or teaching office), as we have already pointed out. One might also describe this as tolerance, matching the character of the communities, which were generally not exclusive. Reciprocal charges of heresy are encountered only rarely.[83]

The office of "leader" (*prostatēs*) seems to have been the most important. It emerges in various sources of the Church Fathers. Hippolytus testifies to it among the Sethians and the

Community organisation

* *Lucian, Peregrinus, ch. 11*

* *Irenaeus, Adv. haer. I 13,6*

See below, p. 323

See above, p. 53

The community leader

* Hippolytus,
Refutatio V 6,3; V 20,1
** Origen, C. Celsum V 63
* Hippolytus
Refutatio V 6,3;
Irenaeus, Adv. haer. I 23,4
** Irenaeus,
Adv. haer. I 21,2
*** Hippolytus,
Refutatio VI 41

Naassenes.* Celsus confirms that "some have (found as their leader) one teacher and daemon, and others another ..."** Other titles are "priests",* "mystagogues",** "bishops"*** (of the followers of Marcus), "prophets" or "prophetesses", "teachers". As we have said, we are denied details (apart from the Manicheans and the Mandeans). Any hierarchical structure of office was largely foreign to the gnostics, and indeed repugnant, since they tended rather towards a charismatic understanding of the Church. In regard to the economic or financial basis also we have little information. Only in connection with the followers of Marcus do we hear that Marcus himself took charge of financial matters and that expenses were defrayed by donations from wealthy members.*

See below, p. 216 f.

* Irenaeus,
Adv. haer. I 13,3

Cultic associations   Viewed in general terms one gains the impression that a comparison might best be drawn between the gnostic communities and the religious societies or "cult associations" (*thiasoi*) which joined together for the worship of some deity. This term is found repeatedly in the sources and is probably appropriate also for the outward form of their relationship to the organs of the state. These associations were so to speak corporations with public rights; they were in charge of their own internal affairs, appointed their own functionaries, cultivated their own festivals and forms of worship. Membership was open to everyone and carried no danger with it. The names of officials mentioned above fit this picture completely. Add to this that we know of initiation rites and "sacraments" from various gnostic communities, which make them like those of the mystery religions. The code of secrecy with respect to certain teachings and procedures engendered in these "mysteries" was just as characteristic of Gnosis as different stages of knowledge and insight into the "secrets" (pneumatics or perfect, psychics), which in some cases were even associated with special ceremonies. As in the mystery religions the gnostic communities were also acquainted with their own secret distinguishing signs. Of the followers of Carpocrates it is reported that they had "branding marks" on the back of the right ear-lobe,* and according to Epiphanius the (Barbeliote) gnostics, by way of greeting, made a tickling stroke on the palm of the hand.*

* Irenaeus,
Adv. haer. I 26,6

* Epiphanius,
Panarion 26,4,2

The majority of gnostic communities probably corresponded to this picture of a kind of mystery religion or "secret cult"; particularly apposite examples are furnished by the Naassenes, the

Ophites, the Barbeliote gnostics and the followers of Marcus. **Mystery**
On the other hand other communities evidently had more the **societies or**
character of philosophical schools, the best example here being **philosophical**
the Alexandrian schools of Basilides and Valentinus in which **schools**
the teacher-disciple relationship was a telling factor. But they
too soon took on the characteristics of a "cult association" as is
shown not least by that Valentinian offshoot the Marcosians.
Consequently different forms could overlap. Here the influence of the "ecclesiastical" organisation is not to be underesti-
mated, although it was not that of the hierarchical mother
church but of the individual community, the efforts of the gnostic missionaries being directed as has been shown at infiltrating
the Christian communities. The concept "church", even if it is **"Church"**
exclusively applied to the "perfect ones", was by no means foreign to Gnosis. "Bishops", too, are attested. The most familiar
examples are the opposition church of Marcion and the establishment in the third century of the Manichean "church". But
these are exceptions; they only prove the rule that in origin
Gnosis did not have a tightly-knit community system with a
hierarchical administration, nor could it do so as long as it proclaimed salvation solely through knowledge. A distinction between "priests" and "laity" is untenable for them, for the community believed that the blessing of salvation was anchored in a
personal and "spiritual" (pneumatic) experience and strictly
speaking encompassed only the "perfect ones", who felt that
they belonged to a non-worldly communion. That the outer
form included also a few advanced students who made more or
less use of cultic or sacramental and magical resources can be
understood as adaptation to the environment; probably also
economical factors and self-preservation have also to be taken
into account.

Tertullian has drawn a picture of the disorderly condition of **The absence of**
the gnostic (Valentinian?) communities ("without authority **discipline**
and ecclesiastical discipline") which, though no doubt over-
charged with polemic, is very instructive, especially because of
the role of women which it attests: "In the first place one does
not known who is a catechumen, who is a believer, they meet
with one another (in the house of assembly), listen to one
another and pray with one another. Even if pagans approach
them they throw that which is holy to dogs, and pearls, though
they be false, before swine. They wish the abandonment of

discipline (*disciplina*) to be taken for simplicity, and our concern for it they call pandering. They maintain (ecclesiastical)
harmony with all making no distinction. As a matter of fact it
exists among them although they hold different doctrines as
long as they wage common warfare against one thing, truth
(i.e. orthodoxy). They are all puffed up, all promise 'knowledge'. Their catechumens are already 'perfected' (*perfecti*)
before they are taught. Even the heretical women – how bare-
faced they are! They make bold to teach, to dispute, to perform
exorcisms, to promise cures, perhaps also to baptize. Their or-
dinations are carelessly administered, capricious and inconsistent. Sometimes they assign position to novices (neophytes), at
another worldly men, at another recreants (apostates), that
they may bind them to themselves for the sake of reputation,
since they cannot by truth. Nowhere is there easier advance-
ment than in the camp of the rebels, where even to be there is a
merit. In this way one man is bishop today, another tomorrow,
today one is deacon, who tomorrow will be reader, today a priest (presbyter), who tomorrow will be a layman. For even to

* *Tertullian,*   laymen they commit priestly duties."*
Praescr., ch. 41
This assessment of Tertullian's is now confirmed by some of
* *cf. NHC I 3,6; VII 3;*   the Nag Hammadi texts,* which engage directly or indirectly in
VIII 2; IX 3; XI 1   polemic against the structure of the ecclesiastical hierarchy and
its authoritative character and in contrast present a conception
of the Church like that of Paul: the community is a spiritual or-
ganism, the Body of Christ, in which "perfect" (pneumatics)
and imperfect (psychics, ordinary Christians) are united in mu-
* *NHC XI 1*   tual understanding and collaboration.* The attitude towards
the "offices" is tolerant to the point of indifference, and they
are considered immaterial; the Spirit, knowledge and law are
to govern the community.[83a] Hence in the Apocalypse of Peter
a warning against the ostensibly authorised church authorities
"bishop" and "deacon" is put in the mouth of Christ: they are
* *NHC VII 3,79,21–31*   only "waterless canals".* Thus over against the established
hierarchic Great Church the gnostics advocated a free com-
munity life that was not marked by any ecclesiastical structure
of authority, such as the gnostic texts depicted, with mythical
trimmings to suggest its origin, in the behaviour of the arrogant
See below, p. 265   and authoritarian Demiurge and his retinue the archons.
What actually guaranteed the coherence of the individual
communities can no longer be ascertained. The wide expansion

of individual branches from the Orient (Syria) to Italy (Rome), **The**
and Egypt (Alexandria) suggests a contact which, in the ab- **unity of the**
sence of any central administration (such as the Manicheans **communities**
alone possessed), was relatively loose. The breaking up of individual schools into various branches, which certainly also had
geographical causes, supports this view. One important contribution to cohesiveness, besides the authority of the founder of
the school and his writings, lay in travelling activity. Reports of
just such activity are frequently made about the gnostics. Leaders of schools and missionaries travelled from great centres like
Alexandria or Jerusalem to Rome and back. Here it was not
only propaganda carried on by itinerant missionaries and merchant men, that was the controlling factor; the visitation of
communities already in existence was also in view. This can be
aptly illustrated in the early Christian church, either by the
journeys of Paul or the legendary undertakings of the apostles
in the apocryphal apostolic histories. Numerous journeys were
undertaken at that time. The outward appearance of such an
"apostle" has been depicted in humorous vein by Lucian in his
"Peregrinus": long hair, shabby clothes, wallet strapped to his
side, staff in hand (in every way like an itinerant Cynic philosopher).

The nature of such undertakings and their results are clearly **Missionary**
reflected at the end of the Poimandres where the recipient of **activity**
the revelation, who has become one with the revealer, proceeds to give thanks to the Father of the All and to make proclamation to men for their conversion: "They heard and came
with one accord. And I said: 'Why, earth-born men, have you
given yourselves up to death, when you have power to share in
immortality? Repent, you who have travelled in company with
error (*planē*) and have made common cause with ignorance
(*agnoia*). Separate yourselves from the dark light, forsake corruption and partake of immortality!' Some of them made fun of
me and went away, and (so) gave themselves up to the way of
death, but the others threw themselves at my feet and begged to
be instructed. But I made them stand up, and became a guide of
the human race, and taught them how and in what way they will
be saved. I sowed in them the words of wisdom, and they were
nourished by ambrosial water. And when evening came and the
radiance of the sun was beginning to set entirely, I exhorted
them to thank God; and when they had completed their thanks-

Corp. Herm. I 27–29   giving they went each to his bed."* Thus "conversion" leads immediately to the founding of a community.

Letters and epistles   Another form of contact employed by the communities was the circulars and letters, of which we have a series (Mani left a collection of letters, which unfortunately has not survived). Generally a decisive importance was attributed to literary activity: on the one hand it gave expression to the vitality of the communities, on the other it was influential in the instruction of disciples and the acquisition of new members. Thus we frequently find missionary discourses interpolated in the texts, as

NHC II 7   in the Hermetic collection, the Book of Thomas,* the Naassene

See above, p. 25f.   sermon etc., which indicate that Gnosis is a missionary religion.

The cult   Like any religious community the gnostic also was a "cult community", an aspect which has already been touched on occasionally and which now must be considered in greater detail. The difficulties with this subject are bound up with the condition of the source material already described. Liturgical or cultic texts have hitherto emerged only in sparse numbers, at least those in Greek or Coptic. Up to now we have not had any archaeological finds of sanctuaries or cultic places. An exception

Plates 9, 34   is the Mandean community where rich evidence, even eyewitness testimony, is available. The Church Fathers leave us largely in the lurch or – and this is even more deplorable – simply indulge in absurd fabrications on this aspect of their opponents; calumny acts as godfather in the ancient tradition of sectarian warfare.

To these difficulties may be added one more, which stems from the nature of Gnosis itself. In its very conception of the world it is really anti-cultic: All "hylic" (material) institutions are disqualified and regarded as futile for redemption. Strictly speaking this is true also of the cultic domain. Sacraments like baptism and last supper (eucharist) cannot effect salvation and therefore do not possess those qualities that are "necessary for salvation"; at most they can confirm and strengthen the state of grace that the gnostics (pneumatics) enjoy already, insofar as they are retained. Only a very few branches however adopted this radical standpoint, like some Valentinians and above all the Manicheans. The majority, as is clear from the limited source material, practised a cult analogous to that of the mystery religions or the Christian church, which contained various ceremonies and rites including outright magical practices like incantations and exorcisms. The thesis has often been advanced that it was only secondarily and in its late phase that Gnosis became a cultic religion. But this conception is unhistorical and is not supported by the evidence. On the contrary it appears that criticism and spiritualization of the cultic institutions belong to a later phase of development, forming as it were an act of critical reflection on their own substructure and perhaps in the face of growing deterioration within this very area. However a final verdict is not yet possible, particularly since little work has been done in this field.[84]

As in the realm of ideology, so also in cultic practice we find a number of behaviour patterns which exist side by side, partly even within the framework of one and the same school. The basic attitudes may be reduced to three or thereabouts:

1. The tacit retention of cultic ceremonies from the surrounding world, adapted to their own thought, which often involves a transmutation of ideas.
2. Amplification, improvement or even innovation of ceremonies, in many cases as the result of a transposition from mythology, i.e. by "ritualizing" mythological events.
3. Rejection or at least rigorous spiritualization of the cult.

The last point, the repudiation of cultic practice, was directed in the first place against the ecclesiastical institutions of baptism and the eucharist (which does not exclude the possibility that these groups enjoyed a communal life with hymns and prayers). Irenaeus tells of a Valentinian (?) group that rejected all water and anointing rites associated with the redemption process, and that they asserted that "the mystery (*mysterion*) of the ineffable and invisible power ought not to be performed through (by means of) visible and corruptible created things, nor the inconceivable and incorporeal by means of what is (sensually) perceptible and corporeal. These hold that perfect 'redemption' (*apolytrosis*, regarded among other groups as a cultic act) is the 'knowledge' (*gnosis*) of the ineffable 'Greatness' ..., therefore knowledge is the 'redemption' (*apolytrosis*) of the inner man. But this, however, is not corporeal, for the body is corruptible, nor psychic, since the soul (*psyche*) descends from a defect and is only the abode of the spirit (*pneuma*); the 'redemption' must therefore be spiritual. The inner and spiritual man is redeemed by means of knowledge (*gnosis*); sufficient for them is the knowledge of the All, and this is the true re-

Hostility to the cult

See below, p. 243f.

Irenaeus,
Adv.haer.I 21,4

demption."* Epiphanius gives an account of a similar attitude taken by the so-called Archontics (probably related to Sethian Gnosis) who during the reign of Constantine the Great established a foothold in Palestine, and also spread to Armenia: "They condemn baptism even though some of them were previously baptized. They reject participation in the (church) sacraments (mysteries) and deny their value, as extraneous and introduced in the name of the (demiurge) Sabaoth ... And when (the soul) acquires 'knowledge' (*gnosis*) and shuns the baptism of the Church and the name of Sabaoth who has given men the Law it ascends from heaven to heaven ..."*

Epiphanius,
Panarion 40,2,6.8

Spiritualization of cultic performances

Hippolytus,
Refutatio V 9,4

** *Corp. Herm. I 31;*
NHC VI 6,57,18f.
* *NHC V 5,85,22–28*
** *NHC II 4,96 (144),*
33–97 (145), 4

* *NHC II 6,131,34–132,2*

* *NHC IX 3,69,7–32*

In other cases cultic acts were "spiritualized" i. e. reduced to spiritual models or interpreted symbolically. "For the worship of the perfect is spiritual, not carnal" (according to the Naassenes).* There are numerous examples where prayers and hymns are taken, as in the Hermetic texts, to be "pure spiritual offerings"** or where the act of "knowledge" (*gnosis*) is understood as baptism as at the close of the "Apocalyse of Adam"*, or as "anointing" in the "Hypostasis of the Archons".** "The purification of the soul is to regain the chasteness of her former nature and to turn herself back (again): that is her baptism."* In the polemical tractate the Testimony of Truth, water baptism is rejected with a reference to the fact that Jesus baptised none of his disciples, and instead the "baptism of truth", i. e. renunciation of the world, is commended.* Sometimes it is very difficult to ascertain whether in the utilization of cultic concepts, to take as an example the repeated one of "living water", it is just a figure for the gift of Gnosis or enlightenment, or whether it is a covert allusion to a water rite which the sect practised. Scholarly opinion has shifted recently in favour of the latter interpretation without having always reached generally accepted conclusions. It is certain, however, that the gnostic texts even in cultic matters favour a metaphorical symbolical manner of speaking and (on account of this?) clearly avoided communicating precise details about their "mysteries".

The exercise of prayer

Several forms of gnostic cultic activity known to us may now be considered. To the traditional usage and certainly practised in every community belong the recitation of hymns and prayers. We have an enormous number of these whether as insertions in theological works or as independent collections. We possess the latter, apart from the rich works of the Manicheans and the Mandeans, in the so-called Odes of Solomon which can be regarded as the song-book or prayer book of a Syrian gnostic-christian community. This collection was also used in Egypt as the admission of several songs from it in the Coptic Pistis Sophia serves to illustrate. From it we obtain a certain insight into gnostic piety:[85]

See above, p. 29

"My arms are lifted up on high
   to the grace of the Lord,
   because he has removed my fetters from me,
   and my Helper has raised me on account of his grace and his
      salvation.
And I put off darkness
and clothed myself with light.
And I myself acquired members for my soul,
in whom were no sickness, affliction or pain.
And the thought of the Lord was exceedingly helpful to me
and his incorruptible fellowship.
And I was lifted up into the light
and I passed before his presence.
And I approached him
while praising and confessing him.
He made my heart bubble over, and it was found in my
      mouth
and came forth upon my lips.
And the joy of the lord and his praise increased upon my face.
Hallelujah!" *

* *Ode Sol. 21*

The stretching out of the hands as a gesture of prayer has symbolic meaning: It is a representation of the Cross, and for the gnostic also symbolic of the "crucifixion of the world".

See above, p. 171

"I stretched out my hands
   and hallowed my Lord.
   For the stretching out of my hands is his sign;
   and my stretching out is the upright wood.
   Hallelujah!" *

* *Ode Sol. 27*

"Repose" and safety are expressions for the possession of redemption which is attained already in this world and is a ready source of praise:

"I found repose on the spirit of the Lord
and he lifted me on high.
And he caused me to stand on my feet in the high place of the
Lord
before his perfection and his glory,
while I continued praising (him) by the composition of his
songs." *

* Ode Sol. 36,1–2

The songs describe the presence of redemption as the soul's already completed "journey to heaven", and it appears that some of those which are dedicated to this theme were sung at a "ceremony of the soul's ascent" or at a "mass for the dead".

"I went up into the light of Truth as on a chariot,
and the Truth led me and brought me,
and made me cross chasms and ravines,
and preserved me from precipices and waves.
And became to me a haven of salvation
and set me on the arms of immortal life." *

* Ode Sol. 38,1–3

"I was carried like a child by its mother,
and he (the Lord) gave me milk, (i. e.) the dew of the Lord.
And I was enriched by his bounty
and found repose in his perfection (or: in his Pleroma).
And I stretched out my hands in the ascent of my soul
and directed myself towards the Most High
and I was redeemed by him." *

* Ode Sol. 35,5–7

The Old Testament psalms were also often used and were understood as an expression of gnostic redemptive piety. In the Pistis Sophia, as is well known, they were interpreted in terms of the fate of Sophia. A few prayers are now to be found in the Nag-Hammadi texts, particularly in those which belong to the Hermetic corpus. *[86] They have the sanction of divine approval. Stress is laid on the fact that the prayer is not a formal precept but an inner requirement of the "mind" (*nous*) which serves wisdom and knowledge. "Let us pray, O my son, to the father of the universe, together with your brothers who are my sons, that he may give the spirit of speech", speaks the revealer Hermes to his son (Thot or Tat is referred to) in order to instruct him in the secrets of the "Eighth" (*ogdoas*) and "Ninth"

See above, p. 156

* NHC VI 6.7

The world snake (*ouroboros*) in the form of an amulet in a Greek magical papyrus of the 3rd century A.D. The amulet, which is the name and seal "of the might of the great God", protects its owner "against demons, against spirits, against all illness and all suffering". The inscription consists of magical words and signs (inter alia *Yaeo*) and the formula: "Protect me, NN, body and soul from all injury".

(*enneas*).* Two prayers will be cited here. The first contains mysterious invocations using letters of the alphabet which we know from magical practices; it shows that the transition to prayer magic was not difficult. Plotinus thought it specially scandalous that the gnostics had recourse to higher beings by means of "exorcisms" to achieve their ends. In this process, he says, "appropriate utterances", "melodies", "shrieks" "whisperings and hissings with the voice" were in common use.* * NHC VI 6,53,27–31

* Plotinus, Enneads II 9,14

"I will offer up the praise in my heart
  as I invoke the end of the universe,
  the beginning of the beginning of man's quest,
  the immortal prize (or: discovery),

the creator of light and truth,
the sower of the word (*logos*), of love (*agapē*) and of immortal life.
No hidden word has the power to speak of you, Lord.
Therefore my mind (*nous*) wants to sing praises to you daily.
I am the instrument of your spirit (*pneuma*),
the mind (*nous*) is your plectrum;
your counsel plays on me.
I see myself: I have received power from you,
for your love has raised us up ...
O grace! After all these things I give thanks to you,
by singing praises to you.
For I have received life from you,
when you made me wise.
I praise you, I invoke your name
that is hidden within me:
a ō ee ō eee ōōō iii ōōōō ooooo ōōōōō yyyyyy
ōōōōōōōōōōōōōōōōōōōōōōōō
You are the one who exists with the spirit.
I sing praises to you with devotion." *

* NHC VI 6,60,17–61,17

The other "prayer that they (Hermes and Thot) spoke" was already known earlier in Latin and Greek:

"We give thanks to you! To you every soul and heart
reaches out, O untroubled name, honoured with
the name God and praised with the name Father.
For to everyone and everything (extends) the pleasure of
the Father, the love and the affection.
And if the instruction is sweet and straightforward, then it
gives understanding (*nous*), the word (*logos*) and knowledge
(*gnosis*):
Understanding, so that we might understand you.
The word, so that we might interpret you.
Knowledge, so that we might know you.
We rejoice, since we have received light by your knowledge.
We rejoice because you have taught us about yourself.
We rejoice because while we were still in the body you have
made us gods through your knowledge.
The gratitude of the man who comes to you amounts to one
thing (only):

that we know you.
We have known you, O (spiritually) perceptible light.
O life of life, we have known you.
O womb of every seed, we have known you.
O womb, you who are pregnant with the nature of the
    Father,
we have known you.
O eternal permanence of the begetting Father, thus have we
adored your goodness.
We have but one wish: we would be preserved in knowledge
    (*gnosis*).
We seek but one protection: that we do not stumble in this
    kind of life."*   * *NHC VI 7,63,33–65,7*

A postscript is added that after the prayer "they kissed each
other and went to eat their holy food, which has no blood in it,"
i. e. the ceremony came to a close with a ritual vegetarian meal
(in contrast to the sacrificial meals of their contemporaries).

To the "divine service of the word" belong also addresses and **Sermons**
sermons which have survived in abundance in gnostic literature; naturally it is not always possible to demonstrate that they
formed part of the cultic practice. It may be assumed however
that this was the case since the meetings held by the communities afforded the single opportunity for reciprocal instruction
and the sharing of information. Various texts connect prayers
and hymns with notes for instruction purporting to give a vision
of the heavenly worlds from the favoured and talented pen of
some legendary author. Thus the Three Stelae of Seth* are a   * *NHC VII 5*
proclamation of Dositheos who "saw and heard" them in the
other world. "Many times I joined in rendering praise with the
powers (above), and became worthy (for the presence) of the
immeasurable great ones". The transmission of the three didactic hymns to the community has the same object in mind. The
recitation encourages the absorption into or rather the elevation to the spheres above. Many of the texts known to us are
written for similar purposes. According to the Book of Thomas
"when you pray you will find rest, for you have left behind the
suffering and sickness of heart".*   * *NHC II 7,145,10–12*

Evidently many gnostics also fostered a cult of images, even **Image worship**
owning statues of gods such as those found among the archaeological remains of mystery cults. In the anonymous Hermetic

tractate mentioned above, there is a probable allusion to one of these: "You invisible God, to whom one speaks in silence, whose image (*eikon*) is moved when one takes care of it, and it
* *NHC VI 6,56,10–14* is cared for (when one moves it)."* Irenaeus describes the Simonians who among other things "possess an image (*eikon, imago*) of Simon, made in the form of Zeus, and Helena (his con-
* *Irenaeus,* sort) in the form of Athena, and these they worship."* The
Adv. haer. I 23,4 same writer submits a similar report of others (the followers of Carpocrates): "They have also images, some painted, some too made of other material, and say they are the form of Christ made by Pilate in that time when Jesus was with men. These (images) they crown, and they set them forth with the images of the philosophers of the world, Pythagoras, Plato, Aristotle, and the rest; and their other observance concerning them they
* *op. cit. I, 25,6* carry out like the heathen."* Unfortunately we have no means of investigating these revealing statements in detail, but it can be shown that even the Manicheans erected an image of their
Plate 25, leader during cultic performances, and wall paintings in their
Colour plate IV central-asiatic sanctuaries (of the 8th C.) have been preserved.
Even synagogues were decorated, as we know today from finds, and Christians from an early date engaged in similar artistic activity in the places where they met, as the catacombs indicate. The gnostics were no exception in this respect. It need not be doubted however that they did not worship statues or images as such, but viewed them only as symbols and emblems.

Further ceremonies which played an important part in the life of the gnostic community include baptisms and washings (lustrations), anointings with oil (so-called "sealings"), festive meals (e.g. the eucharist), death rites (for the ascent of the soul) and some practices peculiar to certain groups. Some short liturgical prayers, relating to the anointing, baptism and the eucharist, have turned up in the appendix to the anonymous
* *NHC XI 2,40–44* (Valentinian) fragment in Codex XI from Nag Hammadi.* At times "five seals" are mentioned, chiefly among the Valentinians but not only by them, and this evidently refers to five cere-
* *NHC II 3* monies which, at least according to the Gospel of Philip,* include baptism, anointing, eucharist, "redemption" (*apolytrosis*) and "bridal chamber".[87] We shall now discuss them briefly.
Baptisms and   To begin with the water rites. Apart from the Mandeans
washings where they stand at the centre of the cult, one does not come across them very much and we are singularly lacking in detailed

descriptions of the actual performance. Complete immersion in "flowing (= living) water" was evidently the rule although sprinkling or douching were not precluded. Although the greater part of the evidence belongs to the Christian gnostic domain and thus presupposes Christian baptism, there are indications that water rites existed in the gnostic communities independent of Christianity, and derived from Jewish purification rites, especially of heretical origin. Jewish baptismal sects evidently had a certain affinity with gnostic movements. This provides the readiest explanation for a series of features connected with the performance of the rite: the cleansing character (for entry into the Pleroma) and the idea of "initiation" into the mysteries of gnostic wisdom. A few (Valentinian) groups practised a special "redemption" rite with the aid of a water baptism and baptized the dying. Baptism also served as an admission rite. "The promise of the washing (in baptism)", said Hippolytus of the so-called Naassenes, "is, they say, nothing less than the introduction into unfading enjoyment of him who in their fashion is washed in living water and anointed with unutterable anointing."* The Sethians also practise baptism and the "cup of living water"* as the means whereby one partakes of immortality. This conception has evidently become characteristic of the gnostic interpretation of baptism, and not that of the blotting out of sins. The latter is disparagingly ascribed to the "psychic" baptism of the earthly Jesus, and is distinguished from the "spiritual" baptism of the Christ who descended upon him.* The most detailed reports come from the Valentinians. As the baptism of Jesus signifies the descent of the Spirit of Christ upon him so the baptism of the gnostic is an act which imparts to him the spirit (*pneuma*) of immortality, redemption and resurrection and thereby makes him a pneumatic. In baptism the gnostic obtains his immortal garment or the "perfect man" (Christ). One formula runs: "In the name of the unknown Father of all things, into Truth, the mother of all, into him who descended on Jesus (i.e. Christ), into union, into redemption (*apolytrosis*), into the communion of the powers."*

The Gospel of Philip uses some impressive definitions and images in the attempt to expound baptism: "The living water is a body. It is fitting for us to put on the living man. Therefore when he (the gnostic) comes to descend into the water, he strips in order that he may put on this one (the living man)."* The

See above, p. 188

See below, p. 244

* Hippolytus, Refutatio V 7,19

* op. cit. V 19,21

* Irenaeus, Adv. haer. I 21,2

* op. cit. I 21,3

* NHC II 3,75 (123), 21–25

possible word-play in Greek between "to baptize" (*baptizein*) and "to dye" (*baptein*) led to the following comparison: "God is a dyer. As the good dyes – they are called 'true' – perish with the things that are dyed in them, so it is (also) with those God has dyed. Since his dyes are immortal, they (the dyed ones) become immortal through his tinctures. But God immerses those

* NHC II 3,61 (109), 12–20 whom he baptizes in water."* The one who is baptized thus becomes immortal thanks to the mediating spirit (who stands for the dyes), in contrast to the corruptible fabrics, whose dyes fade. Two pages further on a piece of legend about Jesus says: "The Lord went into the dye-works of (the disciple) Levi. He took seventy-two colours and cast them into the cauldron (of dyes). He brought them all out white and said: 'So (also) came

* NHC II 3,63 (111), 25–30 the Son of Man (as) a dyer'."* "White" as the colour of life and light is a symbol for the immortality which Christ secures for mankind. The same line of thought is found in the Valentinian Theodotus, who associates the baptism for the dead in the New

* 1 Cor. 15,29 Testament* with the heavenly model of angel baptism: "'Those who are baptized for the dead' are the angels who are baptized for us (who being mortal are as dead), in order that we too, possessing the (baptismal) name, may not be held back (at the as-

* Clem. Alex.,
Ex Theodoto 22,4 cent) and be prevented by the 'border post' (*horos*) from entering into the Pleroma."*

Anointing
with oil   Anointing with oil has a greater representation than baptism in Gnosis and in some texts it is even regarded as more significant. In general, however, it is taken closely with the baptismal ceremony – the anointing taking place either before or after the baptism. This association first appeared in Christendom as a whole in the course of the second century and is linked up with the name of Christ, "the Anointed One". Magical connotations also played an important role: anointing oil expelled demons and gave protection against them; correspondingly it cured and dispelled the "sickness" of the soul and the body. Hence exorcism (driving out) was performed by means of anointing. The ancient magical texts provide abundant evidence for this application of oil. Often the anointing is taken as a "sealing", the ointment as a "seal", i.e. it is a protective act and a declaration of property. The deity in this way assures the believers through the priests and they enjoy its protection. All these interpretations are also found in Gnosis. In the foreground however is the concept of redemption, the gift of immortality which is trans-

mitted by anointing. It was closely bound up with the paradisical "olive tree" which as the sign of life depicted the origin of
the anointing oil. Celsus reports of the Ophite gnostics that *See above, p. 103 f.*
they possessed a "seal" the recipient of which was made a "son"
of the "Father"; his response was: "I have been anointed with
white ointment from the tree of life."* The Gospel of Philip *Origen, C. Celsum VI 27*
says the same: "But the tree of life is in the midst of paradise
and the olive tree from which the oil of anointing (*chrisma*)
comes; through it [came] the resurrection."* This idea is more *NHC II 3,73 (121), 15–19*
fully worked out in another passage of the same text: "The
anointing (*chrisma*) is superior to baptism. For from the anointing we were called 'anointed ones' (Christians), not because of
the baptism. And Christ also was (so) named because of the
anointing, for the Father anointed the son, and the son anointed the apostles, and the apostles anointed us. He (therefore)
who has been anointed has the All. He has the resurrection, the
light, the cross, the Holy Spirit . . ."* The anointing then, as Ire- *NHC II 3,*
naeus tells us, could be made to serve as a special "redemption" *74, (122), 12–21*
ceremony for the "perfect", even displacing baptism: "But
some (Valentinians?) say that it is superfluous to bring people
to the water (to be baptized), but they mix oil and water together and pour it with invocations . . . on the heads of those to be initiated, and this is regarded as being the 'redemption'. They also anoint with balsam."* A similar ritual is also undertaken on *Irenaeus,*
behalf of the dying (a kind of extreme unction) and this needs *Adv. haer. I 21,4*
some comment later. The significance of the anointing is ex- *See below, p. 244*
pressed also in their eschatological stance: It is received not only in the hereafter as a token of the final "release"* but has a *NHC II 3,85 (133),*
protective function when the soul makes its ascent. In some *24–28; Ode Sol. 36,6*
texts like the Pistis Sophia and the Books of Jeu the "spiritual
ointment" is a prerequisite for entry into the pleroma, by which
the highest "mystery" is meant.

Unfortunately we do not know a great deal about the perfor- **The anointing**
mance of the anointing ceremony except that the oil was app- **ceremonies**
lied principally to the head and brow, sometimes in the form of
the sign of the cross, as in the Christian church. Also an anointing of the whole body may have taken place. Prayers and invocations which accompanied the ceremony are preserved in the
apocryphal Acts of Thomas, where the anointing with oil was
accorded a higher significance than baptism. Hence the description of the anointing of a converted noblewoman at the

Indian court: "Mygdonia was standing before the apostle with her head bare. And he lifted the oil and poured it over her head saying: 'Holy oil, given us for sanctification, hidden mystery in which the cross was shown to us, you are the unfolder of the hidden parts (i.e. the seed of light). You are the humiliator of stubborn deeds. You are the one who shows the hidden treasures. You are the plant of kindness. Let your power come. Let it abide on your maid Mygdonia and heal her by this (unction).'"* Then she was baptized in a water-spring and partook of bread and water.

* Acts of Thomas, ch. 121

The sacred meal   Such a "sacred meal", which is either an imitation or the taking over of the Christian eucharist ("thanksgiving") or a reflection of older ideas from the surrounding world, is mentioned again in occasional statements, but these are relatively rare.

See above, p. 225 We already have a reference to "sacred and bloodless food" preserved in the Hermetic writings. Hence it follows that "bloody" sacrificial meals as practised by the traditional cults were not acceptable to Gnosis. In the late gnostic tractates of the Pistis Sophia group the notion of "sacrifice" is understood as a kind of mystery religion observance which serves to remit sins and to purify. Its component parts are wine, water, bread, incense, herbs and plants.* The practical implementation of this ceremony is rather uncertain; its symbolical value is preeminent as can be seen in the metaphorical usage of the terms "baptism" and "seal". The position is much clearer with regard to the partaking of bread and water among the Mandeans, which takes place at the close of the water baptism. The preference of water to wine is evident in various heretical communities of early Christendom and is grounded principally in the preoccupation with abstemiousness (rejection of intoxicants). In Gnosis the idea of the "water of life" as a symbol of illuminating knowledge, which was depicted ritually by a "drink of water", may also have played a part.

* Pistis Sophia, ch. 142; 2nd Book of Jeu, chs. 45–47

See below, p. 361

The celebration of the eucharist   Again it is the Gospel of Philip which at some points supplies us with a certain amount of information on the gnostic Valentinian usage of the eucharist. As in the official church it consists

21, 22
Ruins of Chotsko (Turfan oasis). The K group of ruins which is considered to be a Manichean sanctuary (temple). In it Manichean temple banners (cf. plates 27, 28) were found intact together with numerous Manichean manuscripts and miniatures. Above, a Persian arch from this group. Below, general view of the site from the south west (in the centre the building shown above).

23
Manichean book miniature depicting the sacred meal of the elect at a festival of thanksgiving for
Mani (Bema festival). In the centre stands the "table of God" with its holy fruit (in a basket)
and white bread; on the left sit the male, on the right the female "elect"; below the simple "hearers".
The large figure to the left of the table is the founder of the religion Mani (?).

Iranian Manichean manuscript from Turfan (M4 II V). In the right column, lines 5–10, appears the "Song of Mani" cited on p. 329 f.

25
Distinguished Uigurian benefactors (princes) from a temple frieze in Bäzäklik (Turfan).
Cf. colour plate IV.

26

Iranian Manichean manuscript fragment (M 18 R) with the "passage on the crucifixion (of Christ)".
The page contains the story of the empty tomb.

27
Manichean "elect"
(*electa*) on a temple
banner from Chotsko
(Turfan): Characteristic
are the broad white robes
and the white caps; the
dangling scarves are red.
In front of her she holds
a writing tablet or a book.

28
Manichean "elect" (*electus*) on a temple banner from Chotsko (Turfan). Cf. pl. 27. The long hair is parted into thick strands according to Turkish custom. Beside the two Manichean pneumatics, hearers (laity) kneel in worship.

29, 30
The Cologne Mani codex before conservation.
Greek text on parchment. 5. cent. Enlarged 2½ x and
original size. H. 4.5 c. m., W. 3.5 c. m.

31
Coptic Manichean manuscript
(Papyrus). Lines from the
"Kephalaia". 4. cent. Egyptian
(Medinet Madi).

Chinese Manichean manuscript (London Hymn-book) from Tun-huang. Circ. 800. It contains a prayer of confession and petition for a successful ascent to the kingdom of light.

of "bread and cup". The significance attached to it appears outwardly "Church Christian", but within the framework of the
text as a whole it is manifestly gnostic: "The cup of prayer (i. e.
the thanksgiving, eucharist) contains wine (and) water, (both)
being appointed as the type (*typos*) of the blood over which
thanks is given, and it is full of the Holy Spirit and belongs to
the wholly perfect man. When we drink this (cup), we shall re-
ceive for ourselves the perfect man."* "He (Jesus) said on that *NHC II 3,75 (123),*
day in the eucharist: '(You) who have joined the perfect, the *14–21*
light, with the Holy Spirit, join the angels with us also, the im-
ages'."* The eucharist anticipates the union of the gnostic with *NHC II 3,58 (106), 10–14*
his "angel image"; it effects a realization of the original oneness
of the Pleroma. The "flesh" and "blood" of Christ as they are
represented in the Last Supper are for the gnostic "word" (*logos*) and "Holy Spirit", understood as a celestial pair of aeons.
"He who has received these has food and drink and clothing."* *NHC II 3,57 (105), 3–8*
That is to say, the recipient is in the possession of perfection
and eternal life.

Irenaeus' account of Marcus the Valentinian affords a remarkable and very singular insight into a gnostic celebration of
the eucharist.* As is the case with all such statements its relia- *Irenaeus,*
bility is naturally not altogether certain. "Over a cup mixed *Adv. haer. I 13,2*
with wine he pretends to give thanks, and whilst greatly pro-
longing the invocation (*epiklesis*), he contrives that it (the cup)
should appear purple and red so that 'Grace' (*charis*), who belongs to the (spheres) which are superior to all things, may
seem to be dropping her blood into that cup by means of his invocation, and that those present should fervently desire to taste
of that cup in order that the Grace called hither by that sorcerer
(magician) may flow into them. On another occasion he gives
to women cups already mixed and full and bids them offer
thanks in his presence. When this is done, he produces another
cup much larger than the one over which the deluded woman
has given thanks, and he then pours from the smaller one over
which she has given thanks into the one which he has brought
forward ..., and at the same time he speaks as follows: 'May
Grace (*charis*) who is before all things, who is beyond thought
and description, fill your inner man and multiply in you her
knowledge (*gnosis*), sowing the mustard seed in good soil!'* By *cf. Matth. 13,31f.*
saying such things and by making the wretched woman de-
ranged, he appears as a wonder-worker, when the larger cup is

filled from the smaller one to such an extent that it actually overflows ..."

It is apparent that this ceremony accommodates gnostic ideas, such as, for example, the invocation of "Grace", a gnostic aeon, to strengthen the "inner man" (i. e. the seed of light), to the Christian celebration of the Last Supper. Over and above this, Marcus probably saw that it provided a good opportunity for him to demonstrate his supernatural powers (such as the inspired gnostics liked to claim for themselves) before his followers and in particular before the womenfolk. To what extent conscious deception lay behind these antics can of course no longer be ascertained.

Similar eucharistic prayers to those used by Marcus are also found in quite different areas, which stand close to Gnosis. In the Acts of Thomas the apostle Thomas enunciates the following "epiklesis" over the "bread of the blessing": "⟨Come, gift of the Most High.⟩ Come, perfect compassion; come, intercourse with the male. ⟨Come, holy Spirit (of might).⟩ Come, you who know the mysteries of the elect one; come, you who share in the contests of the noble contestant (athlete). ⟨Come, glorious treasure; come, beloved of the compassion of the Most High.⟩ Come, repose, who reveals the majesty of the whole greatness. Come, you who bring the hidden things to light and cause what is secret to be revealed. Come, holy dove, you who give birth to the twin young. Come, hidden mother; come, you who are manifest by your deeds and supply joy and rest to those bound up with you. Come and take part with us in this eucharist which we perform in your name, and in the love-feast (*agape*) for which we are assembled at your invitation."* The divine first cause is invoked in his female form, the origin of the aeons and active in the spirit (*pneuma*); it is a Sophia figure, such as we have come to know it, who is entreated here to participate in the celebration of the meal like a goddess at one of the ancient sacrifical meals. The expression "twin young" appears to be an allusion to the relation between the heavenly image and its earthly counterpart in the myth of the soul.

* *Acts of Thomas, ch. 50*

Late gnostic ceremonies   In the area of gnostic cult, therefore, the old and the more recent ceremonies are frequently bound closely together. To those of patently late formation belong a series of rites which can be understood only on the basis of the gnostic conceptual world and extend beyond the realm of normal ecclesiastical cult practices. This applies above all to the ceremonies for the dead and the related "redeeming" and "perfecting" procedures of the Valentinians, not to mention a sperm and snake cult practised by certain deviant groups. We have already noted in the discussion of the concepts pertaining to the ascent of souls that the gnostic was not content to rely merely on his abstract "knowledge", but also frequently resorted to safeguards in order to secure the redemption he craved for. In some branches of Gnosis, and probably first in that of the Valentinian Marcus, people went on to perform the "redemption" (*apolytrosis*) also as a ritual act, and to make of it a regular sacrament. "The intellectual act seemed too intangible, and perhaps not certain enough. What was substantial, the action, the sign, the words and formulas, they provided a more positive guarantee of salvation."[88] Here the tendency to stress what could be experienced, to the visible realization of salvation, may also have played an important role, such as we find at the same time also in the development of the Christian divine service into a mystery ceremony. Irenaeus tells us in one chapter of his antignostic work of a whole series of forms under which the "apolytrosis" rite took place. "They affirm" (he is citing the opinion of his opponents) "that it is necessary for those who have attained to perfect knowledge (*gnosis*), that they may be regenerated into the power which is above all. Otherwise it is impossible to enter into the Pleroma, because it is this (only) that leads them down into the depths of the abyss (i.e. of the divine first cause)."* While some celebrate it as a baptism, indeed as the "spiritual" over against the merely "psychic" baptism of the earthly Jesus, others regard it as an anointing rite,* which is also performed for the dying.** Some of the formulas used in this rite have been noted down by Irenaeus, although he did not understand much of them, especially the two fragments in Aramaic. The latter doubtless served, as the Church Father puts it, "to baffle even more those who are being initiated" (we know this belief in strange, unintelligible words from the magical texts), but they also indicate that here we are dealing with ancient liturgical material, which is otherwise seldom the case. The (Greek) translation provided by Irenaeus, as we now realize, is not a correct one, although more recent study has not been able to clear up the obscurities completely.[89] The one, evidently a baptismal formula, runs like this: "In the name of Achamoth

The sacrament of redemption (*apolytrosis*)

* Irenaeus, Adv. haer. I 21,2

See above, p. 228f.

* Irenaeus, Adv. haer. I 21,2–3
** op. cit. I 21,5

(wisdom), be immersed! May the life, the light which is beamed forth, the spirit of truth be in your redemption!" The other is designated as a "formula of the restoration (*apokatastasis*)" and appears to have been recited by the initiates (not as Irenaeus says by those who are being initiated): "I have been anointed and (thereby) my soul has been redeemed from every age (aeon) in the name of Iao, who redeemed himself, and in Jesus of Nazareth." The Greek formula that follows says something similar: "I am established, I am redeemed, and I redeem my soul from this age (aeon) and from all that comes from it, in the name of Iao, who redeemed his soul (or himself) unto the redemption (*apolytrosis*) in Christ, the living one." Those present make the response: "Peace be with all on whom this name rests." "Then they anoint the initiate with the oil from the balsam tree. This oil (*myron*) is said to be a type of the sweet savour which is above all terrestial things." It is thus a divine service for the community with responses and a baptism or an anointing or both.

Sacraments for the dying
* Irenaeus, Adv. haer. I 21,5
The performance of this "redemption" ritual for the dying, as Irenaeus informs us in the same chapter,* involves pouring "oil and water" on their head, together with the above-named invocations, in order that "they may become unassailable by and invisible to the powers and authorities, and that their 'inner man' may ascend above the realm of the invisible, whilst their body remains behind in the created world, and their soul is delivered to the Demiurge". For safe passage through the barriers of the archons the well-known pass-words were imparted to the deceased which we know now also from the Nag Hammadi texts. When he has overcome the dangers "he enters into his own, his fetter, i. e. the soul, shaken off." Such a "mass for the dead" as we have here was evidently practised by a number of the gnostic communities. The Mandeans supply the clearest report on the proceedings in the form of their "ceremony of the ascent" and the richly developed meals for the dead. The songs, prayers and hymns recited at the ceremony form a complete literary *Gattung*, which we meet again in the Manichean Psalmbook and in some of the Coptic texts (e. g. in the second Apocalypse of James).[90]

See above, p. 174f.

See below, p. 362

In the Acts of Thomas Thomas utters the following prayer before his execution:

"My Lord and my God,
my hope and my redeemer,
my leader and my guide in all lands!
May you be with all who serve you,
and guide me as I come to you to-day!
May no one take my soul,
which I have surrendered to you!
May the tax-collectors not see me,
and the creditors not accuse me!
May the (world) snake not see me,
and the dragon's children not hiss at me!
See, Lord, I have finished your work
and fulfilled your command.
I have become a slave,
therefore today I obtain liberty.
Now bring it to fruition,
you who have given it to me.
I say this, not because I doubt,
but so that they may hear (it) who ought to hear (it)." *

         * Acts of Thomas, ch. 167

According to a statement by Irenaeus "some of them (the Valentinians) prepare a 'bridal chamber' and perform a mystic rite (*mystagogia*), with certain invocations, for those who are being consecrated (or perfected), and they claim that what they are effecting is a 'spiritual marriage', after the image of the conjunctions (syzygies)." * This ceremony of the "bridal chamber" has evidently also become a form of the ritually shaped "redemption" as the statements of the Gospel of Philip suggest to us, probably even a kind of sacrament for the dying accompanied by unction and recitations.[91] The bridal chamber is the "Holy of Holies" and ranks above the other sacraments. * The object in view was evidently to anticipate the final union with the pleroma (represented as a bridal chamber) at the end of time and realizing it in the sacrament, although not by a sexual act or a kissing ceremony, as was frequently assumed. Of this Irenaeus himself has nothing to report; it would be contrary to the "spiritual" interpretation of this "marriage". There is an explicit contrast between the earthly and the celestial marriage; the latter is the "unsullied marriage." * Irenaeus has provided the correct background here: Heavenly perfection is envisaged (particularly in Valentinianism) in terms of the union between

The ceremony of the bridal chamber

* Irenaeus, Adv. haer. I 21,3

* NHC II 3,69 (117), 14–28; 74 (122), 36–75 (123), 2
See above, p. 186

* NHC II 3,81 (129), 34–82 (130), 26

a man and a woman and is expressed by the idea of divine conjunctions (syzygies). Since the world and the fall of the soul originated through the disruption of this unity, something that is illustrated by the Sophia mythology, the return of the soul to the arms of her partner or ideal prototype, prefigured in that of Sophia herself, is the decisive event at the end of time. The sacrament of the bridal chamber is correspondingly a perfect delineation of the Pleroma conception of the unity of separated elements. The pneumatics or gnostics are understood as brides of the angels, and their entrance into the world beyond as a wedding-feast "which is common to all the saved, until all become equal and mutually recognize one another."[*] "The pneumatics then lay aside the souls, and at the same time as the mother receives her bridegroom, each of them too receives his bridegroom, the angels; then they enter the bridal chamber within the (Pleroma) border (*horos*) and attain to a vision of the Father, and become spiritual aeons, (entering) into the spiritual and eternal marriage of the union (syzygy)"[*] (Compare also the tomb inscription of Flavia Sophē.)

The Gospel of Philip understands this eschatological state very clearly as dependent upon the earthly consummation of the "bridal chamber" which manifestly served the purpose of a safe ascent. "As for those who have put on the perfect light – the (supramundane) powers do not see them and cannot seize them, but one will put on the light in the 'mystery', in the 'union'."[*] Or: "If someone becomes a child of the 'bridal chamber', he will receive the light. If someone does not receive it while he is in these places (= this world), he will not be able to receive it in the other place (= the Pleroma). He who will receive that light (in the bridal chamber) will not be seen (at his ascent), nor can he be seized."[*] In a detailed statement fundamental to the understanding of the sacraments in Gnosis an attempt is made to elucidate the indispensable correlation between the image-character of earthly (and cultic) activities (the "types" and "images") and their realization in the next world ("rebirth", "resurrection", "restoration"): "Truth did not come into the world naked, but it came in types and images. It (the world) will not receive it in any other way. There is a rebirth and an image (of) rebirth. It is truly necessary to be reborn through the 'image'. What is the resurrection and (its) image? It is necessary to rise again through the 'image'. It is necessary

See above, p. 196

Clem. Alex., Ex Theodoto 63,2

op. cit. 64,1

See above, p. 212

NHC II 3,70 (118), 5–9

NHC II 3,86 (134), 4–9

that the bridegroom (to be read for bridal chamber) and the 'image' through the 'image' enter the truth: that is the restoration (of the Pleroma, *apokatastasis*)."*   *NHC II 3,67 (115), 9–18*

The symbolic transformation of gnostic wisdom into cultic practice indirectly led in some branches to quite scandalous practices, which might be mentioned only in passing since in the older studies in particular they attracted a lot of attention. The oldest informant is Epiphanius, thus a relatively late and not very reliable source. In the section on the so-called Ophites **The serpent** (the "snake people") in his "Medicine Chest" he gives the fol- **cult** lowing account of a ceremonial feast held by this community:[92] "They have a snake which they foster in a particular box; at the hour when they perform their mysteries they coax it out of the hole, and whilst they load the table with bread, they summon forth the snake. When the hole is opened, it comes out ... crawling onto the table and wallowing in the bread: this, they claim, is the 'perfect offering'. And that is also why, so I heard from them, they not only "break the bread" (an old Christian expression for the Lord's Supper) in which the snake has wallowed, and offer it to the recipients, but everyone also kisses the snake on the mouth, once the snake has indeed been charmed by sorcery ... They prostrate themselves before it (in worship) and call this the 'thanksgiving' (eucharist) which originates from its (the snake's) wallowing (in the bread), and furthermore with its help they raise up a hymn to the Father on high. In such a manner they conclude their mystery feast."* Supposing   *Epiphanius,* it was actually performed like this and by the later Ophites (the   *Panarion 37,5,6–8* older sources pass it over in silence) the ceremony only superficially resembles the Christian eucharist, but rather continues older Greek and Hellenistic secret cults (like that of Eleusis and that of the god Sabazios), in which the snake was worshipped as a symbol of the chthonic deity and fertility. For the Ophites or Naassene gnostics the snake was a medium of revelation and mouthpiece of the most sublime God, as we have seen.   *See above, p. 97f.*

More sinister and therefore to be taken with the greater caution, are the other accounts which Epiphanius (as we have already seen he invokes eyewitnesses here) presents of the gnos-   *See above, p. 19* tics whom he introduces as "Stratiotici" (i. e. "soldier-like, warlike"), Phibionites (meaning unknown) or Borborites (i. e. dirty), and who probably all belong to the large group of Barbelo-gnostics ("Barbeliotes").* What is told about their cultic   *Epiphanius, Panarion 26*

Snake crawling from the
cista mystica in the ancient
Greek Demeter Cult
at Eleusis. From a relief in the
Ny Carlsberg Glyptothek,
Copenhagen.

Sperm-cult and orgies celebrations has, as we would say today, pornographic features. They gravitate, if one is to understand the ideological background, around speculations on the collection of the seed of light, which in the form of the male semen and the female menstrual blood must not be allowed to escape, but must get back to God. Bound up with this is the liberal interpretation of the earthly law which extends to its negation (so-called libertinism). They refuse to give birth to children because this only prolongs the sorrowful lot of the seed of light and only serves the purpose of the creator of the world. All the details of Epiphanius' descriptions are not to be taken seriously; in his exposing polemic he exaggerates a good deal. In places he appears to give full rein to phantasy and to indulge in concupiscence. We also find here an old example of the awful "myth of ritual murder,"* which was part of the inventory of religious sectarian polemic (similar stories to those told by Epiphanius of the gnostics are told for example by Celsus and the Mandeans of the Christians, and as is well known, later by the Christians of the Jews). The connections with Christian rites, especially with the Lord's Supper, are indeed not to be overlooked,[93] but they bear only a superficial resemblance, if indeed they are not an insertion by the heresiologist.

> * *Epiphanius, Panarion 26,5,5*

Epiphanius writes* that the men and the women of the sect first sit down together to a sumptuous meal with wine and meat. After they have "filled their stomachs to satiety" the actual love-rite (*agapē*) commences in which men and women have sexual relations with one another. "When they have had intercourse out of the passion of fornication, then, holding up their own blasphemy before heaven, the woman and the man take the man's emission in their own hands, and stand there looking up towards heaven. And while they have uncleanness in their hands they profess to pray .... 'We offer you this gift, the body of Christ.' And so they eat it, partaking of their own shame and saying, 'This is the body of Christ, and this is the Passover; hence our bodies are given over to passion and compelled to confess the passion of Christ.' Similarly with the woman's emission at her period; they collect the menstrual blood which is unclean, take it and eat it together, and say: 'This is the blood of Christ'." Child-bearing is avoided. If pregnancy ensues the infant embryo is forcibly removed and – this quite certainly belongs to the realm of perverted phantasy – is consumed after being torn apart and duly prepared.* Epiphanius also calls this their "Passover". In justification a prayer is uttered: "We have not been deceived by the lord of lust, but we have retrieved our brother's transgression". Finally we are told that the purpose of sleeping together is to present the women who are seduced to the Archon. Since this applies respectively to the 365 Archons and is to be practised in ascending and descending series, 730

> * *op. cit. 26,4,3–8*

> * *op. cit. 26,5,2–6*

"immoral unions" ensue, at the end of which the man in question is made one with Christ.* Evidently misrepresentations

* op. cit. 26,9,6–9

and vicious slanders are embedded in these descriptions. More
credible is what is said in another passage by way of providing
an ideological basis: "The power which resides in the (female)
periods and in the semen, they say, is the soul (*psyche*) which
we collect and eat. And whatever we eat, be it meat, vegetables, bread, or anything else, we are doing a kindness to created
things, in that we collect the soul from all things and transmit it
with ourselves to the heavenly world . . ." This is reminiscent of

See below, p. 341 f.

the Manichean feasts of the "elect", which serve the "gathering

* op. cit. 26,9,4

in of the souls."*

A final judgement on the proceedings described so far is not
easy as we do not as yet have any original source material to act
as a controlling factor. For all that it is nevertheless perplexing
that in other gnostic texts references of a censorious kind are

Repudiation of orgies

clearly made to such rites. The Pistis Sophia curses in the name
of Jesus the people "who take male semen and female menstrual blood and make it into a lentil dish and eat it"; they will in the

* Pistis Sophia,
ch. 147; 251,14–19

"outer darkness be destroyed".* The second book of Jeu also

* 2nd Book of Jeu,
ch. 43; 304,17–21

opposes a similar practice.* The two Egyptian testimonies from
the 3rd – 4th centuries A. D. could have the Phibionite festive
meals in mind. Already at the beginning of the 3rd century Clement of Alexandria imputes to the gnostic Carpocratians licen-
tious gatherings which generated gluttony and sexual dissipa-

* Clem. Alex.,
Strom. III 10,1

tion; these were declared "love-feasts for uniting".* A little
later Origen had to defend himself against similar charges levelled against the "Christians" by Celsus and instead attributed

* Origen,
C. Celsum VI 27 f.

them to the Ophites.* As has been said, behind this lies a good-
ly number of traditional reproaches levelled by religious communities against one another, but the supposition cannot be
ruled out that among some gnostic groups such consequences
for cultic practice were indeed drawn from the traditional ideology. This would accord well with the trend of this time towards
the expansion and "deepening" of the cultic sphere.

The cultic kiss and round dance

Occasion for malicious slanders might also have been provided by other gnostic practices and to some extent this was the
case. Thus we find repeatedly (e. g. in the Hermetica* or in the

* NHC VI 6–8
* NHC II 3

Gospel of Philip**) the cultic kiss as an expression of communion, brotherhood and the confidence expressed by the elect in
their salvation, whether it be in baptism, feasting, anointing or

any other gathering of the faithful. The ancient church also recognized the "holy kiss".* In the Acts of John** we can even find a dance with antiphonal responses which the community of Jesus' disciples performed typologically with their Lord in the midst. It evidently served to depict the joy and the harmony of the redeemed universe and thus has an eschatological significance. "Grace dances. I will play on the flute, every one dances ... Whoever does not dance does not recognize what is taking place."

Rom. 16,16; 1 Pet. 5,14
**Acts of John, chs. 94–96*

Irenaeus deals with an original prophetic ordination (reported by eyewitnesses) among the Marcosians.* It takes place at a banquet held by the community and the candidate is determined by lot. The leader of the sect concerns himself in particular with women and by invocations and suggestive influence endows them with his "Grace" (*charis*) so that they prophesy and are capable of exercising prophetic office in the community. Irenaeus here implies sexual exploitation of the women who fell under the spell of Marcus and wanted not only spiritual communion with him but also physical, "in order that she, with him, may enter into the One (= Pleroma)". Here the symbolism employed is very clear, like "bride" and "bridegroom", "entering into the One" or "becoming One" and the "lifting up of the seed of light", and could easily have been transposed from the ideal image of heavenly conjunctions (syzygies) to the earthly performance of physical consummation such as Irenaeus makes mention of elsewhere* and is further depicted with Epiphanius' usual exaggeration.

Prophetic ordination
Irenaeus, Adv. haer. I 13,3–4

op. cit. I 6,3

Finally there is also a series of festivities which were observed by the gnostic communities, occasionally in agreement with the orthodox church. The celebration of the baptism of Jesus was observed by the followers of Basilides (and probably also by others) on the sixth of January, hence as the Epiphany (Appearance) of the Redeemer. Clement of Alexandria ascribes a new moon celebration to the Carpocratians. The first day of the week, which corresponds to our Sunday, was probably observed as the "day of the Lord" as in the Church; if this had not been the case the heresiologists would have reported deviations. Irenaeus reproaches the gnostics because they are the first to arrive at heathen festival parties (which amounted to state holidays) and relished the spectacle of fights in the circus.* Unfortunately we know nothing else about this aspect of

Festive days

Irenaeus, Adv. haer. I 6,3

the gnostic community life. As in other respects the Mandeans
are an exception, for they have their own calendar of festivals
(with loans from Jewish and Iranian festivals). The Manicheans, too, had their own festivals and remembrance days, or
at least they received different explanations when they co-
incided with those of other religions (particularly the Christian).

Ethics The fore-mentioned cultic practices, of which we have only a
fragmentary knowledge, comprise but one aspect only of the
forms of expression of the gnostic communities available to us;
the other aspect is that of ethical and moral behaviour. This
too, seen from the outside, is not homogeneous; a more precise
analysis of the basic principles is required. Gnostic ideology,
which harbours a strong antipathy towards the world, is strictly
speaking only half-heartedly interested, if at all, in ethical questions (Basilides' successor, allegedly his son Isidoros, composed a book entitled "Ethics" which we shall hear more
about). Its concentration on the world above and the unworldly
nucleus of man bound up with it radically severs any connection
with this world and society and focuses attention on the individuals who are "hostile to the world" as the central subject and
The brotherly object of concern. This consistent individualism, or solipsism,
ethic as an expression of the "unwordly self" revealed by Gnosis resulted in the emergence of a new ethical behaviour, a conception of the brotherhood of the "redeemed" which manifested itself in the esoteric formation of the community. H. Jonas has
unerringly recognised these associations and recorded his im-
pressions:[94] "Associated with solipsism, which follows from the
isolation of the pure self in the alienated world and on the practical level demands complete severance from worldly attach-
ments and the intensification of absolute difference, in short
the cosmic alienation of the isolated self – is a soteriological
ethic of brotherhood which is far removed from the this-world-
ly social ethic of antiquity. No longer, as there, a positive design
of co-existence in this world evolved by common intramundane
interests, having as its ultimate idea the integration of man into
the cosmic order, but, by vaulting all the cosmic processes, and
anything to do with them, the goal of this ethic is solely to promote salvation in the other world and that means severance
from this world; this must be the *vehiculum* of each and every
one. The subject of this ethic is not the actual individual, but

only his impersonal, non-mundane nucleus, the 'spark', which is identical in every one. And the basis which produces this conjunction, wherein a constitutive meeting takes place, is a common solitude in a world become alien."

This so-called "ethic of brotherhood" which demonstrates the "spirit of likemindedness" which joins men together in antipathy to the cosmos, which is deemed subdued, has become the foundation of communion. It has naturally enough become articulate in the formation of certain rules of behaviour, in the first instance probably passed on through oral tradition, then by written formulation and the composition of community regulations. Rules of this kind have not survived; what we have belongs to the Manicheans and the Mandeans, of the latter two complete legal tractates. Also in this area a glimpse into the life of the gnostic community has up to now been barred to us. Axiomatic was the injunction of brotherly love: "Love your brother like your soul, guard him like the pupil of your eye."*

<small>* NHC II 2, Log. 25</small>

Morals/morality

It is a different matter when one comes to deal with outward behaviour, in short the morality of the gnostic. Again it is only intelligible from the point of view of the complete cosmic design of Gnosis, which indeed has found in it a particularly apposite expression. The rejection of the creation and the simultaneous appeal to the possession of celestial knowledge led to a rejection of the conventional conceptions of morality. Two contrary and extreme conclusions could be drawn: the libertine or amoralistic and the ascetic. Both expressed the same basic attitude: a protest against the pretensions of the world and its legislative ruler; a revolution on a moralistic plane. Which of the two fundamental views is the older and more appropriate remains up to the present an unsolved problem.

Amoralism and asceticism

H. Jonas has stated decisively that "libertinism" was the form of expression which by its very nature applied to the "pneumatics", because it expressed in the best way possible their self-esteem and sense of freedom (i. e. from every kind of cosmic coercion).[95] "The whole idea revolves around the conception of the pneuma as the noble privilege of a new kind of man who is subjugated neither by the obligations nor the criteria of the present world of creation. The pneumatic in contrast to the psychic is *free* from the law – in a quite different sense from that of the Pauline Christian – and the unrestrained use of this freedom is not just a matter of a negative license but a positive realization of this freedom itself." This "anarchism" then was stamped by a "determined *resentment* against the prevailing rules of life", an emphasis on "*discrimination* against the rest of humanity" and by "obstinate defiance of the *demands* of the divine cosmic powers who are the guardians of the old moral order." "From the viewpoint of the obliteration of the old standards of duty, which with the insulting of the authorities contained at the same time a kind of declaration of war and even the active uprising itself, the revolution was revealed. To this extent libertinism lay at the core of the gnostic revolution."

This assessment is certainly correct, so far as the central idea – the position of the pneumatics – is concerned; but as to the question whether this attitude was the oldest put into the arena by Gnosis the sources have not yet supplied the answers. It is at any rate striking that thus far no libertine writings have appeared even among the plentiful Nag Hammadi texts. The witnesses for the libertine tendency are restricted to the Church Fathers and even here the evidence is uneven and in particular not easy to put into chronological sequence. At times it looks as if libertinism appeared rather late – we refer to the above-mentioned accounts of Epiphanius – and as if individual sects (for example, the Simonians, the Basilidians and the Valentinians) first arrived at these conclusions in the course of their further development. Gnosis was so wide-ranging in its doctrinal traditions, and evidently equally varied in its understanding of morality, even within the same schools. In addition, the heresiologists had an interest in playing up and denouncing this aspect. In many places one gets the impression that the amoralistic features were first inserted into older accounts by them. Irenaeus himself in one passage* doubts whether the principles of anarchistic behaviour enunciated in the theoretical treatises (of Carpocrates) were put into practice. We can see from this that there was evidently a distinction between theory and practice, which made different forms of behaviour possible. One will have to start with the premise that the abnegation of the Old Testament law stands well to the fore, hence the rejection of its moral prescriptions and the righteousness by works which is bound up with it. The primary factor was not an approach that was completely amoralistic from the outset. Moreover the ascetic attitude is similarly detectable quite early; most of the original sources, which clearly do not belong only to the final

See above, p. 247ff.

* *Irenaeus, Adv. haer. I 25,5*

stages, have their origin in this tendency. That we encounter in them, as in the testimony of the heresiologists, plentiful examples of a community morality of thoroughly provincial variety (the Mandeans afford the best example), points us to a developing accommodation to the world which maintains a persistent protest at most in ideologically covert form. But this in no way demonstrates the primacy (and certainly not on a historical-chronological basis) of libertine practice in Gnosis. Evidently libertine and ascetic deductions were drawn from the beginning, and more or less simultaneously, from the common "anarchistic" deposit, and were practised with different degrees of intensity. One cannot prove a uniform process of development for it.

If we examine some of the evidence concerning "amoralism" **Amoralism** then its "speculative theory" very clearly comes to light, a the- **(libertinism)** ory which was developed from the "pneumatic's" understanding of existence. According to Irenaeus, Simon Magus founded moral "freedom" in association with his own role of redeemer in the following manner: Those who put their trust in him (and his consort Helen), should trouble themselves no further with the (biblical) prophets (to whom according to Jewish belief Moses belonged) because they were "inspired" by the "angels who created the world", "but that they should as free men do what they wish: for through his (Simon's) grace are men saved, and not through righteous works. Nor are works just by nature, but by convention (*accidens*), as the angels who made the world ordained, in order to enslave men by such precepts."* The * *Irenaeus, Adv. haer. I 23,3* grace (of the spirit) cancels out the law; a formulation familiar also to Paul which Marcion then extended into a reformation of the Gospel, without however paying homage to libertinism. Simon also did not have a reputation for libertine practices (apart from the curious liaison with the prostitute Helen). The Exegesis on the Soul, which may stem from Simonian circles, is quite explicit with regard to the saving "rebirth of the soul": "This is due not to ingenious (strictly: ascetic) words or to skills or to book learning, but it is the gra[ce of Go]d (?), rather is it truly the gift of Go[d to me]n."* There is clear evidence in the * *NHC II 6,134,29–33* Testimony of Truth (probably third century) that "the Sim[o-n]ians take wi[ves] (and) beget children."* * *NHC IX 3,58*

Of the "most perfect", about whom Irenaeus* comes to * *Irenaeus, Adv. haer. I 6,3 f.* speak in his portrait of the Valentinian system without making

it clear which viewpoint they actually espoused, he recalls that
they "fearlessly practise everything that is forbidden (in Holy
Scripture)". "They eat with indifference food offered to idols
thinking that they are not in any way defiled thereby. They are
the first to arrive at any festival party of the heathen that takes
place in honour of the idols, while some of them do not even
avoid the murderous spectacle of fights with beasts and single
combats, which are hateful to God and man. And some who are
immoderately given over to the desires of the flesh say that they
are (only) repaying to the flesh what belongs to the flesh, and to
the spirit what belongs to the spirit. And some of them secretly
seduce women who are taught this teaching by them ... Some,
openly parading their shameless conduct, seduced any woman
they fell in love with away from their husbands and treated
them as their own wives. Others again who initially made an impressive pretence of living with (women) as with sisters were
convicted in course of time, when the 'sister' became pregnant
by the 'brother'." These spiritual betrothals were evidently regarded as a consummation of the heavenly conjunctions with
whose "secret" they were greatly pre-occupied, as Irenaeus
See above, p. 245 adds (cf. the concept of the "bridal chamber"). Abstinence and
good works may be important for the psychics (here the ordi-
nary Christians) but they are not necessary for the "pneumatics
and perfect". "For it is not conduct that brings men into the pleroma, but the seed (of light) which was sent out from it in its infancy and is made perfect here (on earth)."

Whatever conclusions may be drawn from these ideas the
same Church Father has passed on information about another
point of view, that of the so-called Carpocratians. They "are so
abandoned in their recklessness that they claim to have in their
power and to be able to practise anything whatsoever that is ungodly (irreligious) and impious. They say that conduct is good
and evil only in the opinion of men. And after the transmigra-
tions the souls must have been in every kind of life and every
kind of deed, if a man does not in a single descent (to earthly
life) do everything at one and the same time ... according to
their scriptures they maintain that their souls should have every
enjoyment of life, so that when they depart they are deficient in
*Irenaeus,
Adv. haer. I 25,4* nothing ..."* Freedom must therefore be gained by a complete
demonstration of it on earth, like a task that has to be accomplished.[96] The so-called Cainites also have the same understand-

ing, that "they cannot be saved in any other way, except they pass through all things."* Fearlessness and independence con- *op. cit. I 31,2* stitute the maxim of the gnostic, only thus does he evidence his "perfect knowledge". In what way this was put into effect in the cult is demonstrated to us by the Phibionites of Epiphanius. *See above, p. 247 ff.* Polluted with their own shamefulness, he recalls, "they pray with their whole bodies naked, as if by such a practice they could gain free access to God."* Nakedness as a sign of the res- *Epiphanius,* tored freedom, of the paradisical innocence of Adam, was also *Panarion 26,5,7* practised at a later date over and again in gnostic or gnosticizing movements, like the mediaeval "Adamites".

We come now to gnostic asceticism or abstinence. It has been **Asceticism** established that the overwhelming majority of the sources give unequivocal support to this aspect of gnostic morality. The Church Fathers are divided over this gnostic attitude, for they themselves in the main favoured and supported the trend towards abstemiousness in Christianity. Therefore, they either resorted to the simple expedient of slander or made out the asceticism to be sheer dissimulation and duplicity, as Epiphanius writes of the Archontics: "Some of them ruin their bodies by dissipation, but others feign ostensible fasts and deceive simple people whilst they pride themselves with a sort of abstinence, under the disguise of monks."* Irenaeus already struck a sim- *Epiphanius,* ilar tone with regard to the followers of Saturnilus (Saturni- *Panarion 40,1,4* nus): "Marriage and procreation, they maintain, are of Satan. Many of his followers abstain from animated things (i. e. animal food), and through this feigned continence they lead many astray."* Consequently rejection of marriage and certain foods *Irenaeus,* (especially meat) are among the first decrees of gnostic asceti- *Adv. haer. I 24,2* cism. The motivation for this, as it is ascribed to Saturnilus, appears to have been widely normative. Woman is regarded as a "work of Satan" among these groups. Hence "those who consort in marriage", say the Marcionite followers of Severus (third century), "fulfil the work of Satan."* For man is from the *Epiphanius,* navel upwards a creature of the power of God, but from the *Panarion 45,2,1* navel downwards a creature of the evil power; everything relating to pleasure and passion and desire originates from the navel and below.* This line of argument is strictly speaking no differ- *op. cit. 45,2,2* ent from that of the other early Christian ascetics including monachism; at this point borders with Gnosis are fluid. The concept of abstinence evidently became a popular bridge which facilitated the incursion of gnostic ideas into the Christian communities.

Moderate views   From some accounts it emerges that precisely in regard to marriage some gnostic schools made use of a graduated conception, adapted to human capacity and with good reason also utilized the New Testament. Thus the above-mentioned Isidore in his treatment of ethical problems, as preserved for us in the form of abstracts by Clement of Alexandria,* interpreted the passage in the gospel of Matthew** on the "eunuchs" in the following way: Those who by nature are averse to women and so do not marry are the "eunuchs from birth" (what the gnostics held themselves out to be); those who are such by necessity are the "theatrical ascetics" who master themselves for the sake of good repute and so "become eunuchs by necessity and not by rational reflection (*logos*)"; but those who have made themselves eunuchs for the sake of the eternal kingdom do so to avoid the unacceptable side of marriage, like the trouble that goes with providing the necessities of life. The latter is frequently mentioned in popular Christian writings, as e. g. the Acts of Thomas, as the reason for abstemiousness: Marriage and children are a burden which obstruct the way to salvation and serve only to divert a man from his true goal. The Pauline passage in the letter to the Corinthians* is taken by Isidore as a recommendation to "those who burn" to endure a "quarrelsome wife" in order through her to be free from passion; should this prove unsuccessful marriage is the only way out. A man that is young or poor or fallible, "who is unwilling to marry in accordance with reason, he should not be separated from his brother. He should say: 'I have entered into holiness, nothing can happen to me'. If he does not trust himself, let him say, 'Brother, lay your hand on me, so that I may not sin.' And he will get help both outward and inward. Only let him be willing to perfect what is good, and he will achieve it."*

The struggle against desire has elsewhere also been described by Isidore as urgent.* It required the "strength of rational reflection (*logos*)" and the "domination over the lower orders of creation" in order to fight the wicked "appendages" of the soul which wanted to drag it down. There is no appeal to the constraint of wickedness; the man who acts badly has no excuse. Therefore Basilides already held the view that only sins committed "involuntarily and in ignorance" will be forgiven.*

See above, p. 252

* Clem. Alex., Strom. III 1

** Matth. 19,11f.

* 1 Cor. 7,9

* Clem. Alex., Strom. III 2,1–5

* Clem. Alex., Strom. II 114,1

* op. cit. IV 153,4

Some human needs, says Isidore, "are necessary and natural, others are natural only. To wear clothes is necessary and natural; sexual intercourse is natural, but not necessary."* This reasoning stands on a high level and shows that the key figures of Gnosis were a match for their orthodox church opponents in this area, if not at times superior to them.

* *op. cit. III 3,1*

Another testimony on this subject is the well-known "Letter of Ptolemaeus to Flora" which Epiphanius has preserved for us.*[97] The text contains, in clear, logically weighed argumentation, reflections on the problem of the validity of the law ordained by Moses. The views aired here correspond to some extent to those of the Church and furnish clear evidence that Gnosis, on this occasion its Valentinian variety, could advocate a conception of morality acceptable to the Christian community, which accepted the Sermon on the Mount as a rule of conduct and evinced no libertine or expressly ascetic traits. The writer works with a threefold scheme in which he (appealing to Jesus!) divides the Old Testament law of the five books of Moses into three parts: the law of God, the additions of Moses and the "precepts of the elders". The law of God is again divided into three sections: the "pure law of God" in the form of the ten commandments, which Jesus did not dissolve but fulfilled; then the section which is to be understood "typically" or "symbolically", and finally the law of retribution which is "bound up with injustice" ("an eye for an eye, a tooth for a tooth ..."), which has been completely abrogated by Jesus. The intensification of the law, as Jesus carried it through in the Sermon on the Mount, is consequently also valid for this gnostic. To Jesus also goes back the "figurative" or "spiritual" interpretation of legal prescriptions; he thus led "from the sensually perceptible and apparent to the spiritual and invisible". To these belong*what is laid down about offerings, circumcision, Sabbath, fasting, Passover, unleavened bread, and other such matters. All these are but "images and symbols" which in their literal meaning are abolished, but so far as their "spiritual meaning" is concerned, are preserved: "The names remained the same, but the content changed." Thus the offerings to be made are no longer those of beasts or with incense, but "through spiritual praise and glorification and thanksgiving (eucharist), and through liberality and kindness to neighbours." We are to be "circumcised" in relation to our"spiritual hearts"*. The Sabbath involves relinquish-

The letter to Flora

* *Epiphanius, Panarion 33,3–7*

* *op. cit. 5,8–15*

* *cf. Rom. 2,28f.*

ing evil actions, which is also true when it comes to the principle of fasting. "External physical fasting is observed even among our followers, for it can be of some benefit to the soul if it is engaged on with reason (*logos*), whenever it is done neither by way of imitating others, nor out of habit, nor because of the day, as if it had been specially appointed for that pupose." It is however a way of remembering the "true fast", its visible demonstration. So with the Passover and unleavened bread: they *1 Cor.5,7* apply to Christ and his community, as Paul already claimed.* It is noteworthy in this document that the creator of the law and the creator of the world are regarded as a sort of middle being who occupies a position mid-way between the "perfect God" and the Devil; he is "just, hates evil but is neither wholly good nor bad, although he is better than the corrupting adversary of darkness". Also in this regard we have before us a moderate "communal Gnosis" which clearly derives from a compromise with Christianity and has forfeited its radical nature, even if in this case because of obvious pedagogical motives which lead to the true "gnosis".

The attitude of the community   This kind of "community morality", which does not reveal very much of the extreme demands (whether they be ascetic or libertine) on the "perfect" or "pneumatics", was according to our records, particularly the new Coptic texts from Nag Hammadi, evidently more widespread than has hitherto been supposed. It is unlikely that this state of affairs is to be explained solely by the chance nature of our sources, for example by the view that we possess in the main only the home-spun literature of the community, viz. that of the "believers" and "psychics" *See above, p.195f.* who according to Valentinian opinion had to be "nurtured" *cf. Irenaeus, Adv. haer. I 6,2; °NHC II 2* through faith and works.* In my view there is no support for this line of argument. Texts like the Gospel of Thomas,* which accepts the ethical claims of the Sermon on the Mount and Jesus' parables of the Kingdom of Heaven (indeed making them more demanding in places) and at the same time appeals to the sympathetic understanding of the initiated to whom this exegesis of the sayings of Jesus is to be imparted, show that the authors of this literature wished to address themselves to all gnostics. The one-sided reports of the Church Fathers who present only an incomplete picture of extreme developments must not be allowed to hoodwink us. The original texts are the only standard for obtaining a relatively correct view of the life of the

community and they certainly offer a good cross-section of
Gnosis in the 2nd and 3rd centuries. On these grounds it is remarkable and incompatible with certain older views on Gnosis
that in these texts a high premium is placed on the exertions of
the gnostic toward the just life and that there are also borrow-
ings from the contemporary literature of wisdom and morality.
We have already seen in the portrayal of soteriology and eschatology that the thesis put about by the Church Fathers to the effect that the gnostic must be "saved by nature" is to be taken
cum grano salis. A life governed by gnostic principles is re-   *See above,*
quired of every true gnostic; this is not a matter of indifference   *esp. p. 117f.*
to his salvation. Only thus can we understand the exhortations
to a proper way of living with its trials and tribulations, together
with the stress on the struggle of the soul on its perilous path to
salvation which also constitutes part of its suffering experience
(cf. Isidore's interpretation). It is the world-renouncing and   *See above, p. 258f.*
therefore ascetic tenor that runs through the mass of this litera-
ture; a few examples suffice to bring this home to us.

In the Acts of Peter and the Twelve Apostles Jesus appears   **Ascetic**
as a pearl merchant who when Peter asks the name of his city   **statements**
(i.e. his origin) and the road to it replies: "Not every man is **in the Nag**
able to go on that road except one who has relinquished all his **Hammadi texts**
possessions and has fasted daily from district to district. For numerous are the robbers and (wild) beasts on that road. Whoever takes bread with him on the road the black dogs kill because of the bread. Whoever wears an expensive garment of the
world, him the robbers kill [because of the gar]ment. [Whoev-
er] carries [wa]ter with him, [the wolves kill] ... Whoever is
anxious about [meat] and vegetables, the lions [ki]ll ... If he
evades the lions the bulls devour him for the sake of the food."*   * *NHC VI 1,5,19–6,8*
This is an intentionally figurative description of the road that
the gnostic has to tread in order to reach his goal. The Gospel of
Thomas speaks briefly of it in one of Jesus' sayings: "Blessed is
the man who has suffered (and so) has found life."* And else-   * *NHC II 2, Saying 58*
where in connection with the Gospel of Matthew**: "But you   ** *Matth. 24,43*
be vigilant against the world! Gird your loins with great
strength lest the robbers find a way to reach you. For the neces-
sity for which you look they will (then) find."* This opposition   * *NHC II 2, Saying 21b*
to all the enticements of the worldly powers is the constant
theme of the Authoritative Teaching, which interprets this
"great struggle" as the will of God since he wished to make con-

testants appear who thanks to their "knowledge" leave things
terrestrial behind.* "In regard to [those who belong to] the
world we do not concern ourselves: if they [slan]der us, we pay
no attention to them; if they curse us and cast shame in our faces we (just) look on without saying a word. For they go to their
work, but we wander about in hunger and thirst, looking toward our dwelling place, the place to which our public conduct
(*politeia*) and our conscience look forward. We do not adhere
to the things which have come into being but draw back from
them, because our hearts repose on the things that (really) exist. We are (indeed) ill, weak and afflicted, but a great strength
is hidden within us."* The same text describes the "food", i. e.
vices, by which the devil seeks to seduce the soul and which
they must resist.* "First he casts sadness into your heart until
you are troubled (even) by a trifle of this life, and (then) he
seizes us with his poisons and thereafter with desire for a garment in which to pride yourself; (then follow) love of money,
ostentation, vanity, envy that is envious of another envy, beauty of body, fraudulence; the worst (vices) of all these are ignorance and indifference. Now all these things the adversary (*anti-
keimenos*) prepares nicely and spreads them out before the
body wishing to make the inner part (actually: the heart) of the
soul incline herself to one of them and it overwhelm her. As
with a net he draws her by force in ignorance and beguiles her
until she conceives evil and bears fruit of matter (*hylē*) and goes
about in defilement covetously pursuing many desires and the
fleshly sweetness draws her on in ignorance. But the soul which
has recognised these desires to be ephemeral withdraws from
them and enters into a new way of life (*politeia*) and from then
on despises this present life because it is transitory and longs for
the food which will lead her to (eternal) life and leaves behind
her those false foods ..."

The ethical   Gnosis has here taken over without hesitation the ancient
imperative   schema of the two ways, which leaves the decision to do what is
right to human endeavour and promises a reward for those who
make the effort and punishment for those who are negligent.
The utilization of popular philosophical ethics and wisdom
teaching therefore gave rise to no problem on this level. It is
now best documented by the appearance of the Teachings of
Silvanus* and a fragment of the Sentences of Sextus** in the
Nag Hammadi library. The former, a collection of miscellane-

* NHC VI 3,26,6–26

* NHC VI 3,27,6–25
Continuation see
above, p. 144
* NHC VI 3,30,26–32,3

* NHC VII 4
** NHC XII 1
Plate 18

ous pieces, has an unequivocally practical-ethical tendency which does not have an explicit gnostic motivation but could readily be made to serve the gnostic disapprobation of the world. The call to a righteous way of life in almost monastic style is found here throughout. "Be vigilant that you do not fall into the hands of the robbers: Give your eyes no sleep nor slumber to your eyelids that you may be saved like a gazelle from snares and like a bird from the great noose!* Fight the * *cf. Prov. 6,4* great fight as long as the fight lasts. While all the powers are looking on at you – not only [the] holy ones, but also all the powers of the adversary. Woe to you if they are victorious over you in the midst of every one who is watching you!"*[98] The * *NHC VII 4, 113,33–114,6* gnostic is thus a "contestant", an "athlete", as the apostle Tho-·mas is called in one of the tractates of the Nag Hammadi codi- ces.* * *NHC II 7*

Gnosis is a stranger to any legal conception and in this con- **Attitude to** nection has just as sharp an anti-Jewish attitude as Christianity, **the Law** which led to the smooth adoption of Christian ethical ways of behaviour, such as for example manifests itself in the Gospel of Thomas, although we are aware of this also through other sour- *See above, p. 257ff.* ces. The determining fact is the internal motivation, not the ex- ternal performance of commandments like fasting, prayers, giving of alms or food laws. Jesus replies to his disciples accord- ingly: "Do not tell lies, and do not do what you hate! For every- thing is exposed before Heaven. For there is nothing hidden that will not be made manifest, and nothing covered that will not be uncovered."* Even more trenchantly the Jewish laws * *NHC II 2, log. 6; cf. Matth. 6,1–8* mentioned in logion 14 are made out to be of no consequence, indeed as detrimental to salvation: Fasting gives rise to sin, praying to condemnation, the giving of alms to harming one's spirit; one should eat everything that is set before one. It is im- portant to heal the sick, by which probably the ignorant are re- ferred to. The saying concludes with a quotation from Mark's Gospel;* later still Luke's** as well as Matthew's*** Gospel * *Mark 7,15* are brought in on this question.* Of sole importance is the "fast ** *Luk. 6,44f.* *** *Matth. 12,34f.* as regards the world" because only that leads to the "king- * *NHC II 2, log. 45* dom".** The "great fast" is taken in this sense also by the Man- ** *NHC II 2, log. 27* deans: It is no external abstention from eating and drinking but a cessation from inquisitiveness, lies, hatred, jealousy, discord, murder, theft, adultery, the worship of images and idols.[99] "Whoever has come to know the world", announces the Jesus

of the Gospel of Thomas, "has found a corpse; and whoever
has found a corpse, the world is unworthy of him" (Saying 56;
in saying 80 the same is said, but instead of "corpse" the refer-

NHC II 2, logia 56 and 80   ence is to the "body" of the world*).

Gnostic   The gnostic and Christian ethos could also be brought to-
freedom and   gether in such a way that dominion over sin (which the gnostic
love of   possesses as a "free" man) and love for the ignorant (who must
neighbour   be "freed" from their condition) were regarded as one and the
same thing, as in the Gospel of Philip: "He who has the knowledge (*gnosis*) of the truth is free. But the free does not sin. For

cf. John 8,34   he who sins is the slave of sin* . . . Those to whom it is not permitted to sin, the world calls 'free' . . . knowledge lifts up (their)
hearts, which means it makes them free, and makes them be
lifted up above the whole place (of the world). But love (*agapē*)

cf. 1 Cor. 8,1   edifies.* But he who has become free through knowledge is a
slave for love's sake to those who have not yet been able to take
up the freedom of knowledge. But knowledge makes them

NHC II 3,77 (125), 15–35   worthy so that [it causes them] to become [free] . . ."* This
"Christian" Gnosis fully justifies its epithet and not only on
grounds of external adaptation.

Criticism   So far we have left the social features of the gnostic pro-
of society   gramme aside in order to devote our attention expressly to this
theme at the close. The view of the world and history held by
Gnosis, as we have depicted it, contains a criticism of all existing things which hardly finds its counterpart in antiquity. The
rejection of the creation together with its creator and the de-
grading and demonizing of the celestial spheres (the stars and
planets) necessarily include a disapprobation and denial of the
socio-political world generated by antiquity. This aspect of the
gnostic "revolt" against the prevailing secular and religious system is not however stated explicitly. The reason for this lies in
the first place in the gnostics' supreme indifference to this
present world. For them the cosmos with its diverse (earthly and
celestial) structures of command is an outworn, infirm product
whose dangerousness is still evident in its attempts to block the
irresistible process of its own annihilation (e. g. by tyranizing
the "seed of light" and trying to interfere with its release) but
whose machinations have only a delaying effect. Gnosis, at
least according to the present state of our knowledge, took no
interest of any kind in a reform of earthly conditions but only in
their complete and final destruction. It possessed no other

"revolutionary" programme for altering conditions, as they appeared to it, than the elimination of earthly structures in general and the restoration of the ideal world of the spirit that existed in the very beginning. This is shown above all by the virtual absence of contemporary historical allusions or even of criticism of the Roman Imperium. Still, one does find a whole series of allusions, direct as well as indirect, to socio-critical views of the gnostics, which differed considerably from those of their own environment.[100] Whether they were themselves conscious of this in detail, in the way in which we interpret it, can obviously no longer be ascertained.

In the portrayal and designation of the supramundane "powers" and "forces", particularly in that of their "commander" (*archon*) a gap is certainly reflected between Gnosis and the sovereign authorities on earth, because these concepts had their origin in the political nomenclature of antiquity. As the first cosmic ruler and demiurge enslaved mankind, as he and his following introduced "unrest" and "discord" into the world, the gnostic had a graphic illustration of Roman and other kinds of rule under which he had to live (including that of the orthodox Church!). Consequently he longed for "rest" and release from the "world's discord", to use a Mandean expression. It is noteworthy that in undermining the legitimacy of the earthly order the gnostic systems, in contrast to contemporary theories of the state which regarded king and state as exponents or as an incorporation of cosmic order (harmony!), considered these relations as "ungodly" and inaugurated solely by the evil and "stupid" creator of the world. Whilst Hellenistic political theory understands earthly sovereignty as a system controlled by divine reason (*nous, logos*), and so provides a justification for it, Gnosis disputes the alleged conformity to reason of the whole world, since this world had its origin in a blunder and a "senseless" act. It was not "reason" that ruled the world, it was the lack of reason. The gnostic who has gained this insight and has recognized the true reason beyond all earthly things, which is at the same time akin to himself, can thereby subdue the world and renounce all obedience to it (manifestly by his ethical behaviour). This position with which we are already fully acquainted has, as H. Jonas put it, "shattered the panlogistical or pantheistic illusion of the ancient world."[101] The ancient system of rule has been divested by Gnosis of its sanctity; it has been

Rejection of earthly authorities

See above, p. 73, 78, 83f.

"degraded from the alleged dignity of an inspired 'hierarchical' order to a naked display of power ... which at the most could exact obedience but not respect".[102] This "ideal rebellion" or "metaphysical emptying" of the old rule did not indeed lead to its actual abolition, but the whole counter-design of the gnostic system as it confronts us in its soteriology and eschatology effected for its advocates a practical devaluation and weakening of political conditions.

A telling witness to this gnostic criticism of sovereignty is the idea found repeatedly in certain texts (e. g. in the Apocalypse of Adam*), that the perfect gnostic belongs to a "kingless race" which excels all "kingdoms" of the past and present and gets its uniquely binding legitimation through the true – albeit unrecognized by the world – Father of men. But the champions of this "kingless race" are "kings as immortal within the mortal (realm); they will pass judgement on the gods of chaos and their powers".* The other races belong to the "kings of the Ogdoad" and in the end come to them*, i. e. they do not attain to the ideal kingless realm, where everyone is a king in his own right and so there are no trappings of sovereignty, but only to the "immortal kingdoms" of the remainder of the pleroma. In the Letter of Eugnostos the Blessed and in the Sophia of Jesus Christ there is a discussion of "the race over which there is no sovereignty", by which is meant the world of immortal spirits, those who are the "self-originate", "of equal age" and "of equal power".* The highest Being himself has understanding, insight, thought, intelligence, reason and strength in perfect measure, which may be dispensed in moderation to the remaining realms of the Pleroma (in this connection there is also some mention of the "ruler" of the upper over the lower level, but as an expression of harmony and of *syngeneia*). In the Book of Thomas* the faithful are promised not only "rest" in the hereafter but sovereignty and unity with the "King", by which God is understood. Along these lines the followers of a certain Prodicus (c. 200) justified their libertine propensities, claiming that they were of "noble descent" and were the "King's children", i. e. children of the "first God", over whom no one had authority.*

The way in which polemic was openly expressed against earthly rulers was laid down by the Mandeans, almost to this day an oppressed community, in a special order:[103] "My chos-

* NHC V 5

See above, p. 137

* NHC II 5,125 (173), 13–14

* NHC II 5,125 (173), 3ff.

See above, p. 205f.

* NHC III 3,75,17f.; Pap. Ber. 92,1ff.

* NHC II 7

See above, p. 185

* Clem. Alex., Strom. III 30,1

en! Do not put your trust in the kings, rulers and rebels of this world, nor in military forces, arms, conflict, and the hosts which they assemble, nor (in) the prisoners which they take in this world, nor in gold and silver ... their gold and their silver will not save them. Their sovereignty passes away and comes to an end, and judgement will be pronounced over them."* The *Right Ginza I, 121* Mandeans also, by virtue of their bad experiences, tolerated an "intellectual reservation" (*reservatio mentalis*), i. e. concealment of their real faith in face of persecutions. It is no wonder that the Mandean texts number among the acts of their heavenly Redeemer the destruction of "citadels" and the punishment of the "mighty of the earth".

See above, p. 201

The question of taxes The gnostics, like the Christians, did not regard the payment of tax as an act of recognition. The Gospel of Thomas takes up the parable on Tribute to Caesar* and slightly modifies it: *Mark. 12,14–17* "They (the disciples) showed Jesus a gold coin and said to him: 'Caesar's men demand taxes from us'. He said to them: 'Give to Caesar what belongs to Caesar, give to God what belongs to God, and give to me what is mine!"* If the latter does not have *NHC II 2, log. 100* a spiritual meaning and is intended only to underline devotion to God, this command could also be a reference to the necessary support of the community by its members.[104]

Social criticism The critical attitude of Gnosis with regard to society emerges also from still other facts. We have mentioned the "brotherly ethic" which eschews distinctions of any kind in the community *See above, p. 252f.* of the "perfect" and to that extent contains a new scale of values running counter to the old ethic. For this Plotinus as representative of the "classical" (Greek) standpoint can again be very instructive. He reproaches the gnostics* for using the name *Plotinus, Ennedas II 9,18* "brother" even of the "basest men", but not of the divine powers of the heavens (the sun and stars) and "our sister the world-soul". For him it was outrageous that "men who are base could claim kinship with those above": this befits only the good and the soulful. Also on the social side the Greek idea of the cosmos with its balanced stratification was undermined. Man, including the base and the humble, has divine rights, in as much as he has secured Gnosis, and stands higher than the whole cosmos which in itself has no value. This "inversion of values" appears also in the removal of the distinction between "slaves" and "free", although in the gnostic texts this is envisaged only as an ultimate goal. Nevertheless the common self-designation "free" clearly expresses the removal of any relationships of dependence here on earth and stands for their complete liquidation in the Pleroma. "In the world (*kosmos*) the slaves serve the free. In the kingdom of heaven the free will serve the slaves", as the Gospel of Philip puts it.* When perfection makes its appearance, "then the perfect light will pour out on every one and all those that are in it will [receive the an]ointing. Then the slaves will be free [and] the prisoners ransomed".* Taking up Paul's word** with reference to the Christian community, the Valentinian Tripartite Tractate describes the final condition as a return from multiplicity, changeableness and inequality to the place of original unity "where there is no male or female, nor slave and free, nor circumcision and uncircumcision, neither angel nor man, but Christ is all in all ... and the nature of the one who is (actually) a slave is conditioned anew and he will take a place with a free man!"* But already in this world "the knowledge of the truth which existed before ignorance ... is liberation from the servile nature in which (all) those suffered who originated from an inferior thought."*

Thanks to certain extracts from the "Carpet-bags"* of Clement of Alexandria we know of a unique book which deals with gnostic social criticism; it stems from the second century and bears the title "On Righteousness".[105] It is ascribed to a certain Epiphanes, supposedly the son of the legendary sect founder Carpocrates, who died young. Starting from the gnostic concepts of the world and freedom, it demonstrates by arguments from natural philosophy and logic that the earthly distinctions between "mine" and "thine", riches and poverty, freedom and slavery, rulers and ruled are untenable and not in accordance with nature; these are human, not divine institutions. The author advocates a kind of gnostic communism and in this way shows the latent disruptive force in the gnostic view of life. "The righteousness of God", he says, "is a communion with equality, for the heaven, equally stretched out on all sides like a circle, embraces the whole earth, and the night shows forth equally all the stars, and the sun, the cause of day and the origin (actually: father) of light, God has poured forth from above equally upon the earth for all who can see; but they all see in common, for he (God) makes no distinction between rich or poor, people or ruler, foolish and wise, female and male, free and slave. Not even any of the irrational creatures does he treat

Margin notes (left column):

* NHC II 3,72 (120), 17–20

* NHC II 3,85 (133), 24–29

** Gal. 3,28

* NHC I 5,132,21–133,1

* op. cit. 117,28–38

* Clem. Alex., Strom. III 6,1–9,3

Epiphanes: On Righteousness

differently ..., he establishes righteousness, since none can have more or take away from his neighbour that he himself may have twice as much light (of the sun) as the other. The sun causes common food to grow up for all creatures and the common righteousness is given to all equally ..." (this is demonstrated with examples from the animal and plant world). "But not even the things of generation have any written law – it would have been transcribed – but they sow and give birth equally, having a communion implanted (inborn) by righteousness ... (this is proved by the common gift of eyes to see for everyone without distinction). But the laws, since they could not punish men's incapacity to learn, taught (them) to transgress. For the private property of the laws cut up and nibbled away the fellowship of the divine law ... (here there is a reference to the epistle to the Romans*). Mine and thine, he says, were intro- *Rom. 7,7 duced through the laws; no longer would the fruits either of the earth or of possessions, or even of marriage be enjoyed in community. In common for all he (God) made the vines, which refuse neither sparrow nor thief, and likewise the corn and other fruits. But since fellowship and equality were violated (by the laws), there arose theft of beasts and fruits. In that God made all things in common for man, and brought together the female with the male in common and united all the animals likewise, he declared righteousness to be fellowship with equality. But those thus born rejected the fellowship which had brought about their birth, and say: 'Who marries one (wife), let him have her', when they could all share in common, as the rest of the animals show ..." Further on it is pointed out that the words of the lawgiver (i. e. the Jewish God) "Thou shalt not covet"* *Exod. 20,17 are laughable, and yet more laughable is it to say, "what is your neighbour's". "For the very one, the lawgiver, who gave the desire as embracing the things of birth commands that it be taken away (again), though he takes it away from no (other) animal. But that he said 'your neighbour's wife' is even more laughable, since he (thus) compels what was common possession to become private property". The conclusions affecting the cult which should be drawn from this community are cited in detail by Clement; we have already described them. Elsewhere, in See above, p. 250 the Iran of the Sassanid king Kavad (489–531), the same brand of socio-critical conceptions were put into practice at a critical period and led to the social revolutionary movement of Mazdak (died 524), who in his communistic doctrine also availed him-self of gnostic and Manichean concepts and by doing so fur-nished proof of the disruptive force of this anti-cosmic dual-ism.[106] For that reason O. Klíma called this trend the "gnostic Manichean Left".

Repudiation of property

The condemnation of wealth, chiefly of property, is usual in Gnosis, and closely connected with the fundamental attitude of eschewing the world and all it stands for. This approach how-ever has at the same time a significant socio-critical component, as some evidence shows, although occasionally it is simply the Christian literature that is employed. Lucian relates of the "Christian" Peregrinus that he handed over his property to the community. The Gospel of Thomas clearly disapproves of monetary interest* and in its own way reiterates Jesus' para-bles* against the accumulation of riches, even increasing the tone of severity in places. The parable of the Great Banquet* concludes on a note against businessmen and merchants: They will not enter into the Pleroma*: "Whoever finds the world (*kosmos*) and becomes rich, let him renounce the world."* The homily The Testimony of Truth is directed against usury and addiction to "Mammon", which includes addiction to sexual in-tercourse.* Revealing is a passage from the tractate The Acts of Peter and the Twelve Apostles, which denounces the preferen-tial status of the rich*: Jesus admonishes his disciples to keep away from the rich men of the city since they did not deem him worthy, but "revelled in their wealth and presumption". "Many", he goes on, "have shown partiality to the rich, for (where there are rich) in the communities (churches) they themselves are sinful, and they give occasion for others to do (likewise). But judge them with rectitude, so that your ministry (*diaconia*) may be glorified and my name too may be glorified in the communities (churches)!" Both the church and Gnosis had to resist secularization early on.*

The position of women

To the socio-critical subjects which are mentioned in Gnosis belongs lastly the relation of the sexes. The equal standing of women in cultic practice in the gnostic communities appears to have been relatively widespread, as we have already seen (there is probably a polemical reference to this in the First Let-ter to Timothy; cf. also Paul in First Corinthians*). On the oth-er hand there is evidence in some branches of the denigration of women and the rejection of marriage. These differing attitudes

Marginal notes:

See above, p. 213

* NHC II 2, log. 95
* NHC II 2, log. 63
* Luk. 14, 16–24

* NHC II 2, log. 64
* NHC II 2, log. 110

* NHC IX 3,68,1–11

* NHC VI 1,11,27–12,13

* cf. James 2,1–4

* I Tim. 2,11 f.;
1 Cor 14,34 ff.

See above, p. 257

may perhaps find an explanation in the fundamental conception which at times crops up in the sources, namely that bi-sexuality is an evil of the earthly world and a mark of its lost unity, in contrast to the complete annulment of division in the Pleroma as portrayed by the male-female couplings of heavenly beings. Frequently bi-sexuality became something of an ideal for Gnosis; it is attributed among others to the highest being. The Mandaic Eve speaks to Adam in the following instructive statement:[107]

"When there was no unevenness (or: inequality),
(then) we had (but) *one* form.
We had (but) *one* form
and we were both made as a *single* mana (spirit)
Now, where there is no evenness (or: equality),
they made you a man and me a woman."*

                                                           * *Right Ginza III*

In the Gospel of Philip this division of the sexes is made out to be the woman's (i. e. Eve's) fault (perhaps simulating the fall of Sophia from the unity of the Pleroma) and is connected with the origin of mortality. That unity is life, separation death is a guiding principle of gnostic thought. "When Eve was (still) in Adam, there was no death. When she separated from him, death arose. When she (or it, death) enters him again and he (Adam) takes her (or it, death) to himself, there shall be no (more) death."* "If the woman had not separated from the man, she would not have died with the man. His separation became the beginning of death. Therefore Christ came that he might set right again the separation which arose from the beginning and unite the two, and give life to those who died in the separation and unite them."*

                                               * *NHC II 3, 68 (116), 22–26*

                                               * *NHC II, 3, 70 (118), 9–17*

The devaluation of the woman and what is female which finds expression here is certainly compensated by the activity of women in the life of the community and the large role which is ascribed to the female aspect in gnostic mythology (cf. Sophia, Barbelo and others), but in the final analysis we are left with the traditional assessment, standard in antiquity, of the woman as a creature subordinated to the man. Consequently there are only the beginnings of an emancipation. That this is the case is clear from certain evidence which regards a redemption of the woman as possible only on the condition of her metamorphosis into a man. Of course a part is played by the idea that for the union with the original heavenly image (often depicted as female) of the soul the returning partner (the copy) must belong to one sex, predominantly the male; hence the change is assumed for the sake of the unity to be recovered. At the end of the Gospel of Thomas the following episode takes place: "Simon Peter spoke to them (the disciples): 'Let Mary (Magdalene) leave us, for women are not worthy of life.' Jesus said: 'Behold, I shall lead her in order to make her male, so that she too may become a living spirit resembling you males. For every woman who will make herself male will enter the Kingdom of Heaven.'"* The same view is also held by the Naassenes and Valentinians; the former maintain that all who reach "the house of the (good) God" "become bridegrooms, being rendered wholly male through the virgin spirit."* The Valentinian Theodotus believed that the "seed of light", so long as it was still unformed (i. e. uneducated, untrained), is a "child of the female", but when it is formed (i. e. trained), it is changed into a man and becomes a son of the (heavenly) bridegroom; no longer is it weak and subjected to the cosmic powers, but having become a man, it becomes a male fruit.* As such it can enter into the Pleroma and unite with the angels. "Therefore it is said that the woman is changed into a man and the community here below (on earth) into angels."* One must bear in mind that in Greek "angel" (i. e. messenger) has the masculine gender. In Valentinianism, at least with Heracleon and Theodotus, the "male", as it was created in Adam*, is the "elect" of the angels, the "female" which corresponds to Eve represents the "calling" of the pneumatics, who must be brought up to the male "elect" in order to become part of the Pleroma and attain again to the angelic status.

* NHC II 2, log. 114

* Hippolytus, Refutatio V 8,44

* Clem. Alex., Ex Theodoto 79

See above, p. 196

* Clem. Alex., Ex Theodoto 21,3

* cf. Gen. 1,27

IV

Prominent Uigur ladies from a temple frieze in Bazaklik (Turfan), which portrays supporters of the Manichean church. Cf. plate 25.

HISTORY

Presuppositions and Causes
The Problem of Origins

It is no exaggeration to number the problems of the genesis and the history of Gnosis among the most difficult which are encountered in research not only into Gnosis but also into the history of the religion of later antiquity. The reasons for this are to be found, on the one hand, in the state of the sources which has been described in the first section; on the other hand, it has to be considered that the gnostics showed no interest in historical matters unless they had some connection with the history of salvation, and this is understandable from their opposition to the world. Up to this day we have no historical tractate from gnostic hands, such as, for instance, the Acts of the Apostles by Luke, or even the Ecclesiastical History by Eusebius of Caesarea, which could help us to write the history of Gnosis. We are on firm ground only where known founders of gnostic schools or sects can be pin-pointed and dated, or where literary investigations of the extant sources lead to corresponding results. The latter is now within the grasp of students of Gnosis in view of the texts from Nag Hammadi. Their analysis, both historical and literary, is as yet in its infancy. Thus the contribution to the history from this side too is still limited. In what follows, therefore, no more than an attempt can be made to summarise in a survey some recent results in research. This cannot be done without hypotheses and without the author giving voice to his predilections, particularly on the subject of the beginnings of Gnosis. Much is still in a state of flux, and to write a complete history of Gnosis remains a task for the future.

The ·Fathers of the Church simply traced back the rise of Gnosis to the devil. The classic formulation of this view was made by the father of ecclesiastical historiography, Eusebius of Caesarea (ca. 264–339) in his Ecclesiastical History: "Like brilliant lamps the churches were now shining throughout the world, and faith in our Saviour and Lord Jesus Christ was flourishing among all mankind, when the devil who hates what is **The view of the Church Fathers** good, as the enemy of truth, ever most hostile to man's salvation, turned all his devices against the church. Formerly he had used persecutions from without as his weapon against her, but now that he was excluded from this he employed wicked men and sorcerers, like baleful weapons and ministers of destruction against the soul, and conducted his campaign by other measures, plotting by every means that sorcerers and deceivers might assume the same name as our religion and at one time lead to the depth of destruction those of the faithful whom they caught, and at others, by the deeds which they undertook, might turn away from the path to the saving word those who were ignorant of the faith" [108]. At the head of these deceivers stands Simon Magus (i.e. the sorcerer), known from the Acts of the Apostles*, who came from Samaria and competed with the apostles. He was already considered by Justin and Irenaeus as the forefather of Gnosis. From his disciple and alleged successor Menander, who was also a Samaritan, there came forth like a double-tongued and double-headed serpent (according to Eusebius) Saturninus (or Satornilos) of Antioch and Basilides of Alexandria. These founded "ungodly heretical schools", the former in Syria, the latter in Egypt. With the help of this line of descent, the rise and expansion of the gnostic heresy was explained for subsequent ages.

Eusebius, Eccles. Hist. IV 7 (Loeb Classical Library)

Acts 8

Results of modern research   To establish the actual course of events which lies behind these statements was not an easy task for modern research. Some light was shed on the problem by careful analyses of the extant source material. The "heretics" mentioned by the heresiologists played in this a less important part than the gnostic writings themselves (many of which had been handed down anonymously), and the relations to gnostic communities which can be deduced from the New Testament and from early Christian literature. It is the undeniable merit of the so-called "religionsgeschichtliche Schule" of German Protestant theology to have done pioneering work here. One of its most important results was the proof that the gnostic movement was originally a non- Christian phenomenon which was gradually enriched with Christian concepts until it made its appearance as independent Christian Gnosis. This development, which we know in rough outline only, is equivalent to the development of Gnosis from a relatively independent Hellenistic religion of later antiquity to a Christian "heresy." Its link with Christian ideas, which began

See above, p. 31 ff.

at an early stage, produced on the one hand a fruitful symbiosis which greatly helped its expansion, but on the other hand contained a deadly germ to which sooner or later it was to succumb in competition with the official Christian Church.

But let us return to the problems of the origin of Gnosis. Essentially they can be reduced to three aspects: social history, history of civilisation and history of religion. These three, as one would expect in antiquity, are of course connected, and we shall try not to neglect this in the following description.

First on the aspect of the history of civilisation and religion. **Cultural** The Fathers of the Church maintained again and again that the **and** first gnostics came from the Orient, more precisely from the **religio-** area of Samaria-Palestine, and that their teachings owed a debt **historical** to the Jewish biblical tradition. These statements can be con- **aspects** firmed by many of the older as well as the new original writings. Particularly the Coptic texts from Nag Hammadi have lent support to the thesis that the majority of gnostic systems came into existence on the fringes of Judaism.

Many of the writings, as we have seen, can be understood as interpretations or paraphrases of Old Testament texts, and otherwise, too, the use of biblical material is striking in spite of the polemic against the traditional interpretation which is often manifest. The Old Testament tradition is appealed to even when its official interpretation is rejected and this shows that Gnosis is also dependent on the authorisation by "Holy Writ". As we have heard, various characters of the Old Testament, as e. g. Adam, Seth, Cain, Shem and Noah, are claimed as ancestors. Even the devaluation of the Jewish God of creation in favour of the "unknown God" cannot disguise that in the last resort there is a Jewish root, for the supreme God has traits of Jewish monotheism, and the revaluation of creation and law can be explained as a revolt within a specific Jewish movement. To trace the background in terms of the history of religion, two early Jewish movements must be mentioned particularly, the apocalyptic and the sapiential. The two are linked together by various threads.[109]

The Apocalyptic which takes its name from the literary **Influence** works it produced, the apocalypses or revelations, can be **of Jewish** traced back to the second century B. C. (first of all in the book **Apocalyptic** of the prophet Daniel). It is characterised by the faith in the early end of the world and God's intervention in favour of his own. This eschatological tendency includes also a pronounced dualistic-pessimistic world view in that it teaches that the present age ("this aeon") is bound to perish and will be followed by the future age of redemption; it is no longer governed by God but by his enemy, the devil and his powers, the archons and demons. World and history are left on an automatic course towards the end. Only "apocalyptic man", who knows himself to be the truly pious and Godfearing, knows more about it: God has revealed it to him. Apocalyptic, therefore, is esoteric, revealed wisdom, and the resulting knowledge has an immediate relation to redemption. The knowledge of God's mysteries guarantees salvation; knowledge, or cognition, and redemption are closely connected.[110] As this knowledge is accessible only to the initiated, this Jewish school strictly distinguishes those who consider themselves to be the righteous or the pious, and the rest, the unrighteous and ungodly.

This division is reminiscent of that which Gnosis makes between spiritual man (pneumatic) and man who is attached to matter and to the flesh (hylic, *sarkikos*). The righteous look upon themselves as estranged from the world; they are strangers in this aeon and set their whole expectation on God's future in a new aeon. In Apocalyptic it is still essentially a process in a horizontal direction, a chronological sequence, while in Gnosis a reinterpretation takes place, resulting in a primarily vertical arrangement, an ontological stratification of the same world view (although the linear-eschatological direction is not excluded). But also in Apocalyptic the heavenly world is already a popular object for speculation. The kingdom of God, furnished with various angelic beings and the preexistent future saviour, the messianic Son of man (meaning actually only "man"), is separated from this world by a series of intermediate worlds (serving as places of punishment) occupied by good and evil spirits. Thus God is removed cosmologically, or ontologically, to a far off distance and stands in need of various intermediaries, such as the already mentioned Son of man, Wisdom, or the Logos, in order to operate. By means of heavenly journeys, which are not without danger as they lead through many heavens, certain elect, as e.g. Enoch, Baruch and Ezra, can reach God in order to receive knowledge about the future of the world and other mysteries. Apocalyptic and Gnosis thus have a whole series of mythological themes in common. In addition to the subject of the ascension to heaven and the predilection for the world of angels and spirits, there is a strong interest not only in cosmology as such, but especially in the primeval time of origin and the end-time of eschatological fulfilment. The Adamites and early Fathers of Judaism are specially favoured authorities in the apocalypses; they serve as illustrations and models for the life of the pious. Apocryphal and pseudepigraphal writings which circulate under their names are the main types of apocalyptic literature, which is continued in gnostic literature, sometimes even with evident literary links.[111] An exegesis, often bold, which uses allegory freely, helps to reinterpret the biblical tradition. (This method is employed most impressively by the greatest Jewish philosopher of Hellenistic times, Philo of Alexandria, first century A. D., who however does not belong to the Apocalyptic school). The Adam event is decisive for the history of the world and of humanity. In Adam's fall the whole human race sinned and corrupted the creation. But in Adam there is also contained the multitude of the souls – he is the "container of the souls" – which are to be made incarnate on earth until the fixed end of the world. This is very much reminiscent of the figure of the primeval man, Adam, of the gnostic texts who represents the seed of light.

See above, p. 92f.

There are points of principle as well as individual mythological features which recur in Apocalyptic and in Gnosis and which suggest a connection, although the differences must not be neglected; here they have been consciously put aside (as e.g. the idea of creation which is maintained in Apocalyptic, the link with Israel and the lack of an acosmic dualism). What is said in a recent description of Apocalyptic is valid for both[112]: "World and history are considered as being completely outside the sphere of God, without salvation, without life, condemned to destruction. All evil comes from the world, viz. from history. Man can find salvation only when he flees from history and the world... In spite of all outward, largely historically conditioned differences, individualism and universalism are equally fundamental for Apocalyptic and Gnosis. Individualism and universalism are the expression of a common basic experience for Apocalyptic and Gnosis, that salvation lies outside this world, viz. outside the course of this world." Correspondingly, in both areas a new collective consciousness is formed, namely that of the eschatological community of salvation, be it as community of the true Israel, as the people of the coming aeon of God, or as race of the seed of light, the pneumatics, who equally repre-

See above, p. 205 ff. sent the new aeon. The social ambitions agree similarly. "Gnosis and Apocalyptic are radically revolutionary. To change the world means for them to do away with it. Their judgement of the world is judgement of history as such. They rebel against all rulers and long for the world without laws. They negate the existent completely for the sake of that which no eye has seen, nor ear has heard. They have no interest in any existing order, for nothing is in order, and they strive for a world that needs no ordering hand. They put God and the world into opposition, thus claiming God entirely for themselves."

Qumran   Since 1947 we know from the Dead Sea Scrolls (Qumran) of a community on the fringe of Judaism which observed a strict piety of the law but at the same time held a range of ideas which exhibit links with Apocalyptic as well as with the emergent Gnosis. To these belong the soteriological concept of know-

1QH ledge as it appears especially in the Hymns*, and a cosmological dualism of two spirits (or angels) of light and darkness who

* Manual of Discipline
1 QS III 13–IV 26
rule the world at the order of God *[113]. Accordingly, men are divided into sons of light and sons of darkness, or of wickedness. The former are the initiated, or wise, or prudent, the elect; the latter are the foolish, the men of lies and of evil. The pious man lives in the evil world which is ruled by the devil (*beliar*) as a stranger. His fate is described, especially in the poetic texts, by adopting the vocabulary and style of the ancient psalter, as the fate of the soul in the corporeal world is described in Gnosis.[114] To be sure, the God of knowledge has created the world and the two spirits, but his power over this world is limited by the operation of the angel of darkness (who is at the same time to be understood as the devil). The design for the world and the salvation of the elect are determined by God and the evil one cannot change this; these are the mysteries of God which are known to the wise only and on which his hope is founded. Thus Qumran offers a certain link on the fringe of Judaism for the illumination of the origin of gnostic ideas.

Jewish   There is yet another catchment area in Judaism which is rele-
Wisdom vant: the tradition of Wisdom teaching. Indeed, the figure of
teaching Wisdom (*Sophia, Achamoth*) which we encounter frequently in the gnostic systems indicates a relationship. In the early Jewish Wisdom literature, which may be dated between the fourth and

first century B. C. (Proverbs, Wisdom of Solomon, and Ecclesiasticus), Wisdom is a figure closely connected with God, and even representing him, whether at the creation*, or in the guidance of Israel, or the guidance of pious individuals*; the whole history of salvation is under her control*. She protects her own and helps them to the knowledge of God; she is like a redeemer who grants immortality*. By equating her with the law, the torah, the knowledge of the law becomes a knowledge of redemption of a special kind: knowledge and Wisdom guarantee salvation. In Gnosis there is to be found a corresponding solution of the Jewish problem of salvation, in that the law is equated with the saving knowledge (*gnosis*)*. But Wisdom finds it difficult to gain a hearing; she has to let her call go forth to win men**. Error and foolishness operate against her***. This led to the concept of the disappointed Wisdom who returns from the earth to heaven*:

* *Prov. 8,22–31*

* *Wisd. 7,22–30*

* *op. cit. 7,10–19*

* *op. cit. 6,18f.; 8,17*

* *NHC V 5,83,11ff.; 84,4ff.; NHC II 3, 74 (122), 3–70*
** *Prov. 8, 1–11,32–36; 9,1–12*
*** *Prov. 9,13–18; Wisd. 2,21–24*
* *1 Enoch 42, transl. R. H. Charles*

"Wisdom found no place where she might dwell;
Then a dwelling-place was assigned her in the heavens.
Wisdom went forth to make her dwelling among the children of men,
And found no dwelling-place:
Wisdom returned to her place,
And took her seat among the angels.
And unrighteousness went forth from her chambers:
Whom she sought not she found,
And dwelt with them,
As rain in a desert,
And dew on a thirsty land".[115]

The pessimism about this world which finds expression here is a chief characteristic of the scepticism as it is already earlier displayed on the fringes of the wisdom tradition, especially in Ecclesiastes (written in about 200 B.C.). In it some conclusions are drawn which go beyond the limits of the ideas about God and the world expressed in the Jewish Old Testament, going even further than Apocalyptic. The workings of God become for man strange and inscrutable. He is removed into the distance and placed high above earthly concerns so that his acts in history and his acts of creation become veiled*. It becomes difficult for the pious to discover sense and purpose in the world*. He

Jewish scepticism

* *Job 28; Prov. 30,1–4*

* *Eccles. 3,9ff.*

feels himself alone and abandoned in a chaotic world in which there is no longer a fixed order of life. Despair and scepticism spread, especially with regard to the sense of a righteous way of life*. The future is uncertain, death alone is certain**. Chance and fate rule the world*. A bitter hedonism spreads**, but also a pessimistic devaluation of the corporeal*. Man, the world and God are irreparably torn asunder. It is a "tragic view of life" (G. von Rad) which is determined by vain striving and labour. The pious still believes in God and his righteous guidance in the last resort*; but it is rather an act of despair and a flight from perplexity.

*Eccles. 7,15; 8,14ff.
** Eccles. 3,1–22; 9,1–3
* Eccles. 9,3,11ff.
** Eccles. 5,17;
8,15; 9,7ff.
* Wisd. 9,15; 3,13–4,9

* Eccles.5,3f.; 9,1; 12,1.13

It seems to me that the gnostic world view could take root and flower on this soil. The separation of the world and God, the loss of confidence in the sense of existence (the social causes of which have yet to be examined) and the pessimism with its hedonistic and world-renouncing tendencies are the precursors of the gnostic view of existence. God becomes a remote being who stands beyond the earthly, chaotic activities; the "unknown God" makes his appearance. The vacuum thus brought into existence between the distant, alien God and the world, connected only by the primeval act of creation, is filled by angels, spirits and demons. It only needs a final act which severs this bond as well, which attributes the senselessness and the ungodly activity of the world to a power opposed to God, while the true God remains in the unchangeable and undefiled world beyond, and the gnostic view of the world is born. For in Gnosis this God as well as the Demiurge shows traits of the Jewish God. It can therefore be said with good reason that the scepticism which was born out of doubt in the power of divine wisdom prepared the way for Gnosis, a way which led out from official Judaism and ended in contradiction to it. We are then dealing with a critical self-dissolution on the fringes of Judaism.

The contribution of Iran

Before we turn to the problems of social history, two religious traditions deserve mention which are also important for the genesis of Gnosis: the Iranian (Persian) and the Greek-Hellenistic tradition. Both can be already found centuries before Christ in the literature, language, religion and art of the Syrian-Palestinian region. It is part of the reliable results of research in the history of religion that Jewish Apocalyptic did not come into existence without the contribution of Iranian-Zoroastrian religious ideas. These include above all the idea of the eschatological judgement, the resurrection of the dead, the scheme of the ages, and dualism. These ideas also form part of the systems of Gnosis, and it must be assumed that they were introduced, to a large extent, through the apocalyptic-Jewish filter. But the matter is still more complicated. For we find in some gnostic writings and systems Iranian elements which are independent of the Jewish tradition, as in the so-called "Song of the Pearl" in the Acts of Thomas* which, in the form of a popular fairy-tale, *Acts of Thomas,* tells of a prince who left his home to save a pearl which is part of *chs. 108–113* himself and was lost abroad. In this impressive text numerous affinities to Iranian (Persian) ideas can be traced, even down to the language.[116] Direct Iranian influence can also be established among the Mandeans and especially in Manicheism. These forms of Gnosis, as we have heard, have actually been *See above, p. 71* described as Iranian Gnosis, because the characteristic dualism of the two principles (light and darkness, God and devil, good and evil), as taught in Zoroastrianism, became in them the main feature of the system. To be sure, this Iranian dualism was decisively altered in that it was transformed into an ontological contrast of matter, or body, and spirit, as is typical for Gnosis generally. Apocalyptic did not represent this form of dualism; it is an essentially gnostic peculiarity. But it is not only the cosmological but also the anthropological dualism that was contributed by Iran. The distinction of soul and body, combined with the notion that the former enters the heavenly realm of light after death, is to be met with in the Orient only in Iran. This concept has become of extraordinary importance not only for Gnosis. Its roots already lie in the ancient Indo-Iranian religion. Some other Iranian theological concepts, which we cannot treat here more fully, have left their unmistakable traits, especially in the so-called Iranian Gnosis, but also in the other systems. To these belong, as already mentioned, the periodic sequence of the ages which are represented by distinct person- *See above, p. 137* ages (compare the 14 kingdoms of the Apocalypse of Adam)*, *NHC V 5* moreover the figure of the ambassador, or messenger of light, the predilection for certain concepts of the spirit and personifications, and finally also thematic ideas of the primeval and the eschatological age (primeval man, the conflagration of the world, judgement). A whole series of gnostic ideas, therefore, must be conceived as having arisen against the Iranian background, even if in part only indirectly (through Judaism).

284   GNOSIS

The Greek- Of equally great importance for the development of Gnosis
Hellenistic was the Greek world of ideas, which influenced the Orient
contribution gradually more and more from the time of Alexander the
Great; it was not so much the traditional-religious tendency of
Greek thought, but rather that of philosophic enlightenment.
The individualism and universalism, set free by the disintegra-
tion of the ancient religion of the *polis*, which marked the Hellenistic age until the end of classical antiquity, also became a
decisive prerequisite for the genesis of Gnosis. This influence
of Greek-Hellenistic thought is already ascertainable early on
in Judaism.[117] The scepticism of Ecclesiastes cannot be fully understood without the Greek rationalism and the early Hellenistic popular philosophy. The remaining wisdom literature, too,
as e.g. Ecclesiasticus, showed itself receptive to Hellenistic
thought. Even traditional Judaism in Palestine, as has been
known for some time, was strongly influenced by Hellenistic
thought, so that recent research more and more refuses to separate strictly a Hellenistic from a Palestinian Judaism. Greek
language, terminology and interpretation deeply influenced all
Oriental traditions and contributed to their transformation in a
new age, the Hellenistic. Syria (Antioch), where we can find
the beginnings of the formation of gnostic communities, and
Alexandria, where Gnosis had its finest flowering, were at the
same time well-known centres of Greek-Oriental (Jewish) culture, in which the representatives of Gnosis were confronted by
the contemporaneous philosophic and religious movements.

Quite apart from the Greek language in which the majority
of the gnostic writings was composed, indeed had to be composed to achieve wide influence, a component that cannot be
overlooked is the vocabulary of most of the gnostic systems,
even the apparently most ancient, derived from the conceptual
language of Greek philosophy; without it Gnosis, as indicated
by the very word, is unthinkable. This impression is strengthened especially when one considers the great gnostic systems of
the 2nd century A.D. which originated almost exclusively in
Gnosis and Alexandria, for here the problems discussed are closely related
Platonic to Greek Platonic philosophy.[118] In the question of the con-
tradition: struction of the world and of theology, the Alexandrine gnosis
Middle was an important link in the tradition of Middle Platonism
Platonism which united early and late Platonism. Mention may be made
of the problems of the transition from the divine unity to the di-

versity of the cosmos in the sense of a development downwards from spirit to matter, which is equal to an alienation of the spirit itself. A whole series of themes of this kind is shared by gnostic and philosophic thought of the era of the early empire (1st – 2nd century): God and the soul, the demiurge, the "unknown God", the origin of evil, the descent and return of the soul, coercion (fate) and freedom. Even when these problems are variously solved and the solution offered by Gnosis is somewhat eccentric, the catalogue indicates a similar climate of questions and thinking. Faith in the nearness of God to man, a certain hostile attitude to the body and the world, as well as the understanding of the limitations of the earthly life and its striving was part and parcel of the philosophy of the era of the empire. The Platonic dualism of spirit and matter, soul and body, God and world, also had considerable importance for Gnosis. It gave to Gnosis points of departure and of contact for the conception of its view of the world and bricks for its theology. No more can be said about it here.

An important witness for the existence of a non-Christian **The Hermetica** Hellenistic-gnostic system of thought is provided by the Hermetica which we have repeatedly cited. They originated in the first two centuries A. D. on Egyptian soil (Alexandria?) and contain a strange mixture of gnostic, gnosticising and non-gnostic features. They have been given the name "proletarian Platonism" (W. Theiler), a designation which however characterises only one aspect. The theosophic mysterious character, which includes esoteric revealed wisdom with the aim of salvation and the vision of God, and the anti-cosmic gnostic tendency present another aspect. In any case, the Hermetica (which also contain reminiscences of Judaism) teach us much about the soil on which the gnostic plants grew. In this connection it is also neces- **Hellenistic** sary to indicate the part played by the Hellenistic mystery reli- **Mysteries** gions in the formation of Gnosis. It is well known that the organisation of the gnostic communities was not dissimilar to that *See above, p. 214f.* of the mystery religions. The basic ideas of the individual mystery religions which were seldom summed up in a proper theology (as e. g. in the Egyptian mysteries of Isis) found a certain echo in Gnosis; they were expanded in a way favourable to the gnostic teaching and so furthered its propagation (cf. the so-called homily of the Naassenes). It is not impossible that specific traditions of the mystery religions found acceptance in certain gnostic communities (Ophites, Naassenes), traditions which encompass the common fate of the divinity and the faithful and which seek to realise salvation by cultic means as was the aim of the mystery cults. It may be the same with the contri-**Orphism** bution allegedly made by Orphism, an ancient Greek theosophic school connected with the cult of Dionysus which exerted its influence more in secret than publicly. Its theology, derived from the Greek sage Orpheus, actually contains a series of affinities with gnostic theology: the fate of the soul full of suffering in the corporeal world caused by the disastrous fate at the primeval beginning, when particles of the divinity (Dionysus) torn asunder by the Titans found their way into the human body, so that the body was called the grave of the soul, in which as in a prison the soul had to endure the cycle of the times. Only the initiated who lead a righteous life and observe a diet free from meat (vegetarianism) find salvation, while the impious are condemned to the eternal transmigration of the souls and the punishments of hell. There are no direct allusions in the gnostic texts to this myth, which in its developed form does not appear before the 3rd century A. D. Neither Orpheus nor Dio-*NHC II 6* nysus is mentioned in the Exegesis on the Soul*. Only general agreements surrounding the idea of the fate of the soul can be traced.

Graeco-oriental syncretism When considering the history of religions within Hellenism since the 4th century B. C. in general terms, a fundamental characteristic to be found is the linking of Oriental and Greek traditions, or ideas. The initial power of penetration of the Greek element is met from the 2nd century B. C. onwards by the ever-growing resistance of the Orient, a movement which manifests itself in artistic change as well as in political events, namely the opposition of the Oriental peoples and empires to the West, the power of Rome. In spite of this, there remains a resulting mixture of the Oriental and Greek body of faith which cannot be easily separated. This syncretism, which must be considered without any attempt to evaluate it (for every religion is strictly speaking a syncretistic product, pure religions only existing as theoretic constructions by scholars), proved to have a strong vitality which made itself felt to the end of the age of classical antiquity and beyond. The Hellenistic religions characterised by it, to which Gnosis belongs, are dominated by a surprising dynamism which comprises at one and the same time change and conservativism. On the one hand, they leave behind their native soil, whether Iran, Asia Minor, Syria or Egypt, to spread abroad throughout the world of that time (they can be called therefore "oecumenical religions"), on the other hand they preserve much of their original traditions which often have an archaic ring, consciously referring back to them in order to reinterpret them from the Hellenistic viewpoint. This flexibility, which corresponds to the whole flux of the Hellenistic world civilisation, put in place of the old, apparently static, popular religions with their strong collective links with custom and tradition, a religious individualism which **Individualism** made possible the rise of confessional religions with a mission- **and esoterism** ary character. This change in the character of religions which is exemplified most strikingly in Christianity also leads to the division of religious communities into an inner and outer circle of the faithful; esotericism is in large measure a characteristic of these religions. In contents they are stamped by a religiosity which concentrates on redemption and on a saviour. The salvation of the individual is mediated through participation in the life and example of the divinity. Salvation is no longer primarily sought in this world, as was the case with most of the ancient cultic religions (even if it was, as in Egypt, a form of this world which was projected into the next), but in another, eternal, spiritualised world in which the change and anxiety of this world are forgotten. The favourite means to reach this aim are, in addition to the traditional but often reinterpreted cultic practices, faith, knowledge, wisdom, i. e. intellectual attitudes. The tendency to spiritualise ancient religions and cultic ideas is another **Spiritualisation** characteristic of the time which must not be overlooked. The growing tendency to see God as the expression of the divine as such and as the summing up of all divinities and divine powers which shape and control the universe moves in the same direction. This monotheistic idea is already found in early Hellenism, as the hymn to Zeus by Cleanthes (about 300 B. C.) impressively demonstrates.

The characteristics here enumerated, to which more could be added, were to show that the gnostic religion was no more than one special case in a changed landscape of the history of religions.

Let us now turn to the economic and social conditions. Here, too, with regard to the place and time of the origin of Gnosis,

Economy and the starting-point is the change which began with Hellenism; it
society in the was a decisive presupposition for Gnosis. In the train of Alex-
Hellenistic ander the Great's campaign of conquest in the Orient, there
Orient followed Greek merchants, artisans and artists. A network of
cities (*poleis*) formed or transformed on Greek models began
to arise and became the backbone of the Hellenistic economic
and intellectual life. Some of them grew into large cities, as e. g.
Seleucia-Ctesiphon on the Tigris, Antioch on the Orontes,
Ephesus and especially Alexandria in Egypt. An expert
writes:[119] "In them something new takes shape, the special essence of the metropolis with its mixture of men of many lands
who are divorced from the rest of the country by a common life
and experience and are concentrated into a unity of their own,
as we see today metropolises which have become distinct from
their home country and have adopted the common life-style of
the metropolis. Those metropolises were Hellenistic through
and through, unthinkable without Hellenism, and supported in
their existence by a developed industry and trade. Caravans
from the Chinese border reach the Syrian coast through Central Asia. Merchant ships bring precious rarities from India and
East Africa. Alexandria procures all the riches of the East for
Rome and puts its own products, wheat, paper, linen and glass,
on to the world market. East and West are opened up economically, have dealings with one another and grow into an economic community, the exponents of which are again the men and
the ideas of Hellenism". Thus arose a world civilisation which
set no limits to the exchange of ideas. But this is only one aspect, the other, more hidden, is revealed by closer inspection;
it is the contrasts which become noticeable within the cities as
well as between city and country. While the relatively small go-
verning class which set the fashion consisted either of Greeks or
of the native ruling class absorbed by them, the vast mass of the
working population (the *laoi* and slaves) was throughout indigenous, i. e. of Oriental descent. This is particularly true of the
real country. M. Rostovtzeff says about it: "The mass of the na-
tives were never absorbed by Greek culture and never Hellenised. They held fast to their traditional life-style, to their religious, social, economic, legal and cultural peculiarities. They
never felt themselves part of a greater unit whose upper class
was formed by the Greek and the Hellenised *bourgeoisie*".[120]
Although we are lacking in a detailed knowledge about the si-

tuation in most areas, it is certain that the class antagonism in the Eastern states was strengthened and complicated by national and cultural-religious differences. "Outwardly the Hellenistic world was a unit, but inwardly it was split into two unequal parts, a Greek and an indigenous; the one had its centre in the cities and townships, the other was living dispersed throughout the country in its villages, hamlets and temples".

It has been established that the situation of the dependent class of serfs (peasants) and slaves did not change in principle in the Hellenistic monarchies compared with earlier times. Dependence and exploitation had remained, indeed in some places (especially demonstrable for Egypt) it had been strengthened on account of the new form of administration organised by the Greeks (bureaucracy). Over and above the taxes to be paid to the crown, there were added those payable to cities exercising rights over landed property and to the landlords residing in them. Thus the majority of the lower classes lived in poverty and did not share to any great extent in the proverbial wealth with which, for example, Syria was credited. This is true primarily for the population of the country whose migration into the cities, as far as this was possible, finds here its explanation. When the Romans made Syria subject to themselves in the 1st century B. C., there was at first no worsening in the economic conditions. Roman businessmen became noticeably active, and the governors sought to stem the marked decline of the Syrian cities, even by engaging in argument with the official tax-gatherers. But the growing burdens, taxes, imposts and the billeting of troops, especially during the civil wars and the campaigns against the Eastern kingdoms of, for example, the Nabataeans and the Parthians, ruined the country's economy. The economically essential caravan trade came in many cases to an end, or was made difficult. It is therefore not surprising that discontent and revolts made an appearance, the best known of which were those of the Jews in the 1st century A. D. which finally ended in the Jewish War (65–70). These movements were not, as was formerly thought, of a purely religious nature; in them there erupted at the same time the contemporaneous social conflicts.[121] As religion, especially in the life of the indigenous oppressed, "played a very important part, their bitterness took the form of a struggle for the ancient gods against the new who were worshipped in the cities".[122] Already the earlier

The situation of the lower classes

events which had led to the establishment of the Jewish state under the Hasmonaeans in the struggle against the policy of Hellenisation of the Seleucids (163/164 B. C.) are to be assessed as such a reaction, indeed as the most important one in the Near East. These events allow us to study particularly well the above mentioned interrelationships of social, religious and national contrasts. They cannot always be kept apart tidily, but rather dovetail in a manner which is not uncommon in antiquity.

The spread of Oriental cults   Of a more peaceful nature was the above-mentioned spread to the West of Oriental cults which outwardly wore Hellenistic dress, for only thus could they gain entry and hope to be understood, as Hellenisation was the expression of the whole civilisation of this period. In the year 204 B.C., Cybele, the great mother, was officially introduced to Rome from Asia Minor as the first Oriental divinity. Further Oriental cults followed, even if only after long resistance by the Roman state, as for example the cult of Isis which had already been disseminated since the 2nd century B.C. among Italian slaves and freedmen, but did not obtain a state temple before the year 38 A.D. The Syrian slave trade as well as Syrian merchants also brought indigenous forms of religion to Rome and the Latin West. Among them the "unvanquished sun god" (*sol invictus*) eventually conquered the whole empire in the third century A.D. Through Syria and the Balkans there came Mithras, the Persian god of covenant loyalty, to be sure in a form much changed and Hellenised, who became the most popular god of soldiers. In this series, the spread of Judaism throughout all centres of the Roman empire must not be forgotten, and in its train the spread of Christianity (from about the middle of the 1st century). It can be demonstrated that the Oriental religions obtained importance and recognition from below upwards, although this was not exclusively so. Their spread, too, was primarily sustained by the lower, i.e. the working, oppressed and exploited classes and was shaped by their desires, hopes and expectations. A series of extant prophecies, oracles and revelations of the first century B.C. and the first century A.D. express themselves differently, more directly, but derive from the same root, as for example the Jewish Sibyl, the oracle of Hystaspes (with obvious Parthian background) and other Jewish-Christian apocalypses, in which the anti-Roman, altogether anarchical, trait cannot be overlooked. Rome will be destroyed, predicts the prophecy of Hystaspes (a legendary Iranian king), and with it all the wicked and impious in a world-wide fire, then comes the sun-like great king from the East to establish the kingdom of righteousness and to deliver the oppressed and weak; this is understood as the victory of the Orient over the West.

If we now attempt to place Gnosis in the socio-economic landscape with its social tensions as we have briefly outlined it, our starting-point is the fact that it was essentially a city religion. We find it in most of the centres of the world of that period (Antioch, Ephesus, Alexandria, Rome, Seleucia-Ctesiphon), more precisely on the border between the Hellenistic Orient and Rome, with a tendency to decline towards the Latin West; the centre of gravity is the Orient (Syria, Mesopotamia, Asia Minor, Egypt). Even if individual leaders or founders of gnostic schools originated in the country (e. g. Simon Magus from Gitta, and his disciple Menander from Capparetaea, both in Samaria), their activities were linked with cities. At most the Mandeans have stronger links with the country, but they represent a special development and through the course of time they never relinquished their link with the city, which today even occupies a place in the forefront. The dual face of the gnostic systems, their Hellenistic dress over an Oriental-Jewish body, can be very easily explained by the situation as sketched in the Hellenistic cities where both traditions met. Furthermore, we must remember the characteristics critical of the social order and of the government and the probable composition of most of the gnostic communities. From this it can be inferred that Gnosis originally represented an ideology related to the dependent classes of the Hellenistic cities which was meant to contribute to the establishing of a new identity after their own intellectual world had largely broken down. Gnosis took account fully of this situation in various ways: it offered a support to the individual, even a certain nearness to God through the idea of a divine kernel in man. A close relationship to God became possible even for the "man in the street" without priestly mediation, without temple and without cultic practices, thus taking account of the mobility of the traffic of trade; fixed cult places were no longer necessary. The idea of the God "Man", moreover, gave essential help towards self-identification of man who had become conscious of his autonomy and independence, at least theoretically. The dependence, on the other hand, was explicit-

Gnosis as a city religion

See above, p. 264 ff.

See above, p. 209 ff.

ly seen as an earthly-heavenly order of existence, which being "disorder" was of a transitory nature. In opposition to the Greek *logos* to which the ruling class was pledged, Gnosis set up a concept of cognition and knowledge which served salvation, indeed included it. At this point, nearness to and distance from the Hellenistic world of ideas are particularly obvious. While the other Hellenistic religions too want to offer salvation from this world, the gnostic soteriology is closely linked with a strict attitude of world-denial, which is the most radical of its kind in all antiquity. Here the mood of weariness of life of the Oriental population, afflicted by internal troubles and wars, seems to have found expression and led to the consequence that the sense of life was no longer seen in activities for this world,

Gnosis as social protest but in a striving pledged to suffering and persevering to overcome this world in conformity with the real social situation. It has to be remembered that the social situation of the oppressed and the exploited was not given much attention anywhere in antiquity (the Cynics represented a wisdom of fools rather than that they grasped the problems). The utopian schemes put forward by many Greek literary men and philosophers like Zeno, Hecataeus, Euhemerus, or Iambulus remained pure ideals and were without effect in practice. On this subject, therefore, the dependent classes, lacking in support and because of their ideological isolation, were left to develop their own concepts, and these could only hope to find an echo, at least in the Near East, if they were somehow linked to religious tradition. Thus Jewish apocalyptic and esotericism and the Oriental faith in salvation in the form of the mystery religions also became means of expression of a social protest. Gnosis was without doubt the most radical voice in this circle. Its rejection of the moral tradition and the visible world of government (including the supernatural) is an attempt to solve the social problems of the time under an unambiguously religious banner, namely through the total overcoming of the world; this is its "protest against the real misery" (K. Marx). Thus Gnosis can be largely understood as an ideology of the dependent petty bourgeoisie which however feels itself called to freedom on the ideological-religious plane; it produced, or brought into play, at the same time a necessary exchange of Oriental and Greek traditions in a new spirit.

But attention must still be drawn to another side. As has been emphasised several times before, the formulating and

framing of gnostic doctrines and systems was not the work of **Religious**
the uneducated but of experts on the older traditions (e. g. of **intellectualism**
the Jewish traditions) including a certain body of Hellenistic **of the laity**
education. Already more than half a century ago, the well-
known German sociologist, Max Weber, drew attention to the
importance of intellectualism for the Near Eastern Hellenistic
religiosity of salvation, especially to the non-priestly "intellectualism of the laity" of Jewish provenance.[123] In his opinion, the
religions of salvation, among which he explicitly includes Gnosis and Manicheism, are "specific intellectual religions as far as
their founders as well as their important exponents are concerned, and also with regard to the character of their doctrine
of salvation". He sees the cause for this development in the
"depoliticising of the intellectualism", which could take place
either by force or voluntarily. According to Weber, such an intellectualism was already effective in pre-Christian times in the
Hellenistic Orient right across the social strata, and produced,
by means of allegory and speculation, soteriological dogmas in
the various sacramental cults of salvation. These comments are
indeed largely apt, but unfortunately they have so far scarcely
been taken into account. It may be assumed that the rule exercised in the regions of the Eastern Mediterranean, first by the
Greeks and then by the Romans, led to the political loss of power of a great part of the middle stratum of education, to which
belonged the officials, or at least to the diminishing of their influence. Thanks to their familiarity with the older mythological, religious and philosophical traditions and to a lively religious interest, which included sometimes prophetic gifts, they
were in a position to operate in the manner described by
M. Weber. In this way a good part of the gnostic products and
their echo in the lower classes can be understood. It is even possible to go further and to refer to the relationship of Gnosis to
the sceptic Wisdom tradition and to Apocalyptic which has
been established above. Clearly, circles of this kind, Jewish
Wisdom schools and institutions of scribal learning, played an
important part in the shaping of gnostic thought. Scribe and
wise man had already converged in pre-Christian times into the
class of the Jewish "scribe", a religious scribal intellectualism of
lay descent, in contrast to the priesthood. In the later Rabbinic
tradition, there is some evidence which suggests that the occu-
pation with cosmological problems was reckoned to be an eso-

teric teaching and led into dangerous by-ways which the rabbis violently rejected. Unfortunately, not much of this has sur- vived, but the little that has points in the direction indicated, to- wards "seductive" esoteric as well as gnostic interpretations of scripture. To follow up the rise of gnostic literature under these aspects is still a task for future research.

Early Schools and Systems

Simon Magus Even if modern research in Gnosis no longer holds the convic- tion that Simon Magus has to be considered the ancestor of all gnostic religion, yet his name is in fact the first to appear in the context of Gnosis. But the most ancient source, the Acts of the Apostles, composed in the 1st century A. D., did not describe him as a proper gnostic, but rather as a megalomaniac and rapa- cious magician who seduced people in Samaria*. His faithful designated him "the power of God which is called Great". Con- verted and baptised by Philip the Evangelist, he wants to traffic in the laying on of hands of the apostles Peter and John, which bestows the Holy Spirit (later called "simony", or buying of ec- clesiastical office). Thereupon he is cursed by Peter and ex- cluded from the congregation. This description hardly does justice to the importance of Simon and reduces him to a mere charlatan. (The Acts of the Apostles also show elsewhere a ten- dency to play down conflicts and to idealise early Christianity.) The apologist and martyr Justin (died in 167), who also comes from Samaria, confirms for us for the first time that Simon worked there in the time of the emperor Claudius (41–54) and was allegedly worshipped by his followers as the "first god". He is also the first to tell us that "at that time a certain Helena went about with him, who had formerly plied her trade in a bro- thel. Of her it was said that she was the "first thought" (*ennoia*) begotten by him"*. Irenaeus, finally, has the most complete ac- count and knows the system of the Simonians more precisely*. To the divine worship of Simon as supreme power, there is now added his claim to be a Christ figure. He bought out the harlot Helena in Tyre (Phoenicia). She is considered to be the mother of all and proceeded from him as "first thought" (*ennoia*) and descended to the lower regions and created the angels and powers. These, in their turn, created the world and kept Hele-

* Acts 8,9–25

* Justin, Apology I 26,1–3

* Irenaeus, Adv. haer. I 23,1–4

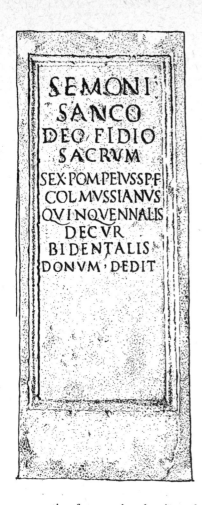

Dedication to the old Roman god of oaths, Semo Sancus, found in 1574 on the island in the Tiber at Rome, where Justin Martyr (or his informant) may once have seen it in the 2nd century (1 Apol. 26, 56) and wrongly considered it a statue of the deified Simon Magus, reading the Latin inscription as *Simoni deo sancto* instead of *Semoni Sanco Deo Fidio Sacrum*. This confusion was repeated by Irenaeus (Adv. haer. I 23.1), Tertullian (Apol. 13.9) and Eusebius (HE II 13). Possibly the Simonians themselves were responsible for the identification, since they worshipped their founder as a divine being (as Zeus among others).

na captive for envy's sake, in order to inflict on her every outrage, so that she could no longer return. Enclosed in a human body, she had to wander throughout the centuries from vessel to vessel in ever changing bodies (also in the body of Helen of Troy) until she ended up in the brothel from which Simon, who had descended as unrecognised redeemer, delivered her. Simon's teaching includes the rejection of the creation and of the law; it has a libertine character. Hippolytus* gives further information about Simon's doctrine in extracts from a treatise by Simon Magus, entitled "The Great Exposition" (*Apophasis Megalē*).[124] This text is hardly to be considered as Simon's work, but is probably a kind of philosophical-speculative interpretation of sayings attributed to him by his school in the 2nd century. Their strongly monistic character is connected with the cycle of the divine element throughout the three periods –

See above, p. 253 ff.

* *Hippolytus, Refutatio VI 9–18*

the primeval, the present and the future – in which Simon saw himself, designating himself as "he who (formerly) stood, stands and (again) will stand". Evidently, this interpretation refers to a honorific title of Simon known from other sources, "he who stands," with which his divine character was described. (The Samaritans use the expression as a description of man's existence determined by God.)

The final stage of the Simon legend is to be found in the apocryphal Acts of Peter and in the pseudo-Clementine romance (about 3rd century).[125] Here, Simon appears as the stereotype opponent of Peter, an underling of Satan, who founds congregations in the Palestinian-Syrian coastal cities from Caesarea to Antioch by his miracles and his rhetoric, but loses them again to the more successful Peter who follows in his footsteps. In this context, some new information about him is given but its historicity is doubtful: e.g. the names of his parents (Antony and Rachel), his Greek education in Alexandria and his discipleship of John the Baptist, who saw in him his most able disciple but could not appoint him his successor, as Simon sojourned in Egypt at the time of the death of John. His other disciple, Dositheos by name, (a Samaritan sectarian leader), filled the office until Simon, on his return, usurped it. He then wandered about with his Helena and 30 disciples, as described, until he mysteriously came to his death in Rome. According to Hippolytus[*] he had himself buried to demonstrate his resurrection but did not come alive again. According to another version, he made an attempt to fly over Rome to demonstrate his miraculous powers to Peter who, calling upon Christ, made him crash down. He broke his thighs and was taken by his followers to Aricia (south of Rome) where he finally died[*] Thus, in the eyes of the Christian community, the magician came to his death by his own machinations.

op. cit. VI 20

Acts of Peter 32; Martyrdom of Peter 3

As already mentioned, these stories are pure legends which at most can only show us that evidently Simon himself came to Rome, or that his disciples spread as far as Rome, and that in the 2nd century they together with other gnostic schools, especially that of Marcion, presented a serious danger to the existence of the Christian communities. The apocryphal "Epistle of the Apostles" (*Epistula Apostolorum*), from the first half of the 2nd century, likewise sees in Simon and in the later Cerinthus anti-apostles, who want to alienate the Christians from their

faith.* The disputations of the pseudo-Clementine writings *See below, p. 307*
possibly contain reminiscences of the doctrines put forward by * *Epistula Apostolorum*
Simon, or handed down by his school, as for instance the doc-   7/18
trine of the "supreme, incomprehensible power", of the lowly
creator of the world and of the captivity of the soul (which
stands here for *ennoia*). In one passage, Simon significantly
speaks about Peter as follows:[126] "But you will, as it were bewil-
dered with astonishment, constantly stop your ears that they
should not be defiled by blasphemies, and you will turn to
flight, for you will find nothing to reply; but the foolish people
will agree with you, indeed will come to love you, for you teach
what is customary with them, but they will curse me, for I pro-
claim something new and unheard of ..."* This is an excellent * *Recognitions II 37,6f.*
analysis of the way in which the gnostic prophet sees himself.

For the historical Simon it must undoubtedly be assumed
that he founded a gnostic community in Samaria which was
considered by expanding Christianity a serious competitor, especially as the Simonians themselves annexed Christian doctrines and thus threatened to subvert the Christian communities, as did most of the later gnostics. The framework of Simon's teaching can be reconstructed in outline only: it must have
been an early form of the so-called Barbelognostic system, according to which the supreme god goes into action through his
first emanation (*ennoia*), the world comes into existence, and
the soul falls into servitude. We now possess in the Nag Hammadi text "The Exegesis on the Soul"* probably a source which * *NHC II 6*
tells us more about it. Simon appeared as redeemer of the hu-   *See above, p. 109f.*
man soul which was, among others, also in Helena; he brought
the revelation necessary for its delivery, the "call". Thus he
was, in the eyes of his followers, the embodiment of the "supreme power", i.e. of the unknown god. This aspect of his
teaching is also a clear indication of his Samaritan origin, for
the term "might, power"is a popular divine attribute of the
Samaritan-Jewish tradition. Here also belongs the above mentioned self-designation "he who stands". Behind it is hidden, in
gnostic understanding, the possession of the *pneuma* which ele-
vates the gnostic above unredeemed man. "He who would
know our great power will become invisible, and no fire will be
able to burn him, and he will be pure..."* The Christian re- * *NHC VI 4,36,3–7*
ports about Simon are often either misunderstandings, as in the
case of Helena who clearly was only a symbol for the fallen soul

which had made its abode in the "brothel" of the world (perhaps elaborated by literary means as in the Exegesis on the
Soul), or they are conscious misrepresentations and slanders to
which already the title "Magus" seems to belong. Naturally, the
heresiologists had no deeper understanding of a teaching hostile and dangerous to them.[127]

Simon was evidently a representative of the above men-
tioned intellectualism of Oriental-Jewish origin with a certain
measure of Greek education. This also is true of his disciples, of
Menander and whom Menander is the next known to us. He, too, comes from
Satornilos Samaria but worked in Antioch of Syria and may have lived un-
til about 80 A.D. To him are attributed an attitude and doc-
* *Justin, Apology I 26;* trine similar to those of Simon, including, of course, magic*. It
Irenaeus, Adv. haer. I 23,5 is different with Satornilos (Latin: Saturninus) who comes from
Syria (Antioch or Daphne, in the region where the Jordan
rises) and, according to the opinion of the heresiologists, holds
* *Irenaeus, Adv. haer.* views which are dependent on Menander*. This is true of the
I 24,1–2 = Hippolytus, creation of the world by inferior angels but not of other features
Refutatio VII 28 of his teaching. There is lacking (only in the sources?) the fe-
male figure of Ennoia or Sophia, instead there is a report in the
gnostic manner of the creation and animation of the first man
See above, p. 185 f. and the first description of the figure of Christ as gnostic redee-
mer. Besides, the Satornilians took the ascetic course and dif-
ferentiated strictly between good and evil men. In the case of
Satornilos we have good cause, therefore, to speak already of a
Christian Gnosis. His lifetime extended certainly to the first
half of the 2nd century, and he was evidently a contemporary of
Basilides.

Two more Christian gnostics are mentioned from early
times: Cerinthus and Carpocrates. The former comes from
Cerinthus Asia Minor and was a contemporary of the martyr Polycarp
from Smyrna (died in 156 or 157), about whom Irenaeus tells
the following amusing story: "And there are those who heard
him (Polycarp) tell that John the disciple of the Lord went in
Ephesus to bathe and seeing Cerinthus within, sprang out of
the baths without bathing, calling out, 'Let us fly lest the baths
* *Irenaeus, Adv. haer.* fall in, since Cerinthus, the enemy of the truth, is within'."* In
III 3,4 = Eusebius, another passage, Irenaeus asserts that the Gospel of John was
Eccles. Hist. IV 14,6 written against Cerinthus*, a view which a little later, from
(Loeb Classical Library) another quarter, was turned into the opposite, it being given
* *Irenaeus,* out as the work of Cerinthus. But, at most, so much is credible
Adv. haer. III 11,1

in this, that the Fourth Gospel had more than a slight contact with Gnosis. The same Irenaeus brings us the little that is authentic of Cerinthus himself*: the doctrines of the supreme unknown god and the lowly creator of the world as well as a docetic Christology.

See below, p. 305 f.
* Irenaeus, Adv. haer. I 26,1
See above, p. 165

The historicity of Carpocrates and of his son Epiphanes has been denied repeatedly.[128] One saw behind his name rather a gnosticising cult association of the late Egyptian god Harpocrates, Horus the son of Isis, and gave credence to the report of Celsus who knew of "Harpocratians"*. Although it is not possible to discuss this question more fully here, it seems to me that there is little reason for doubting the existence of the person of Carpocrates (the name, however, may contain a conscious allusion to Harpocrates). Carpocrates is said to have worked under the emperor Hadrian (117–138), especially in Asia Minor, but to come allegedly from Egypt*. His son, who died at the age of 17, already played an important role (Clement even describes him as the actual founder of the school); the book already cited, "On Righteousness", was composed by him. A female disciple of Carpocrates, Marcellina by name, spread his teaching (in modified form?) in about 160 in Rome (Celsus calls her followers actually "Marcellians"). The sect flourished in about 130. Its system works up earlier gnostic tradition into a consistent antinomianism, or libertinism, which the soul must follow to its redemption, if necessary through several births. Jesus is the example worth striving for on this road, an example that can even be surpassed. Only faith and love are necessary for salvation; the rest, especially laws and regulations, is neutral. We have already got to know the cultic consequences that follow from this, as well as the syncretistic cult of images of the Marcellian gnostics.

Carpocrates

* Origen, C. Celsum V 62

* Clem. Alex., Strom. III 5,2

See above, p. 268 f.

See above, p. 256

See above, p. 250
See above, p. 225 f.

For the early period of Gnosis we have followed so far the sources in the Fathers of the Church. They, however, give us only a very fragmentary picture. A source made more and more accessible by modern research is the writings of the New Testament, those early Christian testimonies which gained universal recognition in the course of the 2nd and 3rd centuries, partly in confrontation with contemporaneous Gnosis. In a series of these, important conclusions on two levels can be drawn for early Gnosis, especially for the Christian variety which was about to arise: on the one hand through the existence of gnostic

The testimony of the New Testament

elements in the texts themselves, i. e. in their statements of content, on the other in the polemic against gnostic teaching, or gnostic communities. The views in this area are still very much divided, as far as particulars are concerned, but the state of affairs was clarified by critical research in principle long ago. The pioneering contribution was made by Rudolf Bultmann and his school.[129] The process which is plain from the New Testament itself is twofold, the Christianising of Gnosis and the gnosticising of Christianity. The result of both processes is the canonising of Christianity as an orthodox Church on the one hand, and the elimination of Gnosis as a heresy on the other. Gnosis as we

Gnosis as inner-Christian movement meet it in the New Testament is understood less as an alien pagan religion; "rather, it is only dealt with so far as it is a *phenomenon within Christianity.*"[130] The gnostics feel themselves as Christians and present themselves as such in the young Christian communities. Thus it is a danger more from inside than from outside about which Paul is already said to have given

Acts 20,29f. warning*. It follows from this that evidently already the pre-Pauline Hellenistic Christianity, as it had developed in the coastal cities of Palestine, Syria and Asia Minor (especially in Antioch), had contacts with Gnosis, apparently through the mediation of an already Hellenistic-gnostic Judaism which we have assumed as the starting-point of Gnosis in the same geographical zone. In this region, therefore, the history of Gnosis continues through symbiosis with Christianity, and attains in its further course worldwide expansion (Alexandria, Rome), which forms part of the presuppositions of the "high-gnostic" systems of the 2nd and 3rd centuries.

A central figure of this development was obviously the apostle Paul, a Jewish artisan of Tarsus in Cilicia, converted in about 30(33) to the Christian faith, which he had formerly opposed as representative of orthodox (Pharisaic) Judaism. He became the most successful early Christian missionary and theologian. His end is unknown; he probably died a violent death in about 60 in Rome. His (genuine) letters, which he composed between 41 and 52, repeatedly contain expressions of passionate opposition to false doctrines which spread among most of the congregations founded by him, and which included

Paul's letters to the Corinthians gnostic doctrines. This was particulary clear in Corinth where Paul had founded a congregation in about 41, to which he later (ca. 49/50) addressed his two famous letters (they are more pre-

cisely a collection of letters). The gnostic origin of his opponents clearly emerges from the polemic.[131] They are pneumatics and "perfect", men who are proud of their "knowledge"*, *I Cor.8,1–3*
and to whom all things are permitted**. Therefore they look **I Cor.10,23*
down upon the weak*. As possessors of the Spirit they already *I Cor.10,23–31*
have the resurrection**. The assembly of the congregation be- **I Cor.15,29–32;*
comes a demonstration of the gnostic indwelling of the Spirit*; *II Cor.5,1–5*
women are active in this sphere**. The Eucharist is degraded to *I Cor.12,3; 14,2–19*
a meal designed to sate the appetite*. Men allow themselves to **I Cor.11,5 *I Cor.11,17–34*
be baptised for the dead**. The earthly Jesus is clearly despised **I Cor.15,29*
in favour of the heavenly Christ*, a feature which is also report- *I Cor.12,3*
ed of the so-called Ophites*. The gnostic understanding of lib- *Origen, C. Celsum VI 28*
erty seems to have corrupted Paul's congregation. The Jewish
origin of these "apostles" is explicitly stated*. Similar condi- *II Cor.11,22*
tions, which arose from gnostic propaganda, evidently pre-
vailed not only in Corinth but also in other Pauline communities, as e.g. in Thessalonica (today's Saloniki), Philippi
(Macedonia), Colossae and Ephesus (in the last two only after *See below, p.302*
Paul). But Paul does not seem to be altogether innocent of this,
for his own concepts are not free from echoes of gnostic doctrines, and later gnostics often appealed to him as witness (a
point already hinted at in Acts*). He knows the differences be- *Acts 20,27*
tween psychics and pneumatics; the latter are a new creation *I Cor.2,10–3,18*
who are partakers of the glory* and who are free of the law**. **Gal.3,28; I Cor.12,13*
Flesh and spirit, like darkness and light, are unbridgeable con- *Rom. 8,5–10; 13,11–13;*
trasts*. This world as fallen creation is ruled by Satan and by *I Thess. 5,4–6*
demonic powers**. The Jewish law, too, only comes from an- **I Cor.2,6–8; II Cor.4,4; Gal.4,3.9*
gelic powers*. Therefore an attitude of world rejection domi- *Gal.3,19*
nates, and marriage is considered dangerous*. Adam's fall *I Cor.7,32–34*
brought sin and death into the world* and, ever since, mankind *Rom.5,12ff.*
has fallen under the sway of the earthly-psychic realm of existence*. Only the redemption through Christ brought the turn- *I Cor.15,21.44.49*
ing-point and made possible a new mankind of the Spirit*. The *op. cit.*
redeemer is for Paul a heavenly being who descended unrecog-
nised and returns again to God*. Only this spiritual Christ is *II Cor.8,9; I Cor.2,8; Phil.2,6–11*
decisive, not Christ "after the flesh"*. He delivers from the de- *II Cor.5,16*
monic powers and from the fall of the world which holds sway
since Adam. The redeemed are united with him in one body, in
contrast to the unredeemed Adamic mankind*. The unity of *Rom.5,12–14; 12,4f.; I Cor.15,22,48f.; 12,12–27*
the community of salvation so created, the Church, is suprana-
tional, ruled by the Spirit. This conception of the community,

oriented to the Spirit and to charismata, was still maintained in Christian Gnosis when it was no longer a vital factor in the

See above, p. 215

Church at large. Faith is accompanied by the knowledge of the

* Phil. 3,8–10;
1 Cor. 2,6ff.
** 1 Cor. 9,1–23

verities of salvation*. The Christian pneumatic has freedom and power, but is bound by love and obedience*. In Paul, therefore, there is to be found an element of gnostic concepts and ideas, evidently derived from the heritage of Hellenistic Christianity and from his own experience, which makes him interesting for the history of Gnosis; he belongs to it, not only as an opponent. Through him, Christianity became a religion of salvation in late antiquity, and Gnosis played its part in it.

On the same level the discussion continues, through assimilation and reinterpretation of gnostic ideas, in some post-Pauline letters, which, however, in part derive from the school of Paul.

The Epistle to the Colossians

The inter-connected letters to the Colossians (about 80) and to the Ephesians (towards the end of the 1st century) have been well known in this connection for some time. In the former, there is controversy with a Jewish-Christian Gnosis in which, in addition to the part played by Christ as redeemer, there are also references to doctrines about cosmic powers and angelic be-

* cf. Col. 2

ings*. These "elements" must be treated with special consideration, obviously because they can influence the way of the soul; ritual-cultic duties play their part here. The author of the epistle emphasises in reply the comprehensive cosmological importance of Christ as "image of the invisible God" and mediator of creation who is above all powers and alone guarantees salvation. Through baptism the Christian partakes of Christ's victory over the powers, for Christ's body nailed to the cross is identical with the old man under the sway of earthly and supernatural powers whom Christ has "put off" in his resurrection.

The Epistle to the Ephesians

Here clearly gnostic ideas were Christianised. A similar process takes place in the Epistle to the Ephesians[132] where gnostic im-

* Eph. 5,25–32
** Eph. 1,10;
2,14–18; 4,8–11
* Eph. 4,3f.,12; 5,23

ages are inserted in the doctrine of the Church: the partnership (syzygy) of Christ and the Church*, Christ as cosmic man** and head of his body, the Church*. In the Epistle to the Hebrews

The Epistle to the Hebrews

(about 80/90), too, gnostic traditions seem to have been ac-

* Hebr. 1,5–2,18;
3,7–4,10; 5,14; 10,20

tive*.

The Pastoral Epistles

The so-called Pastoral Epistles – the two letters to Timothy and the letter to Titus –, which go back to the beginning of the 2nd century and were perhaps written in Ephesus, discuss the

* 1 Tim. 6,20

gnostic heresy, which they explicitly name Gnosis*, less intensively, but they insist the more on a strict separation; the pursuit of Gnosis is thought to be useless*. The soil is here prepared for the later polemic against the heretics: the false teaching is contrasted with the right, sound teaching, the abandonment of which means apostasy from truth, reason and conscience*. The heretics, therefore, are deceivers, liars and avaricious men**, of whom Paul, as fictitious author of the letters, had already warned*, and who are expelled from the community after having been admonished twice**. The process of separation of orthodoxy and heresy, Church and sect, begins to make itself felt; the early Catholic Church declares itself. Little can be learned about the ideas of the rejected heresy; it seems to be a strange mixture of gnostic doctrines and Jewish piety, a Jewish-Christian form of Gnosis. Myths (i.e. fables) and genealogies play a part*, evidently in the sense of gnostic pleroma speculations and interpretations of the law**. One glories in higher knowledge* and makes ascetic demands as e.g. abstinence from marriage and the consumption of certain foods**. The resurrection is said to have taken place already*, as is fitting for the pneumatic. Women were apparently very active in the gnostic communities*. The events in Corinth come to mind, and also the "philosophy" resisted in Colossae could have connections with Gnosis as postulated in the Pastoral Epistles.

* II Tim. 2,16;
Tit. 3,9f.;
I Tim. 1,4

* I Tim. 1,19; 6,5; 4,2;
II Tim. 2,18; 3,8;
Tit. 1,15
** I Tim. 4, 2;
6,5; II Tim. 3,13
* I Tim. 4,1; II Tim. 4,3
** Tit. 3,10

* I Tim. 1,4; 4,7; Tit. 3,9
** Tit. 3,9
* Tit. 1,14; I Tim. 6,20
** I Tim. 4,3; 5,23;
Tit. 1,14f.
* II Tim. 2,18

See above, p. 189

* I Tim. 2,9–15

The line of the Pastoral Epistles is also taken by the letters of Ignatius of Antioch (he suffered martyrdom under Hadrian [117–138] in Rome), which in some passages oppose gnostic errors (docetism, the denial of the resurrection), and thus at the same time indicate the existence of gnostics in Ephesus* and the cities of Asia Minor, Magnesia*, Tralles** and Smyrna***. The basis of the argument is a strict conception of the unity of the Church which centres on the episcopacy. "If any man followeth one that maketh a schism, he doth not inherit the kingdom of God"*. Therefore "the children of the light of the truth" are to shun "division and wrong doctrines"*. But on the other hand, Ignatius is not free of gnostic traits in his Christology and in his doctrine of the Church*.[133] Ignatius' contemporary, Polycarp of Smyrna (martyred in about 156), conducts a similar polemic in his letter to the congregation in Philippi, also aiming at those gnostics who deny the resurrection and at the docetists*.

The brief letter of Jude, which turns against the libertine

Ignatius of Antioch

* Ign., Eph. 7,2; 18–20
* Ign., Magn. 11
** Ign., Trall. 9f.
*** Ign., Smyrn. 1–3,7

* Ign., Phil. 3,3,
transl. Lightfoot Ign
* Ign., Phil. 2,1

* Ign., Eph. 17,19

Polycarp of Smyrna

* Polycarp, Phil. 7,1

The Epistle of Jude

gnostic heretics who penetrated the community (which community remains unknown) and caused divisions, was written at about the same time as the Pastoral Epistles. They, as possessors of the Spirit, despise the angelic powers and "make pompous speeches". Instead of pneumatics they should be called "psychics"; they are "dreamers" and "murmurers". They are accused of defilement of the flesh and intemperance, even at the love-feasts (*agape*), which indicates that they were antinomian representatives of Gnosis.

Here, too, no refutation is offered in detail, but reference is made to the Old Testament judgements which threaten the heretics (perhaps by way of reversing the biblical tradition used by them). To hold fast to the transmitted faith and to revile one's opponents are the chief expedients of polemic.

The Second Epistle of Peter The latest book of the New Testament, the Second Epistle of Peter, which goes back to the middle of the 2nd century and which presupposes the formation of the great gnostic schools, is, in this connection, dependent on Jude. For this reason, the author writes out the Epistle of Jude in the second chapter and argues similarly, using the fiction of the prediction of the apostle Peter with reference to the penetration of the "false prophets" in the Church. The concrete occasion for this was evidently the delay of the appearance of Christ* and the abandonment by Gnosis of eschatological teaching.

* II Pet. 3

The Revelation of John In this connection the "Letters to the Seven Churches" which are inserted into the Revelation of John* are also noteworthy, for in them a libertine-gnostic tendency which spread in the congregations of Asia Minor, Pergamon, Thyatira and Ephesus, towards the end of the 1st century (Revelation may be dated in about 95) is similarly attacked. This party is for the first time given a name: the "Nicolaitans"*. In Thyatira they are led by a prophetess and teacher, Jezebel by name*. About their teaching not much is said: they claim "to know the deep things of Satan"*, and trace themselves back to the "teaching of Balaam"*, of the kind we know from the contact of the gnostics with the Old Testament. In practice they stand for libertinism; they take part, without more ado, in pagan cult meals (idol sacrifices) and commit "fornication"*. The Fathers of the Church, beginning with Irenaeus, included the Nicolaitans in their catalogue of heresies and, for lack of any detailed knowledge (they had already become part of the past), attributed to them all

* Rev. 2–3

* Rev. 2,6–15
* Rev. 2,20

* Rev. 2,24
* Rev. 2,14

* Rev. 2,14.20–23

manner of gnostic teaching. Their name is linked with that of the deacon Nicolas of Antioch, known to us from the Acts of the Apostles*, which may be quite correct, as these gnostics may have appealed to him, as others appealed to other early Christian famous men (e. g. James, Philip). Clement of Alexandria knows apocryphal traditions of Nicolas which, however, his followers falsified in a libertine direction*.

* Acts 6,5; Irenaeus, Adv. haer. I 26,3

* Clem. Alex., Strom. II 118; III 25,5–26,2

One body of writings within the New Testament which holds a very special position and is particularly relevant for Gnosis has not been considered until now, namely the Johannine. These are the writings which allegedly were composed by the apostle John: the Fourth Gospel, or Gospel of John, and the three epistles. The former probably originated in about 100 in Syria, the latter in the same region but somewhat later, in the beginning of the 2nd century. In describing gnostic Christology, we already had occasion to draw attention to the gnostic character of the Gospel of John. Not only is the redeemer Christ depicted in the colours of gnostic redeemer mythology, but other features too show the gnostic background.[134] Dualistic thinking pervades the presentation: light and darkness, truth and lie, "above" and "beneath", God and devil, or the world (*kosmos*), stand opposite one another. The world is subordinate to the evil one, viz. the devil*. In the presence of the heavenly envoy who reveals the true God, mankind is divided into two classes: those who know God and thus come from him, and those who do not know him and thus are of the world, or of the devil, a reference in the first instance to the Jews (an anti-Jewish trait). Knowledge is synonymous with faith, is part of it (the word "Gnosis", however, does not occur). The eschatological ideas are spiritualised, or realised: the redeemer brings judgement, separation, or *krisis*. Resurrection already takes place in the act of faith*. Freedom from the world also means freedom from sin*. The original author has no great interest in sacraments, nor in the concept of the Church. The community is formed by the redeemer gathering together "his own", viz. his disciples*; they live already in this world eschatologically. To be sure, the Gospel of John does not represent a radical cosmological dualism, for it holds fast to the creation of the world by God, or by his "Word" (*logos*); it also lacks the idea of the fate of the soul, the rule of the archons, and the pleroma, as well as the idea of a substantial salvation, but it belongs in the

The Gospel of John

See above, p. 159f.

* John 12,31; 14,30; 16,11; cf. 8, 23 and 8,44

* John 5,24f.; 11,25f.

* John 8,31–36

* John 13,1; 17,21f.

realm of Gnosis, as the new texts have revealed it to us in manifold ways. Clearly, John already had an understanding of Gnosis that had undergone a process of reflection and had been
adapted to Christian tradition, that had largely demythologised
and historicised the mythology. Whether or not there is hiding
behind it a direct polemic against other gnostic tendencies must
remain an open question. This question can perhaps be ans-

The Epistles
of John

wered best by reference to the Johannine Epistles, for in them
such a polemic can be clearly recognised, and in them ecclesiastical interests become more prominent (unless this is caused by

*cf. I John 2,18–27;
3,9; 4,1–6,
5,1.5–*

a later redaction).* What we are dealing with is therefore less a
conflict between Christianity and Gnosis, but rather a dispute
between Christian-ecclesiastical Gnosis and radical-mythologi-
cal Gnosis (as it occurs later, for instance, between Clement of
Alexandria and the gnostics). The view, advocated by E. Käsemann, that in the author (or authors) of the Johannine writings
a heretic has found a place as a Christian witness within the
New Testament is, under these circumstances, fully justified.
The author, unknown to us, (designated as a presbyter in the
2nd and 3rd Epistle of John) "is a Christian gnostic who possessed the altogether unimaginable boldness to write a gospel
of the Christ experienced by him, who addresses the world of
Gnosis".[135]

Moreover, we possess a cycle of gnostic texts which, in style
and language, are closely related to John. There are, on the one
hand, the Odes of Solomon in Syriac, which were written in the
2nd century, and on the other is the Mandean literature which
in its most ancient parts goes back, without doubt, into the same
period. John presupposes a bilingual (Greek-Semitic) milieu,
or was originally composed in Aramaic-Syriac, as has already

*John 1,1–18

been demonstrated earlier for the prologue of the gospel*.

The plurality of
the gnostic
systems

When we look back, in summary fashion, on the contribution
to the history of early Gnosis drawn from early Christian literature, we already encounter a great variety, which does not per-
mit us to construct correlations in order to present falsely a united front of Gnosis which threatened to subvert Christianity. A
certain plurality, adapting to situation and location, seems to
have existed from the start. In spite of this, essentially the same
themes from cosmology, soteriology (Christology), eschatology and ethics are being grappled with, and we also encounter
them in the gnostic original sources. Unfortunately, the time is

not yet ripe for us to trace, by a closer analysis of the Nag Hammadi texts, relationships with the phenomena of the 1st century which illuminate the history of tradition. For the time being, they can only be conjectured. Evidence may possibly be derived from the traditions and systems which we now have in the Apocryphon of John, the Exegesis on the Soul, the Apocalypse of Adam, the Hypostasis of the Archons and the Sophia of Jesus Christ, or the Letter of Eugnostos* and which, at least in *NHC II 1, II 6, V 5, their basic constituent parts, go back to the beginning of the II 4, III 3, III 4 2nd century, and in part even to the 1st century. The relation- **The** ships which existed between Jewish Christianity and Gnosis **relationship** have not been mentioned much. We could only state that in the **to Jewish** early Christian mission field various groups and parties com- **Christianity** peted. To these belonged, in addition to the Jewish-gnostic (Simon Magus), also Jewish Christian (Judaistic)–gnostic groups, the latter being especially in the Pauline mission field. It is interesting to observe how some Coptic texts explicitly appeal to and claim as their own a Jewish-Christian authority like James, brother of Jesus and leader of the Jerusalem community, as do the two Revelations of James* and the apocryphal Let- *NHC V 3.4 ter of James*. Besides, we have known for some time the *NHC I 2 "Pseudo-Clementines", which are influenced by gnostic ideas, and which in part derive from Jewish-Christian groups on the edge of Palestine which were overtaken and pushed aside by the Great Church. We also know groupings like the Elkesaites from the same region who became important for Manicheism. The world of the Jewish baptist sects on the east bank of the Jordan was obviously here and there exposed to gnostic influences.[136] The most outstanding phenomenon in this connection is Mandeism, which has survived to the present day. *See below, p. 343 ff.*

The question has been repeatedly discussed whether it is pos- **The problem of** sible to reconstruct from the individual gnostic systems which **an "original"** have come down to us one "original" system, which could then **gnostic system** be considered the most ancient type of the gnostic world view, from which all later systems were somehow developed, either by elaboration or by transformation. H.–M. Schenke[137], for example, postulated the following system: the "unknown God" is with the Sophia (as his divine consort) in the "Ogdoad", i. e. the eighth heaven; the Sophia brings forth without her husband an abortion, the Demiurge, whose abode is the "Hebdomad", i. e. the seventh heaven; he brings forth six angels, or archons, and so completes the number of the planets; these, in their turn, create from matter the world and man; but as the latter is not able to live and cannot stand erect, the supreme God sends (through Sophia) the soul, or the spirit, into the human body; now man can stand erect, he knows the world for a false work of the archons and knows, at the same time, the true God from whom he descends in his inner being. But this construction only applies to a part of the gnostic tradition, namely to the Syrian-Egyptian, more especially the Barbelo-gnostic, and proceeds from the entirely theoretical hypothesis "according to which in principle the complicated derives from the simple".[138] It is, of course, possible to derive individual systems of schools and sects one from another but, according to the present state of research, it is still too early to posit a common "original" system. Incidentally, this would also presuppose an originator and founder of Gnosis whom we do not know as yet and whom we cannot postulate. Unaffected by this is the fact that Gnosis as a whole has certain basic thoughts in common which characterise its essence and which were from the beginning in the minds of

See above, p. 53 ff. the first gnostics. These basic ideas were elaborated, evidently relatively early, i. e. at least in the 1st century A. D., into theological systems, in the sense of doctrines which were capable of forming schools, and as ideological framework, preponderantly in the form of interpretations of older (Jewish) traditions, and they were developed accordingly in course of time, without always having been in touch one with another. Indeed the gnos-

See above, p. 53, 209 tic theologians, as we have seen before, were often individualists.

The Great Systems of the 2nd Century

The Spread of Gnosis The spread of the gnostic sects since the middle of the 1st century from the Palestinian-Syrian region towards the West reached its first climax in the 2nd century, establishing itself along the coasts of Asia Minor and Greece at the end of the 1st century, and also reaching, probably already in the first two decades of the 2nd century, Egypt, i. e. at first Alexandria, and a little later (in about 130) also the metropolis of the empire, Rome. Thus the two leading cities of that time also became centres of Gnosis. The schools which arose and developed there are, at the same time, the leading schools of the 2nd century. Unfortunately, the evidence for this is very fragmentary, so that it is impossible to sketch a complete picture of the history of Gnosis in the 2nd and 3rd centuries. Nevertheless, the majority of all gnostic literature which has come down to us, including the Nag Hammadi texts, dates from this time. The sects which are often mentioned by the heresiologists, as e.g. the Ophites, the Naassenes, the Cainites, the Sethians and the Peratae, belong to this period; they either only now arose or, for the most part, reached their peak. Especially three gnostic theologians determined the profile of Gnosis in the 2nd century, and we must occupy ourselves with them: Basilides, Marcion and Valentinus.

Basilides (in Greek: *Basileides*) is the first important repre- **Basilides** sentative of a Christian Gnosis who consciously saw himself as such, and who wanted to be a Christian theologian. Hegel, in his lectures on the history of philosophy, described him as one of the most distinguished gnostics. Unfortunately, we know almost nothing about his life, not even the years of his birth and of his death. He was active in Alexandria under the emperors Hadrian and Antoninus Pius (117–161). It is not known whether he came from Egypt, or perhaps from the East (Syria). The Fathers of the Church saw in him, as we have already heard, a disciple of Menander of Antioch, which is not very probable. The sojourn in Persia (as a "preacher"!) attributed to him similarly deserves to be banished to the realm of legend. Of his literary works we know, apart from a few fragments, only the titles. Origen attributes to him the composition of a gospel, apparently a gnostic recension of the gospels of the Church. To this he added an exegesis (*Exegetika*) in 24 books, of which Clement of Alexandria has preserved some extracts. Besides he composed for his congregation psalms, or odes. The value which Basilides attributed to the "apostolic tradition" (parallel to the endeavours of the Church) is attested in reports according to which he allegedly had for his teacher Peter's interpreter, Glaucias, or, as we are told elsewhere, that he received "secret words" of the Saviour from the apostle Matthias*. Other au- * cf. Acts 1,23ff. thorities to whom he appealed are the prophets Barcabbas and Barcoph (sons of Noah?) who are unknown to us. These "and some others who had never existed (Basilides) set up for him-

* Eusebius, Eccles. Hist.
IV 7,6–8
(Loeb Classical Library)

self and he invented barbarous names for them to astonish those who were influenced by such things", as Eusebius writes*, appealing to the "Refutation of Basilides" by Agrippa Castor, which is lost.

The teaching of Basilides ·

* Irenaeus,
Adv. haer. I 24,3–7

* Hippolytus,
Refutatio VII 20–27

As for the teaching itself, it, too, cannot be safely grasped, as there are, apart from the few authentic fragments, two entirely different reports about it.[139] While one set of sources, cited by Irenaeus*, sketches a dualistic system related to earlier gnostic tradition, Hippolytus* presents an essentially monistic, strongly Greek philosophical, system of doctrine. The different explanations for these variations have hitherto still not yielded a satisfactory solution. Probably neither of the two heresiological accounts, as is often the case, is identical with the original system. Irenaeus makes things cruder and likes to paint in Valentinian colours; Hippolytus wants to trace back all gnostic teaching to Greek philosophy and is not very scrupulous in the use of

See above, p. 295 f.

his sources (e. g. he attributes the *Apophasis Megalē* to Simon Magus). It may be assumed that Basilides did not present his teaching systematically (an appropriate work is never mentioned), but communicated it only orally to his disciples by means of his biblical exegesis. It is therefore not suprising if the later school made varying interpretations and transformations. Perhaps it is even to be assumed that the Basilidian Gnosis, as with Manicheism, had different facets, i. e. was, on the one hand, indebted to older gnostic traditions and, on the other hand, had adapted to late Greek philosophy and Christian theology. The formation of a school only strengthened this tendency, as can also be observed in Valentinianism. The surviving fragments cannot be fitted into either of the two descriptions of the system; they also deal more with practical ethical problems. Nevertheless, they show a dualistic, in part clearly an anti-cosmic, background of the system which contained ascetic and libertine beginnings: an initial chaos and mixture set in motion the genesis of the world and brought the soul into the body, where it is due to roam until the final salvation, for it partakes of the universal sinfulness of the world (from which even the earthly Jesus is not excepted). The suffering of the soul (also the martyrdom) here is a punishment for ignorance and transgressions arising from it. The successor of Basilides, his son Isidore, emphasised in addition the lack of homogeneity of the soul: it can have appendages which lay it open to the desire for evil. The gnostics (pneumatics) are a "selection" alien to the world, as they are of supernatural constitution. Basilides prefers the expression "faith" to "Gnosis", but he means the same thing when he takes it to mean "understanding" (*noēsis*), which is not based on proof and free decision but on "supernatural election", and is thus "given by nature". Faith is therefore "a state of being, not freedom, a nature and substance, an eternal beauty of a sudden creation". The ethical problems which present themselves in this doctrine of predestination occupied the school of Basilides a great deal.

See above, p. 258f.

The few authentic statements lack references to mythological speculation; these must be gathered from the sources already mentioned. As Irenaeus has probably preserved correctly, Basilides taught an emanation of beings and angels from the unbegotten Father: at first six spiritual powers which formed the actual Pleroma: "mind" (*nous*) or Christ, "word" (*logos*), "prudence" (*phronēsis*), "wisdom" (*sophia*) and "power" (*dynamis*). From the last pair 365 angelic powers originated in an unbroken descending sequence, each creating a "heaven" according to the model of the preceding. These 365 heavenly spheres correspond to the world year or aeon, here spatially understood, which at the same time symbolises the distance between God and creator. For the lowest class of angels created the world and men. Their leader is the God of the Jews who apparently is also called "Abrasax" (or "Abraxas"), a name that has for its basis the numerical value 365, according to the number of the heavens, but which was probably originally a secret paraphrase of the name of the Jewish God Yahweh written in four (Hebrew: *arba* = *abra*) consonants (tetragram). In order to deliver men from the tyranny of the God of the Jews and creator of the world, the supreme God sent his Christ-Nous who appeared in Jesus, but before the crucifixion he exchanged roles with Simon of Cyrene so that he himself was not crucified but could return unrecognised to his Father. In this process of salvation, men as such do not matter but only their souls (nothing more is said about the descent of the soul); the body is transient and the work of the demiurgic power.

See above, p. 165

The monistic reinterpretation of the Basilidian system reads differently but is similar in the fundamental ideas, for everything speaks for the view that in Gnosis a reverse process, i. e. a later strictly dualistic interpretation of an originally more

The monistic reinterpretation of the system

strongly monistic system of doctrine, is unthinkable. The ineffable "non-existent" God brought forth without volition a "world-seed" (similar to a world-egg) out of which everything that exists proceeds according to a predestined order (as out of a grain of mustard-seed), namely in an upward movement, for the seed is apparently "beneath" (upon the sea of chaos?), while God is "above". The emanation takes place in three "sonships": the first, the lightest, speeds at once to God, the second, the coarser, can only get there with the help of the Holy Spirit, while the third sonship has to remain beneath and needs purification and salvation (it corresponds to the "soul", i. e. the physical world element). From the world-seed there also proceed the ruler of the sphere of the fixed stars (the ogdoad) and the ruler of the planets (the hebdomad) who are here described in terms of Greek worship of the cosmos. Salvation consists of the leading back of the divine elements which, in the form of the third sonship, are still in the lower world. For this purpose, this system, too, uses the Christ event, but it is much transformed: the "gospel" (which here stands for the heavenly Christ) travels like a ray of light through the intermediate worlds, instructing them, until it reaches our world where it enlightens Jesus. His fate follows outwardly (bodily) the course of the gospels, but he initiates by means of a "separation of the species" the eschatological "restoration of all things", in leading back the third sonship that was left behind into the spiritual world above the cosmos. When this has happened, mercy overtakes the "creation", i. e. God spreads the primeval "ignorance" over it, "so that everything remains according to its nature and nothing rebels against its nature". The former spatial order of things is restored. This system of a gifted follower of Basilides (in Rome?) who had received a Platonic education has also preserved the "tragic" feature which is typical for Gnosis: the "unworldly" is, without guilt, closely bound up with the lower world, which is strictly separated from the infinitely distant spiritual upper world, and stands in need of deliverance.

Isidore   The school founded by Basilides was, after his death, presided over by his disciple Isidore, who is explicitly described as his "real son" (which, however, need not mean that he was his natural son). Three writings of his are known: "On the Grown Soul", i. e. that part of the soul which turns towards inordinate

See above, p. 310 f. desires, of which we have already spoken. Then there are his

"Ethics" which has also already occupied us, and finally his *See above, p. 258f.* "Expositions of the Prophet Parchor", an authority unknown to us (perhaps he is identical with the above mentioned Bar- *See above, p. 309* coph who is also legendary). Of all these only small fragments have survived (preserved by Clement of Alexandria), which, however, indicate that Isidore developed the teaching of his master independently. The school of Basilides apparently spread only a little outside Egypt. Epiphanius still knows it there in the 4th century. Remarkable is the fact that the Basilidians celebrated the day of Jesus' baptism on 6th or 10th January (there is no agreement on this), "in that they spend the whole preceding night in reading"*. This entirely corresponds * *Clem. Alex.,* to their idea that it was on this occasion that Christ descended *Strom. I 146,1* (in the form of the dove) upon the earthly Jesus and that thus his activity as saviour began.

Marcion (Greek: *Markion*) was a contemporary of Basilides **Marcion** and one of the most original theologians of early Christianity. His relationship to Gnosis is disputed to the present day, especially because one of his best known interpreters, Adolf von Harnack, vigorously denied any such contact.[140] In the meantime the situation has changed, and nothing prevents the treatment of Marcion in an account of Gnosis. However, in contradistinction to the other gnostic theologians, he occupies a special place in that he, as it were, stood partly in the gnostic tradition and partly took up a Christian-Pauline position, to which he imparted his own individualistic understanding. Besides, Marcion consciously proceeded to found a church (with creed, constitution and service) which no gnostic had done before Mani. Marcion's importance lies in many respects outside Gnosis, but he cannot be understood without it and, therefore, belongs to its history. His opponents in the Church saw him mostly in the context of the gnostic "heresy" and his "church" turned, more strongly than its founder, again to the gnostic world of ideas (particularly in the Orient). In the following, therefore, Marcion will be considered essentially in his importance for the history of Gnosis.

Marcion comes from Asia Minor, namely from Sinope (Sinob) on the Black Sea (Pontus). His year of birth is not known, it may be put at about the end of the 1st century. From his father, he took over the profession of shipowner (*nauclerus*). If the report is correct that his father was at the same time bishop of the local Christian community, then he grew up in a Christian tradition; it remains obscure whether or not this Christianity was of a type (Paulinism) characteristic of his later views. Later he was probably active in the western coastal cities of Asia Minior, such as Ephesus and Smyrna, which were old gnostic centres. Perhaps here already there were dissensions with the orthodox community authorities. It is said that especially Polycarp of Smyrna inveighed against him and called him "firstborn of Satan" (but this may also refer to a later period). It is certain that Marcion appeared in Rome about 139/40 and attached himself to the local congregation to which he donated part of his large fortune. Here he apparently finally elaborated his new teaching, according to information from the heresiologists (mostly Irenaeus), under the influence of the Syrian gnostic Cerdo

Cerdo (Kerdon)

(Kerdon). Cerdo lived in Rome under the Roman bishop Hyginus (in about 136–142). He advocated the antithesis, not unknown to Gnosis, of the Old Testament God of creation and

* *Irenaeus, Adv. haer. I 27,1*

the "good God" of Christ's tidings*. Marcion's attempt to gain recognition for his views at a synod in Rome failed, and he was rebuffed. This happened in July 144, a date that for the Marcionites is the date of the foundation of their own church. We have no information about Marcion's later fate. Apparently he was indefatigable in working for the expansion of his newly created church and theology in the Roman empire. Already in about 150 the apologist Justin complains of his influence and

* *Justin, Apology I 26,58*

puts him side by side with Simon Magus and Menander*. It may be assumed that Marcion died in about 160.

Marcion's teaching

The essential point of his theology is the absolute antithesis of the God of law and the God of salvation. The former is the God of the Old Testament who created the world, and who rules it with the full rigour of the law which is based on retaliation; he is "just" but without mercy and goodness. He is therefore imperfect and despicable, and the same is true of his creation. In contrast to him is the "good" and "strange" God who resides unknown above the lowly God of creation in his own heaven. His essence is perfect goodness and mercy; in other respects he cannot be defined more closely, for our earthly limitation is incapable of it. Against his background, the narrowness and imperfection of the demiurge become manifest. Marcion saw in the description of these contrasts one of his main concerns and sought to substantiate them from the Bible in a treatise with the title "Antitheses", contrasting the entirely differently orientated revelation of the New Testament with the Old Testament. This revelation alone is the work of the "strange God": he sent his son Jesus into the world of hopelessness and misery in order to save men from it. The body which he bore was only a "phantasm"(without it his entry into the evil world would have been impossible), but in it he suffered the death on the cross which the creator God had ordained for him without knowing him. Before returning to his Father, he descended into Hades in order to do there, too, his work of salvation. It is noteworthy that those delivered by him belong to those who are condemned in the Old Testament, such as Cain, the Sodomites, the Egyptians and all Gentiles, while the "righteous" of the Jewish history of salvation remain in the underworld*. The • *Irenaeus, Adv. haer. I 27,3* work of Christ is understood by Marcion, who follows Paul, primarily as "redemption" and as payment of a debt, in contrast to the code of criminal justice of the demiurge. It is a pure act of mercy which is quite unintelligible for the earthly world. The acceptance of Christ's work and thus of salvation is realised for man by faith and by the resulting rejection of the law, as well as by a severely ascetic way of life. Marcion saw in the Sermon on the Mount, and especially in the beatitudes, the essential point of the message of Jesus. In order to give to his community an authoritative basis of scripture, he was the first in the history of Christianity to draw up a "canon" of the New Testament. It was rigorously selected and arranged according to his basic principles and consisted of the Gospel of Luke, purified of its Jewish elements, and of ten Pauline epistles (Galatians, I and II Corinthians, Romans, I and II Thessalonians, Ephesians, Colossians, Philippians and Philemon). Against this "purified" gospel the Church soon fixed its own canon of scripture, including the Old Testament.

As has been remarked, Marcion's teaching cannot be understood without gnostic theology. This is true primarily of the "teaching about the two Gods" already described. For even if this was based by Marcion on an extreme understanding of the Pauline teaching of law and gospel, the devaluing of the creator God and of the creation cannot be deduced from it. The Marcionite demiurge corresponds fully to the demiurge of the gnostics, but he is left, so to speak, hanging in the air for want of any connecting link with the "strange God", while in Gnosis he

Marcions's attitude to Gnosis

meaningfully is a fallen product of the world of light. Also the position and description of the saviour God has its parallels in Gnosis. The kind of treatment meted out to the Old Testament is gnostic, the "exegesis of protest" which is found often in the gnostic texts. In his valuation of the world and of matter, Marcion also stands on gnostic ground, and the ethic (ascetic) consequences which he draws arise from the anti-cosmic attitude that pervades his whole theology. However, there is a clear difference to Gnosis in his anthropology: Marcion knows of no share of man in the supreme God; for him there is no affinity of essence between man and God as prerequisite for salvation, as taught in Gnosis. Not only the body is evil but also the soul is infected by it, for it, too, comes from the demiurge. Man, accordingly, is completely corrupt (here too Marcion stands close to Paul). Only a transformation of the soul – the body has no part in it, as it is transient – makes it capable of final salvation. Marcion apparently saw in the gnostic teaching on creation, which established a fall of the soul into matter, a limitation of the principle of salvation; man is utterly dependent on the mercy of the true God. It is clear that this result does not agree, without difficulty, with the presupposition that man as such is capable of being saved, and this led in the school of Marcion to changes which are attested especially in the Oriental sources (they know of a Marcionite doctrine of the soul which is related to gnostic teaching). Another aspect that separates Marcion from Gnosis is the lack of mythological speculation (the teaching about emanations and aeons) and his limitation to the Bible. In this respect, he is a "biblical theologian" through and through, even if a very critical one. Behind this one can see a conscious rejection of the usual gnostic speculations and a turning back to the essential as he found it in Pauline theology, which indeed was not free from gnostic traits. One is actually encouraged to see in Marcion a consistent continuator of Paul in the gnostic spirit. He worked with the gnostic ideas available in his time, insofar as they corresponded to his theological attitude. This links him with the other great gnostics of his time who similarly proceeded in an original and independent manner.

Apelles   Among Marcion's disciples Apelles, who probably joined gnostic circles in Alexandria, stands out. He guided his master's teaching more strongly back again to the contemporary Gnosis, in that he ascribed to the souls a prehistoric existence with the "good God", and made the demiurge into an angel who was created by the same God, and so blunted the edge of the radical system of the two Gods. As cause of evil and of the body, he introduced a "fiery angel" who had fallen away and who is also the God of the Jews. He then left the Marcionite church and founded his own community in Rome which spread parallel to that of his teacher as far as the Orient, but which did not last as long as his (not beyond the 3rd century). Apelles wrote down his views in two works which have not survived: the "Syllogisms", in which he is said to have proved the untruth of the books of Moses, and the "Revelations" (*Phaneroseis*) of a prophetess, Philumene by name, who was his friend. Moreover it is known that he had, in his old age, a religious debate with the theologian Rhodo from Asia Minor, about which Eusebius reports in some detail*. This may have taken place towards the end of the 2nd century.

Eusebius, Eccles. Hist. V 13

Marcion's church, as its fierce opponent Tertullian said, filled the whole world. It was, without doubt, the greatest danger encountered by the Catholic Church in the 2nd century. We can trace it not only in Italy and Egypt, but also far into the Orient, to East Syria (Mesopotamia) and Armenia where leaders of the Church (especially Ephraem of Edessa) engaged it in dispute. In the West, only the legislation against heresies promulgated by the Christian emperors in the 4th century led to its fall, while before it had survived, together with the Catholic Church, all persecutions of the Christians. In the East it survived longer, especially by its flight into the country; in the region of East Syria there were whole Marcionite villages. But in the 5th and 6th centuries we hear little of them even there. It is very uncertain whether the Arab authors, who still write about the Marcionites in the 10th century, presuppose their existence. It is often supposed that that section which did not return to Christianity merged in Manicheism. There are many agreements between the two religions and Marcion's ecclesiastical organisation prepared the ground for Mani's.

See below, p.339f

Valentinus

The last great gnostic school was founded in the 2nd century, more or less in the same period as the two already described. Its founder was the Christian teacher Valentinus who was probably born in Lower Egypt. Unfortunately, very little is known about him, although the Fathers of the Church occupy themselves much with his teaching. He obtained a Greek education in Alexandria and embraced there Christianity, probably already in gnostic dress. We may recall that Basilides was active there at the same time (but no connection between the two is reported). Valentinus was busy for a while as a free Christian teacher, before he went to Rome at about the same time as did Marcion (in about 140). In Rome, he apparently worked quite successfully. It is even reported (by Tertullian), quite anachronistically, that he was put forward as bishop, and that he only had to withdraw in favour of a martyr (the reference is probably to the election of Pius in 143). But it came to a breach with the community and he was rebuffed as a heretic. As he probably already possessed his own school, he was able to continue his activities in Rome for another twenty years. He is said to have left Rome only under bishop Anicetus (154–165) and to have gone to the East, perhaps to Cyprus, where he found a new sphere (according to Epiphanius). But it is also possible that he died in Rome not long after 160. Even his opponents attest to his great intellectual gifts and poetic talent. This is confirmed by the few fragments of his works which have been preserved for us (mostly by Clement of Alexandria). They show that he composed predominantly sermons (homilies), hymns or psalms and letters; thus he devoted himself largely to practical work for the community and spread his teaching in this form as well as by oral instruction.[141] The only hymn which we possess from him bears the title "Harvest" (or "Summer") and conforms to the early Christian hymnic style:[142]

> "I see that all is suspended on spirit,
> I perceive that all is wafted upon spirit.
> Flesh is suspended on soul,
> And soul depends on the air,
> Air is suspended from ether,
> From the depths come forth fruits,
> From the womb comes forth a child" *

* Hippolytus, Refutatio
VI 37,7, transl. D. Hill

The teaching of Valentinus   The idea of emanation inherent in the system of Valentinus with the primeval beginning, the divine "depth" (bythos) at the beginning, is here expressed poetically. The visionary gift which shines through here becomes manifest also in another communication which indicates at the same time that Valentinus claimed for his teaching divine revelation, and thus gave it authority (he is said to have given himself out to be a pupil of a disciple of Paul Theodas by name). "For Valentinus says (that) he saw a small child, newly born, and asked him who he was, and he answered that he was the Logos. Then he added to this an imposing myth and on this he wants to base the 'sect' that was founded by him"*. To his followers he writes with prophetic confidence: "From the beginning you are immortal and children of eternal life. You wished to take death to yourselves as your portion in order that you might destroy it and annihilate it utterly, and that death might die in you and through you. For when you destroy the world and yourselves are not destroyed, then you are lords over the whole creation and over all decay"*. In a homily "On Friends", we read as follows: "Much that is written in the generally available books is found written also in the church of God. That which is common is this: the words which come from the heart, the law which is written in the heart. This is the people of the Beloved, who are loved by him and who love him"*. The community of Valentinus sees itself as the Church of Christ which finds its wisdom also outside itself in the "inner" tradition of mankind accessible to gnostics.

Hippolytus, Refutatio VI 42,2, transl. D. Hill

Clem. Alex., Strom. IV 89,2–3, transl. D. Hill

op. cit. VI 52,3–4, transl. D. Hill

Only one theological title is attributed to Valentinus: "On the three Natures", in which he is said to have pondered, as the first to do so, on three hypostases (substances) and three persons (Father, Son and Holy Spirit). The Tripartite Tractate* to be found among the Nag Hammadi texts has nothing to do with it, although it probably derives from the Valentinian school (about 150–180). Another text too*, which according to its initial words was entitled "Gospel of Truth", is surely not a work by Valentinus, as was thought in the first enthusiasm of discovery when appeal was made to the information given by Irenaeus who had seen a gospel of this name "recently" come into existence among the Valentinians*, but a homily which shows vague affinities with the Valentinian school.[143] Also not by Valentinus are the two writings, which on good grounds are attributed to Valentinianism generally, the Gospel of Philip* and the Letter to Rheginos*. The same holds for the anonymous Valentinian doctrinal treatise.*

NHC I 5

NHC I 3

Irenaeus, Adv. haer. III 11,9

NHC II 3
NHC I 4
NHC XI 2

In view of this state of the literary remains, it is also not possible in the case of Valentinus to reconstruct his system with any certainty. It is only reflected in manifold ways in the teachings of his great school which revealed a fairly independent growth

* Irenaeus, Adv. haer.
I 1–8,11–12,13–21
** Hippolytus,
Refutatio VI 29–36
*** Origen,
Commentary on the
Gospel of John,
citations from Heracleon
* Clem. Alex.,
Ex Theodoto
** Epiphanius,
Panarion 31,5–8;
35,4; 35–36

See above, p. 53

of ideas. We have no fewer than six more or less complete accounts of the Valentinian system in the heresiological literature[144]: in Irenaeus*, Hippolytus**, Origen***, Clement of Alexandria* and Epiphanius**. From this it has been concluded that there was no fixed system of teaching at all that goes back to the founder of the school. But this is not very likely, as a series of basic features are to be found in all Valentinian sects which can be traced back to him only. Gnostic schools in general share a rather unorthodox attitude in respect of their teaching tradition. Much room was allowed, apparently, to free thought and to the shaping of the teaching that had been handed down. The spirit was meant to reign, not the dead letter. Irenaeus, one of the first "anti-Valentinians", repeatedly found fault with the fact that the disciples of Valentinus boasted of being "improvers of the master", and that therefore they

* Irenaeus, Adv. haer.
I 11,1; 12,1; 13,1

* op. cit. I 11,1,
transl. D. Hill

possess an "inconsistent teaching"*. "Although there are only two or three of them they do not speak with one voice on the same points, but with reference to the subject-matter and the names put forward opposing views"*.

The characteristics of Valentinianism

To the ideas held in common by all Valentinians belong the following which probably were typical for Valentinus too: the Pleroma consists of (at least) 30 aeons or worlds which bear different names and are arranged in pairs (they form 15 pairs). Of greater importance are only the two first tetrads, viz. an ogdoad, which have (according to Irenaeus) the following names: the "primal depth" (*bythos*) or "progenitor" (the head of the whole system) and the (synchronous) "thought" (*ennoia*), also called "grace" (*charis*) and "silence" (*sigē*); then the "understanding" (*nous*) or the "only-begotten" (*monogenēs*) and the "truth" (*alētheia*); the "Word" (*logos*) and the "life" (*zoē*); the "man" (*anthropos*) and the "church" (*ekklesia*). Out of them arise the remaining "world spaces" up to the last aeon, the "wisdom" (*sophia*). This plays an essential role for, in the last resort, the world events take their course by reason of its fall which was caused by its unbridled striving, motivated by inquisitiveness, after the unknown father of the Pleroma, as by the "ignorance" or the "error" thus called forth, the "material substance" arises. It is furthermore characteristic of Valentinianism that these events occur on two levels: inside and outside of the Pleroma, which is protected by a boundary (*horos*). The events in the Pleroma have a consequent continuation towards

the outside which constitutes the actual doom. In order to restore the disturbed peace in the Pleroma the pair of aeons
"Christ" and the "Holy Spirit" is created, the former leading
the (upper) Sophia back into harmony. But this, according to a
statement of Irenaeus*, was not the teaching of Valentinus.
According to him, Christ was a son of the "mother", i. e. of Sophia, brought forth in the "remembrance of those from above",
to which place he also returned, while the mother, thus abandoned, created (from the psychical elements left to her) another son, the Demiurge. In my view, this is not very likely and is
an error of Irenaeus (a confusion with the Barbelo-Gnosis or
with the Logos of the Sophia). The passionate desire (*enthymesis*) of the reintegrated Sophia is separated from her and as "female fruit" outside of the Pleroma becomes the "lower Sophia"
or Achamoth (Hebrew: "Wisdom"). It remains uncertain
whether this duplication of Sophia, which we have already met,
goes back to Valentinus. In order to remove the "sufferings" of
this lower "Wisdom", Jesus or the "Saviour" (*sotēr*) is brought
forth, with the participation of all the aeons, as the "perfect
fruit of the Pleroma". He put her "affects" in order through
"knowledge", but the passions are separated from her and become the (at first non-material) elements of the future creation
of the world. Altogether there are three substances or modes of
being which proceed from the experiences of Sophia: out of
passion the material, out of "conversion" or "repentance" the
psychic (*psychē*), out of that which was brought forth after her
"purification" by the Sotēr the spiritual (*pneuma*, the seed of
light). The Valentinian division of mankind into hylics, or choics, psychics and pneumatics is here firmly fixed ideologically;
it is rooted in the Pleroma. Out of the psychical substance,
Achamoth creates the creator of the world who takes to himself
seven heavens (the "hebdomad"). He takes up an intermediate
position, the "place of the Midst", between Achamoth, which
has its abode in the "Ogdoad" above him, and the psychic and
material objects created by him below him, i. e. the world
whose "lord" and "king" he is. In all other respects he bears the
features of the Demiurge which are usual in Gnosis: ignorance
(concerning the Pleroma) and arrogance. In the version of one
school, a son is attributed to the Demiurge who is the actual ruler of the world (cosmocrator) and who corresponds to the devil. This is a clear softening of the original system, but is, as it

*Irenaeus,
Adv. haer. I 11,1*

See above, p. 154

were, inherent in it as it has a very much weakened dualism. Man is, according to one fragment by Valentinus, a product of lowly angels, which, however, thanks to its hidden supernatural character (as the image of the aeon "Man") surpasses its creator and therefore is capable of attaining saving knowledge. The available sources, however, do not say much about this.

Without being able to reproduce the complex events of the cosmological speculation, details of which are in dispute among the Valentinians, the brief description here given sketches the system drawn up by Valentinus. What is essential, in addition to the teaching about the aeons, is the role of "Ignorance" as the cause of the material-psychic world or matter, and the threefold division into body, soul and spirit, in which a limited capability for salvation is attributed to the soul, which is shaped with the help of the spirit towards the attainment of knowledge.

See above, p. 196

The models of Valentinus Valentinus developed this teaching from older models, and it had apparently even more mythological features than we know in detail. Already in earlier times one thought of the Barbelognostic or Ophite systems as Valentinus' ancestors. The Fathers of the Church also were aware of this. Today we are able to produce an excellent literary model for the teaching of Valentinus, the Apocryphon of John* of which we have written more fully above. It was already known to Irenaeus (in about 180) in a form very near to our extant versions, and may therefore have existed in its essential outline before Valentinus. A comparison, which need not be followed through, shows that Valentinus received his stimuli from this side. Accordingly he stands in a certain gnostic tradition which we have characterised as "Barbelognostic", or "female". Building on his Greek Platonic education, he elaborated this tradition and permeated it with new ideas, so that one of the most impressive and complete systems of gnostic speculation came into existence. It can be described as the climax and goal of this gnostic sect, and it may have made its contribution towards suppressing lesser systems of this kind; they are not mentioned much later on. The system created by Valentinus sees itself as the abolition of the "ignorance" which arose from a fault in the Pleroma, by means of "knowledge"; it is thus at one and the same time an act of knowledge and of salvation.

* NHC II 1; Pap. Ber.

See above, p. 76ff., 102ff.

See above, p. 80

See above, p. 115f.

The Valentinians The school of Valentinus is one of the greatest and most influential gnostic schools before Manicheism. Of no other have we so many names and reports. Some of the disciples of Valentinus were distinguished intellects, such as Ptolemaeus, Heracleon, Theodotus and even Marcus. The division of the Valentinians into two schools, which they themselves called "Anatolian" (i. e. Oriental) and "Italian", is remarkable and significant for their importance. Hippolytus, to whom we are indebted for this information, reports that the point at issue between them was a question of Christology*. While the Italian school attributed to Jesus a psychic body which the spirit (i. e. the logos of the Sophia) entered only at the baptism, the "Orientals" presupposed a pneumatic body for Jesus already at his birth. Additional differences occur in the speculation on the aeons and in the teaching on salvation. As can be seen from the names of the two schools, they had different geographical centres, and this may have contributed to their separation. The Italian school was dominant in Rome and reached as far as Southern Gaul where it was opposed by Irenaeus at Lugdunum (Lyons) on the Rhône. Its leading representatives were Ptolemaeus and Heracleon. The Oriental school was active in Egypt, Syria and Asia Minor; to it belonged Marcus, Axionicus of Antioch (he lived at the time of Tertullian) and Theodotus (the Syrian Bardaisan was also wrongly assigned to it). Most of these Valentinians we know only from their opponents in the Catholic Church. Of some we have detailed reports and even some original works. To these belong especially Ptolemaeus and Heracleon. Ptolemaeus lived in the time of Irenaeus (2nd half of the 2nd century), who based his comprehensive description of the Valentinian Gnosis* on the system of Ptolemaeus. An expert has remarked that in this version we meet a picture of Gnosis "that can compete with Mani's system in its conceptual unity but surpasses it in intellectual depth."[145] Ptolemaeus represents quite a moderate dualism. He sees the basic constituents of the world less in matter than in psychic non-corporeal elements, and he pays much attention to the fate of the psychics; the work of the saviour Jesus is primarily directed towards them. The means of their salvation is the "formation in accordance with knowledge". Ptolemaeus also took a moderate attitude with regard to ethical-practical problems. His letter to his disciple Flora, which is preserved in its original form, instructs us about this. Of Heracleon, who is described by Clement of Alexandria as the most distinguished of the school, we have a few quota-

* *Hippolytus, Refutatio VI 35,5–7*

Ptolemaeus

* *Irenaeus, Adv. haer. I 1–8*

See above, p. 259f.

Heracleon

See above, p. 17

See above, p. 16

See above, p. 241 ff.
Marcus

* Irenaeus,
Adv. haer. I 14,1

tions from his exegetical "memoirs" ("Hypomnemata") in the works of Origen and Clement[146]. His teaching largely corresponds to that of Ptolemaeus and markedly takes into consideration the traditions of the Catholic Church. In the foreground stands the ethical interest, the salvation of man, not the speculation on aeons. Finally, Clement of Alexandria left a whole book of "Excerpta", mainly from the works of Theodotus, who belonged to the Oriental school[147]. In his writings some of the ancient features of the school seem to have been preserved, especially a stronger rejection of the creator of the world, but there is also to be found much that is in general gnostic and cultic, including magic. The latter plays a dominant role, as we have already shown, in the work of the most notorious Valentinian, Marcus (Markos). He also was a contemporary of Irenaeus, who unmasked the followers of Marcus who had reached as far as the Rhône valley. The starting point for his activities seems to have been Asia Minor, or perhaps Egypt. Hippolytus describes him as a disciple of the fictitious Kolarbasos (or Kolorbasos) who owes his existence to a misunderstanding, namely to the Hebrew name of the "tetrad" which was placed by Marcus before the 30 aeons (*kol-arba'* "all is four")[148]. He traces his wisdom back to divine revelation as did his master Valentinus: the above mentioned supreme "tetrad" descended to him in female form as "silence" (Greek: *sigē*) in order to manifest to him the mysteries of the All*. This setting of the scene (perhaps as introduction to the source used by Irenaeus) was necessary, for Marcus transposed the whole Valentinian system into numerical speculations (Gematria) and letter mysticism, as it was in use in the Hellenistic world since the Pythagoreans. Irenaeus and, copying him, Hippolytus have given a detailed account of it.[149] One discovers from it, however, that Marcus preserved the basic ideas of his teacher. The ceremonies practised by him are in part connected with the ancient mystery cults but were also familiar to the Valentinian community in the Orient. It cannot be proved whether this, as is often maintained, means an invasion of "vulgar Gnosis", for we know little about the cultic practice of all gnostics and a pure Gnosis without cult probably never existed. The reports by Irenaeus are not free of spitefulness and malicious distortion. This is attested by the taunt-song of an unknown "divine presbyter and herald of the truth" on Marcus reproduced by him[150]:

"You maker of idols, Marcus, and you interpreter of signs,
Experienced in astrology and magic too,
Whereby you confirm your lying teaching,
And show them miracles to pervert them.
This is the wanton game of dark powers,
Your and their goal is the father Satan.
The devil Azazel gives you strength,
You run along before him, his word is your command" *   * op. cit. I 15,6

Marcus evidently attached importance to the symbolic representation and cultic appropriation of the teaching.

The Valentinian schools continued in various parts of the Mediterranean world of that time, and there is evidence for their existence to the end of the 4th century. In the year 229, Origen specially travelled to Athens, in order to engage in a debate with the most influential Valentinian there, Candidus. Epiphanius knows the school from Egypt and Cyprus. In Syrian Edessa there were still quarrels between Arians and Valentinians in the time of the emperor Julian (361–363). Likewise in Callinicum on the upper Euphrates a Valentinian church was destroyed by enraged monks under Theodosius I (379–395)[151]. It may be assumed that still in the 5th century there were representatives of this gnostic sect living in hiding.

The really productive period of Western Gnosis ends strictly speaking with Valentinus and his great disciples; at least the tradition has nothing essentially new to tell us later. Occasionally names still crop up of persons who stand outside the known gnostic schools, such as Monoimus "the Arab" (i. e. he comes from the Roman province of Arabia) about whom Hippolytus provides some information*, Prodicus, who is mentioned several times by Clement of Alexandria, the head of an antinomian group who see themselves as "sons of the first God" and even reject prayer, and finally the painter Hermogenes. Hermogenes was probably born in Antioch (in Syria) and, in about 180, the bishop of Antioch wrote a polemical tract against him which has not survived. Twenty years later Tertullian wrote against him in Carthage*. This painter, of whom Tertullian maliciously opined that he married more than he painted, evidently influenced his disciples very much ideologically. He must have had a very original mind for, like the Alexandrian gnostics, he combined Greek Platonic ideas with gnostic and Christian

Other gnostics: Monoimus and Prodicus

* Hippolytus, Refutatio VIII 12–15

Hermogenes

* Tertullian, Adversus Hermogenem

ideas into a dualistic cosmology which Hippolytus included in
his book of heresies*. Otherwise we have in the 3rd and 4th
centuries almost exclusively manifestations of the late forms of
the older gnostic schools, inasfar as they still exist. A typical
product of this time are the cumbersome and tedious tractates
of Pistis Sophia and the Books of Jeu, also the later parts of the
Hermetic collection and some of the Nag Hammadi writings.
Epiphanius, because of his powers of invention, has only a limited evidential value, but his description apparently reflects
the final period of the Western Gnosis quite well. The "Archontics" described by him who spread from Palestine as far as
Armenia are probably a late form of Gnosis which centres on
the figure of Seth "whom they also call 'stranger'" (*allo-
genēs*)*[152]. In what way gnostic traditions and ideas gained access into the broader Christian popular piety is demonstrated to
us in the numerous apocryphal Acts of the Apostles, some examples of which we have come to know. While on this level
gnostic features were adopted more or less without reflection,
yet in other realms we find their "transformation" (metamorphosis) into the official Christian world of ideas; on the one
hand in the known systems of the great Alexandrine theologians such as Clement and Origen, on the other in the arising
mysticism of monasticism where one can observe the inner appropriation (internalisation) of gnostic ideas, such as the concept of the soul's heavenward journey, the struggle with the evil
powers, the hostility to the world and asceticism. We shall have
to return to this subject briefly in the concluding section of this
book, as this process forms an essential part of a historical ap-
preciation of Gnosis and its effects.

*Hippolytus,
Refutatio VIII 17*

**Late forms
of Gnosis**

*Epiphanius,
Panarion 40,1–8*

See below, p. 369f.

Manicheism

While in the Roman empire the formation of the great gnostic
schools comes to an end in the 2nd century, there begins in the
3rd century in the East (Mesopotamia) a golden age of gnostic
religion on a world-wide scale. It is the work of one man who as
one of the great founders of religion has passed into the history
of mankind. Manicheism, of which we are speaking, can be re-

garded as one of the four world religions known to the history of religions. This means, it shares a position with Buddhism, Christianity and Islam, but, in contrast to these, lies in the past. R. Haardt has aptly characterised it as "the final and logical systematisation of the Gnosis of late antiquity as a universal religion of revelation with a missionary character".[153] The soil for the origin of this gnostic world religion – this designation is apt in its fullest sense – had been prepared for some considerable time, for Mesopotamia had not only an ancient civilisation but also a wealth of varying religious traditions which had developed and met there in the course of a history of some thousand years. In addition to the offshoots of the ancient Babylonian cults which can be traced here and there down to the late Hellenistic period, there were the Iranian religious ideas which penetrated in the train of the Persian rule (539 B.C.) and, after this since Alexander, Hellenistic civilisation. Furthermore, there arose in the country in the time of the so-called Babylonian exile (597 B.C.) a strong Judaism. In the course of the 2nd century, Christianity penetrated from Syria and, especially in the North, formed centres such as Edessa and Nisibis. It is remarkable that at first those groups predominated which were later declared heretical, such as gnostics (the special heretical school identified in Edessa are the followers of one Quq by name, the Quqites), Marcionites and Jewish Christians. This feature of early Eastern Christianity was apparently typical for its beginning in the 2nd and 3rd centuries and also explains the origin of gnostic and gnosticising works in this region, such as the apocryphal Acts of Thomas with the gnostic "Song of the Pearl", the Odes of Solomon and the figure of Bardaisan (Latin: Bardesanes) who belongs to the immediate forerunners of Mani. This "Aramaic philosopher", as he was called, lived for the better part of his life at the court of king Abgar IX of Edessa (179–216). After the conquest of the city by the Romans (216), he went to Armenia where he died probably in about 222. Bardaisan combined in his person an Oriental-Greek education with a Christianity shaped by Gnosis which he himself had adopted. For his community or school, which apparently strongly influenced the Christian Edessa, he composed a book of 150 hymns in Syriac, modelled on the Psalter, which were preserved in fragments only by his fiercest later opponent Ephraem of Edessa (306–373). One of his disciples, following the

The conditions of its origin

Bardaisan

teachings of his master, wrote a tractate couched in dialogue
form about fate, the so-called "Book of the Laws of Countries", which, in addition to the heresiological sources, is the
only work which allows us an insight at first hand into Bardaisan's thinking.[154] Other works have not come down to us except
for the titles; some (such as the Odes of Solomon or the "Song
of the Pearl") were wrongly attributed to him. An evaluation of
his teaching, which can be reconstructed only in parts, is not
easy and is under debate among researchers to the present
day.[155]

On the one hand he is considered to be an independent-minded
representative of early Syrian Christianity, on the other hand
he is described in a monograph by Hilgenfeld (1864) as the "last
gnostic". This is in part due to the unsatisfactory terminology
used to define the position of early Syrian (Edessene) Christianity, and in part to the deficient sources. If one accepts the
reports of the Church Fathers, particularly the Syrian ones,
Bardaisan's teaching is to be taken as a special form of Eastern
Gnosis. Although Bardaisan was not a disciple of Valentinus as
some heresiologists maintained (e. g. Hippolytus), he obviously used gnostic (including Hermetic) ideas which influenced his
theology and which continued explicitly in his school and facilitated its transition to Manicheism. His view of the world is
throughout pessimistic and is based on a dualism of God and
darkness (*hylē*). Between them stand the four primeval elements, light, wind, fire and water which, through a fateful
breach of the original order, become mingled with the darkness, and this, in turn, leads to the genesis of the world. Only
the "word of thought" or the "power of the first God", which is
equated with Christ, can halt the utter ruin, and can create
some order out of the mixture which is composed of higher
(psychic) and lower (material) parts above which is ranged the
purely spiritual world of God. Body and matter are considered
to be bad and hinder the salvation of the soul which, because of
Adam's fall, cannot return to God. Only through Christ does it
become once more capable of ascending with the help of the divine spirit into the "bridal chamber". An important means for
this is "knowledge", viz. perception. It is consistent with his
presuppositions that for Bardaisan the resurrection of the body
is excluded and that Christ inhabited on earth only an illusory
body, and this demonstrates more than anything else his close

link with the gnostic world view. His graduated evaluation of the world's edifice (the planets and stars are not merely evil powers) derived from Greek thought and his defence of the freedom of the will against the fatalism of astrology, as set out in the above-mentioned dialogic tractate, are thoroughly consistent with this. If one compares the manifold manifestations of Gnosis in the West with Bardaisan, there is good reason to speak of him as the author of an independent system of Eastern Gnosis which, together with other gnostic schools, prepared the ground for Manicheism.

The founder of the religion, Mani, comes from the Southern region of Mesopotamia; he probably was born on the 14th April, A.D. 216, in the vicinity of Seleucia-Ctesiphon on the Tigris, the Persian capital. His parents are said to be of noble Iranian descent, his mother even of Parthian royal lineage, but this is uncertain. The father, Pattak (Greek: Pattikios, Latin: Patecius) had joined a gnostic baptist sect to which he also introduced his son early on. From a recently discovered source, the Cologne Mani Codex, it is clear that this was the heretical Jewish Christian community of the Elkesaites, which claimed to go back to the legendary prophet Elkesai (i.e. the "hidden power of God") who appeared in about A.D. 100 in Syria. The Mandeans, who to this day live in Southern Iraq, also formed part of this baptist sectarian world which surrounded the young Mani. When he was twelve years old, in about 228/29, Mani had his first vision in which his heavenly double, his "twin", his "partner" or "companion", appeared to him and assured him of his constant protection and help. Later, Mani saw in this the effective revelation of the "comforter" (the Paraclete), or the Holy Spirit*, who had revealed to him the "mysteries" of his teaching. In consequence of this experience, he cut himself loose from his environment and began to engage in argument with it, thus attempting to reform the practice and teaching of the baptists. It came to a division in the community and to an official breach which ended with Mani's expulsion; only his father and two disciples stayed with him. In the meantime, he had another experience at the age of 24 which constituted his actual call to be an "apostle of light". It can be dated on the 19th April, 240, and is once more taken as a revelation of the "companion" who acted on the order of God, the king of light. In a hymn Mani briefly described his role:

The Life of Mani

* cf. John 16,17ff.

"I am a grateful hearer (i. e. pupil)
who was born in the land of Babylon.
I was born in the land of Babylon
and I am set up at the gate of the truth.
I am a singer, a hearer,.
who has come from the land of Babylon.
I have come from the land of Babylon
cf. plate 24   to send forth a call in the world".[156]

We have only a rough idea about his later life. After he had fled with his disciples to the capital Seleucia-Ctesiphon, where he apparently established his first community, he began to missionarise actively inside and outside Iran. While messengers were sent to the Western, Roman, provinces, Mani himself journeyed in 241 by boat to India and up the Indus valley to Turan, where he won over the king for himself. In about 242/243 he is back in Babylonia to pay his respects to the new ruler Shapur I (242–273) after the death of Ardashir I. He succeeds in finding favour with him and even in being received into the royal entourage. Already two brothers of the king become his followers. Clearly, the new universal religion commended itself as a suitable ideology for the Persian empire without the omnipotent Zoroastrian priestly caste, the Magi, being involved. Mani is now able to spread his teaching without hindrance; he sends his disciples to Syria, Egypt and Eastern Iran. "I have [sown] the corn of life ... from East to West; as you see [my] hope [has] gone towards the East of the world and [all] the regions of the globe (i. e. the West), to the direction of the North *Kephalaia, p.16* and the [South]. None of the apostles has ever done this ..."*. When Shapur I died, his successor, Ohrmuzd I (273/74), was still favourably disposed towards Mani, but under Bahram I (274–277) his fate changed. Probably the caste of the Magi had, in the meantime, gained enough influence to eliminate the unwelcome rival who threatened to upset Iran's traditional religious order. The head of the Magi, Kartīr (Kardēr), whose aim was a thorough reform of the Zoroastrian church, appears as Mani's chief opponent. Mani's attempt to change the opinion of the Great King who resided in Bēlapat (Gundeshapur) failed; he was thrown into prison there where he died in chains soon after, in the spring of 276. His corpse was mutilated, as was then the custom when dealing with heretics, and was put on show outside the city. In this his community saw the passion and "crucifixion" (martyrdom) of its master who after this was believed to have ascended into the realm of light.

The Manichean "church" now lived through difficult times; persecutions and schisms afflicted it. Mani's successors in the leadership of the community also suffered martyrdom. This led to a decline of Manicheism in the Persian territories (to this the revolutionary movement of the Mazdakites (494–524), which was suppressed with cruel harshness, ultimately contributed), but not elsewhere; on the contrary its spread intensified in the Eastern and Western countries through emigration. Merchants and missionaries (apostles) continued the work of their founder. In about 300 the "teaching of light", as it was called, can be found in Syria, Northern Arabia, Egypt and North Africa (where St. Augustine joined it from 373–382). From Syria it reached Palestine, Asia Minor and Armenia. At the beginning of the 4th century, there is evidence for Manicheans in Rome and Dalmatia, and soon after also in Gaul and Spain. Anti-Manichean polemical writings and imperial edicts against heretics attempt to counter its influence, but only from the 6th century onwards does the religion disappear, though continuing to exert its influence under different guises in other sectarian circles (Paulicians, Bogomils, Catharists) up to the Middle Ages. It could hold its ground even more successfully and more permanently in the East where it flourished at a time when there were no longer any real Manicheans to be found in the West; this is probably due to Islam having put an end to the monopoly position of Christianity and Zoroastrianism. In the early era of the Arab conquest, Mani's religion once more attained toleration in Persia, partly as a fashionable religion among the educated. But Central Asia became its centre (Turkestan, the Tarim basin) where it had come from Eastern Iran (Chorasan). Here it even succeeded in 762 in becoming the state religion of the Uigur empire. After the collapse of the empire (840) it continued to hold its own in the succeeding petty states beside Buddhism and Nestorian Christianity until the 13th century when it fell utterly victim to the devastating Mongolian attack. The importance of Manicheism in Central Asia is illustrated by the many finds of writings and frescos from this period which were made at the beginning of the 20th century in the course of several Turfan expeditions by German, French and Russian scholars.

The spread of Manicheism

plates 21 and 22

In the 7th century Mani's followers also reached China, via Turkestan and along the Silk Road. In 694 the first apostles made their appearance at the Chinese imperial court and competed with Buddhists, Nestorians and Taoists. Several edicts dealt with Manicheism and the Confucian men of letters opposed it fiercely, as it knew how to adapt to Chinese tradition in its missionary practice. In 843/44 it came to a bloody persecution to which most congregations fell victim. But still, at the end of the 14th century, emperors of the Ming dynasty had occasion to take measures against the followers of "the religion of the venerable light". In Southern China (according to Portuguese reports) Manichean traditions are said to have still survived in the 17th century. Manichean influence has also been traced to Tibet. Thus Manichean Gnosis has had a history of more than one thousand years during which period it spread from Spain to China. Mani has therefore been proved right when he said to his community: "But my hope will go to the West and will also go to the East. And they will hear the voice of its preaching in all languages and they will preach it in all cities. My religion surpasses in this first point all earlier religions, for the earlier religions were founded in individual places and in individual cities. My religion will go out to all cities and its message will reach every land".[157]

The Manichean writings   In order to protect his work from falsification, and to ensure that it should not be forgotten, Mani set great store by keeping a written record of his doctrinal system. Here, too, he aimed at surpassing his predecessors, the earlier prophets and founders of religion, who in his opinion had composed no works of their own and whose message therefore had been preserved only incompletely. For this purpose, he developed a new, practical, script and composed a number of works in Iranian and Syriac for the calligraphic production and copying of which he showed great concern. The superior culture of the Manicheans expressed by script and book which thus came into existence earned him later the epithet "the painter". Unfortunately only scanty remnants of his own works have survived either in quotation by his opponents or in the writings of his community.[158] But we know at least the titles: "Shahpuhrakān", a work dedicated to the Great King Shapur I, the "Great" or "Living Gospel", the "Treasure of Life", the "Pragmateia" (i. e. composition, work of history), the "Book of Mysteries", the "Book of the Giants", a collection of letters or missives, some psalms and prayers as well as a kind of picture book ("Eikon" or "Ard-hang") which illustrated his view of the world in pictures. Up to the end of the 19th century there were hardly any original sour-ces of the Manicheans except the few preserved by the Chris-tian, Zoroastrian and Islamic heresiologists. Only the above mentioned Turfan expeditions (1898–1916) yielded an unex-pectedly rich spoil of Manichean literature (in Iranian, Old Turkish and Chinese) and art.[159] The most important pieces came to Berlin; their publication is not yet concluded. There are doctrinal texts, hymns, prayers, rituals, confessional for-mularies, catechisms, letters of exhortation and epistles, com-mentaries, narrative material of historical and mythological-legendary content, mural paintings and miniatures. The writ-ings are for the most part badly damaged and fragmentary, but they have afforded us, for the first time, direct access to this strange religion, even if they are derived from its late phase (6th–10th centuries). Nevertheless they contain fragments of the works of Mani, e. g. the Shahpuhrakān. A few decades later (in 1930) Carl Schmidt, who has already been mentioned in another context, discovered the Manichean texts in Coptic *See above, p. 27f.* from Medinet Madi (south-west of the Faiyūm oasis in Middle Egypt) which came partly to Berlin and partly to London.[160] In contrast to the finds at Turfan, these Coptic texts are relatively well preserved books (codices) which also are much older; they come from about 400 and therefore were written only 150 years after the rise of Manicheism. The writings were probably trans-lated from Greek and Syriac in the course of the 4th century in Upper Egypt. Their edition too is not yet concluded; moreover some parts unfortunately were lost in the second world war. There have been published the *Kephalaia* (i. e. "principal arti- *See plate 31* cles"), an encyclopaedic handbook in the form of lectures of Mani to his disciples, which is so far our best introduction into his world of thought; then a collection of homilies and a psalm book, both valuable witnesses to the piety of the Manichean community. Recently there appeared a Greek parchment manu-script in pocket book format (3.5cm. × 4.5cm.) of the 4th/5th century which bears the title "On the Genesis of his (Mani's) Body", and which is part of a biography of Mani compiled by his community according to the traditions of his first disciples. This text, which has only just been published, also comes from *See plates 29 and 30*

Egypt and belongs to the Cologne collection of papyri.[161] It is the first extant original Manichean text in Greek which is based on Oriental traditions of the earliest community.

The teaching of Mani   In spite of the remarkable addition to original sources, it is still a much disputed problem which fundamental system Mani himself advocated or taught, for the writings and other reports which we possess always reflect particular varieties or drafts of this system which arose from missionary concerns and from adaptations to the Iranian-Persian, the Christian and the Buddhist environment in which Manicheism spread. This kind of adaptation was a special characteristic of Manichean teaching and, in order to solve the problem of the authentic system, it was assumed that Mani himself had formulated a system of doctrine that was flexible enough to adapt itself readily to other traditions and ideas. We already know this same phenomenon *See above, p. 53ff.* from the remaining world of Gnosis. Mani, who did not regard himself as a philosopher but a gnostic theosophist and prophet, saw his task as fusing the religious tradition of the Orient of his time into a universal religion of the salvation of man. For this purpose of a "conscious syncretism", he created a strongly mythological system with a pellucid theoretical basic structure which did justice to the practical aim of being a gnostic teaching of salvation. Parts of the mythological apparatus could easily be exchanged, and Mani himself seems to have demonstrated this as is shown by his predilection for series of concepts and catalogues. Moreover, modern research rightly inclines more and more to the view that the tradition preserved in the Coptic Manichaica (especially the Kephalaia) comes closest to the original system and is supplemented by the corresponding material from Iranian texts which, however, is younger. Thus the Christian-gnostic tenor of Mani's system and its mediation through the Syrian-Mesopotamian environment of a heretical-gnostic Jewish Christianity, which was recently confirmed by the Cologne Mani Codex,[162] become explicable. Mani clearly tapped this reservoir in many features of his religion, in the Christology, the cyclic doctrine of revelation, the eschatology and in ascetic and other precepts, without losing sight of the goal that his religion was also to be able to be amalgamated with other religions, in particular with the Iranian Zoroastrianism with which it was closely connected by descent. His disciples, whom he must have consciously trained in this sense, only continued this tendency and went on to form Manicheism in this way, as it confronts us in Roman North Africa in the time of St. Augustine (4th century), in Arabic (8th century) and in the Central Asiatic-Chinese sources (6th–10th centuries). As it was apparently on the apostle's own initiative that he was regarded as the "Paraclete" of the Christians, as a Messianic son of Zarathustra and as the Buddha of the future (Maitreya), the absorption of the respective body of faith becomes intelligible. He probably followed this practice himself on his travels to the East. Mani says in the Kephalaia: "The writings and the wisdom and the apocalypses and the parables and the psalms of all earlier churches (religions) were gathered everywhere and came to my church (religion) and were added to the wisdom which I revealed. As water will be added to water and becomes much water, so were the ancient (earlier) books added to my writings and became a great wisdom, the like of which was not proclaimed (hitherto) in all ancient (earlier) generations. The books as I have written (them) were neither written nor revealed (hitherto)"*.[163] However, he did not derive his teachings from human book wisdom but, as we are told elsewhere, the "most blessed father" viz. his "light-spirit" (*nous*) elected and called him "out of the congregation of the multitude that does not perceive the truth" to reveal to him his "mysteries" and those of the whole cosmos*.[164] With this wealth of divine knowledge he could "if the whole world and all men would listen to it ... make them rich and ensure that the wisdom is sufficient for the whole world"*.[165] This is the theological authorisation for his truly astonishing knowledge which he incorporated in his work and which bears witness to a remarkable level of education in the contemporary Orient in the realms of the philosophy of religion and of the natural sciences, and also to the above average imagination and literary talent of the author.

Mani's teaching is based on the well-known gnostic dualism of spirit and body, light and darkness, good and evil, but advocates it most radically in dependence on his Iranian heritage. Also the course of the world was seen as recurring periods and was completely systematised in a way which Gnosis hitherto knew only embryonically. Here also Iran seems to have stood godfather. The cosmic development, understood as an irreversible process of time and as an expression of temporalness as

* *Kephalaia, chap. 154*

* *Cologne Mani Codex, p. 64*

* *op. cit., p. 68*

such, is seen against the background of a gradual liberation of light from darkness. It was Mani who, for the first time, described the fundamental gnostic idea really rigorously: the cosmology is subservient to the soteriology. The universe, the earth and man are subject to a process which has as its goal the liberation by God (of a part) of God and in which man is a decisive means to that end. The insight (*gnosis*) into this world process guarantees to man, as a potential bearer of light, salvation and makes him at the same time into an active promoter; this leads to a "cosmic feeling of responsiblity" which is typical of gnostic-Manichean piety.

The essential and probably oldest characteristics of the system are the following:[166]

The Manichean system   At the beginning stands the undeducible antithesis of the world of light and the world of darkness or of the good and the evil principle. The ruler of the realm of light, which is located in the North, has various names: "Father of Greatness", "King of the Paradise of Light", "most blessed Father" or simply God (in the Iranian texts: Zurvān, i. e. God "Time"). His being manifests itself in five spiritual attributes or hypostases which are also thought of as "members" or "worlds" (aeons): reason, thinking, insight, speculation and reflection. Moreover, he is surrounded by a great number of aeons and light worlds. Darkness or Hylē (matter), which is located in the South, also has a king and five "worlds": smoke, fire, sirocco, water, darkness, each of which is populated by demons and ruled over by an "archon". Driven by its inherent agitation, the night of darkness (*hylē*) comes to the borders of the realm of light and begins, filled with jealousy, to fight against it. This is the occasion for the (second) stage of the mixture of the two principles. The God of light, in order to be able to meet the challenge of darkness, creates three "evocations" which form the basic framework for the action of the light world in the following world process. First the "Great Spirit" or the "Wisdom" (*sophia*) is created from which the "Mother of the living" proceeds. She brings forth the Urmensch (primeval man, called Ohrmazd in the Iranian version) who is furnished with five elements who also are called his "garments" or "sons": fire, wind, water, light and ether. This pentad is also called: "Living Soul". The Urmensch now descends to fight with the darkness but is vanquished and leaves his fivefold "soul" to the underworld. This process, however, is interpreted by the Manicheans not as a defeat but as a preventive measure in which the Urmensch, or his "soul", was only bait to catch Hylē. At all events, the king of light arranges another, the second, "evocation" for the salvation of the Urmensch in the form of the "beloved of the beings of light", the "great architect" and the "living spirit" (called in Persian Mithra), who again has five sons or "gods" (among them the "Light-Adamas"). By sending out an awakening "call" to the Urmensch below to which he reacts with the "answer" ("call" and "answer" together constitute the "thought of life"), the "living spirit" begins his work of salvation which ends with the bringing up of the Urmensch. This salvation is the model for the later salvation of Adam and, finally, of all men. As the five elements or the "soul" of the Urmensch remained in the power of the darkness, the process is not yet concluded, but the "living spirit" sets into motion the creation of the world for their delivery. It comes to pass through the archons who according to the amount of light swallowed by them (in the form of the fivefold "soul") serve as building material for stars, heaven and earth. Thus arises the cosmos from particles of light and darkness; according to Mani it is therefore not subject to being entirely demonised, as becomes clear especially in the positive evaluation of the sun and the moon. For the maintenance of the cosmic order the five sons (gods) of the "living spirit" are responsible, each of whom protects a part of the cosmos. Ten firmaments and eight earthly spheres are mentioned. For the purpose of the actual salvation of the particles of light the cosmos must be set into motion. To this end the third "evocation" ensues, the main figure of which is the "third envoy" or the "God of the realm of light"; his abode is the sun, his female aspect, viz. his daughters, are the twelve virgins of light who represent the zodiac. He sets in motion the mechanism of the purification of light in the form of the three wheels of fire, water and wind. For the reception of the purified particles of light he creates the "pillar of glory" which is also called "perfect man" (as a restoration of the Urmensch). It becomes visible in the Milky Way. On it the liberated particles of light ascend to the moon which gathers them up to its fulness (full moon), in order to pass them on afterwards, thus emptying itself (new moon), to the sun, whence they go to the "new aeon" which in the meantime was designed by the "great architect". In order to de-

prive the dark archons of the light that they had received, the
"third envoy" shows himself uncovered in his male and female
aspect, whereupon the lewd archons either defile themselves or
abort. The semen falls, on the one hand, on dry land and brings
forth the world of plants, on the other hand, it falls into the sea
and produces a sea monster which is vanquished by the "Light-
Adamas". The aborted embryos, too, fall upon the earth, become demons and devour the fruit of the plants, i. e. the seed of
darkness mixed with light, fertilise themselves and thus produce the animal kingdom. Accordingly, the particles of light
are to be found in the plants (here particularly strongly), the
animals and the demons. As the darkness fears the final loss of
the particles of light, it endeavours to bind them to itself as
closely as possible and plans a creation in opposition to that of
the third envoy. By means of two chosen demons, Saklas
("fool") and Nebroēl (also called Namraēl), the first human
pair (Adam and Eve, Persian: Gēhmurd) is procreated in accordance with the male – female "image" of the third envoy in
such a way that the two previously devour all other demons in
order to receive in themselves the light that remained in them.
All further events now depend on the fate of the first man. The
counter measure of the world of light consists of the calling by
the third envoy of the "Jesus Splendour", whom he sends to
Adam to enlighten him about everything and thus to lead to
saving "knowledge". So the plan of darkness has been frustrat-
ed once more. For the salvation of mankind which originated in
Adam, the Jesus Splendour summons the "mind of light" (light-
nous, Persian: the great Manūhmēd) who is the father of all
apostles; by their liberating message he enters all men who are
to be saved. Through the fivefold gifts of the "light-nous", the
soul is led to become conscious of itself and is strengthened in
its power of resistance. So man is the central subject of world
events. His soul, as part of the light (i. e. of God), is the element
to be saved, and the saving element is the "spirit" (nous or
pneuma) that was granted to him by revelation or knowledge.
The body is the dark, evil, component of man, which in death
returns to its origin, the darkness, in order to let the soul ascend, in its liberated state, to its place of origin. But the soul
that remains unawakened is reborn on earth unto a new life
(transmigration of souls) until it is either redeemed or finally
judged. This end of the whole world drama occurs when the de-

liverance of the light is to some extent complete. Then follow the events known from Christian and Iranian tradition: the appearance of Jesus as king, the judgement of the world and the dissolution of the material world by means of a conflagration which purifies the last remaining elements of light. The *hylē* (matter) is incarcerated and care is taken to see that no new cosmos comes into existence. Thus the original state is restored even more radically. In the later communities it came to divisions over the problem whether all particles of light really return again or, after all, bear too heavy an admixture of darkness.

See above, pp. 203 f.

For Mani the event of redemption consists essentially of the awakening of the soul through knowledge, for which the messengers of light are needed, who in the course of history appear variously in space and time, yet mediate only one message, the saving truth in accordance with Manichean teaching. Biblical and extra-biblical figures are considered to be such "apostles of light" and thus forerunners of Mani, such as Seth(ēl), Noah, Enosh, Enoch, Shem, Abraham, Buddha, Aurentes, Zoroaster, Jesus and Paul. Mani himself is the consummation and the apostle of the last generation, the predicted Messiah and the fulfilment of all religions. This is how he saw himself, and his community accordingly saw in him the "redeemer", "illuminator", "physician" (of the soul), even God, as is clear from the graphic descriptions in the rich hymnic literature. In Mani's system the figure of Jesus was broken up into several individual figures, as often happens in Gnosis: the "Jesus Splendour" as heavenly figure of revelation, which corresponds to the gnostic Christ of the pleroma, and the earthly Jesus as messenger of light who acts on the orders of the heavenly or light-*nous*, and suffers only seemingly (the crucifixion, therefore, has no redemptive value and is at most of symbolic worth); in North African Manicheism there is also the "suffering Jesus" (*Jesus patibilis*) as symbol of the suffering particles of light, of the "living soul" of the Urmensch, while in other texts there is mentioned instead the "boy Jesus" who looks forward to redemption.

The doctrine of redemption

See above, p. 156

The "church" organised by Mani is the final community of salvation which has the task of looking after the light that is still in the world by avoiding tormenting it any further and also by trying to purify it and to lead it back. The ascetic attitude to life which follows from this consists of "reducing all relations of life to a minimum" (H. Jonas) and in practice can be accomplished

The Manichean church

See plates 27 and 28

only by few. The result, therefore, is a division of the community into two distinct groups. The real core of the "church" is formed by the "elect" (*electi*) or "perfect", who are also called "righteous" or "true", around whom gather the great circle of the "hearers" (*auditores*) or "catechumens". The hierarchy was recruited only from the "elect": the "head of the church" (*archegos, princeps*) as Mani's successor, the twelve apostles or "teachers" (*magistri*), the 72 bishops or deacons, the 360 "elders" (presbyters) and the plain elect. Women can attain the station of the elect but cannot take office. The monastery became the outward form of the Manichean church in Turkestan, probably under Buddhist influence.

In accordance with the bipartite structure of the community, the standards set for ethic-moral behaviour also vary. The harsh demands made by Manichean ethics, the basic idea of which lies in the acquisition of salvation by renunciation, can only be met by the elect. They are subject to the "three seals of the mouth, the hand and the sexual organs", i.e. they have to keep away completely from consuming meat and wine, from lying and hypocrisy, and from damaging nature by work and sexual intercourse. Ill-treatment of animals, damage of plants (the elect, therefore, walked with downcast eyes), pollution of water, all involve the "tormenting" of the light enclosed therein and are sacrilege. The "perfect" must dedicate themselves to the study, copying and translating of religious writings, and this, as the finds show, they have done in exemplary fashion. They were famous for the use of good paper and writing material. "When the Manicheans expend effort on the production of their holy writings, it is like the Christians doing the same for the churches"; this is the judgement of an Arab author (al-Jāhiz). The possession of material riches was prohibited to the individual, but the community was allowed to possess capital in the form of debentures and could thus attain wealth as the finds at Turfan show. "Whosoever lends on usury does not in-

* Augustine, Ennarationes in Psalmos 140,12

jure the cross of light", says St. Augustine*. The later German popular etymology which derives Manicheans from "*Mahn*-nicheans", creditors, usurers, perhaps, goes back to this. Otherwise the life of the elect was Spartan; they were allowed only one vegetarian meal which was further curtailed by fasting. As such a life could not be led without support by others, the circle of the "hearers" (*auditores*) was a necessity of life for the elect, as are the workers for the drones in a beehive. The "hearers" had to provide the livelihood of the elect and this was accounted to them as good works ("alms"). The guilt which they necessarily took upon themselves by reason of their work, the elect forgave them, but their salvation, i. e. the deliverance of their souls, was delayed; an opportunity for it lay only in their rebirth in one of the plants full of light, or in one of the elect. They were only second-class representatives of the community for whom the observance of ten commandments was enough to prove their Manichean faith. These commandments were: monogamy, the renunciation of fornication, lying, hypocrisy, idolatry, magic, the killing of animals, theft and any doubt of their religion, as well as the duty of the indefatigable care of the elect. Without them, however, the Manichean church would not have been viable, and the rich merchants who attached themselves to it as "hearers" were, without doubt, its economic backbone and account for the quite impressive display of luxury to be found here and there.

Our information about the life of the communities, and especially about their services, is inadequate. As only knowledge is able to save, the Christian sacraments were rejected as institutions of darkness. In spite of this, there were, of course, ceremonies and rites which consisted of prayers, recitations of hymns, singing of psalms, reading of the scriptures, music, fasting and feasts. For the elect seven prayers, or songs of praise, daily were prescribed, for the "hearers" four. Numerous regulations on fasting pervaded the life of the faithful. The elect had to fast 100 days a year, once 30 days running. The central event in the life of the community was the common meal ("the table") of the elect which was taken once daily, and which was especially sacred as it served the purification of the light. It consisted of plants with a high content of light, such as cucumbers and melons, of wheat bread and of water or fruit juice. The "hearers" served it ceremonially and received for these "alms" forgiveness of the "sins" committed in providing it. By consuming this food, the light contained in it, which is described as "the slaughtered, killed, oppressed, murdered soul", was delivered from the admixture of darkness or matter, and cleansed and purified, and thus enriched in "the elect" (as in a still). The elect, St. Augustine tells us, "breathes out of it angels, yea, there shall burst forth particles of divinity, at every moan or

The life of the community

See plate 23

groan in his prayer, which particles of the most high and true God had remained bound in that fig, unless they had been set at

* The Confessions of St. Augustine III 10, transl. E. B. Pusey

liberty by the teeth or belly of some 'Eiect' saint"*. It is not surprising that Christian controversialists interpreted this "mystery meal" as an imitation of the Eucharist.

Feasts and ceremonies   The chief feast was the so-called Bēma feast which was celebrated in memory of Mani's death in February/March and was considered to correspond to the Christian feast of Easter. It was introduced by a fast of thirty days and by confession. On the

See plate 23   feast day Mani's picture was set up on a "rostrum" or "tribune" (Greek: *bēma*), and the apostle of light was invoked with psalms of petition, praise and thanksgiving, such as can be found in the Manichean Book of Psalms. Further ceremonies, such as the laying on of hands and the extending of the right hand, perhaps also an anointing, seem to have played a role at the ordination of the elect and at the admission into the circle of "hearers". There was also a kind of "mass for the dead" which helped to conduct the dead to his rest. A peculiarity of the Manicheism of Eastern Iran and Central Asia was the institution of confession and penitence which had perhaps been devised on a Buddhist prototype. Formularies of confession have been preserved; they show an acute consciousness of sin. This aware-

The understanding of sin   ness of the power of sin and the possibility of a relapse into sin characterises Mani's teaching in comparison with most of the other gnostic sects. To be sure, the soul is guiltless, good and pure, and the seat of sin is only the body, or the earthly world, but without the assistance of the divine spirit, the light-*nous*, the soul is powerless and without protection against the dark powers in the form of the body and the world. So it is needful for the soul to be strengthened by ecclesiastical regulations and commandments. The entry into the community banishes the influence of the power of darkness but is not able entirely to prevent the body from occasionally getting the upper hand. A simple "repentance" (*metanoia*) is sufficient to restore the purity of the soul; for this reason confession became an important institution in Manicheism. Unforgivable is only the sin of the conscious resistance against the redeeming knowledge, the illumination by the light-*nous*, the Holy Spirit; this leads without fail to the final subservience to the darkness (*hylē*).

A Relic: the Mandeans

Only one gnostic sect has survived to the present day; it has therefore been placed at the end of our historical review, although its origins probably go back to pre-Christian times.[167] It is the community of the Mandeans, a baptist sect, comprising about 15,000 followers, and to be found especially in the southern region of the Euphrates and Tigris in the Republic of Iraq. Its present-day centres are Baghdad and Basra where all travellers are able to meet them on the gold and silver market which they practically dominate. They also can often be found in the smaller towns, such as Amarah, Nasiriya and Suq esh-Shujuch. Up into the 20th century their range of distribution was predominantly in smaller market towns and villages of the marshland in southern Iraq, the Batiha, which corresponds to the ancient region of Mesene (Maisān). Their traditions have been preserved most purely among the Iranian Mandeans who dwell along the river Karūn in the province of Khuzistān, especially in Ahwaz and Shushtar. Their Muslim compatriots call them Sabians (in the vernacular: Subba), i. e. "baptists, baptizers", a name which also occurs in the Koran and which enabled them to belong to those religions which are tolerated by Islam.

Expansion and name

The earliest self-designations to be found in Mandean literature are "elect of righteousness" (*bhirī zidqa*) and "Nasoreans" (*naṣuraiyī*), i. e. "guardians" or "possessors" of secret rites and knowledge. "Mandeans" (*mandayī*) is of more recent date but refers back to the ancient Mandean word for "perception, knowledge, Gnosis" (*manda*); it therefore means "the knowing ones, the gnostics". Nowadays the term denotes more generally the laity in contradistinction to the priests (*tarmidī*) or initiates (*naṣoraiyī*). As Christian missionaries of the 17th century saw in them the descendants of the "disciples of John the Baptist", they were known in European literature for a long time under this name or as "John-Christians". They themselves gladly accepted this title, for they actually consider John the Baptist to be a representative of their faith, and this gave them certain advantages in their dealings with the Islamic and Christian authorities. They are traditionally famous as skilled silversmiths ("Amarah-work"), and in the country also as ironsmiths and boat-builders. In European research however they

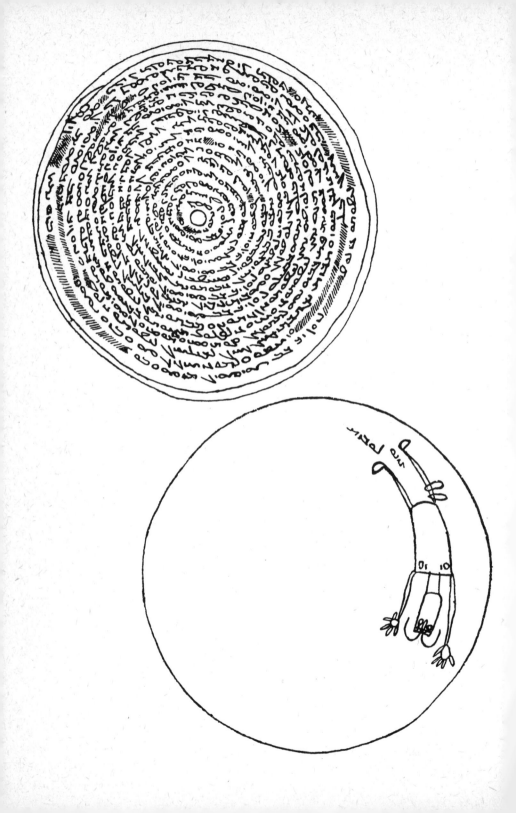

have since the 19th century attracted particular attention by their literature. This is composed in a Semitic dialect (East Aramaic) of its own and in a specially developed script; it is known as "Mandean". The extent of the literature, considering the relative smallness of the community, is surprising; it forms a remarkable body of gnostic writings, the authors and compilers of which are not known to us by name. We have already made the acquaintance of some examples.

See above, pp. 111 ff., 175 ff., 188, 199 f., 204, 266 f., 271

The most important Mandean works are the following: the "Treasure" ("*Ginza*") or the "Great Book" ("*sidra rabba*"), the most comprehensive compilation consisting of two main parts the "Right Ginza" and the (smaller) "Left Ginza". The former consists of a number of (18) mythological-theological moral and narrative tractates, the latter essentially of the hymns for the mass for the dead. It is really a liturgical book which is devoted to the ascent of the soul. The "Book of John", or the "Books of the Kings" (i. e. angels) as it is also called, is a compilation, too, which supplements the Ginza. It bears its name on account of the "discourses" of John the Baptist con-- tained therein, which, however, are entirely couched in Man- dean language and are without direct historical value. Of great importance is a compilation of the liturgical prayers, hymns and recitations which are used at the various ceremonies (baptism, mass for the dead, consecration of the banners, wedding etc.). The work is known under the title *Qolasta* which means 'praise' (later more generally: "liturgical collection"); in European re- search it was simply designated as "Mandean Liturgies" (fol- lowing Lidzbarski) or "Canonical Prayerbook" (following Drower). To the cultic texts belong a further series of scrolls which have come to light only recently and which have been published only in part. There are rituals for the ordination to the priesthood or "crowning", the consecration of the temple, the feast of the end of the year and the wedding, and there are "commentaries" on the ritual events which use for the most part a mysterious micro-macrocosmic symbolism. Some of these scrolls are considered to be "secret" and are accessible only to the priests, such as the voluminous "1012 Questions"

The Mandean literature
See plate 43

Mandean magic bowl of the 5th century, found with 30 others at Chouabir in Iraq in 1894. Above, the inside with the incantation; below, the outside with a drawing of the demon Libat (wrongly written Labit), who is identified with Venus. Cf. also plate 40.

which are meant to introduce the aspirant to the priesthood into the Mandean cultic wisdom (*nasirutha*). Also remarkable are a number of illustrated scrolls, the so-called *Diwanê*, which are published only in part, such as the *Diwan Abathur*, a description of the supernatural places which the soul has to traverse. The drawings show a very distinctive "cubist" style which can also be found in magical texts of late antiquity.[168] The Mandeans also possess an astrological "Book of the Signs of the Zodiac" (*Sfar Malwāshi*) which served the priests for horoscopes and for the giving of names. In addition to this official literature, there is a great mass of magical texts and exorcisms on lead tablets, clay bowls and, more recently, on leather and paper. The most ancient go back to the 4th century and are the testimonies of Mandean literature that can be dated most reliably. The great mass of this literature can be dated only with difficulty. Investigations have shown that the existence of liturgical-poetic writings must be assumed already in the 3rd century. The Mandean script was probably developed in the 2nd century by an inventive personality (comparable to Mani) on the basis of older models, and immediately served for the writing down of the even more ancient religious tradition which the Mandeans brought from their original habitat in Palestine and Syria to Mesopotamia. The collection of the most important tractates, books and rituals already began before Islam, but was hastened by its demand for "books" as proof of a "book religion". The oldest texts are to be found, without a doubt, in the Ginza, the "liturgies" and in the "Book of John". They also supply the proof for the gnostic character of the ancient Mandean religion and they are connected in many ways with the ancient gnostic tradition as we encounter it especially in Syria (Gospel of John, Odes of Solomon).

Only painstaking analyses of Mandean literature, which was not exactly composed and collected on logical and consistent lines, make it possible to separate older material from younger

See plates 44–48

See plates 40 and 41

33
A traditional Mandean sanctuary (*mandi*) at Qal'at Salih on the Tigris. In front of the cult-hut the baptismal pool (Jordan), in the background the surrounding wall. Cf. the drawing on p. 361

34
Mandean priests at the meal for the dead "Blessed Oblation" (*zidqa brikha*) in the Mandi at Qal'at Salih. In the right foreground an acolyte (*shganda*) with a bunch of myrtle as a sign of eternal life.

35
Ganzivra ("treasurer") Abdullah of Baghdad, head of the Mandean community in Iraq, in his priestly robes of office.

36
Mandean baptism in the Tigris near Baghdad. On the left the priest, on the right the baptizand during the (threefold) self-immersion.

37
Mandean priest in ceremonial robes (baptismal ceremony). He has put on the face-veil (*pandama*; part of the turban) and holds his staff *(margna)* in his arm as a sign of his priestly office. On the left in front of him the holy banner (*dravsha*), which is set up at every ceremony (cf. also plate 39).

38
The holy draught of water (*mambuha*) after baptism, which is given to the candidate by the priest after the bread (*pihta*).

39
Close of the baptismal ceremony (on the bank of the Tigris in Baghdad). Beside the squatting candidate the banner, and below it a bowl and a flask for the *mambuha* (cf. plate 38).

40, 41
Mandean magic bowl, outside and inside. Clay, from Nippur (?), pre-Islamic period (5th/6th cent.).
The text contains incantations against all manner of demons, and the sickness caused by them,
for the benefit of a pregnant woman. Cf. the drawing on p. 344

42

Mandean manuscript roll: "Means of Protection (amulet) of Radiance-Hibil" (*Zrazta*
d^eHibil-Ziwa). Paper, copy made in 1925.

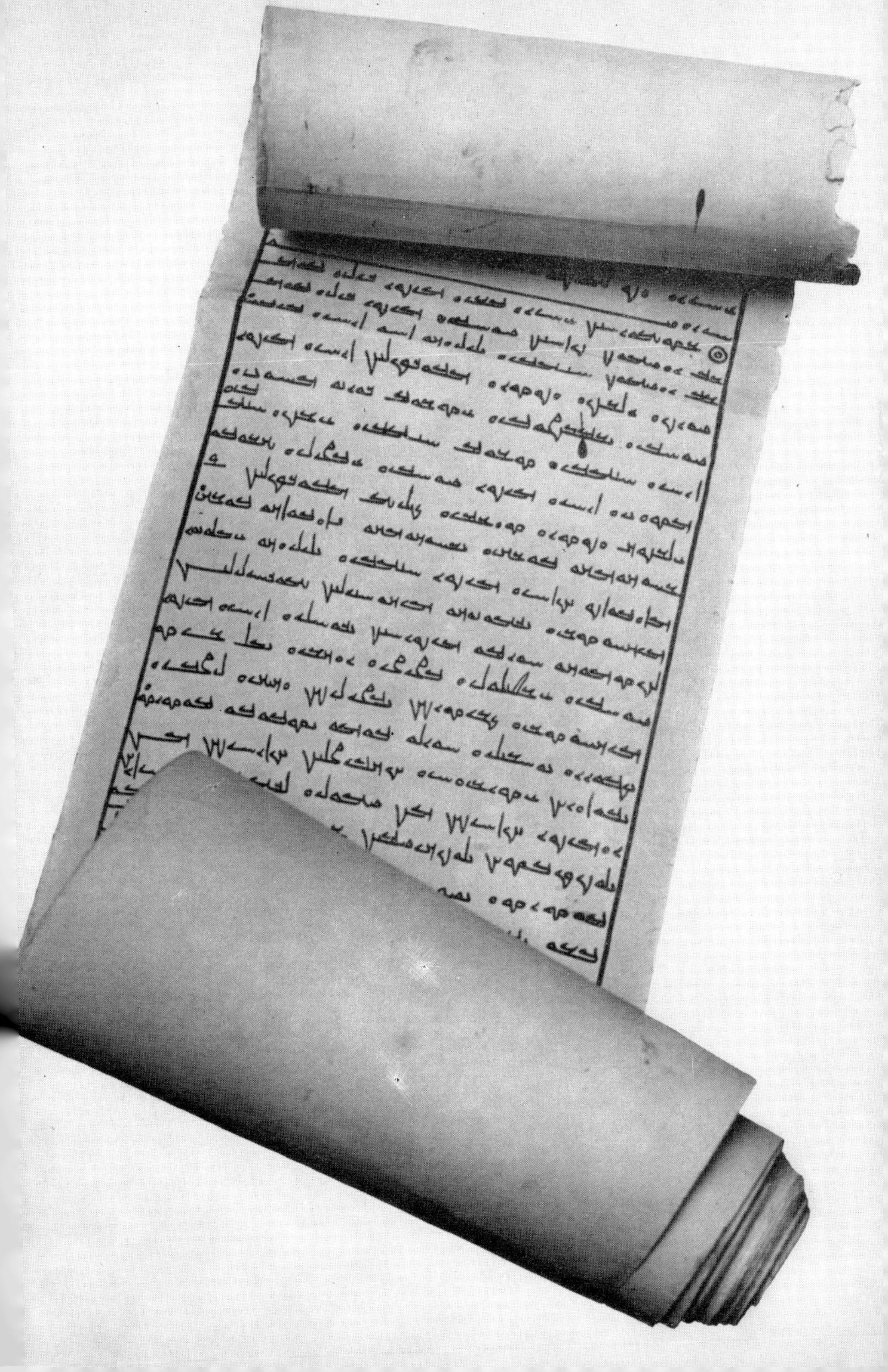

44–48
From the Mandean Diwan Abathur: "stations" on the journey of the soul.

44
The boat of the Sun, manned by male and female demons, such as Ruha (evil "spirit"), Venus (Libat), Adonaios, Schamisch (the Sun) etc. In its "cubist" style the representation of the figures is characteristic for all Mandean Diwans.

45
Beginning of the planetary stations with their "guardhouses", in which various menaces await the soul: (from right to left) a lion (guarding the entrance gate), an ape, a well full of menstrual blood (intended for women who disregard the rules of purity), three demons with musical instruments (music for the Mandeans is something devilish), and a spirit striking copper plates.

43
Mandean codex: beginning of the Right Ginza. Paper, copy made in 1837.

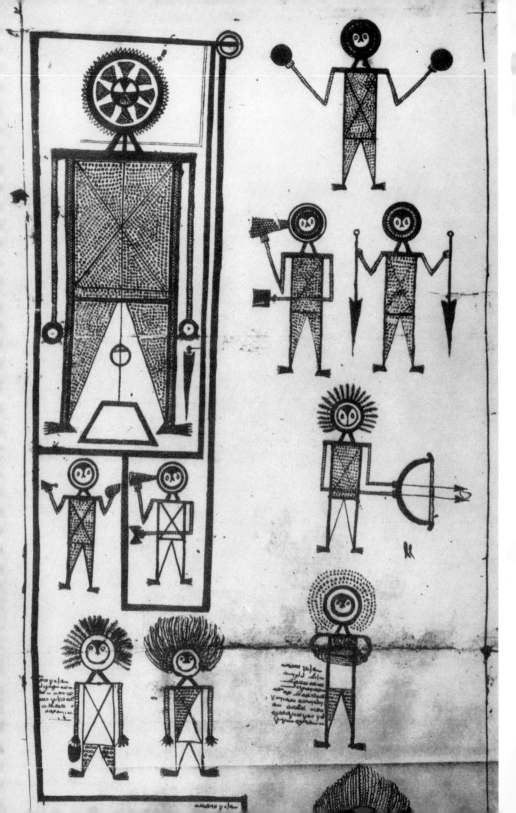

46

Stations with armed demons (between the Sun and the planets). The large figure on the left has no inscription, but Ignatius à Jesu, who first brought this Diwan to Europe in the 16th century, identified it as Mohammed, who in Mandean opinion is destined for one of the hells above the earth. It is however probably Ur, the ruler of darkness, represented on guard.

47

The boat which brings the souls of the righteous to the house of Abathur. The form of the boat corresponds to the old round boats of Iraq (*guffa*), which are still in use today.

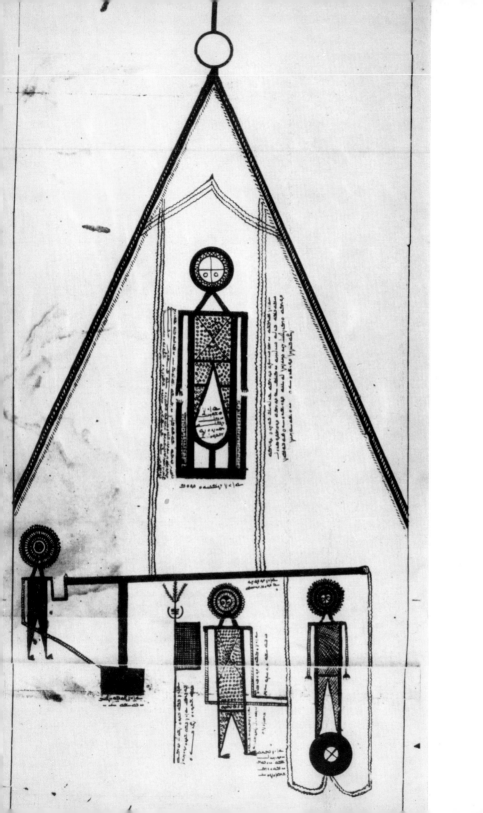

and thus to obtain a moderately clear idea of the ancient Mandean (Nasorean) doctrine.[169] We can only offer here a brief
sketch of it.

The world of darkness (located in the south) stands opposite   **The main**
the world of light (located in the north); each is led by a ruler.   **features of**
The lord of the world of light has various names of which the   **Mandean**
most ancient and most frequently used is "Life" (*haiyī*) or   **teaching**
"Great Life"; next comes "Lord of Greatness" or "Mighty Spirit" (*mana*), and more recently "King of Light". He is surrounded by a countless number of beings of light who are called
mostly Uthri (sing. *uthra*), which means "riches", or less often
"kings" (*melki*). They inhabit countless worlds of light and, like
the faithful on earth, carry out ritual acts and above all praise
the "Life". The worlds of life came into existence through a series of emanations from the supreme being or "First Life". The
stages of the "Second", "Third" and "Fourth Life" are repeatedly mentioned, which also bear the names "Joshamin" (an ancient god of heaven), Abathur ("Keeper of the Scales") and
Ptahil (the creator god). Behind this is clearly the idea of the
defection from the divine primeval unity of the "Life", which
finally ends in the creation of the world by Ptahil. The world of
darkness, too, has an origin, namely in the chaos or "dark water" which is its oldest manifestation. According to one version,
the "King of Darkness" arises from it, according to another it is
the "Lord of Darkness", who is described as a giant, monster or
dragon, and who bears the name Ur (i. e. probably a distortion
of the Hebrew '*ōr* "light"), the product of the evil "Spirit" (*rūhā*), who is considered to be the disaffected adversary of the
world of light. The ruler of darkness creates a realm for himself
with demonic beings of every kind, the "wicked", "monsters",
"dragons", "angels" (the Hebrew name being revalued), but
above all the "Seven" (planets) and the "Twelve" (signs of the
Zodiac) who, together with Rūhā, are the chief representatives
of the darkness. Hostile relations between the two primeval
principles of light and darkness, life and death, good and evil
begin from both sides. The defecting tendency of the worlds of
light leads to a creation ("consolidation") of the earth (*tibil*) in

48
The scales of the soul (below), with above Abathur, the "Lord of the scales", on his throne. On the
right-hand balance stands Shitil, whose purity the righteous soul must outweigh if it is to enter the
kingdom of light.

the "dark water", which is not allowed by the King of Light,
and in this the powers of darkness, i. e. especially Rūhā with the
"Seven" and "Twelve", participate. The process cannot be
reversed by the world of light, but it is at least possible to limit
the ruler of darkness in his activity, when a messenger of light,
the "Gnosis of Life" (*manda dᵉhaiyī*) puts him in fetters. The
demiurge himself is condemned and is not allowed to return into the world of light until the end of the world. The climax of
creation is the making of the first man, Adam, whose body is
formed by Ptahil and his dark helpers, but whose animating
substance, the soul or the "inner (hidden) Adam", has its origin
in the world of light. Around this event a great number of narratives has grown which are not always in harmony one with
another, but which clearly show the influence of the gnostic an-
thropos-myth. In the earthly Adam one sees a counterpart of
the heavenly or "great Adam", also called Adakas (i. e. "hidden Adam"). Just as this one had a wife (Eve) and sons, so had
the other: the "cloud of light" (heavenly Eve) and the heavenly
Adamites Hibil (Abel), Shitil (Seth) and Anosh (Enosh). The
Mandeans derive their origin from Adam and Eve as the "race
of Life", for their souls come from the world of light and have
since had to take up their abode in the "darkness" or the "corporeal (earthly) world". The salvation of these "souls" (*nishim-
ta*) or spirits (*mana*) is now a main concern of the Mandean religion. It is believed that the world of light sends forth its "messengers", "helpers", "envoys", in order to teach the faithful by
their "call" and to save their souls. As first and most important
of these messengers of light there appears the "Gnosis of Life"
(*manda dᵉhaiyī*) who is also called "Son of Life" or "Counterpart of Life" and who is a personification of the redeeming
knowledge. At his side stand the three heavenly Adamites,
Hibil, Shitil and Anosh of whom the first is later often inter-
changeable with the "Gnosis of Life". The redemption of
Adam serves as a prototype. He is enlightened by the "Gnosis
of Life" about the "mysteries" of the cosmos and thus is redeemed, i. e. his soul or the "inner Adam" (= man) can return
to the world of light. The Mandean soteriology originally
knows no "historical" redeemers but only "mythological" ones,
who appear throughout the various ages of the Mandean world
history and who only offer a repetition of the "primeval revelation" to Adam. For the faithful they are always present and can

be invoked, above all at the cultic ceremonies. Only as an after-
thought the Mandeans created, in opposition to Christianity
which they reject, a legend according to which one of their messengers of light (Anosh and Manda d°Haiyi are mentioned) appeared in Jerusalem as an opponent of Jesus Christ in order to
unmask him as a lying prophet. It follows from this that the
Mandeans are descended from a Gnosis that is independent of
Christianity and that they have preserved its features until the
present day.

The "deliverance" of the soul from the perishable body and **Soteriology and**
the transitory world is the centre of Mandean soteriology. **eschatology**
Death is the "day of deliverance" when the soul leaves the body
and begins a long and dangerous journey leading through seven
or eight supernatural "places of detention" (the planetary
spheres, including the sun and the moon and that of Rūhā). *See above, p. 175ff.*
These places are considered altogether evil and hostile to the
soul. They, therefore, seek to detain it, but can only succeed in
the case of sinners and non-Mandeans, who then have to endure the punishments of hell. (For this reason these "places of
detention" may also be called "purgatories".) The cultic rites *See plates 45 and 46*
yet to be mentioned also play a decisive role in this, for they can
influence the soul's ascent. (Especially in the younger commentaries to the rites there are references to the "rebirth" of the
soul and to other doctrines.) When the soul with the help of its
passwords has overcome the dangers, it has to face the "scales"
of Abathur on which its good works are weighed. Only when it *See plate 48*
is found to be full weight – and this includes the "spirit" which
only the good soul can redeem, i. e. draw along with it – it attains the realm of light, being accompanied by "helpers" or
"companions" over the frontier rivers, to obtain eventually, as *See plate 47*
tokens of victory, robe and wreath and to unite with its heavenly counterpart which is primarily "Life" himself. In addition to
this eschatology ("the day of the end") which refers to the individual soul, the Mandeans also have a more general eschatological notion, the "great day of the end" or "judgement", when
the final decision is made on the souls which are in the heavenly
hells, as to whether they should fall into the "blazing fire" or the
"Sea of Sūf (a reinterpretation of the Hebrew "Sea of Reeds")
and thus suffer the "second death", or, after all, be received in-
to the Pleroma like the disaffected beings of light. All unbeliev- *See above, p. 181*
ers and evil powers are destroyed, for this day is the "end of the

world(s)" when "the light ascends and the darkness returns to
its place".

Ethics   Mandean Gnosis occupies a special position in its ethic-
moral pronouncements, for it does not make either radically ascetic or libertine demands. Only certain indications (the devaluation of woman and of the cosmos) show that at some time
there were more rigorous ascetic features. But monogamy and
the procreation of children are already prescribed in the old
"moral code", similarly good works, especially alms-giving, the
observance of dietary laws, ritual slaughtering and rules of purification, such as baptisms and lustrations. The precept of love
for one's neighbour refers primarily to the fellow-believer. As
See above, p. 266f. we have already heard, *reservatio mentalis* is sanctioned. In
spite of the rather pedestrian ethics which are not very different
from their Jewish basis, the Mandean world of ideas is pervaded by a hostile attitude to the world which is apparent,
above all, in the ancient hymns and which led to the rejection of
riches and of music (which is considered demonic). But the
Mandeans, as one can observe today, have otherwise made
themselves quite comfortable in this world and have come to
terms with it, even contributing as silver- and goldsmiths to the
circulation of earthly trinkets; they could hardly have survived
to the present day otherwise.

The cult   The great importance which the Mandeans attribute to their
cult practices shows their special character even more clearly. It
is not "knowledge" alone that redeems but the cultic rites,
primarily baptism and the "mass for the dead", are necessary
for salvation. From this it may be deduced that here the gnostic
ideology was amalgamated with that of an older cultic community, a heretical Jewish baptismal sect as is suggested by the
water rites, and that thus an original Mandean-Nasorean system came into existence, probably already in pre-Christian
Baptism times. The central cultic rite is baptism or "immersion" (*mas-
buta*, pronounced *maswetta*) in flowing ("living") water which
is called "Jordan". It can be administered in any river, but in
practice it is confined to certain sites which are in the vicinity of
the dwelling places of the Mandeans. On the site there is traditionally a small mud-hut which is designated as "temple"
(*mashkna*) or "Manda-house" (*bit-Manda, bimanda*) and
which may have been larger in earlier times, a pool with an in-
flow and an outflow and a wall which surrounds the whole area

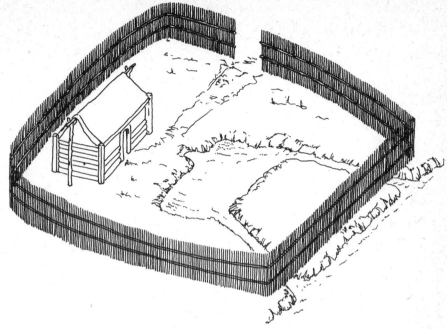

Traditional Mandean sanctuary (*mandi*). In front of the cult-hut is the baptismal pool, the "Jordan", connected with the nearby river through two channels and thus supplied with the necessary "flowing (living) water". The area is surrounded either by a high fence of reeds or by a wall (cf. Plate 33).

which is called Mandi. Only few of these modest sanctuaries have survived. At present the Mandeans turn to building well cared for tiled bathing places which resemble swimming pools, which, however, do not appeal to the priesthood. Baptism can be administered every Sunday, i.e. on the "first day of the week" (*habshabba*) which is for Mandeans, as for Christians, a holiday. It consists of a threefold complete immersion in the white sacral robe, a threefold "signing" of the forehead with water, a threefold draught of water, the crowning with a myrtle wreath and the laying on of hands, all administered by the priest. There follows on the bank an anointing of the forehead with oil, a simple communion of bread and water, and the "sealing", i.e. the protection against evil spirits (exorcism). The hand-clasp with the right hand which priest and neophyte exchange at the ceremony, which is accompanied by prayers and recitations, is of special sanctity. It is called "truth" (*kushta*) and is a demonstration of upright disposition, viz. a symbol of the union with the world of light. For the Mandean believes that he is not only "purified" of sins and trespasses at this

See fig. above and plate 33

See plates 36–39

ceremony, but that he also enters into contact (*laufa*, i. e. "communion") with the world of light, for the "Jordans" rise in it and are a counterpart of the divine element of life. Without baptism no "soul" is able to reach the next world. Baptisms take place at all cultic feasts, including weddings. Great sins even require several baptisms. Recent researches have shown that the fundamental features of the Mandean baptismal rite are derived *See above, p. 226f.* from early Jewish baptismal practices in the Jordan region.[170]

The mass for the dead   The second chief ceremony of the Mandeans is the mass for the dead, which is called "ascent" (*masiqta*, pronounced *massechtha*). It is celebrated at the death of a believer and serves the "ascent" of his soul into the realm of light. It, too, includes lustrations with "Jordan", viz. river water, anointing with oil *See plate 34* and crowning with the myrtle wreath. But the main ingredient is the recitations from the Left Ginza which begin on the third day after death when the soul is divorced from the body and are continued at fixed intervals until the end of the forty-five days' journey of the soul. Certain ceremonial meals are combined with this which begin during the funeral and are repeated during the specified period; they serve, it is said, the nourishment of the soul but also have a symbolic value in connection with the already mentioned idea of the rebirth of the soul and the creation of the body of the soul. As the way of the soul leads through the dangerous supramundane "purgatory", the Mandean never felt entirely safe and gradually introduced into this area of his faith various safety devices which led to an extensive **Meals in** elaboration of the ceremonies for the dead. Three different **memory of** forms of meals in memory of the dead primarily belong to this **the dead** ceremonial. One has the name "blessed alms", which clearly indicates its purpose; it is to give the soul the benefit of "good works" (alms), an idea which contradicts the ancient Mandean concept. In this area much still remains unexplained, especially the genesis, origin and age of the individual forms of these "rites of the soul". Apparently their roots lie in the Iranian-Zoroastrian sphere where there are similar ceremonies that serve the soul. Besides, the idea of "provisions for the journey" of the soul is an ancient notion which found an especially fruitful soil in Mandeism. Meals in memory of the dead, like baptismal ceremonies, belong almost to every Mandean feast and thus reveal an essential side of the Mandean world of faith. It is also characteristic that the traditional graves of the Mandeans

are unmarked, for here rests only the transitory body. (In recent times Islamic burial customs have been widely adopted.)

Unfortunately very little can be established with any certainty about the history of the Mandean religion, as the information
available is very scanty. Up to the present day only one Mandean text has emerged which refers, but in a very confused
manner, to the history of the sect. It is the *"Diwan* of the great
Revelation, called 'Inner Haran'" (*"Haran Gawaita"*).[171] In the
other writings there are occasionally allusions to the persecution of the community in Jerusalem by the Jews in the course of
which the city was destroyed as a punishment; the reference is
probably to A. D. 70. In the *Haran Gawaita* scroll the legend of
John the Baptist as a Mandean prophet and "envoy of the king
of light" is interpolated into these events. He appears here, and
in other texts, as adversary of Christ. However, he is never described as founder of the community but only as a particularly
great "disciple" or "priest" of the Mandean religion. The attempt has been made to deduce from this that we have here historical traditions of the disciples of the Baptist, but this cannot
be proved up to now. It is more likely that the Mandeans took
over legends of this kind from heretical Christian, possibly
gnostic, circles and shaped them according to their ideas. In any
case, the figure of John is not fundamental for them. The relations, which have already been mentioned, between the Mandean baptismal ceremony and the world of baptist sects in the
east Jordan region at this time (1st century A. D.) are an entirely different matter. Numerous elements in vocabulary and tradition, moreover, demonstrate very clearly that, in spite of the
fierce anti-Jewish polemic – the Jewish God Adonai ("my
Lord") is seen as a false god and Moses accordingly as prophet
of Rūhā, the evil spirit –, the Jewish origin of the community
cannot be denied. We are, therefore, ultimately dealing with a
heretical Jewish sect which, like other comparable groups of
late Jewish religious history, stood in opposition to the official
Judaism and was wide open to non-Jewish influences, above all
Iranian and gnostic. Unfortunately, nothing can be ascertained
about the probable social background. In the context of the
Jewish wars of independence and the growing consolidation of
Judaism after the destruction of Jerusalem (A. D. 70), its position in opposition evidently led to persecutions of the commu-
ity and ultimately to its emigration from the Jordan territory –

**The History of
the Mandeans**

Jordan is today still the name of the baptismal waters – to the east. The *Haran Gawaita* scroll reports the flight of a large group of "Nasoreans" during the rule of a (Parthian) king Ardbān (Artabanus) from the Jewish rulers to the "inner Haran" territory or the "Median hill-country" (*Tura d^eMadai*). The reference is clearly to the penetration by the community, or part of it, of the north-west Iranian territory between Harran and Nisibis or Media during the period of the later Arsacids (1st or 2nd century A.D.). The same document attests immediately afterwards the foundation of a community in Baghdad, i.e. in Mesopotamia, and the appointment of Mandean governors in this region. The Sassanids brought this expansion to an end. Apparently in connection with the consolidation of the Zoroastrian state church which began under Shapur I (241–272) and introduced the persecution of foreign religions, they ordered the destruction of many Mandean temples. In the 3rd century, Mani had contacts with the Mandean community. Both religions show in various ways a mutual dependence which, however, also included polemics against one another. Evidence for a controversy with the followers of the "lord Mani" is to be found in the 9th book of the Right Ginza which is altogether full of polemics against other religions and sects. After Iraq was conquered by Islam (636), no change occurred in the community's lot of suffering, although it succeeded in obtaining toleration under the name of Sabeans as a recognised "religion of the book". At all events, the history of the sect was always one of oppression and persecution as can be seen, not least, from the often deeply affecting references of the copyists in their colophons. There are warnings against "Christ the Roman" (i.e. Byzantine), and Mohammed is cursed mostly under a codename (the demon Bizbat). It is not surprising, therefore, that the oppressed community withdrew more and more to the remote marshlands of southern Iraq, whence they have increasingly returned to the larger cities only recently, so that today ancient Mandean centres in the country seldom still harbour Mandeans, and the sanctuaries there fall into decay.

The structure of the community   The hierarchy, which developed in the course of history and which is not to be found in the ancient texts, consists of the simple priests or "disciples" (*tarmidi*), the bishops or "treasurers" (*ganzivri*), and the ethnarch or "head of the people". The office of the latter has been vacant for at least a century. In 1831 a cholera epidemic is said to have carried off all bishops and priests so that one was forced to fall back on educated laymen. This break is seen as an interruption of the old oral tradition and thus as the beginning of the decay of the priesthood. At present there is only one very aged bishop (*ganzivra*) active, Sheikh Abdullah in Baghdad, who is the real head of the com- *See plate 35* munity. Since 1975 the other bishopric in Basra has been vacant. Between the two there are certain differences which have old roots and resemble different schools. In Basra the priesthood is more active in reforms and has erected a modern cultic centre (Mandi) with a tiled baptismal place in the court of the house. There are only about half a dozen priests left. There is a shortage of candidates for the priesthood or "pupils" (*shwalya*), and of deacons or "messengers" (*asganda*). The priests are regarded as "kings" (*melki*), their consecration is a "coronation" at which they receive their insignia, crown (a strip of cloth), staff (of olive wood) and ring, which they wear at all ceremonies. Their symbols also include a banner (*dravsha*) *See plates 37–39* which is set up at the place of worship.

Today's community is not only in a state of crisis because of **The situation** the shortage of priests but also because of the heightened self- **today** confidence of the laity. Many of them are academics and teachers and thus greatly superior to the priests in education; these, on the other hand, anxiously guard their heritage and are suspicious of the reforming aspirations of the younger generation, which moreover often have socialist-communist tendencies. The ignorance of the laity about their own traditions is disastrous; they do not know the old language and script (even among the priests its knowledge is often deficient). The relation, therefore, of the young Mandeans to their religion is no longer close. They attend the ceremonies only when it cannot be avoided, as e. g. at a wedding. In spite of this there is, on the other hand, great interest in their own "culture", of which they proudly say that it is older than Judaism, Christianity and Islam. They seek to identify with it anew and, in this connection, pay considerable attention to the scholarly researches pursued in Europe. In Baghdad a centre, a club, was founded which is not intended only to serve meetings but also the fostering and collecting of Mandean traditions. Mention has already been made of the improvement and refurbishing of the places of worship, for the pollution of rivers has increased considerably in

Iraq too. The continued existence of the community will essentially depend on whether or not it succeeds in solving the problems of a necessary adaptation to the modern world. Only in this way will the oldest gnostic religion, with its two millennia of history in which it developed its independent Aramaic idiom and life style as did no other gnostic sect of the past, be able to survive in the future.

EPILOGUE

A Historical Survey of the Changes and Consequences of Gnosis

The beginning and end of Gnosis in late antiquity **cannot be** pin-pointed exactly. It makes its appearance at the **beginning of** the Christian era and disappears again at the latest **in the 6th** century, at least in as far as its western manifestations are concerned. One can only speculate on the causes of its disappearance just as one can only speculate about its origin. These speculations are of a hypothetical character rather than being based on direct sources. It would hardly be wrong to assume that a number of causes has contributed and is responsible. The gnostic schools, with the exception of Manicheism, did not succeed in becoming broad mass movements; for this they were too narrow-mindedly esoteric and, above all, too hostile to the world. The Manichean church succeeded in getting a secure foothold for any length of time only with the help of the laity, the body of "hearers", which was consciously incorporated in its organisation; this consistent organisational form probably was its great advantage over its gnostic predecessors. Moreover, account must be taken of the fact that the Christian Church, by adapting to its environment, and by accepting the legitimate concerns of gnostic theology into its consolidating body of doctrine, developed into a forward-looking ideology and community structure, which ultimately made it heir to the religions of antiquity.[172] By avoiding extremes and by transforming the radical traits of the early Christian message into a form acceptable to the world, thus not persisting in mere protest but at the same time accepting the cultural heritage of antiquity, it increasingly reduced the influence of Gnosis until it ultimately, after having been invested with the authority of the state (in the 4th century), succeeded in mobilising the physical political power against it which the remaining adherents could not resist for any length of time. Also in conformity with this process was the inner stagnation of gnostic doctrine; in its pre-Manichean phase

The end of Gnosis

it had no longer any future. Its intellectual and creative power was largely exhausted in the ideological and theological debate. Nevertheless, the problems once posed by Gnosis – the question of the origin of evil, the position vis-à-vis the world, the relationship between creation and redemption, the role of "knowledge", the relation of body and spirit or soul etc. – remained, as before, a motive for speculative endeavours in Christian theology; they were kept in reserve and, in the further course of the history of the Church, proved their disruptive force more than once. As H. Blumenberg said: "The gnostic trauma of the first post-Christian centuries goes deeper than that of the bloody persecutions . . ."[173] One can almost say that Gnosis followed the Church like a shadow; the Church could never overcome it, its influence had gone too deep. By reason of their common history they remain two – hostile – sisters.

The after-effects of Gnosis   This raises the question of the after-effects of Gnosis beyond its concrete historical existence. It can be traced in various ways and has varying forms: on the one hand, the acceptance of its problems and even the retention of gnostic positions in Christian theology, on the other hand, a kind of transformation (metamorphosis) of gnostic ideas and traditions, including their reformulation in view of the changed historical and social situation, and finally the more or less conscious, sometimes even amateurish, reception of gnostic ideas and fragments of systems in modern syncretistic-theosophic sects. It is difficult to prove continuity in any detail, as the connecting links often are "subterranean" channels, or else the relationships are based on reconstructions of the history of ideas which have been undertaken especially in the realm of the history of philosophy. F. C. Baur, in his classic monograph *Die christliche Gnosis oder die christliche Religions-Philosophie* (1835), treats, in accordance with his theme, not only of the anti-gnostic representatives of the early Christian "philosophy of religion", but also exhaustively of the "ancient Gnosis and later philosophy of religion", dealing with Jakob Böhme, Schelling, Schleiermacher, and especially Hegel, as its heirs. We are not aiming to go so far in these final observations, although it would be very attractive to re-examine the problems posed by Baur and to continue the investigation beyond Hegel to the present day.

First of all it is sufficient to trace the immediate effects of Gnosis on the edifice of early Christian thought, and afterwards to recall the historical after-effects in the medieval sectarian world. Both aspects also are of considerable importance for the future. The former has already been discussed repeatedly in the course of our survey. The oldest Christian theological systems were those of the Christian gnostics. Herder has aptly called them "the first religious philosophy in Christianity,"* and they had a far-reaching effect, negatively as well as positively, on the subsequent formation of Christian doctrine. "The will of Gnosis to create systems forced the consolidating Church to create dogmas in its turn"[174]. This observation was already made by A. von Harnack in his *History of Dogma*. The first authoritative ecclesiastical system, that of Irenaeus of Lyons, arose directly out of his opposition to Gnosis. His theology, which takes its bearing from Adam's fall and the "restoration" (recapitulation) of man's lost image of God through Christ, has not only the character of a scheme made in answer to Gnosis but follows the gnostic projection in plan and sometimes in execution[175]. This simultaneous delimitation and acceptance is continued particulary in the "Alexandrine theology" of Clement and Origen. While Clement understands "thought" and "knowledge" as essential factors of the process of redemption of the Christian faith and builds the bridge to God with the help of the god-like "spirit" in man[176], Origen, in his system "On the prime origins" (*De principiis*), transposed the gnostic (specifically Valentinian) myth of the soul with its descent and ascent into a Christian scheme in such a way that it was largely "demythologised"; in spite of this, even in this form it was soon recognised to be heretical[177]. The movement towards the "inwardness" of the gnostic scheme of ascent and its gradation runs from Origen to the experience of Christian monastic mysticism, as it appears first in Evagrius Ponticus (4th century), an Egyptian monk. In these circles, which can also be traced almost simultaneously among the "Messalians" or "Euchites" (i.e. "they who pray") in east Syria, the ascent of the (divine) soul to God already in this life is taught and acted upon in anticipation of the eschatological state. The notions, well-known from Gnosis, of the ascent of the soul with its dangers and its stages become psychic experiences. Gnosis (as cognition of God) is here transposed into ecstasy. The myth objectified in theory can now be experienced in the practice of mysticism, an intellectual mysticism which is linked to the spirit (as means of cognition of

Gnosis and Christian dogma

See above, esp. p. 62f., 148ff.

* *Works (Suphan) vol. 20, p. 249*

The Alexandrines: Clement and Origen

Monastic mysticism

God). This tradition can be found above all in Syrian (Nestorian) monastic mysticism up to the 8th century and was thence continued in Islamic mysticism.

Lactantius and Augustine   Lactantius (about 300) was also a theologian who stood in the tradition of the "philosophical Gnosis" of Alexandria. He developed his doctrine of redemption in obvious dependence on the gnostic, especially the Hermetic, but clothed it, following Clement, at the same time in the dress of official theology[178]. St. Augustine (354–430) was, for the time being, the last in this chain of development. With his Manichean past stretching over almost ten years, he had acquired personal experience of the gnostic heresy, and had reflected on its dangers and value*. He appropriated this heritage most clearly in the impressive historical review of the two "realms" (*civitates*), the devil's or that of the wicked (*civitas diaboli* or *impiorum*,) and God's (*civitas Dei*), and thus shaped the Christian historical metaphysics of the Middle Ages. Other aspects of his teaching, too, cannot be understood without this heritage which is linked closely with the related late Platonic, such as the famous faith in predestination (grace and election), the role of the soul as being in the image of God and thus an immortal element and, above all, the concept of original sin. This latter is the result of man's fall from the divine original state brought about by his own guilt. Its position in Augustine's teaching is an echo of the Manichean idea of the fateful "mixture" of light and darkness, spirit and matter, which necessarily determines human existence[179]. One has attributed to St. Augustine, because of his turning away from Manichean Gnosis and because of his overcoming the problems raised by it, a decisive importance in the final acceptance of the ancient understanding of the cosmos as a good creation of God in opposition to the gnostic hostility to the world[180]. "It was the principal concern, from Augustine to high scholasticism, to rehabilitate the world as creation from the negative position of its demiurgical origin and to save the cosmos-dignity of antiquity for the Christian system." The Christian theology of the Middle Ages with its final acceptance of Aristotle as chief witness can therefore "be taken as an attempt to insure finally against the gnostic syndrome"[181]. As the old question of the origin of evil, which was asked so urgently by Gnosis, was not settled in this way, St. Augustine attempted to answer it with the responsibility or freedom of man, who by

* *Augustine Confessions VII 1–8, etc.*

his fall into sin had destroyed the original order of God. But this was only a shifting of the problem, not a solution, for man's trespass evoked his punishment. Was not then the freedom of will to decide an evil when it resulted in evil? Thus man's independence and self-assertion came into ill repute and the doctrine of predestination, which led to the division of men into the saved and the condemned, was only a way out of this dilemma. "The gnostic dualism was set aside for the metaphysical principle of the world, but it continued to be alive within mankind and its history as absolute separation of the called and the rejected. This crudity thought up for God's justification has its hidden irony, in that in a roundabout way, through the idea of predestination, that very authorship of the absolute principle for the cosmic corruption was reintroduced, the elimination of which was the aim of the exercise."[182] At the back of it is, in the last analysis, the sworn faith of Gnosis (especially of Marcion) in the hidden and incomprehensible God who signified for Christianity God's absolute sovereignty. Man's self-assertion which vis-à-vis this hidden God (*Deus absconditus*) was condemned to absurdity and resignation was a heritage of Gnosis which had not been fully overcome but was only "translated Gnosis"[183].

Although the process of demonising the cosmos which was introduced by Gnosis was received and reversed by Christianity, there yet remained a certain aloofness from the world which from time to time could become more articulate and which became closely linked with the idea, also accepted by Christianity, of the devil and adversary of God. Christian piety has preserved this heritage to the present day, as can be seen from the third verse of Luther's hymn "A safe stronghold our God is still" where it is graphically expressed: "And let the prince of ill look grim as e'er he will, he harms us not a whit; for why? – his doom is writ". A gnostic would be able to sing this too. In a different way, Sweden's greatest religious poet, J. O. Wallin (died 1839), put into words the following idea of redemption in a hymn preserved to this day in the Swedish hymnal: "Grievously fallen, separated from the Lord, the spirit bound to matter sees its Father's abode from afar and is unable to loose the bonds. But it has a presentiment of the Father's design and the secretly nurtured sorrow in concord with its longing is the guarantee of its redemption."[184] This could be taken from a gnostic book of

Hostility to the world in Christianity

hymns (cf. the Odes of Solomon and the Song of the Pearl). Further examples could easily be found. It is not widely known thar Heinrich Heine ascribed to Gnosis and to Manicheism a decisive part in the development of the "idea" of Christianity, and here he had this hostility to the body particularly in view.[185]

In opposition to the gnostic challenge, Christian theology held fast to the unity of the creator and the redeemer God, and thus preserved a decisive bond of the Jewish-Christian history of salvation. But even so, all problems did not disappear. This is apparent not only in the outlined discussion of creation and **Christology** cosmos but also in the realm of Christology. It is well known that gnostic soteriology, by accepting the historical redeemer figure of Jesus, transferred its dualism on to it and arrived at the so-called Docetism. We have already, when dealing with this *See above, p. 158 ff.* subject, drawn attention to the fact that the official Christian theology at first struggled in vain to draw clear boundaries, because it too had introduced a duality of the earthly Jesus and the heavenly Christ (*logos*), of sufferer and redeemer, of humanity and divinity. The early Christian Fathers, foremost Irenaeus and Tertullian, strove hard to find forms which make intelligible in a non-gnostic sense the prevailing division of the one Jesus Christ. Strictly speaking they did not succeed. Already Harnack was forced to say: "Who can maintain that the Church ever overcame the gnostic doctrine of the two natures or the Valentinian Docetism?"[186] Even the later councils of the Church, which discussed the Christological problems in complicated, nowadays hardly intelligible, definitions, did not manage to do this; the unity of the Church foundered precisely on this. Thus Gnosis raised a problem which could not be solved with the categories of the dualism current in antiquity in a way entirely different from that propounded by Gnosis itself, although it must be admitted that the gnostic formulations were sometimes rather extreme. It has often been forgotten that gnostic theologians saw Christ as being "consubstantial" with the Father, before ecclesiastical theology established this as a principle, in order to preserve his full divinity. With the elimination of gnostic Christology the radical form of early Christian ideas about Christ was set aside, but not the consequences which are at its root.

Faith and Another effect of Gnosis on Christian theology was obvious-
knowledge ly more decisive: the effect of "knowledge" itself. For Gnosis,

as the name indicates, knowledge and redemption were identical. With this is connected that the gnostic systems sought the prime cause of the world and of existence in "depths" or "heights", often in a way hitherto unknown, which redounds to the honour of human intellectual curiosity (*curiositas*), even when it slipped in doing so into fantasy and absurdity. The antignostic controversialists, therefore, liked to jeer at this trait and to represent it as human pride. Acquiescence and acknowledgement of the divine mysteries are fitting for man, faith not unbridled search for knowledge. "It is better", Irenaeus says, "if a man knows nothing and does not perceive a single cause of things created but abides in faith in God and in love, rather than that, puffed up by such knowledge (*scientia*), he falls away from the love that makes man alive ... and rather than that he falls into godlessness through the subtleties of his questioning and through hair-splitting (*per quaestionum subtilitates*)" *[187]. Here * *Irenaeus, Adv. haer. II 26,1* the gnostic quest for knowledge is very clearly pronounced the forerunner of scientific curiosity in comparison with which "sound, safe, cautious reason that is devoted to the truth is zealously concerned only for that which God has given under man's authority and which he has made subject to our knowledge (*scientia*) ... To this belongs what lies obviously and clearly before our eyes and what is unambiguously and explicitly laid down in Holy Writ"*.[188] These "competing claims of know- * *op. cit. II 27,1* ledge and acceptance in faith" (H. Blumenberg) which are here revealed ultimately lead to a momentous decision, which is taken particularly by Tertullian when he includes "thirst of knowledge" in the catalogue of vices and banishes it from among the positive virtues. "The freely chosen *ignorantia* thus can become *See above, p. 209* the act of recognition of the exclusively divine right of ownership of the truth and of its disposal".[189] Thus a dogma is proclaimed which sets up the simple scriptural faith in opposition to the improper quest for knowledge as point of departure and guiding principle. Only reason guided by God is the ideal of Christian learning which does not let itself be influenced by the "temptations" of worldly learning as St. Augustine describes them. "Thus a fundamental decision is made against the gnostic dualism which was to influence not only the Middle Ages but also the beginning of modern times which protested against this ruling".[190] This does not, however, mean that a scientific value in the proper sense, or even actual progress, can be attributed to the gnostic quest for knowledge, it is subject to the contemporary barriers of its view of the world as is the rest of its religious environment. But it is distinguished by the ruthlessness and boldness of its questioning in the field of the philosophy of religion and theology, which does not stop before any religious authority but rather pushes it aside or reinterprets it. For Gnosis the universe had lost its (religious) reliability, and this posed a challenge to search for a new foundation. This was the motive for the theoretical efforts of Gnosis.

The decisions of ecclesiastical theology, as outlined, in the face of the gnostic challenge had accordingly both negative and positive after-effects. A series of medieval heretical movements saw to it that this challenge did not cease throughout the Middle Ages but made its appearance in a new historical context. These movements were either direct continuations of the Gnosis of late antiquity, or gave renewed importance to its traditions and ideas, and this from within the Church itself. The best known of these "neo-gnostic" or "neo-Manichean" groups formed at the same time the most important opposition churches known in the Middle Ages. One such group came into existence in the middle of the 10th century in Bulgaria and was **The Bogomils** named after its legendary founder Bogomil, a priest, "Bogomils". It has often been assumed that an important source of the Bogomilian ideology was the warlike sect of the Paulicians who, in about 872, coming from Asia Minor, were compulsorily settled in Macedonia (Thracia). They (named according to their predilection for St. Paul) originally came from Armenia and Syria where they are to be found already in the 7th century, and had adopted gnostic-Manichean or -Marcionite traits; but the Bogomils' descent from the Paulicians is by no means certain. The gnostic character of the Bogomilian doctrine is however clear: the history of the world is dominated by the struggle between the good God and the fallen Satanaēl who created the material world and man. Man's soul is derived from the good God and for its salvation from the evil body the "Word of God" (*logos*) was sent in the phantasmal body of Christ. The hierarchy, the sacraments, the cult of the saints, the relics and the icons of the Church were rejected as inventions of Satan. Only the Lord's prayer and confession were retained. Reception into the community was by a "spiritual baptism" which took the form of a laying on of hands. In the Bible the Old Testament

was considered a work of Satan, while in the New Testament
only the Gospel of St. John was considered to be an authentic
proclamation of the true God. The Bogomilian community
consisted of three groups: the "perfect", the "hearers" and the
simple believers. The first, as the actual pillars of the community, lived a severely ascetic life; they avoided the consumption of
wine and meat and any shedding of blood. The leadership was
in the hands of "elders" and apostles or "teachers", who composed their own works. The Bogomils exerted particular power
of attraction by their sharp criticism of the wealth and luxury of
the Byzantine Church as well as of the wars and oppressions of
the state. In this way they acquired for themselves a broad basis
of support and could only be overcome after bloody persecutions in the 12th century. But before this they succeeded in getting a foothold in Serbia and Bosnia where they formed their
own Bosnian church which lasted into the 15th century and the
remnants of which later on converted to Islam. But their influence was not confined to the Balkans but made itself felt east
and westwards. The Bogomilian writings in Old Church Slavonic still enjoyed throughout the Middle Ages great populari-
ty and strongly influenced the Old Slavonic popular literature.
The songs of the beggars at the doors of Russian churches still
preserved Bogomilian thought patterns. Even stronger was the
effect in Italy and France where apparently Bogomilian ideas
penetrated at the beginning of the 11th century, which combined with the local resistance movements against the official
Church and against society. Here, too, the basic features include: the dualism of soul and body, the rejection of marriage,
a spiritualisation of the faith which becomes apparent in the rejection of the sacraments, and the high esteem of the spirit as
well as the division of the community into the "perfect" and the
"hearers". This "gnostic-spiritual heresy" in the 11th century
covered the whole of northern Italy and France and became the
expression of a changed understanding of Christianity and
Church.[191] It found its most strongly marked expression in the
Catharists, i.e. the "pure", or Albigensians (named after the **The Catharists**
city of Albi in southern France). They formed, from about
1150–1300, a church of their own with a network of bishoprics
in southern France (Languedoc), but also had representatives
in northern Italy (where they were called "Patarenes"), in Germany and in northern France. This "neo-Manichean church"

could be subdued only by the harsh action of the Inquisition (which was brought into existence in this connection) and by proper crusades. Its after-effects were still felt for a long time in other later "heresies". The Catholic Church itself could only overcome this crisis internally by recognising the "orders of mendicant friars" which arose in the same period, and which formed part of the protest against the hierarchy and against the wealth of the Church. Thus this revival of gnostic religion was of importance for the self-understanding of the Christian Church. A reminder of the controversy with the "Catharists" has been preserved in our vocabulary to this day by the word "Ketzer" (i. e. heretic; the German word is derived via the Italian *gazzari*).

The continuing effect in the Orient   In the brief historical survey of the consequences of Gnosis, we have only considered the European Christian side; a similar investigation deserves to be made of the after-effects in the Orient, as these are no less interesting and many-sided. The Hermetic Gnosis continues its life in the Islamic history of heresies under the key-word "Sabaism" (Sabean); some gnostic ideas are to be met with in Islamic mysticism and in the literature influenced by it. But especially it is the extreme Shi'ite sect of Ismailism which can be related in its beginnings (ca. 850) with gnostic traits and therefore has been called "Islamic Gnosis" by modern scholars[192]. Manicheism, which flourished longer in the Orient, found its reflection in early Islamic theological trends, apparently most effectively in the book of the Arab prophet himself. Mohammed, according to the Koran, advocates the same cyclic theology of revelation as the gnostic prophet Mani from Mesopotamia, and stands similarly at the end of a series of forerunners who proclaimed the same as he did, but with less success, and whose teaching was falsified by their followers. Mohammed has the same predilection for the Old Testament figures from the Pentateuch as has Mani. But their view of the world and their doctrine of salvation are almost in opposition and separate them; they are united in their claim to be the last prophet of a very ancient history of salvation. Mani's work has vanished in history, while Mohammed's foundation, thanks to a different point of departure that had a more positive attitude to the world, developed into the greatest post-Christian world religion, a fame which Mani was also able to claim for a time.

APPENDIX

Chronological table

	Formation of Poimandres (Corpus Hermeticum I)?	293–300	Amr ibn Adi, king of Hira, protector of Manicheism
	Apophasis Megalē (Simonianism)	297	Edict of Emperor Diocletian against the Manichees
	Oldest Hekhaloth traditions (Jewish Esotericism)	C.300	Anti-manichean letter by an Alexandrian bishop (Theonas?)
C.150–200	Irenaeus of Lyons (Lugdunum)		Alexander of Lycopolis (Assiut),
	The Valentinians' Ptolemy, Heracleon, Theodotus, Marcus.		polemical treatise against the Manichees
	Odes of Solomon (Syria)		Acta Archelai (an anti-manichean
C.150–211/215	Clement of Alexandria		work by Hegemonius)
C.150–223/225	Tertullian		Completion of Corpus Hermeti-
C.160	Death of Valentinus		cum (?)
	Marcellina in Rome (Marcellians)		The Manichean Bundos in Rome (?)
	Death of Marcion. Activity of Apelles		Composition of Pistis Sophia (?)
178	Irenaeus Bishop of Lyons. Adversus haereses.	306–337	Constantine the Great
		306–373	Ephraem of Edessa: antimarcionite and anti-manichean polemic
	Celsus' treatise "The True Logos"		
C.180	Hermogenes	311	First draft of Church History by Eusebius of Caesarea
C.180–216	Bardaisan in Edessa (d.c.222)		
180–253/4	Origen	315–403	Epiphanius of Salamis Panarion (371–377)
C.200	Books of Jeu (?). Acts of Thomas (Hymn of Pearl). Acts of John (?)	C.320	Founding of Coptic monasticism by Pachomius
C.200–235	Hippolytus active in Rome. Refutatio (Philosophoumena)	324/5	Last (4th) edition of Eusebius' Church History
205–270	Plotinus (244–270 in Rome)		
216	Birth of Mani in Babylonia	C.330	Pseudo-clementine Homilies
C.220	Alcibiades the Elchasaite in Rome	C.350	Nag Hammadi Codices (Egypt)
227–651	Sassanid rule. Rivalry with Rome for predominance in Western Asia. Renaissance of Zoroastrianism	350/360	Spread of Archontics in Palestine
		C.350/360	Pseudo-clementine Recognitions
		361–363	Emperor Julian
228/29	First vision of Mani	C.363	Titus of Bostra Adversus Manichaeos
240	Mani's call to be "Apostle of Light"		
241	Mani's journey to India. Conversion of King of Turan	372	Edict of Valentinian I against the Manichees
243	Mani's audience with Shapur I (reigned to 272)	373–382	Augustine a Manichee ("hearer") in North Africa
250–275	Composition of Manichean Psalms of Thomas	379–395	Emperor Theodosius I.
250–300	Redaction of Mandean ritual book (Qolasta)		Sharpening of legislation against Manicheism, which now ranks as crime and sacrilege and hence carries the death-penalty.
C.260	Manichees in Egypt		Appointment of inquisitors.
	Redaction of *Grundschrift* of Pseudoclementine romance		Under following emperors these laws were extended and the
274	Manichees in Syria and Palestine		Manichees deprived of all legal
277	Imprisonment and death of Mani at Belapat (Gundeshapur)		protection (445)

388–399	Augustine's anti-manichean treatises
C.400	Coptic Manichean texts from Medinet Madi (Fayyum)
450–519	Relaxing of antimanichean Edict. Revival of Manicheism?
494–524	Social revolutionary movement of the Mazdakites in Iran
519–527	Justinian I. Resumption of anti-manichean legislation with the aim of wiping out the Manichees
526	The great Latin abjuration formula (*prosperi anathematismi*)
561	Anathematisms of Synod of Braga (Spain)
C.600	Milan Anathematisms
622–632	Mohammed in Medina
from 635	Arab Islamic conquests
C.650	Anōsch bar Danqa, head of the Mandeans, effects the protection of his community by Islam. Redaction of Mandean literature by Rāmowī in Tib
651–750	Omayyad rule
694	Manichees at the Chinese imperial court
719	Building of a Manichean church in Peking
732	Antimanichean edict by Chinese emperor
750–1258	Abbasid rule
762–840	Manicheism the state religion among the Uigurs (Chotsko)
775–932	Struggle by the Caliphs al-Mahdi and al-Muqtadir against the Manichees and dualists (Zindiqs)
791/2	Scholia of Theodore bar Konai (from Kashkar)

8–10th cent.	Main bulk of Central Asian Manichaica (Turfan)
9th cent.	Great Greek abjuration formula
843/44	Persecution of Manichees in China
C.850/60	Abū Īsā al-Warrāq and his disciple Ibn ar-Rawandī, Arabic Manichees. Combatted in the "Book of the Triumph" (Kitāb al-Intiṣār) of al-Khajjāt (d.912) Beginnings of the Ismailite (extreme Shiite) "Gnosis" in Khuzistan, Irak and Syria (missionaries are Abdallah and al-Husain al-Ahwazi)
872	Migration of Paulicians from Asia Minor to Thrace (centre: Philippopolis)
C.925	Removal of head of Manichean Church to Samarkand
C.950	Activity of the Bogomil (Theophilus) in Bulgaria
988	Fihrist of Ibn an-Nadīm
11th cent.	Patarenes (Cathari) in North Italy
1120	Antimanichean edict in China (Wen-Chou province, where there were still 40 Manichean places of worship)
1150–1300	Cathari and Albigensians
1217–1258	Mongol conquests in Central and Western Asia End of the Manichean communities
C.1450	Cessation of "Balkan dualism" (Bogomils, Bosnia)
17th cent.	Catholicising of last Paulicians in Bulgaria

Notes

Full details for works cited by abbreviated titles will be found in the Bibliography.

1. The best-known reconstruction is that of A. Hilgenfeld, *Ketzergeschichte* 21 ff. Other views were advanced by R. A. Lipsius and A. von Harnack.

2. See on this the important remarks of F. Wisse, The Nag Hammadi Library.
3. H. von Campenhausen, *Griechische Kirchenväter*, Stuttgart [4]1967, 27 (ET London 1963, 20).
4. J. Frickel, *Die "Apophasis Megale" in Hippolyts Refutatio.*

5. Quoted after K. Preysing, 15 ff. (BdKV).

6. Quoted after K. A. H. Kellner, G. Esser, 314 (BdKV).

7. H. von Campenhausen, *Lateinische Kirchenväter*, Stuttgart 1960, 24 (ET London 1961, 20).

8. Quoted after O. Stählin, *Clemens von Alexandrien, Ausgewählte Schriften* Bd. 5, 11 (BdKV).

9. Cf. J. Dummer, Ein naturwissenschaftliches Handbuch als Quelle für Epiphanius von Constantia, in *Klio* 55 (1973) 289–299.

9a. Schmidt's text of these works has been published with new English translations by V. MacDermot (*Nag Hammadi Studies* vol. IX Pistis Sophia; vol. XIII Bruce Codex).

10. On this I have published a comprehensive dossier containing the most important works since F. C. Baur, with brief introductions: *Gnosis und Gnostizismus* (WdF *CCLXII*).

11. In the following account I rely on the information supplied by J. Doresse, M. Krause, G. Quispel, H. C. Puech and J. M. Robinson (see Bibliography, p. 391).

12. *The Jung Codex* 13 f.

13. According to a brief report in the Bulletin of the Institute for Antiquity and Christianity at Claremont Graduate School, Vol. II/4, Dec. 1975 (American Research Centre in Egypt, Newsletter 96 (1976) 18–24) 6 f. Further details in a report by J. M. Robinson and B. van Elderen on "The First Season of the Hamra Dom Excavation 27 Nov.– 19 Dec. 1975". See now *Biblical Archeologist* 42 (1979) No. 4.

14. This survey is based on the reports of M. Krause and J. M. Robinson (see bibliography pp. 400 and 402). A brief account of the content of most of the documents is contained in *Gnosis und Neues Testament*, ed. K. W. Tröger, 21–76.

14a. Engl. trans. by C. J. de Catanzaro, JTS 13 (1962) 35 ff.; trans. with commentary by R. McL. Wilson, *The Gospel of Philip*; London 1962.

15. Cf. his editions already mentioned above and his selection of Coptic sources from Nag Hammadi in W. Foerster, *Gnosis* II (ET Oxford 1974).

16. So Irenaeus Adv. haer. I 30.15 (referring to the Valentinian school); also I 30.1 (many heresies have proceeded from the serpent, the archdevil); Hippol. Ref. V 11 (referring to the Naassenes).

17. U. Bianchi, *Le Origini dello Gnosticismo* XX ff. German version also in W. Eltester, *Christentum und Gnosis* 129 ff. See on this my remarks in ThR 36 (1971) 13 ff.

18. *Plotins Schriften* übers. von R. Harder, Bd. 5, Leipzig 1937, 25 f. The two following citations are from pages 39 and 36 f.

19 Op. cit. Bd. 3, Leipzig 1936, 55–87. The quotations are from pages 76, 73, 79 f. Harder had earlier published a translation and commentary on this document: *Die Antike V*, (1930) 53–84.

19a. Cf. on this K. Koschorke, Die "Namen" im Philippusevangelium, ZNW 64 (1973) 305–322.

20. Berlin Codex (Papyrus Berolinensis 8502) ed. W. Till, pp. 22 ff. (MS) or 84 ff. (edition). Till's translation is also printed (with minor alterations) in W. C. van Unnik, *Evangelien aus dem Nilsand* 185 ff. M. Krause's translation, which I frequently follow, is in W. Foerster, *Gnosis* I, 141 ff. (ET 105 ff.). Square brackets indicate restoration of lacunae.

21. M. Krause, *Gnosis* II 37 f. (ET 28); W. Till, Sophia Jesu Christi (Papyrus Berolinensis 8502) 83 f. (MS), 206 f. (edition).

22. R. Kasser et al., *Tractatus Tripartitus* I, 51 ff. (text); after the German translation by Kasser and W. Vycichl, 177 ff. (English trans. 233 ff.).

23. *Gnosis* [4]1955, 168–173 and the diagram at p. 32 (Leisegang in his second edition revised the interpretation he had given in the first). Other explanations in A. Hilgenfeld, *Ketzergeschichte* 277 ff. and Th. Hopfner, Das Diagramm der Ophiten, in *Charisteria A. Rzach zum 80. Geburtstag*, Reichenberg 1930, 86–98 (an important work; cf. H. Chadwick, *Origen Contra*

Celsum, Cambridge 1965, 337ff.). The two descriptions (Orig. c. Cels. VI 25–38) are presented separately in R. Haardt, *Gnosis* 78–81. See also W. Foerster, *Gnosis* I, 124ff. (ET 94ff.).

24. Cf. H. Jonas, *Gnosis und spätantiker Geist* I, 33ff. Cf. also pp. 96 and 123f.

25. Ed. A. Böhlig/P. Labib; cf. also H. M. Schenke, Vom Ursprung der Welt, in ThLZ 84 (1959) 243–286. As has only recently been discovered, the British Museum has possessed since 1895 forty fragments of this gnostic text, from an independent Coptic translation. Twelve of these were published by C. Oeyen in M. Krause (ed.), *Essays on the Nag Hammadi Texts in Honour of Pahor Labib* 125–144. They are deliberately not taken into account in the following extracts.

26. So the recent and illuminating interpretation by G. Scholem in *Mélanges d'histoire des religions offerts à H.-Ch. Puech,* Paris 1974, over against the explanation hitherto current, "child of chaos", which can indeed be supported from the text cited (NHC II 5, 103 (151) 24) but is grammatically impossible. On the other hand the same document offers, alongside the clearly secondary interpretation "Young man, pass over" (NHC II 5, 100 (148) 12), a confirmation for the view advanced above at 103 (151) 32f.: "Sabaoth, the son of Jaldabaoth". In the gnostic texts the original meaning of the plural Sabaoth has been lost, and it has become the name of one of the spirits who originally surrounded the Creator.

26a. Cf. F. T. Fallon, *The Enthronement of Sabaoth* (NHS X), Leiden 1978; B. Barc, Samaèl-Saklas-Yaldabaoth in: *Colloque international sur les textes de Nag Hammadi* (Québec 1978), 123–149.

27. For the sake of simplicity we again use the Berlin version in Till's edition, drawing also upon other translations (especially by M. Krause and R. Haardt). No attempt is made to go into the divergent traditions with regard to the sequence of the aeons in particular.

28. Text and (German) translation in M. Krause and P. Labib, *Gnostische u. hermetische Schriften aus Codex II und Codex VI,* 122–132. Cf. also G. W. MacRae in: *The Coptic Gnostic Library* (CGL) (NHS XI ed. D. M. Parrott), 231–255. I use the translation of the Berlin *Arbeitskreis* in ThLZ 98 (1973) 97–104, but without taking over its interpretation of the title ("Nebront"), which can be justified neither from the original nor from its content, and has now been given up by H.-M. Schenke himself (TU 120, p. 216). Possibly there is in the redeemer-figure some thought of the "heavenly Eve", to whom a similar brief hymn in the anonymous treatise refers (NHC II 5, 114 (162) 8–15). At any rate she ranks here as daughter of Sophia, and thus is one of her forms of existence. A justification for the transmitted title "Thunder" in the sense of the "heavenly voice" of Athena-Sophia has meanwhile been provided by M. Tardieu, *Le Muséon* 87 (1974) 523–529; 88 (1975) 365–369.

29. A. D. Nock/A. J. Festugière, *Corpus Hermeticum* I, 7f. I use the translations of R. Haardt, *Die Gnosis* 143ff., and W. Foerster, *Gnosis* I. 421ff. (ET 329ff.).

30. Cf. on this H. Jonas, *Gnosis* I 212ff. See further the section on community organisation (p. 204ff. below).

31. There is an analysis of the whole complex in H.-M. Schenke, *Der Gott "Mensch" in der Gnosis* (the source material can now be further augmented).

32. H. Jonas, *Gnosis u. spätantiker Geist* I, Ergänzungsheft, 383. Cf. also id. in *Journal of Religion* XLII (1962) 267f.

33. Thus the title of my article in ZRGG IX (1957) 1–20, which however requires amplification.

34. Whether this figure belongs to the original content remains uncertain; it is missing in the other versions, and does not appear again in the later context, Cf. S. Arai, NTS 15 (1969) 308ff.

35. Edited and translated by M. Krause, *Gnostische und hermetische Schriften* (ch. IV, pp. 68–87). Krause's translation

also in W. Foerster, *Gnosis* II 125 ff. (ET
102 ff.). On the significance of the document for the interpretation of the Fourth
Gospel see K. M. Fischer in *Gnosis und
Neues Testament,* ed. K. W. Tröger 245 ff.
(here also a graphic account of the basic
ideas).

36. In what follows I use the texts translated in
my selection of source material in W.
Foerster, *Gnosis* II p. 257 f. (GR 104 f. Petermann; ET 193), 266 f. (GL 61 f. Petermann; ET 200 f.), 268 (GR 92 Petermann;
ET 202), 291 f. (GL 75 f. Petermann; ET
222 f.), 293 (GL 84 Petermann, 14 Petermann; ET 223 f.).

37. After M. Krause in Foerster, *Gnosis* II 139
(ET 111 f.).

38. L. Schottroff, Anima naturaliter salvanda,
in W. Eltester, *Christentum und Gnosis.*
See my comments in *ThR* 36 (1971) 12 f.
The point had however already been made
by Koffmane, *Die Gnosis nach ihrer Organisation,* Breslau 1881, 3 f. (reprinted in
my WdF volume *Gnosis u. Gnostizismus,*
122). Cf. now also K. W. Tröger in *Kairos
XXIII,* 1981, 40 ff.

39. Cf. on this the critical study by C. Colpe,
Die religionsgeschichtliche Schule, and my
remarks in *ThR* 34 (1969) 9 ff.

40. I have used the edition of P. Nagel, *Das
Wesen der Archonten aus Codex II der
gnostischen Bibliothek von Nag Hammadi,*
and the important supplements of
M. Krause in *Enchoria* II (1972) 1–19.
Krause offers his own translation in Foerster *Gnosis* II 53–62 (ET 44–52). Cf. now
the French edition by B. Barc, *L'Hypostase des Archontes* (BCNH 5), with an important introduction.

41. Text and translation in A. Böhlig/P. Labib,
Koptisch-gnostische Apokalypsen, 96–
117. Cf. also M. Krause in Foerster, *Gno-
sis* II, 17–31 (ET 13–23) and G. W. Mac-
Rae in *The Coptic Gnostic Library* (NHS
XI, ed. D. M. Parrott), 151–195.

42. I use the edition by J. Doresse in *Journal
Asiatique* 1966, 330–429 and the transla-
tion prepared thereafter by H.-
M. Schenke in *NTS* 16 (1969–70) 196–208,

as well as the edition of the two versions
now available, by A. Böhlig and F. Wisse,
Nag Hammadi Codices III 2 and IV 2
(NHS IV).

43. Text and translation in M. Krause/P. Labib, *Die drei Versionen des Apokryphon des
Johannes,* 195 f. Cf. also R. Haardt, *Gnosis*
172 ff. and H.-M. Schenke in J. Leipoldt/
W. Grundmann, *Umwelt des Urchristentums* II 352. English translation of Codex
II version by S. Giversen, *Apocryphon Jo-
hannis,* Copenhagen 1963.

44. In addition to the facsimile edition
(vol. 10, 1973) I use the translation prepared by G. and H.-M. Schenke (*ThLZ* 99
(1974) 734–746). Some passages in translation are to be found in K. W. Tröger,
Gnosis u. Neues Testament 75. No attempt
is made to reproduce the *parallelismus
membrorum.* French translation by
Y. Janssens, *La Protennoia trimorphe*
(BCNH "Textes" 4), Quebec 1978.

45. K. W. Tröger, *Gnosis u. Neues Testament*
76. On the Fourth Gospel see below,
p. 305. Cf. the comparison by C. Colpe in
JAC 17 (1975) 122–124.

46. Text and translation in M. Krause, *Gnostische u. hermetische Schriften* 133–149. I
use the revision by W. P. Funk in *ThLZ* 98
(1973) 251–259, to which is prefaced an introduction to the document. Cf. also
G. W. MacRae in *The Coptic Gnostic Library* (NHS XI ed. D. M. Parrott), 257 ff.

47. Cf. text and translation by M. Krause,
"Neue Texte" 135–137. There is a translation by H.-M. Schenke and H. G. Bethge
in *ThLZ* 100 (1975) and now by L. Painchaud, *Le Deuxième Traité du Grand Seth*
(BCNH 6), Québec 1982.

48. This has been shown beyond a doubt by
R. Bultmann (*The Gospel of John*); it has
recently been confirmed again by H.-
M. Schenke (in K. W. Tröger, *Gnosis u.
Neues Testament* 226 f.).

49. Cf. H.-M. Schenke, op. cit. 218 ff.

50. I use in particular the new editions by
T. Wolbergs, *Griechische religiöse Ge-
dichte der ersten nachchristlichen Jahrhun-
derte* I: Psalmen und Hymnen der Gnosis

und des frühen Christentums, Meisenheim (Main) 1971 (Beitr. z. klass. Philologie 40), and A. Kehl, Beiträge zum Verständnis einiger gnostischer und frühchristlichen Psalmen und Hymnen, in *JAC* 15 (1972) 92–119. The first part (lines 1–13) is textually very corrupt and a translation therefore uncertain. New translations in R. Haardt, *Gnosis* 90f.; W. Foerster, *Gnosis* I 363 (ET 282); M. Elze *ZThK* 1974, 401f. M. Marcovich in B. Layton (ed.) *The Rediscovery of Gnosticism* II, 770–778.

51. W. Till, *Papyrus Berolinensis*, ²1972, 194–295 (quotation p. 290ff.). With this should be compared the Letter of Eugnostus with the variants and supplements or expansions of the version of SJC contained in NHC III, as presented by M. Krause in W. Foerster, *Gnosis* II 32f. and 153ff. (ET 24ff. and 35ff.; our text is on p. 159, ET p. 38f.)

52. A. von Harnack, *Lehrbuch der Dogmengeschichte* I 215ff., 285ff., 797ff. (Examination of the background of the concept of pre-existence).

53. Cf. op. cit. 211f.; *Dogmengeschichte*, Tübingen ⁷1931, 51f. (the following quotation is also from this account).

54. *Lehrbuch der Dogmengeschichte* 215.

55. L. Schottroff, *Der Glaubende und die feindliche Welt* 295. On this important book see my remarks in ThR 37 (1972) 297ff. and 304ff.

56. L. Schottroff, op. cit. 289. See also below p. 305

57. Cf. S. Arai, *Die Christologie des Evangelium Veritatis*, Leiden 1964, with my comments on it in ThR 34 (1969) 198ff.

58. After the translation by H. Duensing in Hennecke-Schneemelcher, *Neutestamentliche Apokryphen* 1, pp. 132 and 138 (ET 198f. and 205f.)

59. Translated after K. W. Tröger, *Gnosis und Neues Testament* 68f. Cf. now the edition and translation by S. Giversen and B. A. Pearson in *The Coptic Gnostic Library* (NHS XV ed. B. A. Pearson), 48f.

60. *Lehrbuch der Dogmengeschichte* 286 n. 1

61. Text and translation in M. Krause, *Neue*

Texte 118ff. Cf. K. W. Tröger, *Gnosis und Neues Testament* 61, where this passage is also translated. A new edition and translation is given by L. Painchaud (BCNH 6; cf. note 47) with some different interpretations (38ff., 100ff.).

62. I quote according to the translation by K. Schäferdiek in Hennecke-Schneemelcher, *Neutestamentliche Apokryphen* 2. 157f. (ET 232f.).

63. Text and translation in M. Krause, *Neue Texte* 152–179. There is a new translation by H.-M. Schenke and A. Werner in ThLZ 99 (1974) 575–583. On 82. 3–9 see especially H.-M. Schenke in M. Krause, *Essays on the Nag Hammadi Texts* (NHS VI) 283ff.

64. Cf. A. Böhlig/P. Labib, *Koptisch-gnostische Apokalypsen*, p. 42–45, W. R. Schoedel in *The Coptic Gnostic Library* (NHS XI ed. D. M. Parrott), 84–91. I have also consulted the reconstruction of the damaged text by H.-M. Schenke in J. Leipoldt/ W. Grundmann, *Umwelt des Urchristentums II*, p. 354f. (cf. also Schenke in *OLZ* 61, 1966, 28f.).

65. Lidzbarski, p. 430. Cited from my translation in W. Foerster, *Gnosis. A Selection of Gnostic Texts* II, (ET) p. 275. The passage is also found in the Book of John ch. 5 (Lidzbarski, transl. p. 184f.).

66. The following citations from the Left Ginza also come from my selection in W. Foerster, p. 265 (GL III 12), 254 (GL II 1), 257 (GL II 8), 258 (GL II 12), 271 (GL III 56), 266f. (GL III 15).

67. Citations from my selection op. cit., p. 272 (GL III 57), 268 (GL III 25), 230 (GR II 3), 267f. (GL III 24), 268 (GL III 23), 246f. (GL I 4).

68. Text and translation by M. Krause, *Gnostische und Hermetische Schriften*, p. 99f., W. Foerster, *Gnosis* II, 116f.

69. Text and translation in M. Krause, *op. cit.*, p. 144 f., W. P. Funk/H.-M. Schenke, ThLZ 98, 1973, p. 258, G. W. MacRae in *The Coptic Gnostic Library* (NHS XI), 280–283.

70. Cf. for this n. 44.

71. Text and translation: *De Resurrectione* (Epistula ad Rheginum). Ed. M. Malinine, H.-Ch. Puech, G. Quispel, W. Till, Zurich 1963. Particularly useful for the study of this text are the translation and commentary of R. Haardt in *Kairos* XI, 1969, p. 1–5; XII, 1970, p. 241–269, further H.-G. Gaffron, Eine gnostische Apologie des Auferstehungsglaubens, in *Die Zeit Jesu*. Festschrift für H. Schlier, Freiburg (Breisgau) 1970, p. 218–227, and M. L. Peel, *The Epistle to Rheginos*, London 1969. There is a translation by Schenke in J. Leipoldt/W. Grundmann, *Umwelt des Urchristentums* II, p. 309–372. See now the new translation and interpretation by B. Layton, *The Gnostic Treatise on Resurrection*, Missoula 1979, who emphasizes the philosophical and Platonic traits without denying the Gnostic content. Id. Vision and Revision: a Gnostic View of Resurrection, in B. Barc (ed.), *Colloque international sur les textes de Nag Hammadi* (Québec 1978), 190–217.

72. *Gnosis I*, p. 261. For the whole problem and for the following cf. the arguments of R. Haardt, Das universaleschatologische Vorstellungsgut in der Gnosis, in *Vom Messias zum Christus*, ed. by K. Schubert, Vienna 1964, p. 315, 336.

73. *Mandäische Liturgien* ed. Lidzbarski, p. 205f. (Oxford Collection I 38), cited after my translation in W. Foerster, *Gnosis II*, p. 242.

74. Cf. n. 44.

75. Text and translation in M. Krause/P. Labib, *Gnostische und Hermetische Schriften,* p. 150–165, F. Wisse in *The Coptic Gnostic Library* (NHS XI ed. D. M. Parrott), 294–323. The treatment by K. M. Fischer in *ThLZ* 98, 1973, p. 169–176 was also consulted. Cf. also the remarks in K.-W. Tröger, *Gnosis und Neues Testament*, p. 50ff.

76. Cited from H.-M. Schenke in J. Leipoldt/W. Grundmann, *Umwelt des Urchristentums II*, p. 363f. A translation of this section also appears in R. Haardt, *Gnosis*, p. 208f. For the text cf. the references in n. 25.

77. Text and translation in M. Krause, Neue Texte, p. 2–105.

78. Cf. Lidzbarski's edition p. 311, 11ff.; my selection in W. Foerster, *Gnosis II*, 275f.; from the latter also the following citation; p. 478, 17ff. in Lidzbarski.

79. Cf. my remarks in *ThR* 38, (1978) 6f. and the translation by Koschorke, ZNW 69 (1978) 110ff. with the comments in his work *Die Polemik der Gnostiker* 152ff. An edition of the text with a new translation is given by S. Giversen and B. A. Pearson in *The Coptic Gnostic Library* (NHS XV ed. B. A. Pearson), 122–203 (cf. espec. 170–175); they suggest that the author is Julius Cassianus, a pupil of Valentinus (c. 170), or one of his intimate followers (p. 118ff.).

80. Cf. n. 22

81. *Die Gnosis nach ihrer Organisation*, Bresláu 1881, p. 5f.; reprinted in K. Rudolph, *Gnosis und Gnostizismus*, p. 123.

82. Cited from Haardt, *Gnosis*, p. 138. Text in A. Ferrua, *Revista di Archeologica Christiana* XXI, 1944/45, p. 185ff.

83. What Celsus writes here (Origen, *Contra Celsum* V 63) is certainly exaggerated and applies rather to the doctrinal disputes within the church. However the polemic against other gnostic groups in the Testimony of Truth (NHC IX 3) shows that this was not altogether alien to Gnosis.

83a. Cf. on this the pioneer work of K. Koschorke, *Die Polemik der Gnostiker gegen das kirchliche Christentum* (deals especially with NHC VII 3 and IX 3); Eine gnostische Pfingstpredigt, in ZThK 74 (1977) p. 325–343 (on NHC VIII 2); Der gnostische Traktat "Testimonium Veritatis" aus NHC IX, in ZNW 69 (1978) p. 91–117; Eine neugefundene gnostische Gemeindeordnung, in ZThK 76 (1979) p. 30–60. Similar reflections in E. Pagels, The Demiurge and his Archons – a Gnostic View of Bishop and Presbyter? in *Harv. Theol. Rev.* 69 (1976) p. 301–324, *The Gnostic Gospels* ch. 2.

84. Koffmane, *Gnosis*; W. Bousset, *Hauptprobleme der Gnosis*, p. 276–319;

L. Fendt, *Gnostisches Gemeinschaftsleben*, p. 117–139; H.-G. Gaffron, *Studien zum koptischen Philippusevangelium*, p. 71–99 (important comments); Koschorke, *Die Polemik der Gnostiker*, 142–148; L. Koenen, From Baptism to the Gnosis in Manichaeism, in B. Layton (ed.), *The Rediscovery of Gnosticism* II, 734–756.

85. Text and translation in W. Bauer, *Die Oden Salomos*, and now M. Lattke, *Die Oden Salomos* vol. I, Ia (standard work).

86. Cf. M. Krause/P. Labib, *Gnostische und hermetische Schriften*; K.-W. Tröger, Die 6. und 7. Schrift aus Nag-Hammadi-Codex VI, in: ThLZ 98, 1973, p. 495–503. The Greek and Latin versions of NHC VI 7 are reproduced in A. D. Nock/A. J. Festugière, *Corpus Hermeticum* II, p. 353–358. Cf. also P. A. Dirkse, J. Brashler, D. M. Parrott in *The Coptic Gnostic Library* (NHS XI ed. D. M. Parrott), 341–387.

87. Cf. for this the examination by H. G. Gaffron, *Studien zum koptischen Philippusevangelium*.

88. H.-G. Gaffron, *op. cit.*, p. 198

89. The best explanations hitherto are those of G. Hoffmann, *ZNW* 4, 1903, p. 298 and H. Gressmann, *loc. cit.*, 16, 1915, p. 193.

90. Cf. here W.-P. Funk, *Die Zweite Apokalypse des Jakobus aus Nag-Hammadi-Codex V*, p. 211 ff. (See p. 62, 16–63, 29 for the dying prayer of James); Probleme der Zweiten Jakobus-Apokalypse aus NHC V, in P. Nagel, *Studia Coptica*, p. 147–158.

91. Cf. here primarily H.-G. Gaffron, *Studien zum koptischen Philippusevangelium*, p. 185–219.

92. Cf. here L. Fendt, *Gnostische Mysterien*, p. 22 ff.; H. Leisegang, Das Mysterium der Schlange, in *Eranos-Jahrbuch*, 1939, p. 151–250, especially p. 205 ff. The authenticity of Epiphanius' statements is dubious if one starts from the fact that he attributed Hellenistic mystery practices to the Ophites. Thus the *cista mystica* (at the feet of Demeter) out of which a snake crawls is met with frequently on Greek re-

liefs and coins. Cf. E. Küster, *Die Schlange in der griechischen Kunst und Religion*, Berlin 1913 (*Religionsgeschichtliche Versuche u. Vorarbeiten* 13, 2), p. 146 ff.

93. Cf. especially L. Fendt, *Gnostische Mysterien*, p. 3 ff. Further literature on the "sperm cult" in H.-G. Gaffron, *Studien zum koptischen Philippusevangelium*, p. 355, n. 1. W. Speyer, *JbAC* 6, 1963, p. 129–135, maintains that the descriptions are largely authentic. Minucius Felix also in his *Dialogue with Octavius* deals with obscene meals and associations (ch. 8–9).

94. H. Jonas, *Gnosis und spätantiker Geist I*, p. 170 f.

95. Cf. *op. cit.*, p. 233 ff. The following citations on p. 234.

96. H. Jonas, *op. cit.*, p. 236.

97. Translation in W. Foerster, *Gnosis I* (ET) p. 154–161; R. Haardt, *Die Gnosis*, p. 125–132.

98. Cited after the translation of W.-P. Funk, ThLZ 100, 1975, p. 21. The text is being edited by J. Zandee and M. Peel.

99. *Right Ginza I*, §110–118 Lidzbarski; cf. W. Foerster, *Gnosis II*, p. 290 f.

100. Several in H. G. Kippenberg, Versuch einer soziologischen Verortung des antiken Gnostizismus, in: *Numen* XVII, 1970, p. 211–231, esp. p. 219 f.; G. Theissen, *Kairos* XVII, 1975, p. 296; cf. also already H. Jonas, *Gnosis I*, p. 214–215. For gnostic criticism of the official hierarchy of the Church cf. the essay by E. Pagels mentioned in n. 83 a.

101. *op. cit.*, p. 170

102. *op. cit.*, p. 226 f. n. 1. Included here too are the ensuing citations but following a somewhat different line of argumentation.

103. Lidzbarski. Here from my translation in W. Foerster, *Gnosis II*, p. 290.

104. Cf. J. Leipoldt, *Thomasevangelium*, p. 74. In Hippolytus, *Ref.* V 8, 28 there is an interesting exegesis of Mt. 21, 31 by Gnostics (Naassenes): they are the true publicans who received the last of the tax, i. e. divine semen.

105. Translations in W. Foerster, *Gnosis I*, p. 38 ff. and R. Haardt, *Gnosis*, p. 58 f. The

text in Clement of Alexandria, *Werke*, Band 2, Leipzig 1960, p. 197–200.

106. Cf. O. Klíma, *Mazdak*, p. 183–231, esp. p. 208 ff. On the basis of a singular and doubtful item of information in the Byzantine chronographer John Malalas (6th. cent.), Klíma conjectures that the teaching of Mazdak or his teacher Zartusht goes back to a sect-founder called Bundos (c. 300) who advocated a peculiar kind of Manicheism in Rome and Persia (op. cit., p. 156 ff.). The information we have about the ideology of the Mazdakites is sparse and very contradictory. Worthy of note is the middle Persian information from the Dēnkart about the dris(t)-dēn, "the true religion", i. e. the old Mazdakite self-designation; see M. Shaki in *Archív Orientálny* 46 (1978) 289–306.

107. Lidzbarski, Ginza p. 130, 5 ff. Here from my translation in W. Foerster, *Gnosis II*, p. 203.

108. Eusebius von Caesarea, Kirchengeschichte (new edition) p. 198.

109. On the following see my remarks in *Kairos* IX (1967) 105–122, reprinted in the collection *Gnosis und Gnostizismus* 768–797, esp. 780 ff.; also *ThR* 36 (1971) 89–119, esp. 108 ff. Cf. also W. Schmithals, *Die Apokalyptik*, Göttingen 1973, 67 ff. and 93 ff. (ET Nashville 1975). On the problem of a *religionsgeschichtlich* understanding of Apocalyptic, see the essay of that title by H. D. Betz in *ZThK* 63 (1966) 391–409 (he stresses the hellenistic influence).

110. See the remarks of I. Gruenwald, "Knowledge and Vision", in *Israel Oriental Studies* III (1973) 63–107, esp. 72 ff.

111. Cf. A. Böhlig, *Mysterion und Wahrheit*, 80 ff., 119 ff., 135 ff., 149 ff.; J. E. Ménard, "Littérature apocalyptique juive et littérature gnostique", in *Revue des sciences religieuses* 47 (= *Exégèse biblique et Judaisme*), Strasbourg 1973, 301–307.

112. W. Schmithals, *Die Apokalyptik* (n. 109), 77, 80, 82.

113. Cf. the collection of evidence for both ideas in my article "War der Verfasser der Oden Salomos ein 'Qumran-Christ'"?

Revue de Qumran 4 (1964) 523–555, esp. 544 ff.

114. Cf. op. cit. 550 ff.

115. After P. Riessler, *Altjüdisches Schrifttum ausserhalb der Bibel*, Augsburg 1928, 380. ET from R. H. Charles, *The Book of Enoch*, London 1917, 61 f.

116. Cf. G. Widengren, Der iranische Hintergrund der Gnosis, ZRGG 5 (1952) 87–114; partly reprinted in K. Rudolph, *Gnosis und Gnostizismus* 410–425; cf. also id. 696 ff.

117. Cf. on this the large monograph by M. Hengel, *Judentum und Hellenismus*, Tübingen 1969 [2]1973 (ET London 1974), and his comprehensive study *Juden Griechen und Barbaren. Aspekte der Hellenisierung des Judentums in vorchristlicher Zeit*, Stuttgart 1976 (Stutt. Bibelstudien 76). (ET London 1980).

118. Cf. my survey of research in *ThR* 38 (1973) 12 ff. on the important works of W. Theiler and H. J. Krämer, and A. H. Armstrong, Gnosis and Greek Philosophy, in B. Aland (ed.), *Gnosis. Festschrift Jonas*, 86–124.

119. W. Schubart, *Glaube und Bildung im Wandel der Zeiten*, Munich 1947, 37 f. For a detailed and basic account see M. Rostovtzeff, *Social and Economic History of the Hellenistic World*, 3 vols., Oxford 1941 (German, Darmstadt 1955/56; Stuttgart 1955/56, [2]1962). Cf. also now E. C. Welskopf (ed.), *Hellenische Poleis*, 4 vols., Berlin 1974.

120. *Social and Economic History* vol. II, 1106; here too the following quotation.

121. Cf. H. Kreissig, *Die sozialen Zusammenhänge des Judäischen Krieges*, Berlin 1970 (Schriften z. Gesch. u. Kultur d. Antike 1); F. M. Heichelheim, Geschichte Syriens und Palästinas, in B. Spuler (ed.), *Handbuch der Orientalistik* II, 4: Orientalische Geschichte von Kyros bis Mohammed, Lief. 2, Leiden 1966, 178 ff.; H. G. Kippenberg, *Religion u. Klassenbildung im antiken Judäa*, Göttingen 1978 (Studien z. Umwelt des NT 14).

122. Rostovtzeff, *Social and Economic History* vol. II, 1105.

123. *Wirtschaft und Gesellschaft*, ed. J. Winckelmann, Tübingen [5]1972, I. Halbband, 304–310 (the section on sociology of religion was written c. 1912/13). Cf. on this and what follows my remarks in the collection *Gnosis und Gnostizismus* 776 f.

124. See the fundamental study by J. Frickel, *Die "Apophasis Megale"*. Cf. my comments, *ThR* 37 (1972) 325 ff.

125. Cf. E. Hennecke/W. Schneemelcher, *Neutestamentliche Apokryphen*, 2nd ed. 215 ff. and 231 ff.; 3rd ed., vol. 2. 188 ff. (ET 276 ff.).

126. *Die Pseudoclementinen*. II Rekognitionen in Rufins Übersetzung, ed. B. Rehm, Berlin 1965 (GCS 51) 73 f. Quoted also in H. Jonas, *Gnosis* I 357. The occasional anti-Marcionite tenor is not affected by this.

127. On the state of research relating to Simon see my reports in *ThR* 37 (1972) 322–347 and 42 (1977) 279–359 (includes detailed discussion of the two latest major works on Simon by K. Beyschlag and G. Lüdemann).

128. Cf. on this H. Liboron, *Die karpokratianische Gnosis*, Leipzig 1938 (he maintains the historicity); H. Kraft, Gab es einen Gnostiker Karpokrates?, in *Theol. Z.* 8 (1954) 434–443.

129. Succinctly in *Theologie des Neuen Testaments*, Tübingen 1953, [6]1968; Berlin [3]1959, esp. §15 (ET London 1952, 1955); E. Haenchen, Gnosis und Neues Testament, RGG[3] II cols. 1652–1656. Cf. also the contributions by J. M. Robinson "Gnosticism and the New Testament", and G. W. MacRae, "Nag Hammadi and the New Testament", in the Jonas Festschrift *Gnosis*, ed. B. Aland, 125–157.

130. Bultmann, *Theologie des Neuen Testaments* (1st ed.) 169 (ET 170).

131. Cf. W. Schmithals, *Die Gnosis in Korinth* (ET 1971); id. "Zur Herkunft der gnostischen Elemente in der Sprache des Paulus" in the Jonas Festschrift *Gnosis*, ed. B. Aland, 385 ff. U. Wilckens, *Weisheit und Torheit*. On the social situation of the Corinthian church see most recently G. Theissen, ZNW 65 (1974) 232–272.

The dates for Paul are now given according to G. Lüdemann, *Paulus* I (Studien zur Chronologie).

132. See on this P. Pokorný, *Der Epheserbrief und die Gnosis*; K. M. Fischer, *Epheserbrief*, esp. 173 ff.

133. See on this still H. Schlier, *Religionsgeschichtliche Untersuchungen*.

134. Fundamental: R. Bultmann, *Das Evangelium des Johannes*, Göttingen 1941, [18]1964, (ET Oxford 1971); *Theologie des Neuen Testaments* §41–50. Carried further by E. Käsemann. *Exegetische Versuche und Besinnungen*, Göttingen 1964, I. 168–187; II. 155–180 (ET of latter in *NT Questions of Today*, London 1971, 138–167); *Jesu letzter Wille nach Johannes* 17, Tübingen 1966 (ET *The Testament of Jesus*, London 1968); S. Schulz, *Johannesevangelium*; L. Schottroff, *Der Glaubende und die feindliche Welt*; W. Langbrandtner, *Weltferner Gott oder Gott der Liebe*; M. Lattke, *Einheit im Wort*, Munich 1978 (Studien z. AT und NT 41). Cf. also K. W. Tröger, Ja oder Nein zur Welt, in *Theol. Versuche* VII, Berlin 1976, 61–80, and K. M. Fischer, Der johanneische Christus und der gnostische Erlöser, in K. W. Tröger, *Gnosis und Neues Testament*, 245–266.

135. Käsemann, *Exegetische Versuche* I 178

136. On the Jewish Baptist sects cf. my account in the *Cambridge History of Judaism*, vol. 2 and *Antike Baptisten* (SBSAW).

137. In *Kairos* 7 (1965) 123 (now reprinted) in Rudolph: *Gnosis und Gnostizismus* 599); J. Leipoldt/W. Grundmann, *Umwelt des Urchristentums* I 413.

138. So H. C. Puech in 1933/34 in an essay "Où en est le problème du gnosticisme?", now reprinted in *En quête de la Gnose*, vol. 1, 143–183 (quotation from p. 151); German translation in *Gnosis und Gnostizismus* 306–351 (quotation at p. 315).

139. The best presentation of the sources in translation is in W. Foerster, *Gnosis* I 80–110 (ET 59–83). Cf. also R. Haardt, *Gnosis* 41–54. For the state of research, see my survey in *ThR* 38 (1973) 2 ff.

140. Harnack's book on Marcion remains the best collection of material, even though his interpretation is no longer fully shared (on p. 28f. H. admits loose connections with Gnosis). The modern standpoint is admirably presented by B. Aland, Marcion, in *ZThK* 70 (1973) 420–447. Cf. also my brief report in ThR 37 (1972) 358ff.

141. Translation of the fragments in W. Foerster, *Gnosis* I 309–34 (ET 238–43); R. Haardt, *Gnosis* 105–107.

142. In Wendland's edition, p. 167. I use the new revision by T. Wolberg and A. Kehl (*JAC* 15 (1972) 93ff.), to which Haardt, *Gnosis* 107, also comes close.

143. Cf. on this H. C. Puech in Hennecke/Schneemelcher, *Neutestamentliche Apokryphen* 1, 160–166 (ET 233–241). For criticism, see E. Haenchen, *ThR* 30 (1964) 47ff.; K. Rudolph, *ThR* 31 (1969) 195ff.

144. The best presentation of the sources is now in W. Foerster, *Gnosis* I, 162–314 (ET 121–243). Parts also in R. Haardt, *Gnosis* 107–138. H. Jonas (*Gnosis* I, 363–375) gives a good survey on the basis of the report in Irenaeus. G. Quispel sought to reconstruct "the myth of Valentinus" (*Gnosis als Weltreligion*, 78–84).

145. W. Foerster, Grundzüge der ptolemäischen Gnosis, *NTS* 6 (1959/60) 16–31 (quotation from p. 18). The reasons for the identification, suggested by Harnack and recently advanced again by G. Lüdemann (ZNW 70 (1979) 97ff.), of the Valentinian Ptolemaeus and the teacher and martyr of the same name (d. c. 152 A. D.) mentioned by Justin (2 Apol. 2) are to my mind not valid.

146. Translated in W. Foerster, *Gnosis* I, 214–240 (ET 162–183); A. E. Brooke, *The Fragments of Heracleon*. Cf. E. Pagels, *The Johannine Gospel in Gnostic Exegesis;* B. Aland, Erwählungstheologie und Menschenklassenlehre, in M. Krause (ed.) *Gnosis and Gnostizism* (NHS VIII) 148–181.

147. Translated and analysed by W. Foerster, *Gnosis* I 193–204 (with reference to Ptolemaeus), 287–302 (ET 146–154; 222–233). Edition with detailed commentary by F. Sagnard, *Extraits de Théodote*. NHC I 5 and XI 2 evidently belong to the "western" school.

148. This was already pointed out by G. Volkmar in 1855 (*Zs. f. hist. Theol.* IV 603f.); only Hilgenfeld (*Ketzergeschichte* 288f., 313f., et al.) was not convinced. Recently it has again begun to appear in the literature (thus in H.-M. Schenke, in *Umwelt des Urchristentums* I 408).

149. Well set out in H. Leisegang, *Gnosis* 326ff. Cf. also the translation in Foerster, *Gnosis* I 265ff. (ET 203ff.).

150. Quoted after the translation by E. Klebba, *Irenäus, Buch I–III* (BdKV 3), 53.

151. Cf. J. Leipoldt, *Der römische Kaiser Julian in der Religionsgeschichte*, Berlin 1964 (*SB SAW*, Phil.-hist. Kl. 110:1) 18 (referring to Julian, Letters 115); H. Lietzmann, *Geschichte der Alten Kirche* 3, 284; 4, 78 (ET 3, 280; 4, 87). Cf. further K. Koschorke, Patristische Materialien zur Spätgeschichte der Valentinianischen Gnosis, in M. Krause (ed.), *Gnosis and Gnosticism* (NHS XVII).

152. Extracts in Foerster, *Gnosis* I 378–82 (ET 295–298).

153. *Sacramenta Mundi*. Theol. Lexikon für die Praxis, Freiburg/Breisgau (Herder), vol. 3, 1969, col. 328 (ET London 1969, 373). Cf. also A. Böhlig in *Die Gnosis* III (Der Manichäismus), 27ff.

154. New edition and English translation of the Syriac version by H. J. W. Drijvers, *The Book of the Laws of the Countries*, Assen 1964. German translation: A. Merx, *Bardesanes von Edessa*, Halle 1863, 25–55; H. Wiesmann in *75 Jahre Stella Matutina*, Feldkirch 1931, 553–572.

155. Cf. the large monograph of H. J. W. Drijvers, *Bardaisan von Edessa*, and my survey of research, *ThR* 34 (1969) 223f.; 37 (1972) 349ff. The gnostic character of Bardaisan's teaching has been shown in particular by B. Aland, *ZKG* 81 (1970) 334–351; more recently in Dietrich, *Synkretismus* 123–143.

156. Quoted after A. Adam, *Texte zum Manichäismus* 111. The text is taken from one of the Turfan fragments (M4). Cf. plate 24. ET J. P. Asmussen, *Manichaean Literature* 8f.

157. Unpublished; quoted after C. Schmidt/ H. J. Polotsky, *Ein Mani-Fund in Ägypten* 44 (text p. 86).

158. A convenient collection in A. Adam, *Texte zum Manichäismus*, 1–35, 111–128. To this may now be added the material from the Cologne Mani codex (cf. A. Henrichs/L. Koenen in *ZPE*). Cf. now also A. Böhlig and J. P. Asmussen, *Die Gnosis III*, 221–239.

159. Cf. the graphic report by A. v. Le Coq, *Auf Hellas Spuren in Ostturkestan*, Leipzig 1926. According to the latest reports, considerably more material has since been found, which now rests in the museums of Turfan and Urumchi (in the Chinese province of Sinkiang). Cf. now H. J. Klimkeit, *Manichaean Art and Calligraphy*, 23 ff., plates IV, V, VI (fig. 6–9).

160. Cf. C. Schmidt, *Neue Originalquellen des Manichäismus aus Ägypten*, Stuttgart 1933; C. Schmidt/H. J. Polotsky, *Ein Mani-Fund in Ägypten*.

161. Cf. the preliminary report and edition by A. Henrichs and L. Koenen in *ZPE* 1970, 1975, 1978, 1981, 1982.

162. Cf. on this my studies: "Gnosis und Manichäismus nach den koptischen Quellen"; "Die Bedeutung des Kölner Mani-Codex für die Manichäismusforschung", and P. Nagel, Die apokryphen Apostelakten des 2. und 3. Jahrhunderts in der manichäischen Literatur, in K. W. Tröger, *Gnosis und Neues Testament* 149–182.

163. Cf. Schmidt/Polotsky, *Ein Mani-Fund in Ägypten* 41 (text p. 85).

164. A. Henrichs/L. Koenen, *ZPE* 5 (1970) 108; 19 (1975) 65.

165. A. Henrichs/L. Koenen, *ZPE* 5 (1970) 98; 19 (1975) 69.

166. Here, as often in the foregoing section, I draw upon my article "Mani" in the Kindler Encyclopedia "Die Grossen der Weltgeschichte", esp. 533 ff.

167. For this section I refer to my publications listed in the bibliography. I have also made use of my own experiences on travel, and of information by letter from Mandeans in Iraq.

168. Cf. my pictorial atlas "Mandeism", plates III and IV.

169. Cf. my study *Theogonie, Kosmogonie und Anthropogonie in den mandäischen Schriften*. My selection of source material in Foerster, *Gnosis* vol. II, takes this particularly into account. My contribution to K. W. Tröger, *Gnosis und Neues Testament* 121–148 (revised German version of "Problems of a History of the Development of the Mandaean Religion" in *HR* 8, 1969), and to the Jonas Festschrift *Gnosis*, ed. B. Aland, 244–277, gives a survey of present research.

170. Detailed discussion of these questions in my book *Die Mandäer II Der Kult*, and E. Segelberg, *Masbutā*. Cf. now also my *Antike Baptisten*.

171. Edited and translated by E. S. Drower, *The Haran Gawaita and Baptism of Hibil-Ziwa*. The most important passages are included in my selection in Foerster, *Gnosis* II 397 ff. (ET 314 ff.). See also R. Macuch in *ThLZ* 82 (1957) 401–408, my remarks in the survey in Tröger, *Gnosis und Neues Testament* 129 ff. (ET "Problems" 221 ff.), and "Quellenprobleme zum Ursprung und Alter der Mandäer".

172. Cf. my essay "Das frühe Christentum als religions-geschichtliches Phänomen" in *Das Korpus der Griechischen Christlichen Schriftsteller*, ed. J. Irmscher and K. Treu, Berlin 1977 (TU 120) 29–42.

173. *Säkularisierung und Selbstbehauptung*, 2. Frankfurt (Main) 1974, 144.

174. Blumenberg, op. cit. 150

175. In addition to Harnack's *Lehrbuch der Dogmengeschichte* I 556 ff., reference may be made especially to R. A. Lipsius, Die Zeit des Irenäus von Lyon und die Entstehung der altkatholischen Kirche, *Hist. Zs.* 28 (1872) 241–295, esp. 293 ff., P. Schwanz, *Imago Dei* 117–143, and B. Aland, Gnosis und Kirchenväter, in

Gnosis: Festschrift H. Jonas, 158–215, esp. 163–176.

176. Cf. P. Schwanz, op. cit. 145–169, and B. Aland, op. cit. 181–215.

177. Cf. the excellent interpretation of H. Jonas, *Gnosis und spätantiker Geist* II/1. 175–223. For discussion see U. Bianchi in the Jonas Festschrift, 57–59.

178. Cf. A. Wlosok, *Laktanz und die philosophische Gnosis*.

179. On these points, as on Augustine generally, cf. esp. A. Adam, *Lehrbuch der Dogmengeschichte* I, 225–302; id., *Sprache und Dogma*, Gütersloh 1969, 133–166. Luther's view was still markedly determined by Augustine's understanding of sin, and he even turned it back more strongly into "substantial" thinking and so earned for himself the reproach of Manicheism. Clearly visible in his Hungarian disciple Flacius, who ascribed to man since Adam's fall a totally corrupt nature. In the contempt for concupiscence and the body as the seat of sin, which destroys man's good will (cf. Paul already in this regard), there lurks a gnostic legacy in evangelical Christianity. On Luther from this point of view see now the thorough study by Th. Beer, *Der fröhliche Wechsel und Streit*, Leipzig 1975, Part 1, 126 ff. and 148 ff.

180. Cf. Blumenberg, *Säkularisierung* (n. 173) 150 ff.

181. op. cit. 150

182. op. cit. 155 f.

183. op. cit. 157.

184. Quoted after H. H. Schaeder's translation in H. S. Nyberg's essay "Das Urchristentum als religions-geschichtliches Problem", *Zs. f. Missionskunde u. Religionswiss.* 50 (1935) 303 note.

185. *Zur Geschichte der Religion und Philosophie in Deutschland*, ed. G. Erler, Leipzig (Reclam) 1970, 54 f. Cf. on this E. Peters and E. Kirsch, *Religionskritik bei Heinrich*

Heine, Leipzig 1976 (Erf. Theol. Schr. 13), 82 f.

186. *Lehrbuch der Dogmengeschichte* I. 287 note; Cf. also his *Grundriss der Dogmengeschichte*, Tübingen ⁷1931, 132 ff.

187. W. W. Harvey, I. 345, quoted after Blumenberg, *Der Prozess der theoretischen Neugierde*, Frankfurt (Main) 1973, 84. What is set forth in the text is much indebted to this presentation (esp. pages 79–121). B. however has overlooked the fact that in the philosophy of late antiquity *curiositas* was equally depreciated in comparison with the virtue of "awe" or "prudence" (Greek *eulabeia*) (cf. H. Dörrie in *Kirchengeschichte als Missionsgeschichte* I. Die alte Kirche, ed. H. Frohnes and U. W. Knorr, Munich 1974, 257). On the "limits of gnostic thought" see W. Schultz, *Dokumente der Gnosis*, Jena 1910, XVII f. (now reprinted in Rudolph, *Gnosis und Gnostizismus* 258 f.).

188. W. W. Harvey I. 347.

189. Blumenberg, op. cit. (note 187) 95.

190. op. cit. 99.

191. Cf. E. Werner, *Pauperes Christi*, Leipzig 1956; most recently: *Häresie und Gesellschaft im 11. Jahrhundert*, Berlin 1975 (SB SAW Phil. hist. Kl. 117: 5). Brief surveys are offered by H. Grundmann, *Ketzergeschichte des Mittelalters*, Göttingen 1963 and Berlin 1969, and G. Sfameni Gasparro in *Gnosis. Festschrift H. Jonas*, ed. B. Aland, 316–350. Detailed: M. Loos, *Dualist Heresy in the Middle Ages*, Prague 1974.

192. Cf. H. Halm, *Kosmologie und Heilslehre der frühen Ismāʿīlīya. Eine Studie zur islamischen* Gnosis, Wiesbaden 1978 (Abh. f. d. Kunde d. Morgenlandes XLIV, 1), and my comment on this pioneer work in *BiOr* 38, 1981, 551–557. German translations of the relevant Arabic texts in H. Halm, *Die islamische Gnosis*, Zürich 1982.

Select Bibliography

SOURCES (ORIGINAL TEXTS AND TRANSLATIONS)

German translations in the Bibliothek der Kirchenväter series have been replaced by English translations where these are available.

Church Fathers

Augustine

Jolivet, R., and M. Jourjon, *Six traités anti-Manichéens*. Oeuvres de St. Augustin 17. Brussels 1961.

Clement of Alexandria

Works, ed. O. Stählin, 3 vols., Leipzig 1936–1970 (GCS Bd. 12, 15, 17); vol. 1 in 3rd ed., Berlin 1972; vol. 2 freshly edited by L. Früchtel, Berlin 1962; vol. 3 in 2nd ed. by L. Früchtel, Berlin 1970.

The Writings of Clement of Alexandria, trans. W. Wilson, 2 vols., Edinburgh 1867–9 (Ante-Nicene Christian Library).

Casey R. P., *The Excerpta ex Theodoto of Clement of Alexandria*, London 1934 (Studies and Documents 1).

Sagnard, F. M. M., *Clément d'Alexandrie, Extraits de Théodote*. Texte grec, introduction, traduction et notes, Paris 1948 (quoted in text as Ex Theodoto).

Ephraem of Edessa

Mitchell, C. W., *S. Ephraim's Prose Refutations of Mani, Marcion and Bardaisan* 2 vols., London 1912, 1921

Des Heiligen Ephräms des Syrers Hymnen gegen die Irrlehren tr. A. Rücker, Munich 1928 (BdKV, Bd. 61)

Epiphanius

Ancoratus und Panarion, ed K. Holl 3 vols., Leipzig 1915, 1922, 1933; 2nd rev. ed. of Vol. 2 ed. by J. Dummer, Berlin 1980 (GCS Bd. 25, 31, 37; quoted in text as Panarion)

Ausgewählte Schriften, tr. J. Hörmann, Munich 1919 (BdKV, Bd. 38).

Quispel, G., *Ptolémée. Lettre à Flora*, Paris 1949, 2nd 1966 (Sources chrétiennes 24)

Eusebius of Caesarea

Kirchengeschichte, ed. E. Schwartz, *editio minor* Berlin 5th 1952.

Ecclesiastical History, trans. with introd. and notes by H. J. Lawlor and J. E. L. Oulton, 2 vols., London 1927–28 (quoted in text as HE).

Hippolytus of Rome

Refutatio omnium haeresium, ed. P. Wendland (Works, vol. III), Leipzig 1916; reprint Hildesheim/New York 1977 (GCS Bd. 26; quoted in text as Refutatio).

Philosophumena or the refutation of all heresies, trans. F. Legge, 2 Vols., London 1921 (Translations of Christian Literature, Series 1, Greek texts).

Ignatius of Antioch

Die Apostolischen Väter, revision of the Funk edition by K. Bihlmeyer, Part 1, Tübingen 1924 (SQS II 1).

Neutestamentliche Apokryphen, ed. E. Hennecke, Tübingen 1904, 2nd 1924.

The Apostolic Fathers, with an English trans. by K. Lake, 2 vols., London/New York 1912–13 (Loeb Classical Library).

The Apostolic Fathers, a new translation and commentary, vol. 4 Ignatius by R. M. Grant, New York 1966.

Irenaeus of Lyons

Adversus haereses, ed. W. W. Harvey, 2 vols., Cambridge 1857; reprint Ridgewood, New Jersey 1965 (quoted in text as Adv. haer.)

Irénée de Lyon. Contre les hérésies I, ed. A. Rousseau and L. Doutreleau 2 vols., Paris 1979 (Sources chrétiennes 263/64).

The treatise ... against the heresies, a translation of the principal passages, by F. R. M. Hitchcock, 2 vols., London 1916 (Translations of Christian Literature, Series 1)

Five books ... against heresies, translated by ... J. Keble, Oxford 1872 (Library of the Fathers 42).

Justin Martyr

Die Apologien, ed. G. Krüger, Tübingen
(SQS I 1)
The writings of Justin Martyr and Athenago-
ras, trans. M. Dods, G. Reith, B. P. Pratten,
Edinburgh 1867 (Ante-Nicene Christian
Library 2).
Apologies, ed. A. W. F. Blunt, Cambridge
1911.

Origen

Gegen Celsus, ed. P. Koetschau (Works,
vol. I. II), Leipzig 1899 (GCS Bd. 2, 3; quot-
ed in text as Contra Celsum).
Chadwick H., Origen: Contra Celsum,
trans. with introd. and notes, Cambridge
1953, ²1965.
Der Johanneskommentar, ed. E. Preuschen
(Works, vol. IV), Leipzig 1903 (GCS
Bd. 10).
The Commentary of Origen on St. John's
Gospel, the text revised with a critical in-
trod. and indices by A. E. Brooke, 2 vols.,
Cambridge 1896.
Brooke, A. E., The Fragments of Hera-
cleon, Cambridge 1891 (Texts and Studies I
4).

Tertullian

Opera, ed. A. Reiferscheid, G. Wissowa,
Ae. Kroymann, H. Hoppe, V. Bulhart and
Ph. Borleffs, 4 vols., Vienna 1890–1957
(Corpus Scriptorum Ecclesiasticorum La-
tinorum, vols. 20, 47, 69, 76).
The Writings of Q. S. F. Tertullianus, trans.
P. Holmes, S. Thelwall and R. E. Wallis, 3
vols., Edinburgh 1869–70 (Ante-Nicene
Christian Library 11, 15, 18).
Waszink, J. H., Tertullian: The Treatise
against Hermogenes (Ancient Christian
Writers, vol. 24, Westminster Md. 1956).

Theodore bar Konai

Liber scholiorum XI, ed. A. Scher, Paris/
Leipzig 1912 (Corpus Scriptorum Christian-
orum Orientalium, Syriac Series II,
vol. 66). Reprint: Leuven 1960.
Pognon, H., Inscriptions mandaites des
coupes de Khouabir II, Paris 1899 (with
French translation). Reprint: 1979.

Hermetica

Corpus Hermeticum. Text établi par A. D.
Nock et traduit par A. J. Festugière, 2 vols.,
Paris ²1960.

Odes of Solomon

Harris, J. R./A. Mingana, The Odes and
Psalms of Solomon, 2 Vols., Manchester
1916, 1920
Die Oden Salomos, ed. (and trans.) W. Bauer,
Berlin 1933 (KIT 64).
Gressmann, H., Die Oden Salomos, in
E. Hennecke, Neutestamentliche Apokry-
phen, Tübingen ²1924, pp. 437–472.
Charlesworth, J. H., The Odes of Solomon,
Oxford 1973. Rev. ed. Missoula 1977 (SBL
Texts and Transl. 13)
Lattke, M., Die Oden Salomos in ihrer Bedeu-
tung für Neues Testament und Gnosis, 2
vols. and 1 booklet (Syriac text), Fribourg/
Göttingen 1979, 1980 (Orbis Biblicus et
Orientalis 25/1.1a.2)

Apocryphal Gospels and Acts

Preuschen, E., Antilegomena, Giessen ²1905.
Acta apostolorum apocrypha, ed. R. A. Lipsius
and M. Bonnet, 3 vols., Leipzig 1891–1903;
reprint Darmstadt 1959.
Neutestamentliche Apokryphen, ed. E. Hennecke, Tübingen ²1924. 3rd edition ed.
W. Schneemelcher, 2 vols., Tübingen 1959/
1964; Berlin 1961/1966.
New Testament Apocrypha (English translation) London 1963/1965; second impression
1973/1974.
Handbuch zu den Neutestamentlichen Apokryphen (on 1st edition), ed. E. Hennecke, Tübingen 1904.
The Apocryphal New Testament, ed. M. R.
James, Oxford 1924.

Coptic gnostic texts, including the Nag Hammadi Library.

Barc, B., L'Hypostase des Archontes (NH II,

4), M. Roberge, *Noréa* (NH IX, 2), Québec 1980 (BCNH Sect. "Textes" 5)

Barns, J. W. B./G. M. Browne/J. C. Shelton (ed.), *Nag Hammadi Codices. Greek and Coptic Papyri from the Cartonnage of the Covers*, Leiden 1981 (NHS XVI, The Coptic Gnostic Library)

Böhlig, A., *Das Ägypterevangelium von Nag Hammadi*, Wiesbaden 1974 (Göttingen Orientforschungen VI/I).

Böhlig, A./ F. Wisse / P. Labib, *Nag Hammadi Codices III 2 and IV 2. The Gospel of the Egyptians*, Leiden 1975 (NHS IV).

Böhlig, A./ P. Labib, *Die koptisch-gnostische Schrift ohne Titel aus Codex II von Nag Hammadi im Koptischen Museum zu Alt-Kairo*, Berlin 1962 (DAW, Institut für Orientforschung, No. 58)

Böhlig, A. / P. Labib, *Koptisch-gnostische Apokalypsen aus Codex V von Nag Hammadi im Koptischen Museum zu Alt-Kairo*, WZ der Martin-Luther-Universität Halle-Wittenberg, Sonderband 1963.

Bullard, R. A., *The Hypostasis of the Archons*, Berlin 1970 (PTS 10).

Catanzaro, C. J. de, The Gospel according to Philip, in JTS 13 (1962) pp. 35–71.

Doresse, J., "Le Livre sacré du Grand Esprit Invisible" ou "L'Evangile des Egyptiens", in *Journal Asiatique* 1966, pp. 317–435; 1968, pp. 289–386.

The Facsimile Edition of the Nag Hammadi Codices
Published under the Auspices of the Department of Antiquities of the Arab Republic of Egypt in Conjunction with UNESCO, Leiden. Codex I (1977); Codex II (1974); Codex III (1976); Codex IV (1975); Codex VI (1972); Codex VII (1972); Codex VIII (1976); Codices IX and X (1977); Codices XI, XII, XIII (1973); Cartonnage (1979).

Funk, W. P., *Die Zweite Apokalypse des Jakobus aus Nag-Hammadi-Codex V*, Berlin 1976 (TU 119).

Grant, R. M. / D. N. Freedman, *The Secret Sayings of Jesus according to the Gospel of Thomas*, London 1960.

Guillaumont, A. / H. Ch. Puech / G. Quispel /

W. C. Till / Y. Abd al-Masih, *The Gospel according to Thomas*, London 1959.

Haardt, R., Die "Abhandlung über die Auferstehung" des Codex Jung aus der Bibliothek gnostischer Schriften von Nag Hammadi, in *Kairos* XI (1969), pp. 1–5; XII (1970) pp. 241–69.

Janssens, Y., Le Codex XIII de Nag Hammadi, in *Le Muséon* 87 (1974) pp. 351–414.

Janssens, Y., *La Protennoia Trimorphe* (NH XIII 1), Quebec 1978 (BCNH Sect. "Textes" 4).

Kasser, R. / M. Malinine / H. Ch. Puech / G. Quispel / J. Zandee, *Tractatus Tripartitus, I De Supernis*. Codex Jung f. XXXVI–LII, Bern 1973. *II De Creatione Hominis. III De Generibus Tribus. Oratio Pauli Apostoli*. Codex Jung f. LII–LXX. LXXII (?), Bern 1975.

Koschorke, K., Der gnostische Traktat "Testimonium Veritatis" aus Nag-Hammadi-Codex IX, in ZNW 69 (1978) pp. 91–117.

Krause, M./ P. Labib, *Die Drei Versionen des Apokryphon des Johannes im Koptischen Museum zu Alt-Kairo*, Wiesbaden 1962 (ADAIK, Kopt. Reihe 1).

Krause, M./ P. Labib, *Gnostische und hermetische Schriften aus Codex II und Codex VI*, Glückstadt 1971 (ADAIK, Kopt. Reihe 2)

Krause, M., Neue Texte, in: F. Altheim / R. Stiehl, *Christentum am Roten Meer*, Bd. 2, Berlin 1973, 1–229 (NHC VII 1, 2, 3, 5).

Labib, P., *Coptic Gnostic Papyri in the Coptic Museum at Old Cairo*, vol. 1, Cairo 1956.

Layton, B., The Hypostasis of the Archons or the Reality of the Rulers, in *Harvard Theological Review* 67 (1974) pp. 351–425.

Layton, B., *The Gnostic Treatise on Resurrection from Nag Hammadi*, Missoula, Montana 1979 (Harvard Dissertations in Religion 12).

Leipoldt, *Das Evangelium nach Thomas. Koptisch und Deutsch*, Berlin 1967 (TU 101).

Leipoldt, J. /H.-M. Schenke, *Koptisch-gnostische Schriften aus den Papyrus-Codices von Nag Hammadi*, Hamburg-Bergstedt 1960.

Mahé, J. P., La Prière d'Actions de Grace du

Codex VI de Nag Hammadi et le Discours Parfait, in *ZPE* 13 (1974) 40–60.

Mahé, J. P., *Hermès en Haute-Egypte* (NH VI 6, 7), Quebec 1978 (BCNH "Textes" 3).

Malinine, M. / H. Ch. Puech / G. Quispel / W. Till, *De Resurrectione (Epistula ad Rheginum)*. Codex Jung f. XXII–XXV, Zürich 1963.

Malinine, M. / H. Ch. Puech / G. Quispel, *Evangelium Veritatis*. Codex Jung f. VIII–XVI, XIX–XXII, Zürich 1956. *Supplementum* Codex Jung f. XVII–XVIII, Zürich 1961.

Malinine, M. / H. Ch. Puech / G. Quispel / W. Till / R. Kasser / R. McL. Wilson / J. Zandee, *Epistula Jacobi Apocrypha*. Codex Jung f. I–VIII, Zürich 1968.

Ménard, J. E., *L'Evangile selon Philippe*, Strasbourg/Paris 1967.

Ménard, J. E., *L'Evangile de Vérité*, Leiden 1972 (NHS II).

Ménard, J. E., *L'Evangile selon Thomas*, Leiden 1975 (NHS V).

Ménard, J. E., *La Lettre de Pierre à Philippe*, Quebec 1977 (BCNH Sect. "Textes" 1).

Ménard, J. E., *L'Authentikos Logos*, Quebec 1977 (BCNH Sect. "Textes" 2).

Nagel, P., *Das Wesen der Archonten aus Codex III der gnostischen Bibliothek von Nag Hammadi*, Wiss. Beiträge der Martin-Luther-Universität Halle–Wittenberg 1970/6 (K 3), Halle (Saale).

Painchaud, L., *Le Deuxième Traité du Grand Seth* (NH VII, 2), Québec 1982 (BCNH Sect. "Textes" 6)

Parrott, D. M. (ed.), *Nag Hammadi Codices V 2–5 and VI with Pap. Berolinensis 8502, 1 and 4*, Leiden 1979 (NHS XI, The Coptic Gnostic Library).

Pearson, B. A. (ed.), *Nag Hammadi Codices IX and X*, Leiden 1981 (NHS XV, CGL).

Peel, M. L., *The Epistle to Rheginos*, London 1969.

Quecke, H., Das Evangelium nach Thomas übersetzt, in *Theologisches Jahrbuch*, Leipzig 1961, pp. 224–236.

Roberge, M., *Noréa* (NH IX 2) s. Barc, B., *L' Hypostase des Archontes*.

Robinson, J. M. (ed.), *The Nag Hammadi Li-* brary *in English*, San Francisco and Leiden 1977.

Schenke, H. M., Das Ägypter-Evangelium aus Nag Hammadi Codex III, in *NTS* 16 (1969/ 70) pp. 196–208.

Schenke, H. M., Das Evangelium nach Philippus, in *ThLZ* 84 (1959) cols. 1–26.

Schenke, H. M., *Die Herkunft des sogenannten Evangelium Veritatis*, Berlin 1958.

Schenke, H. M., Die Taten des Petrus und der zwölf Apostel. Die erste Schrift aus NHC VI, in *ThLZ* 98 (1973) cols. 13–19.

Schenke, H. M. / H. G. Bethge, "Nebront". Die zweite Schrift aus NHC VI, in *ThLZ* 98 (1973) cols. 97–104.

Schenke, H. M. / W. P. Funk, "Authentikos Logos". Die dritte Schrift aus NHC VI, in *ThLZ* 98 (1973) cols. 251–259.

Schenke, H. M. / K. M. Fischer, Der Gedanke unserer grossen Kraft (Noēma). Die vierte Schrift aus NHC VI, in *ThLZ* 98 (1973) cols. 169–175.

Schenke, H. M. / K. W. Tröger, Die sechste und siebte Schrift aus NHC VI, in *ThLZ* 98 (1973) cols. 495–503.

Schenke, H. M. / H. G. Bethge, "Zweiter Logos des grossen Seth". Die zweite Schrift aus NHC VII, in *ThLZ* 100 (1975) cols. 97–110.

Schenke, H. M. / A. Werner, Die Apokalypse des Petrus. Die dritte Schrift aus NHC VII, in *ThLZ* 99 (1974) cols. 575–583.

Schenke, H. M. / W. P. Funk, "Die Lehre des Silvanus". Die vierte Schrift aus NHC VII, in *ThLZ* (1975) cols. 7–23.

Schenke, H. M. / K. Wekel, "Die drei Stelen des Seth". Die fünfte Schrift aus NHC VII, in *ThLZ* 100 (1975) cols. 571–580.

Schenke, H. M. / H. G. Bethge, "Die Exegese über die Seele". Die sechste Schrift aus NHC II, in *ThLZ* 101 (1976) cols. 93–104.

Schenke, H. M. / H. G. Bethge, Der sogenannte "Brief des Petrus an Philippus". Die zweite Schrift aus NHC VIII, in *ThLZ* 103 (1978) cols. 161–170.

Schenke, H. M. / D. Kirchner, "Das Buch des Thomas". Die siebte Schrift aus NHC II, in *ThLZ* 102 (1977) cols. 793–804.

Schenke, H. M. / G. Schenke, "Die dreigestaltige Protennoia". Eine gnostische Offenbarungsrede in koptischer Sprache aus dem Fund von Nag Hammadi, in ThLZ 99 (1974) cols. 731–746 (NHC XIII).

Schmidt, C., *Koptisch-gnostische Schriften* Bd. 1: *Die Pistis Sophia. Die beiden Bücher des Jeu. Unbekanntes altgnostisches Werk.* 3rd ed. rev. W. Till, Berlin 1962 (GCS Bd. 45 [13]).

Schmidt, C., *Pistis Sophia*. Text edited. Translation and notes by V. MacDermot, Leiden 1978 (NHS IX, The Coptic Gnostic Library).

Schmidt, C., *The Books of Jeu and the Untitled Text in the Bruce Codex*. Text edited. Translation and notes by V. MacDermot, Leiden 1978 (NHS XIII, The Coptic Gnostic Library).

Tardieu, M., Les trois Stèles de Seth, in *Revue des sciences philosophiques et théologiques* 57 (1973) pp. 545–575.

Till, W., Das Evangelium der Wahrheit, in ZNW 50 (1959) pp. 165–185.

Till, W., *Das Evangelium nach Philippus*, Berlin 1963 (PTS 2).

Till, W., *Die gnostischen Schriften des koptischen Papyrus Berolinensis 8502*, Berlin 1955. 2nd ed. rev. H. M. Schenke, Berlin 1972 (TU 60).

Turner, J. D., *The Book of Thomas the Contender* from Codex II of the Cairo Gnostic Library from Nag Hammadi, Missoula, Montana 1975 (SBL Diss. Series 23).

Wilson, R. McL., *The Gospel of Philip* (trans. and commentary), London and New York 1962.

Coptic Manichean Texts

Allberry, C. R. C., *A Manichaean Psalm-Book* Part II, Stuttgart 1938 (Manichaean Manuscripts in the Chester Beatty Collection, Vol. 2).

Böhlig, A. / H. J. Polotsky / C. Schmidt, *Kephalaia* 1. Hälfte, Stuttgart 1940 (Manichäische Handschriften der Staatlichen Museen Berlin, Bd. 1).

Böhlig, A., *Kephalaia* 2. Hälfte, Lfg. 11/12 (S. 244–291), Stuttgart 1966.

Nagel, P., *Die Thomaspsalmen des koptisch-manichäischen Psalmenbuches*. Berlin 1980 (Ausgew. Texte aus d. Gesch. d. christl. Kirche N. F. 1).

Polotsky, J. *Manichäische Homilien*, Stuttgart 1938 (Manichaean Manuscripts in the Chester Beatty Collection, Vol. 1).

Schmidt, C., *Neue Originalquellen des Manichäismus in Ägypten*, Stuttgart 1933.

Schmidt, C. / H. J. Polotsky, *Ein Mani-Fund in Ägypten*, Berlin 1933 (SB PAW, Phil.-hist. Kl. 1, 1933).

Cologne Mani Codex

Henrichs, A. / L. Koenen, *Ein griechischer Mani-Codex* (Papyrus Coloniensis, No. 4780) in ZPE 5 (1970) H. 2, 97–216. Ergänzungen: ZPE 8 (1971) 243–250.

Henrichs, A. / L. Koenen, *Der Kölner Mani-Kodex*. Edition of pages 1–72, in ZPE 19 (1975) 1–85. Edition of pages 72–99: ib. 1978, 87–199. Edition of pages 99–120, in ib. 44 (1981) 201–318. Edition of pages 121–192, in ib. 48 (1982) 1–59 (319–377, the end).

Cameron, R. / A. J. Dewey, *The Cologne Mani Codex* (SBL Texts and Translations 15, Early Christian Literature Series 3), Missoula, Montana 1979.

Iranian Manichaean Texts

Andreas, F. C. / W. B. Henning, *Mitteliranische Manichaica aus Chinesisch-Turkestan* I–III, Berlin 1932–1934 (SB PAW 10, 1932; 8, 1933; 27, 1934). Reprinted in Henning, W. B., *Selected Papers* (see below).

Asmussen, J. P., *Manichaean Literature*, New York 1975 (UNESCO Collection of representative works, Persian Series No. 22).

Boyce, M., *A Catalogue of the Iranian Manuscripts in Manichean Script in the German Turfan Collection*, Berlin 1960 (DAW Inst. f. Orientforschung No. 45).

Boyce, M., *A Reader in Manichean Middle Persian and Parthian*, Leiden 1975 (Acta Iranica, 3e Série, Vol. II).

Boyce, M., *The Manichaean Hymn-Cycles in Parthian*, Oxford 1954 (London Oriental Series 3).

Henning, W. B., *Ein manichäisches Henochbuch*, Berlin 1934 (SB PAW 5, 1934, 27–35).

Henning, W. B., *Ein manichäisches Bet- und Beichtbuch*, Berlin 1937 (Abh. PAW 10, 1936).

Henning, W. B., *Selected Papers*, Leiden 1977. 2 Bde. (Acta Iranica, 2ᵉ Série, V and VI).

MacKenzie, D. N., *Mani's Šāhbuhragān*, in BSOAS XLII (1979) 501–534, XLIII (1980) 288–310.

Müller, F. W. K., *Handschriftenreste in Estrangeloschrift aus Turfan I und II*, Berlin 1904 (SB PAW 1904, 348–352; Abh. PAW 1904, Anhang).

Sundermann, W., *Mittelpersische und parthische kosmogonische und Parabeltexte der Manichäer*, Berlin 1973 (Schriften zur Geschichte und Kultur des Alten Orients, Berliner Turfantexte IV).

Sundermann, W., *Mitteliranische manichäische Texte kirchengeschichtlichen Inhalts*, Berlin 1981 (Schriften zur Geschichte und Kultur des Alten Orients. Berliner Turfantexte XI).

Turkish Manichean Texts

Bang, W., Manichäische Laienbeichtspiegel, in *Le Muséon* 36 (1923) 137–242.

Bang, W., Manichäische Hymnen, op. cit. 38 (1925) 1–55.

Bang, W., Manichäische Erzähler, op. cit. 44 (1931) 1–36.

Gabain, A. von / W. Winter, *Türkische Turfantexte* IX, Berlin 1958 (Abh. DAW, Kl. f. Sprachen, Lit. u. Kunst, Jg. 1956).

Le Coq, A. von, *Türkische Manichaica aus Chotscho* I–III, Berlin 1912, 1920, 1923 (Abh. PAW 1911, 1919, 1922).

Le Coq, A. von, *Die Buddhistische Spätantike in Mittelasien*. Bd. II: Die manichäischen Miniaturen, Berlin 1923. New impression Graz 1973.

Sprachwissenschaftliche Ergebnisse der deutschen Turfan-Forschung. Text-Editionen und Interpretationen von A. von Le Coq, F. W. K. Müller, W. Bang, G. R. Rachmati, W. Thomsen. Akademieschriften 1908 bis 1938, 2 Bde., Leipzig 1971.

Zieme, P., *Manichäisch-türkische Texte*, Berlin 1975 (Schriften zur Geschichte und Kultur des Alten Orients, Berliner Turfantexte V).

Chinese Manichean Texts

Chavannes, E. / P. Pelliot, Un traité manichéen retrouvé en Chine, in *Journal asiatique* 1911, 499–617; 1913, 99–199, 261–394.

Haloun, G. / W. B. Henning, The Compendium of the Doctrines and Styles of the Teaching of Mani, the Buddha of Light, in *Asia Major* NS III (1952) 184–212.

Waldschmidt, E. / W. Lentz, *Die Stellung Jesu im Manichäismus*, Berlin 1926 (Abh. PAW ⁴1926).

Waldschmidt, E. / W. Lentz, *Manichäische Dogmatik aus chinesischen Texten*, Berlin 1933 (SB PAW 13, 1933).

Mandaica

Brandt, W., *Mandäische Schriften*, Göttingen 1893; reprinted Amsterdam 1973.

Drower, E. S., *A Pair of Naṣoraean Commentaries* (Two Priestly Documents), Leiden 1963.

Drower, E. S., *Diwan Abathur or Progress through the Purgatories*, Città del Vaticano 1950 (Studi e Testi 151).

Drower, E. S., *Šarh d-Qabin d-Šišlam-Rba*. Explanatory Commentary on the Marriage Ceremony of the Great Šišlam, Rome 1950 (Biblica et Orientalia 12).

Drower, E. S., *The Book of the Zodiac (Sfar Malwašia)*, London 1949.

Drower, E. S., *The Canonical Prayer-Book of the Mandaeans*, Leiden 1959.

Drower, E. S., *The Coronation of the Great Šišlam*, Leiden 1962.

Drower, E.S., *The Haran Gawaita and the Baptism of Hibil-Ziwa*. Città del Vaticano 1953 (Studi e Testi 176).

Drower, E.S., *The Thousand and Twelve Questions (Alf Trisar Šuialia)*, Berlin 1960 (DAW, Institut für Orientforschung 32).

Lidzbarski, M., *Das Johannesbuch der Mandäer*, 2 Teile, Giessen 1915. Reprinted Berlin 1965.

Lidzbarski, M., *Ginzā. Der Schatz oder das grosse Buch der Mandäer*, Göttingen 1925 (Quellen der Religionsgeschichte Bd. 13). Reprint: Göttingen 1979.

Lidzbarski, M., *Mandäische Liturgien*, Berlin 1920 (Abh. der Kgl. Gesellschaft der Wissenschaften zu Göttingen, Phil.-hist. Kl. NF 17, 1). Reprint: Hildesheim 1962.

Rudolph, K., Mandäische Quellen, in *Die Gnosis*, hrsg. von W. Foerster, Bd. 2, Zürich 1971, 173–418 (ET Oxford 1974, 123–319).

Rudolph, K., *Der mandäische "Diwan der Flüsse"*, Berlin 1982 (Abh. SAW Leipzig, Phil.-hist. Kl. 70, 1)

Yamauchi, E.M., *Mandaic Incantation Texts*, New Haven 1967 (American Oriental Series 49).

Anthologies of Sources

Adam, A., *Texte zum Manichäismus*, 2. verb. u. verm. Auflage, Berlin 1969 (KlT 175).

Foerster, W., *Die Gnosis*. Bd. 1: Zeugnisse der Kirchenväter. Unter Mitarbeit von E. Haenchen und M. Krause, Zürich 1969, ²1979; Bd. 2: Koptische und mandäische Quellen, Eingel., übers. und erläutert von M. Krause und K. Rudolph. Mit Register zu Bd. 1 und 2, Zürich 1971; Bd. 3: Der Manichäismus, unter Mitwirkung von J.P. Asmussen eingel., übers. u. erläutert von A. Böhlig, Zürich 1980 (Bibliothek der Alten Welt). ET: vol. 1 Oxford 1972; vol. 2, 1974.

Grant, R.M., *Gnosticism*. A Sourcebook of heretical Writings from the Early Christian Period, London and New York 1961.

Haardt, R., *Die Gnosis. Wesen und Zeugnisse*, Salzburg 1967 (ET Leiden 1971).

Latte, K., *Die Religion der Römer und der Synkretismus der Kaiserzeit*, Tübingen 1927 (Religionsgeschichtl. Lesebuch. Hrsg. von A. Bertholet, 2. Aufl., Heft 5).

Schenke, H.-M., Die Gnosis, in Leipoldt, J./W. Grundmann (Hrsg.), *Umwelt des Urchristentums II*. Texte zum Neutestamentlichen Zeitalter, Berlin ²1970, 350–418.

Schultz, W., *Dokumente der Gnosis*, Jena 1910.

Völker, W., *Quellen zur Geschichte der christlichen Gnosis*, Tübingen 1932 (SQS NF 5).

Essays and Monographs

Adam, A., *Lehrbuch der Dogmengeschichte*, Bd. 1: Die Zeit der Alten Kirche, Gütersloh 1965; Berlin 1970.

Adam, A., *Die Psalmen des Thomas und das Perlenlied als Zeugnis vorchristlicher Gnosis*, Berlin 1959 (BZNW 24).

Aland, B., (Ed.), *Gnosis*. Festschrift für Hans Jonas, Göttingen 1978.

Altaner, B., *Patrologie*. Leben, Schriften und Lehre der Kirchenväter. 6. Aufl. hrsg. von A. Stuiber, Freiburg (Breisgau) 1963. (ET of 5th ed. Edingburgh/London 1960).

Asmussen, J.P., *Xᵘāstvānīft. Studies in Manicheism*, Copenhagen 1965 (Acta Theologica Danica 7). With detailed Bibliography.

Barc, B. (ed.), *Colloque international sur les textes de Nag Hammadi (Québec, 22–25 août 1978)*, Québec/Louvain 1981 (BCNH Sect. "Etudes" 1)

Bauer, W., *Rechtgläubigkeit und Ketzerei im ältesten Christentum*, 2. Aufl. mit einem Nachtrag von G. Strecker, Tübingen 1964 (ET Philadelphia 1971).

Baur, F.C., *Die christliche Gnosis oder die christliche Religions-Philosophie in ihrer geschichtlichen Entwicklung*. Tübingen 1835. Reprint: Darmstadt 1967.

Baur, F.C., *Das manichäische Religionssystem nach den Quellen neu untersucht und entwickelt*, Tübingen 1831. Reprint: Göttingen 1928.

Bernhardt, J., *Die apologetische Methode bei Klemens von Alexandrien*, Leipzig 1968 (Erfurter Theologische Studien 21).

Betz, O., Das Problem der Gnosis seit der Entdeckung der Texte von Nag Hammadi, in *Verkündigung u. Forschung* 21 (1976) 46–80.

Beyschlag, K., *Simon Magus und die christliche Gnosis*, Tübingen 1974 (Wiss. Untersuchungen zum NT 16).

Bianchi, U. (ed.), *Le Origini dello Gnosticismo*. Colloquio di Messina 13–18 Aprile 1966. Testi e Discussioni, Leiden 1967, ²1970 (Studies in the History of Religions, Supplement to *Numen* XII).

Bianchi, U. (ed.), *Selected Essays on Gnosticism, Dualism and Mysteriosophy*, Leiden 1978 (Supp. *Numen* 38).

Biblical Archeologist, Autumn 1979 = vol. 42 No. 4 (contains richly illustrated contributions by J. M. Robinson on the story of the discovery and by B. van Elderen on the excavations at Nag Hammadi).

Böhlig, A., *Mysterion und Wahrheit*, Gesammelte Aufsätze zur spätantiken Religionsgeschichte, Leiden 1968.

Böhlig, A. / F. Wisse, *Zum Hellenismus in den Schriften von Nag Hammadi*, Wiesbaden 1975 (Göttinger Orientforschungen VI/2).

Bornkamm, G., *Mythos und Legende in den apokryphen Thomas-Akten*, Göttingen 1933.

Bousset, W., *Hauptprobleme der Gnosis*, Göttingen 1907, ²1973.

Bousset, W., Gnosis, Gnostiker, in PWRE Bd. 7, Stuttgart 1912, 1503–1547.

Bousset, W., *Religionsgeschichtliche Studien*. Hrsg. von A. F. Verheule, Leiden 1979 (Suppl. to NovTest 50).

Brandenburger, E., *Adam und Christus*, Neukirchen-Vluyn 1962.

Brandt, W., *Die mandäische Religion*, Leipzig 1889. Reprint: Amsterdam 1973.

Broek, R. van den, and M. J. Vermaseren (ed.), *Studies in Gnosticism and Hellenistic Religions* pres. to G. Quispel on the Occasion of his 65th Birthday, Leiden 1981 (EPRO 91).

Brox, N., *Offenbarung, Gnosis und gno-*

stischer Mythos bei Irenaeus von Lyon, Salzburg/Munich 1966.

Bultmann, R., *Das Evangelium des Johannes*, Göttingen ¹⁰1941, ¹⁸1964 (Krit.-exeget. Kommentar über das NT). ET Oxford 1971.

Bultmann, R., *Exegetica*, ed. E. Dinkler, Tübingen 1967.

Bultmann, R., *Theologie des Neuen Testaments*, Tübingen 1953, ⁶1968; Berlin ³1959 (ET London 1952–55).

Bultmann, R., *Das Urchristentum im Rahmen der antiken Religionen*, Zürich 1949; Hamburg 1962, ⁵1969 (ET London 1956).

Burkitt, F. C., *Church and Gnosis*, Cambridge 1932.

Burkitt, F. C., *The Religion of the Manichees*, Cambridge 1925. Reprint: New York 1978.

Cerutti, M. V., *Dualismo e Ambiguità*. Creatori e creazione nelle dottrina mandea sul cosmo, Roma 1980.

Chwolsohn, D., *Die Szabier und der Szabismus*, 2 vols., Petersburg 1856. Reprint: New York 1965.

Colpe, C., *Manichäismus*, in RGG³ IV (1960) 714–722.

Colpe, C., *Die religionsgeschichtliche Schule*, Göttingen 1961.

Colpe, C., Die Thomaspsalmen als chronologischer Fixpunkt in der Geschichte der orientalischen Gnosis, in *JbAC* 7 (1964) 77–93.

Colpe, C., Heidnische, jüdische und christliche Überlieferung in den Schriften aus Nag Hammadi I–IX, in *JbAC* 15 (1972) 1–18; 16 (1973) 106–126; 17 (1974) 109–125; 18 (1975) 144–165; 19 (1976) 126–138; 20 (1977) 149–170; 21 (1978) 125–146; 22 (1979) 98–122; 23 (1980) 108–127; 25 (1982) 65–101.

Cumont, F. / M.-A. Kugener, *Recherches sur le Manichéisme* I–II, Brussels 1908–1912.

Decret, F., *Aspects du Manichéisme dans l'Afrique romain*, Paris 1970 (Etudes Augustiniennes).

Decret, F., *L'Afrique manichéenne*, Paris 1978, 2 vols. (with bibliography).

Decret, F., *Mani et la tradition manichéenne*, Pair 1974 (Maitres spirituelles 40).

Dietrich, A. (ed.), *Synkretismus im syrisch-persischen Kulturgebiet*, Bericht über ein Symposion in Reinhardshausen bei Göttingen 1975 (Abh. AWG 96).

Doresse, J., *Les livres secrets des gnostiques d'Égypte*. I. Introduction aux écrits gnostiques coptes découverts à Khénoboskion, Paris 1958.

Doresse, J., *The Secret Books of the Egyptian Gnostics*, New York/London 1960, [2]1970.

Drijvers, H. J. W., *Bardaisan of Edessa*, Assen 1966.

Drower, E. S., *The Mandaeans of Iraq and Iran*, Oxford 1937; new edition Leiden 1962.

Drower, E. S., *The Secret Adam*, Oxford 1960.

Drower, E. S., *Water into Wine*, London 1956.

Ehlers, B., Bardesanes von Edessa – ein syrischer Gnostiker, in *ZKG* 81 (1970) 334–351.

Ehlers, B., Marcion, in *ZThK* 70 (1973) 420–447.

Elsas, Chr., *Neuplatonische und gnostische Weltablehnung in der Schule Plotins*, Berlin 1975 (RGVV 34).

Eltester, W. (ed.), *Christentum und Gnosis*, Berlin 1969 (BZNW 37).

Essays on the Coptic Gnostic Library. An Offprint from Novum Testamentum XII 2, Leiden 1970.

Faye, E. de, *Gnostiques et gnosticisme*, Paris [2]1925.

Fendt, L., *Gnostische Mysterien*, Munich 1922.

Fischer, K. M., *Tendenz und Absicht des Epheserbriefes*, Berlin 1973.

Flügel, G., *Mani, seine Lehre und seine Schriften*, Leipzig 1862; reprint: Osnabrück 1969.

Foerster, W., Das Wesen der Gnosis, in *Welt als Geschichte* XV (1955) 100–114; reprinted in Rudolph, K., *Gnosis und Gnostizismus* 438–462.

Frickel, J., *Die "Apophasis Megale" in Hippolyts Refutatio* (VI 9–18), Rome 1968 (Orientalia Christiana Analecta 182).

Gabain, A. von, *Das uigurische Königreich von Chotscho 850–1250*, Berlin 1961 (SB DAW, Kl. f. Sprachen, Lit. u. Kunst 5, 1961).

Gaffron, H. G., *Studien zum koptischen Philippusevangelium unter besonderer Berücksichtigung der Sakramente*, Theol. Diss. Bonn 1969.

Grant, R. M., *Gnosticism and Early Christianity*, New York [2]1966.

Haenchen, E., Gab es eine vorchristliche Gnosis? in ZThK 49 (1952) 316–349 and in *Gott und Mensch*. Ges. Aufsätze, Tübingen 1965, 265–298.

Haenchen, E., Literatur zum Codex Jung, in *ThR* 30 (1964) 39–82.

Haenchen, E., Literatur zum Thomasevangelium, in *ThR* 27 (1961) 147–178; 306–338.

Harnack, A. von, *Geschichte der altchristlichen Literatur bis Eusebius*. 1. Teil: Überlieferung und Bestand, Leipzig 1893; 2. Teil: Chronologie, Bd. 1 1897, Bd. 2 1904.

Harnack, A. von, *Lehrbuch der Dogmengeschichte*. Bd. 1: Die Entstehung des christlichen Dogmas, Tübingen [4]1909 (ET from 3rd ed. London 1894).

Harnack, A. von, *Dogmengeschichte* (Grundriss), Tübingen [7]1931.

Harnack, A. von, *Marcion. Das Evangelium vom fremden Gott*. Neue Studien zu Marcion, Leipzig [2]1924. Reprint: Berlin/Darmstadt 1960.

Henrichs, A., Mani and the Babylonian Baptists, in *Harv. Stud. in Class. Philol.* 77 (1973) 23–59.

Henrichs, A., The Cologne Mani Codex Reconsidered, in *Harv. Stud. in Class. Philol.* 83 (1979) 339–367.

Hilgenfeld, A., *Die Ketzergeschichte des Urchristentums urkundlich dargestellt*, Leipzig 1884. Reprint: Hildesheim 1963.

Horst, P. W. van der / J. Mansfeld, *An Alexandrian Platonist against Dualism. Alexander of Lycopolis' "Critique of the Doctrines of Manichaeans"*, Leiden 1974 (= Theta-Pi 3 (1974) 1–97).

Jackson, A. V. W., *Researches in Manicheism*, New York 1932.

Jervell, J., *Imago Dei*. Genesis 1. 26 f. im Spätjudentum, in der Gnosis und in den paulinischen Briefen, Göttingen 1960.

Jonas, H., *Gnosis und spätantiker Geist*. Teil 1:

Die mythologische Gnosis, mit einer Einleitung zur Geschichte und Methodologie der ‣Forschung, Göttingen 1934, ²1954, ³1964 mit Ergänzungsheft zur 1. und 2. Aufl. Teil 2/1: *Von der Mythologie zur mystischen Philosophie*, Göttingen 1954, ²1966.

Jonas, H., *The Gnostic Religion*, Boston 1958, ²1963, ³1970.

Kippenberg, H. G., Versuch einer soziologischen Verortung des antiken Gnostizismus, in *Numen* XVII (1970) 211–231.

Klíma, O., *Manis Zeit und Leben*, Prague 1962.

Klíma, O., *Mazdak. Geschichte einer sozialen Bewegung im sassanidischen Persien*, Prague 1957.

Klíma, O., *Beiträge zur Geschichte des Mazdakismus*, Prague 1977 (Dissertationes Orientales 37. Hrsg. v. Orient. Inst. der Tschechoslowak. Akad. d. Wiss.).

Klimkeit, H.-J., *Manichaean Art and Calligraphy*, Leiden 1982 (Iconography of Religions XX).

Koenen, L., Augustine and Manichaeism in Light of the Cologne Mani Codex, in *Illin. Class. Stud.* 3 (1978) 159–195.

Koschorke, K., *Hippolyt's Ketzerbekämpfung und die Polemik gegen die Gnostiker*, Wiesbaden 1975 (Göttinger Orientforschungen VI/4).

Koschorke, K., *Die Polemik der Gnostiker gegen das kirchliche Christentum*, Leiden 1978 (NHS XII).

Koschorke, K., Eine neugefundene gnostische Gemeindeordnung, in *ZThK* 76 (1979) 30–60.

Kraft, H., *Gnostisches Gemeinschaftsleben*, Theol. Diss. Heidelberg 1950 (typescript).

Kraft, H., *Kirchenväter-Lexikon*, Munich 1966.

Krause, M., Der koptische Handschriftenbestand bei Nag Hammadi: Umfang und Inhalt, in *Mitt. ADAIK* 18 (1962) 121–132.

Krause, M., Zum koptischen Handschriftenfund bei Nag Hammadi, in *Mitt. ADAIK* 19 (1963) 106–113.

Krause, M., Die Texte von Nag Hammadi, in B. Aland (ed.), *Gnosis*. Festschrift Jonas, 216–243.

Krause, M., (ed.), *Essays on the Nag Hammadi Texts. In Honour of Alexander Böhlig*, Leiden 1972 (NHS III).

Krause, M. (ed.), *Essays on the Nag Hammadi Texts. In Honour of Pahor Labib*, Leiden 1978 (NHS VI).

Krause, M. (ed.), *Gnosis and Gnosticism*. Papers read at the 7th International Conference on Patristic Studies (Oxford, Sept. 8th–13th 1975), Leiden 1977 (NHS VIII).

Krause, M. (ed.), *Gnosis and Gnosticism*. Papers read at the 8th International Conference on Patristic Studies (Oxford, Sept. 3rd-8th 1979), Leiden 1981 (NHS XVII).

Langbrandtner, W., *Weltferner Gott oder Gott der Liebe*. Der Ketzerstreit in der johanneischen Kirche, Frankfurt/M. 1977 (Beitr. z. bibl. Exegese u. Theologie 6).

Langerbeck, H., *Aufsätze zur Gnosis*. Aus dem Nachlass hrsg. von H. Dorries, Göttingen 1967 (Abh. AWG, Philos.-hist. Kl. 3, Nr. 69).

Layton, B. (ed.), *The Rediscovery of Gnosticism*. Proceedings of the International Conference on Gnosticism at Yale, New Haven, Connecticut, March 28–31, 1978, Vol. I The School of Valentinus, Leiden 1980; Vol. II Sethian Gnosticism, Leiden 1981 (Suppl. to *Numen* 41).

Leisegang, H., *Die Gnosis*, Leipzig 1924, Stuttgart ⁴1955 (Kröner Taschenausg. 32).

Lidzbarski, M., Alter und Heimat der mandäischen Religion, in *ZNW* 27 (1928) 321–327.

Lietzmann, H., *Geschichte der Alten Kirche*, 4 Bde., Berlin ²⁻³1953 (ET 1937–1955).

Lieu, S. N., *The Religion of Light*. An Introduction to the History of Manichaeism in China, Hongkong 1979.

Loos, M., *Dualist Heresy in the Middle Ages*, Prague 1974.

Lüdemann, G., *Untersuchungen zur simonianischen Gnosis*, Göttingen 1975 (Göttinger Theol. Arbeiten 1).

Lüdemann, G., *Paulus, der Heidenapostel*. Bd. 1 Studien zur Chronologie, Göttingen 1975 (FRLANT 123).

Lüdemann, G., Zur Geschichte des ältesten Christentums in Rom, in *ZNW* 70 (1979) 86–114.

Macuch, R., Alter und Heimat des Mandäismus nach neuerschlossenen Quellen, in *ThLZ* 82 (1957) 401–408.

Macuch, R., Anfänge der Mandäer, in Altheim, F./ R. Stiehl, *Die Araber in der alten Welt*, Bd. 2, Berlin 1965, 76–190.

Macuch, R., Der gegenwärtige Stand der Mandäerforschung und ihre Aufgaben, in *OLZ* 63 (1968) 5–14.

Macuch, R. (ed.), *Zur Sprache und Literatur der Mandäer*. Mit Beiträgen von K. Rudolph und E. Segelberg, Berlin 1976 (Studia Mandaica I).

Mead, G. R. S., *Fragments of a Faith Forgotten*, London 1900.

Ménard, J. E. (ed.), *Les Textes de Nag Hammadi*. Colloque du Centre d'Histoire des Religions (Strasbourg, 23–25 Oct. 1974), Leiden 1975 (NHS VII).

Nagel, P. (ed.), *Studia Coptica*, Berlin 1974.

Nagel, P. (ed.), *Menschenbild in Gnosis und Manichäismus*, Halle (Saale) 1979 (wissenschaftliche Beiträge der Martin-Luther-Universität Halle–Wittenberg, 1979/39 [K5]).

Nilsson, M. P., *Geschichte der griechischen Religion*. Bd. 2, Munich ²1961 (Handbuch d. Altertumswissenschaften V 2).

Nock, A. D., Gnosticism, in *Harvard Theol. Review* 57 (1964) 255–279; *Essays on Religion and the Ancient World*, ed. by Z. Stewart, London 1972, vol. 2, 940–959.

Ort, L. J. R., *Mani. A Religio-Historical Description of his Personality*, Leiden 1967 (with Bibliography).

Pagels, E., *The Johannine Gospel in Gnostic Exegesis*. Heracleon's Commentary on John, Nashville/New York 1973 (SBL Monograph Series 17).

Pagels, E., *The Gnostic Paul*, Philadelphia 1975.

Pagels, E., *The Gnostic Gospels*, London/New York 1979.

Pallis, S. A., *Essay on Mandaean Bibliography 1560–1930*, London/Copenhagen 1933. Reprint: Amsterdam 1974.

Perkins, Ph., *The Gnostic Dialogue*. The Early Church and the Crisis of Gnosticism, New York 1980 (Theol. Inquiries).

Poirier, P.-H., *L'Hymne de la Perle des Actes de Thomas*, Louvain-la-Neuve 1981.

Pokorný, P., *Der Epheserbrief und die Gnosis*, Berlin 1965.

Pokorný, P., *Počátky gnose*, Prague 1968, ²1969 with English summary (Rozpravy českosl. Akademie věd, Radu společ věd 1968, R. 78:9).

Polotsky, H. J., Manichäismus, in *PWRE*, Supplement-Bd. 6, Stuttgart 1935, 241–272. As separate print: *Abriss des manichäischen Systems*, Stuttgart 1934. Reprinted in *Collected Papers*, Jerusalem 1971, 645 ff.

Puech, H.-Ch., *Le Manichéisme. Son fondateur – sa doctrine*, Paris 1949.

Puech, H.-Ch., Les nouveaux écrits gnostiques découverts en Haute-Égypte, in *Coptic Studies in Honor of W. E. Crum*, Boston 1950, 91–154.

Puech, H.-Ch., Die Religion des Mani, in König, F. (ed.), *Christus und die Religionen der Erde*, Bd. 2, Freiburg (Breisgau) 1951, 499–563.

Puech, H.-Ch., *En quête de la Gnose*, 2 vols., Paris 1978 (Bibliothèque des Sciences Humaines).

Puech, H.-Ch., *Sur le manichéisme et autres essais*, Paris 1979.

Quispel, G., *Gnosis als Weltreligion*, Zürich 1951.

Quispel, G., *Gnostic Studies*, 2 vols., Leiden 1974, 1975.

Reitzenstein, R., *Poimandres*, Leipzig 1904.

Reitzenstein, R., *Die hellenistischen Mysterienreligionen*, Leipzig ³1927. Reprint: Darmstadt 1956. ET Pittsburgh 1977.

Reitzenstein, R., *Das iranische Erlösungsmysterium*, Bonn 1921.

Reitzenstein, R./ H. H. Schaeder, *Studien zum antiken Synkretismus aus Iran und Griechenland*, Leipzig/Berlin 1926 (Studien der Bibliothek Warburg VII). Reprint: Darmstadt 1965.

Ries, J., Introduction aux études manichéennes, in *Ephemerides Theologicae Lovanienses* 33 (1957) 453–482; 35 (1959) 362–409.

Ries, J. (ed.), *Gnosticisme et monde hellénistique*: Actes du Colloque de Louvain-la-

Neuve (11–14 Mars 1980), Louvain 1982.

Robinson, J. M., The Coptic Gnostic Library Today, in *New Testament Studies* 14 (1967/ 68) 356–401; Claremont Graduate School, The Institute for Antiquity and Christianity, Occasional Papers No. 1, 1971.

Robinson, J. M., The Facsimile Edition of the Nag Hammadi Codices, in *Occasional Papers* No. 2, 1972.

Robinson, J. M., The Jung Codex. The Rise and Fall of a Monopoly, in *Religious Studies Review* 3 (1977) 17–30.

Robinson, J. M., From Cliff to Cairo. The Story of the Discoverers and the Middlemen of the Nag Hammadi Codices, in B. Barc (ed), *Colloque international sur les textes Nag Hammadi* (Québec) 21–58.

Rose, E., *Die manichäische Christologie*, Wiesbaden 1979 (Studies in Oriental Religions 5).

Rudolph, K., Gnosis und Gnostizismus, ein Forschungsbericht, in *ThR* 34 (1969) 121–175, 181–231, 358–361; 36 (1971) 1–61, 89–124; 37 (1972) 289–360; 38 (1973) 1–25.

Rudolph, K., Simon – Magus oder Gnosticus? in *ThR* 42 (1977) 279–359.

Rudolph, K. (ed.), *Gnosis und Gnostizismus*, Darmstadt 1975 (WdF Bd. CCLXII).

Rudolph, K., Nag Hammadi und die neuere Gnosisforschung, in Nagel, P., *Von Nag Hammadi bis Zypern*, Berlin 1972 (BBA 43) 1–15.

Rudolph, K., *Die Mandäer* I. Prolegomena: Das Mandäerproblem, Göttingen 1960. II. Der Kult, Göttingen 1961.

Rudolph, K., *Theogonie, Kosmogonie und Anthropogonie in den mandäischen Schriften*, Göttingen 1965.

Rudolph, K., *Mandaeism* (Iconography of Religions, ed. by Th. P. van Baaren et al., Section XXI), Leiden 1978.

Rudolph, K., Die mandäische Literatur, in *Studia Mandaica* I, ed. R. Macuch, Berlin 1975, 147–170, and in *Das Corpus der Griechischen Christlichen Schriftsteller*, ed. J. Irmscher and K. Treu, Berlin 1977 (TU 120) 219–236.

Rudolph, K., Problems of a History of the Development of the Mandaean Religion, in:

History of Religions 8 No. 3 (Febr. 1969) 210–235.

Rudolph, K., Quellenprobleme zum Ursprung und Alter der Mandäer, in J. Neusner (ed.), *Christianity, Judaism and other Grèco-Roman Cults*. Studies for M. Smith at Sixty, Leiden 1975, Part IV, 112–142.

Rudolph, K., Die Religion der Mandäer, in Gese, H. / M. Höfner / K. Rudolph, *Die Religionen Altsyriens, Altarabiens und der Mandäer*, Stuttgart 1970 (Die Religionen der Menschheit Bd. 10/2) 403–464.

Rudolph, K., Zum gegenwärtigen Stand der mandäischen Religionsgeschichte, in K. W. Tröger, *Gnosis und Neues Testament*, 121–148.

Rudolph, K., Der Mandäismus in der neueren Gnosisforschung, in B. Aland (ed.), *Gnosis*. Festschrift Jonas, 244–277 (with chronol. table for Mandean history).

Rudolph, K., Die Bedeutung des Kölner Mani-Codex für die Manichäismusforschung, in *Mélanges d'histoire des religions offerts à H.-Ch. Puech*, Paris 1974, 471–486.

Rudolph, K., Gnosis und Manichäismus nach den koptischen Quellen, in *Koptologische Studien in der DDR*. WZ der Martin-Luther-Universität Halle–Wittenberg, Sonderheft 1965, 165–190.

Rudolph, K., Mani, in *Die Grossen der Weltgeschichte*, ed. K. Fassmann, vol. II, Zürich 1972, 544–565.

Rudolph, K., *Antike Baptisten*. Zu den Überlieferungen über frühjüdische und -christliche Taufsekten, Berlin 1981 (SB SAW Philol.-hist. Kl. 121, 4).

Runciman, S., *The Mediaeval Manichee*, Cambridge 1947.

Sagnard, F. H. M., *La gnose valentinienne et le témoignage de s. Irénée*, Paris 1947.

Salles-Dabadie, J. M. A., *Recherches sur Simon le Mage*. I. L'"Apophasis megale", Paris 1969 (Cahiers de la Revue biblique 10).

Schaeder, H. H., Bardesanes von Edessa in der Überlieferung der griechischen und syrischen Kirche, in *ZKG* 51 (1932) 21–74 and in *Studien zur orientalischen Religionsgeschichte*, ed. C. Colpe, Darmstadt 1968, 108–160.

Schaeder, H. H., Manichäismus, in RGG² III (1929) 1959–1973.

Schaeder, H. H., Urform und Fortbildung des manichäischen Systems. *Vorträge der Bibliothek Warburg 1924/25*, Leipzig 1927, 65–115. Reprinted in *Studien zur orientalischen Religionsgeschichte* (see above) 15–107.

Schenke, H.-M., Die Gnosis, in Leipoldt, J./ W. Grundmann (eds.), *Umwelt des Urchristentums*, I. Darstellung, Berlin 1965, ³1971, 371–415.

Schenke, H.-M., *Der Gott "Mensch" in der Gnosis*, Berlin 1962.

Schlier, H., *Religionsgeschichtliche Untersuchungen zu den Ignatiusbriefen*, Gießen 1929 (BZNW 8).

Schmithals, W., *Paulus und die Gnostiker*, Hamburg-Bergstedt 1965 (ET Nashville 1972).

Schmithals, W., *Die Gnosis in Korinth*, Göttingen 1956, ²1965, ³1969 (ET Nashville/ New York 1971).

Schmithals, W., Das Verhältnis von Gnosis und Neuem Testament als methodisches Problem, in *NTS* 16 (1970) 373–383.

Schmithals, W., Gnosis und Neues Testament, in *Verkündigung und Forschung* 21 (1976) 22–46.

Schmithals, W., Zur Herkunft der gnostischen Elemente in der Sprache des Paulus, in B. Aland (ed.), *Gnosis*. Festschrift Jonas, 385–414.

Schoeps, H. J., *Urgemeinde, Judenchristentum, Gnosis*, Tübingen 1956.

Scholer, D. M., *Nag Hammadi Bibliography 1948–1969*, Leiden 1971 (NHS I). Supplemented in *Novum Testamentum* 13 (1971) 322–336; 14 (1972) 312–331; 15 (1973) 327–345; 16 (1974) 316–336; 17 (1975) 305–336; 19 (1977) 293–336; 20 (1978) 300 bis 331; 21 (1979) 357–382; 22 (1980) 351–384; 23 (1981) 361–380.

Schottroff, L., *Der Glaubende und die feindliche Welt*. Beobachtungen zum gnostischen Dualismus und seiner Bedeutung für Paulus und das Johannesevangelium, Neukirchen-Vluyn 1970.

Schulz, S., Die Bedeutung neuer Gnosisfunde für die neutestamentliche Wissenschaft, in *ThR* 26 (1960) 209–266, 301–334.

Schulz, S., *Das Evangelium nach Johannes, übersetzt und erklärt*, Göttingen 1972, Berlin 1975 (NT Deutsch 4).

Schwanz, P., *Imago Dei als christologisch-anthropologisches Problem in der Geschichte der Alten Kirche von Paulus bis Klemens von Alexandrien*, Halle (Saale) 1970.

Segal, A. F., *Two Powers in Heaven*. Early Rabbinic Reports about Christianity and Gnosticism, Leiden 1977 (Studies in Judaism in Late Antiquity 25).

Segelberg, E., *Masbūtā. Studies in the Ritual of Mandaean Baptism*, Uppsala 1958.

Sidorov, A. J., Plotoni i gnostiki, in *Vestnik drevney istorii* 1979, H. 1 (147), 54–70.

Söderberg, H., *La religion des Cathares*, Uppsala 1949.

Söderbergh, T. Säve, *Studies in the Coptic Manichaean Psalmbook*, Uppsala 1949.

Sundermann, W., Iranische Lebensbeschreibungen Manis, in *Acta Orientalia 36 (1974) 125–149*.

Sundermann, W., Namen von Göttern, Dämonen und Menschen in iranischen Versionen des manichäischen Mythos, in *Altorientalische Forschungen* VI, Berlin 1979, 95–133.

Tardieu, M., *Trois mythes gnostiques*. Adam, Éros et les animaux d'Égypte dans un écrit de Nag Hammadi (II 5), Paris 1974.

Trofimova, M. K., *Istoriko-filosofskije voprosy gnosticisma* (Nag Hammadi II, 2, 3, 6, 7), Moscow 1979 (Akademie Nauk SSSR).

Tröger, K.-W., *Mysterienglaube und Gnosis in Corpus Hermeticum XIII*, Berlin 1971 (TU 110).

Tröger, K.-W., *Die Passion Jesu Christi in der Gnosis nach den Schriften von Nag Hammadi*, Theol. Dissertation B, Humboldt-Universität Berlin 1977 (typescript).

Tröger, K.-W. (ed.), *Gnosis und Neues Testament*. Studien aus Religionswissenschaft und Theologie, Berlin 1973.

Tröger, K.-W. (ed.), *Altes Testament – Frühjudentum – Gnosis*. Neue Studien zu "Gnosis und Bibel", Berlin 1980.

Unnik, W. C. van, *Newly Discovered Gnostic Documents*, London 1960.

Vallée, G., *A Study in Anti-Gnostic Polemics. Irenaeus, Hippolytus, and Epiphanius*, Waterloo/Ont.1981 (Studies in Christianity and Judaism 1).

Vielhauer, Ph., *Geschichte der urchristlichen Literatur*, Berlin 1975.

Völker, W., *Der wahre Gnostiker nach Clemens Alexandrinus*, Berlin 1952 (TU 57).

Waldschmidt, E., *Religiöse Strömungen in Zentralasien, in Deutsche Forschung*. Aus der Arbeit der Notgemeinschaft der Deutschen Wissenschaft, Heft 5, Berlin 1928, 68–99.

Widengren, G., *Mesopotamian Elements in Manichaeism*, Uppsala/Leipzig 1946.

Widengren, G., *Mani und der Manichäismus*, Stuttgart 1961 (Urban-Bücher 57). ET New York 1965 (History of Religion Series).

Widengren, G. (ed.), *Der Manichäismus*, Darmstadt 1977 (Wege der Forschung Bd.168).

Widengren, G.(ed.), *Der Mandäismus*, Darmstadt 1982 (Wege der Forschung Bd.167).

Widengren, G. and D.Hellholm (eds.), *Proceedings of the International Colloquium on Gnosticism*, Stockholm Aug.20–25, 1973, Stockholm and Leiden 1977 (Kungl. Vitterhets Historie och Antikvitets Akademiens Handlingar. Filol.-filos. Serien 17).

Wilckens, U., *Weisheit und Torheit*, Tübingen 1959 (Beitr. z. hist. Theol. 26).

Wilson, R.McL., *The Gnostic Problem*, London 1958, ²1964.

Wilson, R.McL., *Gnosis and the New Testament*, Oxford 1968.

Wilson, R.McL. (ed.), *Nag Hammadi and Gnosis*. Papers read at the First International Congress of Coptology (Cairo, Dec. 1976), Leiden 1978 (NHS XIV).

Wisse, F., The Nag Hammadi Library and the Heresiologists, in *VigChrist*. 25 (1971) 205–223.

Wlosok, A., *Laktanz und die philosophische Gnosis*. Untersuchungen zu Geschichte und Terminologie der gnostischen Erlöservorstellung, Heidelberg 1960 (Abh. HAW, Phil.-hist. Kl.2, 1960).

Zandee, J., Gnostic Ideas on the Fall and Salvation, in *Numen* XI (1964) 13–74.

Zandee, J., *The Terminology of Plotinus and Some Gnostic Writings, mainly the 4th Treatise of the Jung Codex*, Istanbul 1961 (Nederlands Hist.-Archäol. Inst. in het Nabije Oosten).

Zandee, J., *"The Teachings of Silvanus" and Clement of Alexandria*, Leiden 1977 (Mém. de la Soc.d'Etudes Orient. "Ex Oriente Lux" 19).

Index